P9-EDT-872

GEOGRAPHY AND RESOURCE ANALYSIS

Second edition

GEOGRAPHY AND RESOURCE ANALYSIS

Second edition

BRUCE MITCHELL

Copublished in the United States with
John Wiley & Sons, Inc., New York

To my wife, Joan

Longman Scientific & Technical,
Longman Group UK Limited,
Longman House, Burnt Mill, Harlow,
Essex CM20 2JE, England
and Associated Companies throughout the world.

Copublished in the United States with
John Wiley & Sons, Inc., 605 Third Avenue, New York, NY 10158

First published 1979
Second edition 1989
Reprinted 1991, 1993

British Library Cataloguing in Publication Data

Mitchell, Bruce, *1944–*
Geography and resource analysis. —— 2nd ed.
1. Natural resources. Management. Role of geography
I. Title
333.7

ISBN 0-582-46364-5

Library of Congress Cataloging-in-Publication Data
Mitchell, Bruce, 1944–
Geography and resource analysis/Bruce Mitchell. —— 2nd ed.
p. cm.
Bibliography: p.
Includes index.
ISBN 0-470-21190-3 (Wiley, USA only).
1. Geography —— Research. I. Title.
G74.M66 1989
910′.72 —— dc 19 88-18736
CIP

Set in 10/12 Linotron 202 Century Schoolbook

Produced by Longman Singapore Publishers (Pte) Ltd.
Printed in Singapore

CONTENTS

LIST OF FIGURES

LIST OF TABLES

PREFACE TO THE SECOND EDITION

In preparing this revised edition, I have considered comments from faculty and students, especially the latter since the book was conceived and written for them. The overall orientation and structure of the first edition have been maintained, since both undergraduate and graduate students have indicated that the approach is useful. Effort also was taken to provide an extensive set of references, since again students have indicated that this feature is valuable.

In terms of changes, several considerations guided the revisions. First, changes in research activity and emphasis since publication of the first edition have been noted. Second, new examples have been introduced throughout to reflect work in resource analysis during the 1980s. Third, in providing new examples, explicit attention has been given to broadening the range of studies from Third World or developing nations. Fourth, as new material was added, some of the work in the first edition has been condensed or removed in order to avoid making the second edition excessively long and thereby too expensive. The publisher's guidelines in that regard were that the second edition should not be more than ten per cent longer than the first edition.

The following specific changes have been made. Chapter 1 has been shortened by removing from the first edition the section which covered general trends in geographical research. The second chapter is longer, with new material on ethical considerations in research. This discussion has been strongly influenced by the work done with Dianne Draper and published by Longman as *Relevance and Ethics in Geography* (1982). This addition is viewed as important as it emphasizes that in research, as well as in other aspects of their work, resource analysts must balance concern for technical efficiency against ethical questions.

The substantive chapters (3 to 12) have been altered in various ways. In Chapter 3, new material is presented regarding remote sensing and geographic information systems as well as end-use forecasting methods. The concept of backcasting also is introduced.

There has been a reduction of some of the discussion in the fourth chapter, especially related to the technical details of diffusion research. New examples are presented.

Chapter 5 begins a group of chapters which are based in the ecological or man-land research tradition. In the fifth chapter much more attention is devoted to public participation regarding both conceptual and practical issues. From the resource manager's perspective, public participation is one of the key practical consequences associated with recognition of varying perceptions, attitudes and behaviour. Chapter 6, on landscape evaluation, is updated by incorporating some of the debate among investigators regarding theoretical and conceptual foundations. The seventh chapter focuses on carrying capacity. The first edition focused exclusively upon carrying capacity research in developed nations and emphasized recreation. In revised form, this chapter includes consideration of carrying capacity as it relates to population–food relationships. This issue has been of great concern and practical significance in the Third World, and many geographers in such countries have been conducting research on it.

The eighth chapter has been renamed and substantially rewritten. The original discussion on natural hazards has been condensed so that research associated with technological hazards (noxious industrial wastes, pesticides and herbicides, nuclear radiation, biotechnology) can be reviewed. Substantial changes also appear in Chapter 9. Administrative aspects of environmental impact assessment are explored. In addition, the development of social impact assessment is discussed more fully compared to the first edition.

Chapter 10 incorporates some of the more recent ideas associated with evaluation research, and includes a more complete review of benefit–cost analysis. A much wider range of examples is provided in the eleventh chapter on institutional arrangements, which was the shortest chapter in the first edition. There still are difficult research issues to overcome in the research on institutional arrangements, but the growing number of studies indicates that its significance has begun to be recognized. The basic ideas and models of policy making remain intact in Chapter 12. However, new material has been added regarding bargaining, negotiation and mediation. This reflects the emergence of 'environmental mediation' during the 1980s as an alternative to the legalistic and adversarial approach which has been so influential, especially in the United States.

The concluding chapter has been totally reorganized. In the first edition, Chapter 13 was a summary and review of the accomplishments by geographers and others. It was primarily retrospective. In this revised edition, the final chapter traces the evolution of resource analysis in geography and highlights major achievements. However, it also considers where current and future effort might be directed. In that sense, it is more future-oriented than in the first edition.

I believe that the reader will find the second edition to be substantially different from the first, even though on the surface it may appear to be similar because of the decision to maintain the original orientation and structure. This revised edition is appearing about two years later than originally had been planned by both the author and the publisher. The reason for this delay was a serious accident in February 1985 which made it initially impossible and subsequently difficult for me to work. Four operations over a nineteen-month period created a situation in which regular progress on the revisions was difficult to sustain.

Since the first edition appeared in late 1979, many people have been helpful in providing comments and suggestions. I have found particularly useful the observations offered by undergraduate students at the University of Waterloo and other institutions. Visiting professorships at the University of Leeds in England, the University of Edinburgh in Scotland and the University of Madras in India, as well as Visiting Fellowships at the University of New England and the Australian National University in Australia have been of great value in exposing me to the ideas of students, faculty and resource managers from diverse cultures and in different environmental contexts. The experiences at each of those institutions have influenced my thinking and the second edition of this book, and I would like to acknowledge my appreciation to each of them.

Cathy Giesbrecht, a Master's student in geography at the University of Waterloo, participated as a research assistant in the work of preparing the revised edition. She searched literature, provided critical assessment of work in several areas, verified sources and reviewed the manuscript. I am grateful for her contributions, especially in helping to ensure that the material is presented in a way that is appropriate from the students' perspective.

Several people typed various drafts of the manuscript for the second edition. At the University of Waterloo, word processing was done efficiently by Jacky Forabosco, Susan Friesen, MaryLynn Reinhart and Jay Van Laar. At the University of New England, similar work was done by Megan Wheeler.

At Longman Scientific and Technical, prompt, thoughtful and constructive advice was given by their staff.

The first edition was dedicated to my wife, Joan. I would like to rededicate this revised edition to her. She continues to support me in my various endeavours, and simultaneously has always ensured that they are kept in proper perspective.

Bruce Mitchell
Waterloo, Ontario
September 1987

PREFACE TO THE FIRST EDITION

Several experiences and principles have influenced my ideas and approach in this book. The first of these concerns my search for a textbook which could be used in a resource management course for advanced undergraduate students.

Existing books seem to fall into one of several categories. First, are books which are mainly *content-oriented*. They focus upon the distribution and use of a variety of resources. Such texts are rich in facts and information, but offer little in the way of principles and concepts. Furthermore, they do not encourage examination of the adequacy of the research upon which the information is based. A second type might be labelled as *crisis-oriented*. These books draw attention to problems of resource and environmental management, and were particularly prominent in the early 1970s. While increasing awareness of problems, they give little attention to fundamental research issues, questions, and strategies which must be handled prior to identifying alternative solutions.

A third type is *perspective-oriented*, emphasizing ecological, economic, political, social or other aspects of resource management. Each provides an in-depth treatment of a fairly narrow range of material. While principles and concepts are emphasized, little explicit attention is given to research issues. In geography courses, it is necessary for students to acquire a number of these books, which is expensive. It also assumes that the students have the necessary background in the respective disciplines to understand and appreciate the material, which is not always the case. A fourth category is *integrative-oriented*, in which an attempt is made to touch upon two or more perspectives. The emphasis is upon principles rather than information. These books usually assume a broad familiarity with the resource management literature, which most undergraduates do not have. They also are selective in coverage. Furthermore, few explicitly consider the problems to be overcome in the research process.

Simply stated, I could not find a text which adequately covered the material which I thought necessary for advanced undergraduates.

In my view, such a book would demonstrate the relevance of work in both physical and human geography, would illustrate the relevance of different research thrusts (ecological, spatial and regional) in geography, would identify fundamental research issues, and would relate geographic research to policy needs and problems.

A second aspect is closely tied to a principle. I believe that an interdisciplinary approach is desirable and necessary for analysis of many resource management problems. At the same time, if an individual is to participate on an interdisciplinary team, he must be able to define his area of competence. Thus, one of my concerns has been to ensure that geography students become aware of their disciplinary heritage, without being overly concerned about disciplinary boundaries.

Experience at the University of Waterloo emphasized the importance of this belief. I began teaching in the year that a Faculty of Environmental Studies was established. The faculty consists of four units, two 'academic' departments (geography, man-environment studies) and two 'professional' schools (architecture, planning). My classes normally had a mix of students from the different units, but with a majority of geography students. In talking with the students, it became clear that many were searching for an 'identity' from which they could relate their work to a faculty commitment to interdisciplinary study.

The third consideration behind this book relates to a principle. In all of my courses, my ultimate goal has been to encourage development of a critical but constructive approach to problem-solving. If students were to develop this approach, they required a framework against which they could judge the adequacy of research. In brief, they had to be able to identify a *problem*, to evaluate *evidence*, and to appraise *arguments*. One of my roles as an instructor was to draw students' attention to the considerations, some of which conflicted, involved in appraising and conducting research.

My experience with both undergraduate and graduate students was that, with some exceptions, they did not know how to systematically evaluate the adequacy of research. In my first class of a term, I often asked the students to write an essay on 'What constitutes excellence in research?'. A great majority did not know how to address that question. This raised concern. In my view, the enduring value of a university education is the cultivation of a critical and constructive mind. Such a mental framework, modified through time, would have value long after the details of a specific resource management program had become dated or forgotten.

As a result, in my resource management classes with both undergraduates and graduates, I have attempted to integrate concern about fundamental research issues with attention to resource management problems. Initially, this approach has generated confusion for many students. They have had difficulty in linking these different considerations, and in developing their personal research framework. In the longer run, however, the students seem to find this a challenging and worthwhile exercise. Indeed, in an age when 'relevance' and 'utility' seem to be watchwords, most students acknowledge that this approach is 'relevant'.

From the above experience and principles, the form of this book emerged. The basic approach has evolved over a nine-year period of teaching and conducting research in the field of resource management. Undoubtedly, my ideas and approach will continue to evolve. Despite future modifications, the basic objectives are believed to have long-term merit. First, students should become aware of the contributions by geographers and those in related disciplines to resource management. To this end, students should be aware of the major research thrusts in geography, and how these have been influenced by and have had influence upon other issues in the discipline. Second, students should be able to identify basic research issues, and to judge how well these have been handled by geographical studies in resource management.

The book is organized to meet these ends. The first chapter identifies some key ideas as well as discusses research thrusts and issues in geography. The second chapter then outlines some of the issues which arise in research. Based upon personal values and ethics, it is hoped that each student will use this material as a departure point to identify a position relative to the various issues which are identified. The subsequent chapters are each devoted to a substantive area of inquiry in resource analysis. Each chapter concludes with a discussion of the implications for resource management and the conduct of research. The concluding chapter offers more general implications and speculations.

The book is oriented to advanced undergraduate students in geography. It may also be of use to graduate students, as well as to students in related disciplines interested in resource analysis and management. It assumes a background in both physical and human geography. Although an understanding of research methods and quantitative techniques will be helpful to the student, it is not essential. A conscious effort has been made to discuss such material in relatively non-technical and non-jargonistic terms. Where reference to technical aspects could not be avoided, references are provided so that the student can seek clarification and elaboration.

The metric system of measurement (International System of Units) has been emphasized in the text. This approach required the changing of the data in some studies from non-metric to metric equivalents. A metric conversion table is provided in Appendix I.

Considerable help has been received during the preparation of this book. A Canada Council Leave Fellowship and a sabbatical leave from the University of Waterloo provided the opportunity to reflect on teaching and research experience, to complete further reading, and to start writing. Funds from the Leave Fellowship allowed Rob Cook,

Shirley Fenton, Karen Kubis and Barbara Veale to serve as research assistants. Further financial support came from the University of Waterloo Research Grant Subcommittee and the Faculty of Environmental Studies which both provided funds to cover the typing and editing of the manuscript on the computer SCRIPT system.

A number of colleagues read one or more chapters. These included Novia Carter, Chad Day, Dianne Draper, Dave Erb, Jim Gardner, Len Guelke, Ralph Krueger, Geoff McBoyle, Gordon Nelson, Roy Officer, George Priddle, and Geoff Wall. Other colleagues who provided suggestions about ideas, approaches or material were Kiyo Izumi, Richard Preston, Sally Lerner and Sally Weaver. Further suggestions were received from undergraduate and graduate students who were exposed to the ideas and approach during seminars and lectures. Valuable comments and criticisms were offered, not all of which I was able to respond to adequately. Any errors or weaknesses remain my responsibility.

Typing was done with accuracy and speed by secretaries in the geography department. While Rosemary Ambrose and Susan Friesen did most of the typing, others included Jean Fraser, Pat Forgett, Bonnie Roth and Karen Steinfieldt.

Encouragement and support was offered continuously by the Longman Group Ltd. Their cooperation and interest was and is much appreciated.

My wife, Joan, was an active participant in the preparation of this book. In addition to taking on additional responsibilities to provide me extra time for writing, she served as a sounding board and critic. This book is dedicated to her.

Bruce Mitchell
Waterloo, Ontario
October 1978

ACKNOWLEDGEMENTS

We are grateful to the following for permission to reproduce copyright material:
Academic Press Inc. (London) Ltd. and the author, Prof. W. R. Derrick Sewell for fig. 12.1 from fig. 1 and fig. 12.5 from fig. 2 (Sewell 1974); Addison-Wesley Publishing Company for fig. 10.1 from fig. 2.1 and table 10.1 from table 2.1 and an extract (Holsti 1969) © 1969 Addison-Wesley, Reading, Massachusetts; Aldine Publishing Company and the author, Prof. Roger E. Kasperson for fig. 12.3 from fig. 40.1 (Kasperson 1969a) © 1969 by Roger E. Kasperson and Julian V. Minghi; Almqvist and Wiksell International for table 4.2 from table 2 (Aldskogius 1967); American Museum of Natural History for table 6.2 from table 1, table 6.3 from table 2, table 6.4 from fig. 1 and an extract (L. B. Leopold 1969) copyright © the American Museum of Natural History 1969; Associated Business Press for fig. 13.2 from fig. 15.2, p. 223 (Jantsch 1072); Association of American Geographers for table 4.3 and an extract (Jones 1954); the author, Ian Burton for table 8.2 from table 3, p. 12 (Burton, Kates & White 1968); Butterworth Scientific Ltd. for table 3.3 from table 1 (after Robinson 1982c); Cornell University, Center for Environmental Research for fig. 11.1 compiled from data (Canada-United States University Seminar 1973); *Economic Geography* for fig. 4.1 from fig. 4, fig. 4.2 from fig. 5 (Wilson 1967) and fig. 4.3 from fig. 1 (Williams & Zelinsky 1970); Federal Environmental Assessment and Review Office, Ottawa for fig. 9.1 from fig. 8 of *The Assessment and Review of Social Impacts* by R. Lang and A. Armour (1981); Harper and Row Publishers Inc. for fig. 1.1 from fig. 1.2 and two extracts from pp. 2 and 14 (Zimmermann 1951); Holt Rinehart and Winston for fig. 2.2 from fig. 4.1, p. 85 and an extract from p. v (Runkel & McGrath 1972) copyright © 1972 by Holt Rinehart and Winston Inc.; the Institute of British Geographers for fig. 6.4 from fig. 2 (Penning-Rowsell 1975); the Institute for Environmental Studies (University of Toronto) for fig. 2.1 from fig. 2 (Whitney & Dufournaud 1982); Intermountain Research Station, Forest Service (U.S. Dept. of Agriculture) for fig. 7.2 from fig. 1 (Stankey *et al.* 1985); *Journal of the American Institute of Planners* and

the author, Sherry R. Arnstein for table 5.2 from table 2 (Arnstein 1969); *Journal of the American Institute of Planners* and the author, K. H. Craik for table 5.1 and extracts (Craik 1968 & 1970a) McGraw-Hill Book Company for table 2.3 modified from pp. 21–30 (Siegel 1956) copyright © 1956 McGraw-Hill Book Co.; Methuen Publications (Canada) for fig. 1.2 from fig. 1, p. 7 and extracts from p. 6 (Krueger & Mitchell 1977) and fig. 13.1 from fig. 1.1 (Downs 1972); National Recreation and Park Association for fig. 6.3 from fig. 2 and an extract from p. 14 (Shafer, Hamilton & Schmidt 1969); *Norsk Geografisk Tidsskrift* on behalf of the author, T. H. Digernes, for fig. 4.7 from fig. 7 (Digernes 1979); *Operational Geographer* for fig. 1.3 from fig. 1 (Sewell & Mitchell 1984); Penguin Books Ltd. for table 3.2 and an extract from pp. 107–11 (Stamp 1960) © The Estate of L. Dudley Stamp 1960, 1961, 1963; Pergamon Press Inc. and the author, Mr. K. D. Fines for fig. 6.1 from fig. 1 (Fines 1968); Rand McNally College Publishing Co. for table 2.2 from data on pp. 8 & 40 (Campbell & Stanley 1966); Regional Science Research Institute and the authors, Prof. Jack B. Ellis and Prof. Carlton S. Van Doren for table 4.1 from table 1 and an extract from p. 56 (Ellis & Van Doren 1966); Royal Scottish Geographical Society for fig. 6.2 from fig. 5, table 6.5 from table 1 and extracts from pp. 219, 227 & 231 (Linton 1968); Ryerson Polytechnical Institute (Department of Geography) for table 5.4 from fig. 1 (Smith 1983b); Sage Publications Inc. and the author Timothy O'Riordan for fig. 12.4 from fig. 2, p. 202 (O'Riordan 1971b); School of Urban and Regional Planning (University of Waterloo) for table 5.3 from table 3 (after Shrubsole 1986); the University of Liverpool (Department of Geography) for fig. 12.2 from fig. 12, p. 88 (Mitchell 1971); University of New Mexico School of Law for fig. 7.1 from fig. 2 (Lucas 1964), and table 8.1 from table 1 and an extract from p. 440 (Burton & Kates 1964a); Wilfrid Laurier University for fig. 9.3 from fig. 2 (Gardner 1972–73).

Whilst every effort has been made, we are unable to trace the copyright owners of fig. 9.2 (Day *et al.* 1977) from fig. 1, p. 173 of *Environment Impact Assessment in Canada: Processes and Approaches* edited by M. Plewes and J. Whitney and would appreciate any information which would enable us to do so.

CHAPTER 1
RESOURCE ANALYSIS AND GEOGRAPHY

1.1 INTRODUCTION

The goals of this book are: (1) to introduce the reader to contributions by geographers and by those in related disciplines to resource analysis; (2) to indicate how geographical research in resource analysis has evolved out of several major traditions in the discipline; (3) to identify research issues which must be considered in resource analysis and how these have been handled by geographers; and (4) to identify resource management issues and how geographical research has contributed to their understanding and solution. In this chapter attention is directed towards explaining some key concepts (natural resources, resource analysis, resource management, resource development), identifying the range of dimensions that are involved in studying natural resources, and identifying major themes in geographical research.

1.2 THE NATURE OF NATURAL RESOURCES

Zimmermann (1933; 3–9) provided a functional interpretation of resources which is as relevant today as when first proposed in 1933. He argued that neither the environment as such nor parts of the environment are resources until they are, or are considered to be, capable of satisfying human needs. That is, resources are an expression of appraisal and represent an entirely *subjective* concept. To illustrate, he explained that coal was not a resource without people whose wants and capabilities gave it utility. He thus viewed the concept of a resource as a subjective, relative and functional one.

In a revised edition, Zimmermann (1951; 3–20) elaborated upon this functional interpretation of resources. He stressed that natural resources are dynamic, becoming available to man through a combination of increased knowledge and expanding technology as

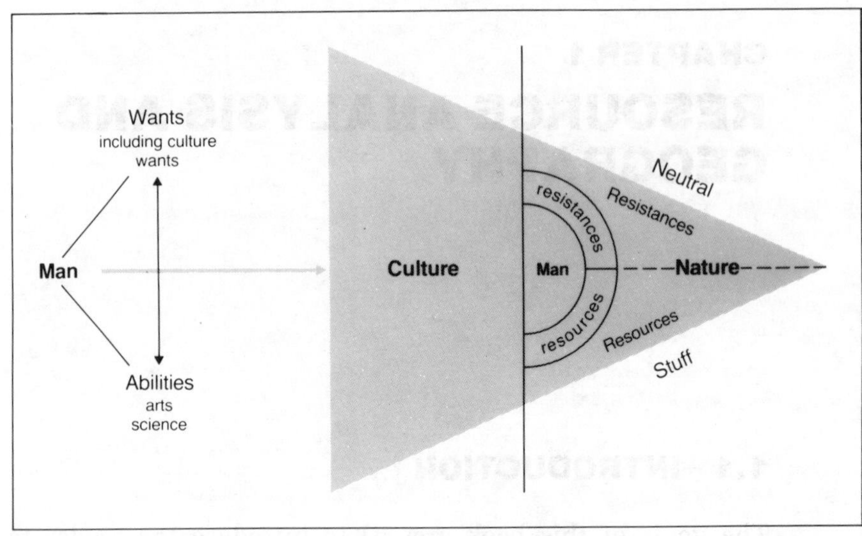

Fig. 1.1 Man, culture and nature (*after Zimmermann, 1951*)

well as changing individual and societal objectives. From this position, attributes of nature are no more than 'neutral stuff' until man is able to perceive their presence, to recognize their capacity to satisfy human wants, and to devise means to utilize them (Fig. 1.1). Consequently, resources evolve from a three-way interaction of natural, human and cultural assets. In other words, in the frequently quoted words from his book, 'Resources *are* not, they *become*; they are not static but expand and contract in response to human wants and human actions' (Zimmermann, 1951; 15).

In summary, natural resources are defined by human perceptions and attitudes, wants, technological skills, legal, financial and institutional arrangements, as well as by political customs. What is a natural resource in one culture may be 'neutral stuff' in another culture. Resources, to use Zimmermann's words, are subjective, relative and functional.

1.3 RESOURCE ANALYSIS

The term 'analysis' is often used to mean the 'examination of a thing's parts to find out their essential features' (*World Book Dictionary*, 1975; Vol. 1). Following this definition, four types of geographical research in resource analysis suggest themselves. These are: (1) studies of natural resources themselves: surveying, mapping and measurement of the supply of and demand for resources as well as their characteristics and properties (Chs 3, 6, 7); (2) studies of alternative allocations (spatial, temporal, functional) of resources in terms of users, facilities and activities (Chs 4, 7, 8, 9); (3) studies of variables (biophysical, technological, economic, social, political, institutional, legal) which condition resource allocation or development (Chs 5, 7, 9, 11, 12); and (4) studies of the impact of specific resource allocations (Chs 10, 11, 12).

The orientation of these types of research activity indicates a role for the geographer as resource analyst. They indicate a predisposition towards the compilation and manipulation of data about natural resources, or the inquiry into the manner in which resources are allocated among competing uses and users. The focus is upon determining the way in which resources are actually located and used, as well as upon exploring alternative ways in which they could or should be utilized. *As resource analyst, the geographer seeks to understand the fundamental characteristics of natural resources and the processes through which they are, could be, and should be allocated and utilized.* The actual allocation of resources lies in the domain of the manager who may or may not be a geographer. A key consideration in this book is to determine what distinctive role the geographer has played and may play as a resource analyst (section 1.6).

1.4 RESOURCE MANAGEMENT AND RESOURCE DEVELOPMENT

If resource analysis concentrates upon understanding the characteristics of natural resources and the processes through which they are allocated, resource management emphasizes the control or direction of resource development. In other words, *resource management represents the actual decisions concerning policy or practice regarding how resources are allocated and under what conditions or arrangements resources may be developed.* In O'Riordan's (1971a; 19) words, resource management

> may be defined as a process of decision making whereby resources are allocated over space and time according to the needs, aspirations, and desires of man within the framework of his technological inventiveness, his political and social institutions, and his legal and administrative arrangements. Resource management should be visualized as a conscious process of decision involving judgement, preference and commitment, whereby certain desired resource outputs are sought from certain perceived resource combinations through the choice among various managerial, technical and administrative alternatives.

More succinctly, resource management may be viewed to be about power and politics (Fernie and Pitkethly, 1985; vii). Resource management in this sense may involve either the management of production from a specific resource (a forest) or the overall planning of the development and use of resources in an area or region. It is generally

Table 1.1 The roles of resource analysts, managers and developers

Example	Analyst	Manager	Developer
A. Regarding a specific resource: *water*	1. Determine quantity, quality, availability, dependability 2. Determine demand 3. Evaluate alternative strategies regarding efficiency, equity . . . 4. Analyse constraints upon alternative allocation patterns 5. Identify alternative methods of allocation	1. Establish regulations to govern allocations 2. Mediate among conflicting uses and users 3. Ensure that regulations are enforced	1. Translate 'neutral stuff' into a resource by building dam, waste treatment plant, irrigation system . . .
B. Regarding a specific resource management issue: *carrying capacity* for a wilderness area	1. Identify nature of the resource and users 2. Conduct research to establish thresholds beyond which biophysical environment and user satisfaction deteriorates 3. Examine relative impacts of possible regulations to minimize deterioration 4. Monitor use	1. Establish regulations to govern use 2. Design facilities (trails, campgrounds)	1. Build or provide desired facilities and activities

executed by elected or appointed officials in the public or private sector. In reaching decisions, the resource manager will frequently seek guidance from the resource analyst, although the latter's advice usually represents only one of many inputs to be considered in the decision process. In contrast, *resource development represents the actual exploitation or use of a resource during the transformation of 'neutral stuff' into a commodity or service to serve human needs and aspirations.*

Although the activities of analyst, manager and developer may overlap, it is useful to differentiate among them, especially since the initial education of a geographer is usually oriented towards preparing individuals to be analysts. This statement is not meant to imply that managers or developers never have geographical backgrounds. They often do, particularly in the area of resource management. While the geographer's initial education often makes him best qualified with professional expertise as a resource analyst, subsequent study or work, individual qualities or other considerations may result in the geographer becoming highly competent as a manager or developer. Table 1.1 illustrates some of the different activities which may be characteristic of the analyst, manager or developer in selected situations.

1.5 A VARIETY OF DIMENSIONS

Firey (1960; 20) has identified three broad groupings of concern regarding natural resources: physical habitat, human culture, and economic scarcity. If these three groups are combined with the ideas advanced by Zimmermann, the following perspectives emerge: biophysical, economic, social, political, legal, institutional, and technological. In other words, analysis of resource problems may be pursued through one or more of these perspectives. If temporal and spatial components are added, a matrix is created which emphasizes the importance of achieving in-depth knowledge about specific perspectives, time periods and spatial scales, as well as an appreciation of their interactions (Fig. 1.2).

Whether considering a resource sector (air, water, land, wildlife, minerals), a resource topic (demand, supply, quality), a resource problem (carrying capacity, public involvement, environmental assessment) or a resource issue (conflicts among recreationists on a lake or river), this framework emphasizes the substantial mix and difficulty of considerations involved in reaching decisions (Krueger and Mitchell, 1977; 6). To develop a thorough grasp of even one perspective, time period or spatial scale represents a monumental task. This situation emphasizes the importance of being able to identify and define problems, to assess the adequacy of evidence, and to separate conclusions based upons evidence from those not supported by proof or

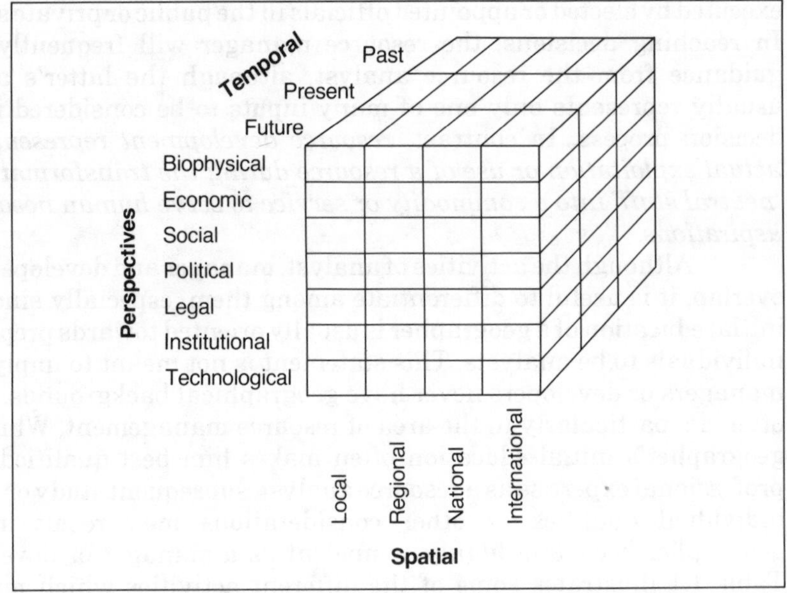

Fig. 1.2 Dimensions of resource analysis (*after Krueger and Mitchell, 1977*)

logic. These aspects are crucial, because as Krueger and Mitchell (1977; 6) have observed, 'Those in management positions do not have the luxury of studying and contemplating forever before making decisions. Conflicting demands for the use of resources increase, problems occur, issues arise and action must be taken.' As a result, in addition to seeking in-depth understanding, the analyst must be able to balance the need for more understanding against the necessity of completing an investigation in time so that its results can be used in a management decision.

As it is necessary to be aware of the variety of dimensions in resource analysis, so it is essential to be aware of the different stages in resource management to which the analyst will be expected to contribute. In addition, it is desirable to have an appreciation of the different levels at which geographical input may be made. Sewell and Mitchell (1984; 25) provided some comments in this regard when discussing the achievements by and prospects for geographers in public policy. They suggested that policy making consists of four stages; (1) identification of a significant problem, for which either there is no policy or else present policies are inadequate; (2) formulation of a policy which attempts to solve the problem; (3) implementation of policy; and (4) monitoring the effects of policy. They noted that the second stage has primarily been decided in the political arena. The contribution of geographers to public policy has more often been in the first and fourth stages of the process.

Concerning levels at which geographical input can be made to policy, they noted that the effectiveness of input is conditioned not only by individual abilities but also by the level of the administrative hierarchy at which it is made. With reference to a national level of policy making in a parliamentary system, at one end of the scale is the policy maker himself. At the other end is the interested academic whose primary concern is understanding the problems to be faced by the policy maker. In between these extremes, a range of other roles exist (Fig. 1.3).

When functioning as a professional geographer, an individual is unlikely to have a role as policy maker. In democratic societies, that

Stages of policy evolution →

Inputs from policy-makers and technical advisors	Problem identification and strategy specification	Policy formulation	Policy implementation	Policy evaluation
Policy makers e.g. ministers	▬▬▬▬▬▬▬▬▬	▬▬▬▬▬▬▬▬▬	▬▬▬▬▬▬▬▬▬	---------
Other politicians e.g. Members of Parliament	OOOOOOOOO	OOOOOOOOO	OOOOOOOOO	OOOOOOOOO
Internal advisors e.g. senior officials	▬▬▬▬▬▬▬▬▬	---------	OOOOOOOOO	---------
External advisors e.g. advisory boards	■■■■■■■■■	---------	---------	---------
Research consultants e.g. ad hoc advisors	■■■■■■■■■	---------	■■■■■■■■■	---------
Critics e.g. involved academics and interest groups	OOOOOOOOO	---------	---------	OOOOOOOOO
Uninvolved observers and researchers	---------	---------	---------	---------

Degree of influence on policy (Low → High)

Contributions

Key

Continuous	▬▬▬▬▬▬▬▬▬
Frequent and important	■■■■■■■■■
Frequent but less important	OOOOOOOOO
Occasional	---------

Fig. 1.3 Stages and levels of policy involvement (*after Sewell and Mitchell, 1984, 24*)

role is usually held by elected officials who are responsible and accountable for their decisions. As a professional, the geographer is more likely to function in one of the roles of Internal Adviser, External Adviser, Consultant, or Critic (Fig. 1.3). In these roles the geographer may exert considerable influence in shaping policy. Because elected officials do not always have the time or expertise to understand the complexities of a resource management problem, they often rely heavily on the advice of their advisers. All of these roles demand an ability to bring geographical concepts, methods and techniques to bear on problems, to appreciate fundamental research issues which must be overcome, and to recognize basic resource management problems. In addition, as a scholar, the individual should be able to visualize the implications of analytic work for other work in the discipline as well as to appreciate the potential that ongoing work in the discipline has for the immediate problem under investigation. In this spirit the remainder of this chapter briefly discusses major traditions in geographical research.

1.6 MAJOR THEMES IN GEOGRAPHICAL RESEARCH

Numerous definitions have been developed concerning the nature of geography. When various statements are examined, three themes appear dominant. These themes are spatial analysis, ecological analysis, and regional analysis. Each of these themes has its proponents, and each underlies a substantial number of investigations.

1.6.1 SPATIAL ANALYSIS

The theme of spatial analysis has been developed in many ways. Ackerman (1958; 2, 19) wrote that geography is the 'science of spatial distribution' and believed that an objective of geographic research must be an 'understanding of the evolution of space content as it is influenced by the physical, biotic and cultural processes'. McCarty (1963; 3) offered a similar viewpoint when stating that geography's focus was 'to account for the locations and spatial arrangements of phenomena on the earth's surface'. Morrill (1970; 3) stated that the core elements of geography were space, spatial relations, and change in space. More precisely, he maintained that geographers were concerned about how physical space is structured, how men relate through space, how men have organized their societies in space, and how the conception and use of space have changed. Abler, Adams and Gould (1971; 61) explained that geography differentiated itself from other sciences by the questions posed about 'location, spatial structure and spatial process'. They also asserted that in the future questions will shift from a concern with where things are or have been to where things can be or should be. In brief, the theme of spatial analysis focuses attention upon locations and distributions of phenomena; interactions of people, goods and services between places and regions; spatial structure, arrangements and organizations; and spatial processes.

As Taafe (1974; 9–10) observed, a strength of spatial analysis has been its capacity to generate cumulative generalizations to a greater degree than other themes. As a result, the spatial analysts have probably progressed furthest in attempts to build theory. On the other hand, Taafe also noted that spatial analysis has had at least two shortcomings. A progressive abstracting of spatial patterns increases the danger of overconcern with 'sterile geometric patterns'. Furthermore, research on this theme suffers from a danger that a disproportionate share of research might be allocated to problems which are as socially trivial as they are theoretically tractable. When examining research in resource analysis, the reader should seek to determine what significance the spatial analysis theme has had for the types of questions posed, the research strategies applied and the contribution toward development of theory. This theme has been particularly influential on the studies discussed in Chapters 3 and 4.

1.6.2 ECOLOGICAL ANALYSIS

Ecological analysis, or the study of man–environment relationships, enjoyed a revived interest with the emergence of concern with environmental issues during the late 1960s and early 1970s. Prior to this revival, it had been neglected due to events in the early years of the twentieth century. Analysis of man–environment relationships was an important facet of geographical research in the early 1900s. Unfortunately, researchers became preoccupied with describing and explaining human behaviour in terms of the physical environment. This work, in its extreme form known as 'environmental determinism', became too simplistic. Reasons for human behaviour were seen as a result only of physical factors, with other possible explanatory variables being overlooked or ignored. Furthermore, having been frustrated in attempts at explanation, many geographers then focused upon description without regard to explanation or prediction (section 2.1.1). During the latter part of the 1960s, however, ecological analysis started to become more fashionable with the arrival of the 'environmental crisis' (Carson, 1962; Udall, 1963; Ehrlich, 1968; Commoner, 1972a).

Despite the rejection of man–environment relationships as a focus of research in the early 1900s, prominent geographers continued to urge research on this theme. Barrows (1923; 3) suggested that geography should be defined as human ecology, with the aim of determining 'the relationships existing between natural environments and the distribution and activities of man'. Aware of the negative connotations from the era of environmental determinism, Barrows emphasized that geographers should study this relationship

> from the standpoint of man's adjustment to the environment, rather than from that of environmental influence. The former approach is more likely to result in the recognition and proper evaluation of all the factors involved, and especially to minimize the danger of assigning to the environmental factors a deterministic influence which they do not exert.

Barrow's viewpoint of geography as human ecology, focusing upon human adjustment to the environment, has become the conceptual foundation upon which hazard research has grown (Ch. 8).

Sauer (1941, 1956) reinforced Barrow's ideas by urging geographers explicitly to incorporate an historical dimension when studying the processes through which different cultures adjusted to and modified the landscape. The importance of appreciating the historical context within which man–environment adjustments evolve is gaining renewed attention (Guelke, 1982a). Sauer visualized ecological and regional analysis themes as overlapping and complementing one another, as geographical research documented the evolution of culture and landscape interaction within given localities.

In the early 1960s, Ackerman (1963; 435) placed ecological analysis into a systems framework. During a presidential address to the Association of American Geographers, he argued that geography was concerned with systems and that its overriding problem was '. . . nothing less than an understanding of the vast, interacting system comprising all humanity and its natural environment on the surface of the earth'.

As with the spatial analysis theme, later chapters will strive to ascertain how the ecological theme has influenced the type of work undertaken by geographers in resource analysis (Chs 5, 6, 7, 8, 9). The latter theme has led to fewer cumulative generalizations than the spatial viewpoint. However, the study of man–environment relations has often focused geographers' attention upon pressing environmental problems (Biswas, 1981).

1.6.3 REGIONAL ANALYSIS

Regional studies and geography are frequently thought of as synonymous. For many people, their only introduction to geography has been studying of foreign places, and learning numerous facts about regions. This facet of regional analysis, sometimes alluded to as 'capes and bays' geography, is regional geography at its worst. Innumerable facts are memorized with little or no attention to principles, concepts or problems. At the other extreme, the careful and thorough synthesis of the attributes of an area which give it a particular quality, set of problems and range of opportunities is extremely difficult (Hart, 1982). And, while such a regional exercise often is primarily of educational value, it also is a frequent prerequisite for regional and resource planning (Ginsberg, 1957), or for appreciating attitudes toward local environments (Parsons, 1985).

Regional analysis has a long tradition as a major theme within geography. Fenneman (1919; 7) was blunt when exclaiming that '... the one thing that is first, last, and always geography and nothing else, is the study of areas in their compositeness and complexity, that is *regional* geography'. Sauer (1925; 21), interrelating the ecological and regional themes, wrote that the field of geography is 'the knowledge of landscapes or of lands' while Hartshorne (1939; 1959) became well known for his argument that 'geography is a study which looks at all of reality found within the earth surface from a particular point of view, namely that of areal differentiation' (1939; 374). Lukermann (1964; 167) asserted a similar view by claiming that geography is the knowledge of the world as it exists in places. In his view, the basic geographic question is why the world is, or why the world is seen to be, divided into places and regions. An interpretation by Broek (1965; 3–4) touches upon many of the ideas already mentioned. He believed that geography was distinguished from other disciplines through its '... concern with the character of "place", that is, the integrated whole of a people and its habitat, and the interrelations between places'. Broek thought that geographers do not study people, crops, customs, minerals, towns and other phenomena for their own sake, but because they are perceived as parts of an interrelated complex that gives character to a place.

Like the other themes, regional analysis has strengths and weaknesses. At its weakest, it becomes an encyclopedic list of facts concerning an area, lacking either structure or a problem-oriented focus. At its strongest, regional analysis integrates spatial and ecological analysis within a defined area. This type of synthesis, requiring understanding of an array of variables and their interrelationships, defines the character of a place (Chs 5 and 6). Such a holistic viewpoint is a prerequisite to human intervention in natural systems if undesirable repercussions of management decisions are to be avoided (Chs 10, 11 and 12).

1.6.4 OVERVIEW

In the preceding discussion (sections 1.6.1 to 1.6.3), the characteristics of three identifiable research themes were outlined. Although some investigations recognized the interdependence of two or more themes, the majority advocated one theme as the core for the discipline. Other writers have taken the position that all themes are valid foundations for geographical inquiry. Pattison (1964) is representative of the second group when stating that a small number of distinct but affiliated traditions characterize geographical research.

His traditions – spatial, area studies, man–land, earth science – are all viewed as legitimate ones.

Pattison's reference to a fourth tradition or theme – earth sciences – draws attention to the important role of physical geography in resource analysis. The contribution from physical geography may include improved understanding of specific natural processes or greater appreciation of the interactions occurring in complex ecosystems (Marcus, 1979). Geomorphologists have demonstrated that knowledge regarding landforms can assist in efforts to minimize environmental impact during resource development (Cooke and Doornkamp, 1974; Mensching, 1982). Fluvial geomorphologists also have shown how water systems may be modified through human manipulation (Aegerter and Messerli, 1983; Adams, 1985). Similar managerial lessons emerge from research in biogeography (Vale and Parker, 1980; Cole and Smith, 1984; Price, 1985), soils (Rodda, 1980), and climatology (Bryson, 1974; Trilsbach and Hulme, 1984). It also should be stressed that the physical geographer's work may be applied directly to urban areas (Detwyler and Marcus, 1972; Berry and Horton, 1974), regarding problems associated with vegetation (Detwyler, 1972), soils (Gray, 1972) or wildlife (Gill and Bonnett, 1973).

A general question must be raised at this stage. Geography does not enjoy an exclusive claim to these separate themes or traditions. Other disciplines and professions such as ecology, economics, anthropology, sociology, psychology, planning, engineering and medicine have a direct interest in the man–environment or ecological theme. Similarly, the spatial, regional and earth sciences research themes are of interest to other disciplines. If geographers are to have a substantive role in resource analysis, they have to demonstrate how their input is different from that of other disciplines and professions.

This question is addressed by those who present the view that geography's distinct contribution arises from integrating the three major research themes (spatial, ecological, regional). Berry (1964) offered the thesis that the geographic point of view is spatial, and that the integrating concepts and processes of the geographer relate to spatial arrangements and distributions, to spatial integration, to spatial interactions and organization, and to spatial processes. Nevertheless, Berry concluded that a spatial perspective is not the geographer's sole prerequisite since other scientists also are concerned with space. In his view, geography's contribution results from applying the spatial perspective to understanding the earth as the home of man. He defined such a system as the complex worldwide man–earth ecosystem. Although biologists, botanists and ecologists may study such ecosystems from a spatial viewpoint as well, Berry claimed (1964; 3) that 'the geographer is the person who concentrates upon the spatial analysis of that worldwide ecosystem of which man is a part'. And, while many social sciences study man-made environments, none emphasize a spatial point of view as does the geographer.

An Ad-Hoc Committee on Geography of the National Academy of Sciences–National Research Council (1965) offered a similar view. Restating Ackerman's definition (section 1.6.2), the Committee designated geography's overriding problem as the full understanding of the vast system on the earth's surface comprising man and his natural environment. This definition was qualified, however, with the comment that the man–environment system is treated primarily from the point of view of space in time.

In contrast to these positive views about the concept of integration, Buttimer (1986) has questioned the value of integration as a unifying concept for geography. In the context of resources management, Ferguson and Alley (1984; 36) have noted that while geographers often believe that they have skill regarding integration, these views are too often internal to the discipline and not recognized by other professions. Thus, as with most issues, conflicting viewpoints can exist.

This discussion of major themes in geographical research has a simple objective. The student should identify one or more themes or perspectives which are personally satisfying and which serve to make clear geography's contribution to resource analysis relative to other disciplines. Furthermore, such an exercise will ensure that individual geographers will be able to identify where study in a specialized subfield relates to geography as a whole (Davis, 1906; 3).

Having urged the development of a definition of geography, a cautionary note is in order. Although it is desirable to have a working definition of the discipline, the individual who becomes over-concerned with disciplinary boundaries may lose desirable flexibility. The important point is to see where your background allows you to make substantial contribution to resource analysis, not to eliminate problems because they do not fit neatly into disciplinary bounds. Several prominent geographers have issued similar warnings. Writing in 1941, Sauer (p. 4) noted that

> Particularly depressing has been the tendency to question, not the competence, originality, or significance of research ..., but the admissibility of work because it may or may not satisfy a narrow definition of geography. When a subject is ruled, not by inquisitiveness, but by definitions of its boundaries, it is likely to face extinction. This way lies the death of learning.
>
> A healthy science is engaged in discovery, verification, comparison, and generalization. Its subject matter will be determined by its competence in discovery and organization.

Just over 30 years later, Gilbert White, one of the major geographical innovators in resource analysis, re-echoed Sauer's sentiments. White (1972a; 102) remarked that 'One of the common and commonly destructive questions about research runs "But is it geography?" I would like to see us substitute "Is it significant?" and "Are you competent to deal with it?".' In replying to White, Browning (1974; 137–9) leaves us with good advice. He basically agreed with White, but was concerned that geography faces a danger of becoming fragmented in its interests and superficial in its research. Thus he felt that identification of the 'central concerns and concepts of geography' was essential. If the student is successful in this endeavour, then he or she will have a firm base from which to launch studies in resource analysis, will be able to identify his or her contribution as a geographer to the investigation and resolution of resource issues, and will be able to determine what consequences the student's research contains for the discipline of geography.

1.7 INTERDISCIPLINARY INQUIRY

The complexity of resource analysis suggests that more than one disciplinary viewpoint is required to conduct the necessary research. This had led to calls for interdisciplinary or transdisciplinary research in which the problem rather than disciplinary orientation is the overriding concern (Jantsch, 1972). An interdisciplinary orientation should not create a problem for the geographer. In adopting quantitative techniques, geographers have had to become conversant with the language of mathematicians and statisticians. The conduct of behavioural research has forced greater awareness of, and interaction with, psychologists, anthropologists and sociologists. Concern with environmental impact assessments has necessitated greater familiarity with the ideas of scientists from biophysical disciplines, especially those from ecology. Paradoxically, this recognition of the need and desirability for interdisciplinary studies requires the geographer to define the nature of his own contribution to resource analysis. If he is to have a viable role in research involving other disciplines, the geographer must be aware of the overriding research problem(s) at the core of his discipline as well as the relevance of traditional research themes to these problems (Birch, 1977; 420).

Man–environment relationships and spatial analyses are not the exclusive domain of geographers. The former is shared with many social science disciplines, and the latter with such diverse interests as management science, economics and regional science. The earth sciences tradition is shared with geology and other physical sciences. As a result, this first chapter has attempted to identify and describe the characteristics of the discipline. With this background and an appreciation for the questions demanding attention in resource analysis and resource management, the student should develop a research philosophy and framework to which investigations can be related.

Changing technologies make it even more imperative that the

geographer pursuing resource analysis should have a clear image of his discipline, its strengths and weaknesses. Ever more powerful computers with their scope for handling larger amounts of data and for facilitating sophisticated ways of producing visual displays through computer cartography require the geographer to know the extent to which he must be conversant with such technologies. The appearance of remote sensing to monitor the earth's resources suggests that the geographer competent only in conventional aerial photographic interpretation is lacking a significant research tool. Again the question arises, however, as to the extent to which every geographer should become competent with the various displays available through remote sensing. Only by having a clear appreciation for the nature and scope of his own discipline will the geographer be able to determine at what point such technologies cease being means to an end and become ends in themselves.

In summary, the thrust of this chapter is to increase the geographer's awareness of his own discipline as it relates to resource analysis and resource management. It is not a comprehensive survey of how the discipline has evolved. It does attempt to clarify what is meant by resource analysis and management. It outlines the major traditions of research in geography. This material should allow the student a perspective from which he can judge what the geographer's contribution might be in resource analysis, and what implications work in resource analysis might have for the discipline as a whole. Davis (1906; 3) expressed similar feelings when commenting

> Our work will become more serviceable to others if it is presented in such a manner that its relations to the whole subject are made clear. ... we may often benefit ourselves by systematically setting forth the place of our individual studies in geography as a whole, for we may be thereby led to discover that the systematic sequence of parts is interrupted here and there by gaps, which can be filled by well-directed effort.

CHAPTER 2
THE RESEARCH PROCESS

2.1 INTRODUCTION

This chapter outlines the nature of the research process, and identifies some basic considerations which require attention when conducting resource analysis studies. The intent is to make the student more aware of what is involved in conducting research. At least two benefits should result. First, the student will be in a better position to improve the quality of his own research. Second, the student will be able to more critically assess research done by others. The chapter is divided into four parts. The first section (2.1) considers different ways in which research can be categorized. The following section (2.2) addresses the matters of research philosophy, ideology and theory. The next (2.3) identifies some basic considerations associated with technical efficiency, ethical considerations and practical value which are encountered in research. The fourth (2.4) discusses more general considerations (compromise, subjectivity, serendipity, and others) deserving attention.

Before examining the different types of research, however, the major components of an inquiry must be identified. The quality of research rests upon three aspects: *problem, evidence,* and *conclusion.* Although interrelated, each of these is an identifiable foundation for investigations. If any one of these is weak or falters, the entire research effort may become suspect.

The first foundation identifies the nature of the problem to be investigated. In resource analysis, particularly when studying the processes through which resources are allocated, it is important that symptoms be distinguished from causes and effects. This consideration is important in resource analysis, for all too often resource management policies, programmes or projects are not focused upon basic problems. Irrigation projects are designed to increase agricultural production by a specified number of tonnes per hectare. A hydroelectric dam is constructed to generate a predetermined number of megawatts. However, as White (1972b; 914) and Sewell (1973; 36–37) have argued, such procedures state goals in terms of *means* rather than of *ends*. Ends should represent goals involving changes in national income, income redistribution, political equity, aesthetics and environmental protection rather than specific levels of production of goods or services. More detailed discussion of problem definition is contained in section 2.3.1.

Once the problem has been defined, collection of evidence becomes critical. *Evidence* represents information pointing towards, but not necessarily proving, the truth or falsehood of something. In contrast, *proof* implies evidence that leaves little doubt, and *testimony* indicates something said or done to demonstrate something to be true or false. In resource analysis, the investigator often deals with evidence rather than proof, and testimony from respondents may be collected as part of the evidence. Since the force of a report is often governed by the nature of supporting evidence, it is desirable to have some standards against which such evidence may be judged. In sections 2.3.2 and 2.3.3 the main focus is upon describing the factors which determine the adequacy of evidence.

In *the conclusion*, the researcher offers his decision or judgement about the problem. The conclusion frequently has at least two components. One component represents judgements based upon the assembled evidence. Insofar as the evidence is adequate and the reasoning logical, these conclusions are based upon a solid base. The other component may more properly be called *speculation* which is based upon the evidence as well as the investigator's experience, intuition and beliefs. Such speculation may centre upon possible explanations for unaccountable patterns, or views about the implications of the findings for management or research procedures. This component is legitimate, needed and important. However, the investigator has an obligation to differentiate conclusions based upon evidence from those founded upon experience and intuition. Such a distinction allows the reader to judge the sources from which conclusions are drawn. Greater elaboration on this aspect is found in section 2.3.4.

2.1.1 DESCRIPTION, EXPLANATION, PREDICTION, PRESCRIPTION

One method of categorizing research is on a description–prescription hierarchy. The implication is that each level in the hierarchy precedes the one after it, although exceptions exist. *Description* emphasizes 'what', 'where' and 'when' without attention to 'how' or 'why'. It normally is considered the most basic level of research. Associated with description is classification, a procedure in which phenomena are arranged into classes according to some method or system. Land use classification systems (Ch. 3) represent this level of inquiry in resource analysis. *Explanation* shifts the focus to 'how' and 'why' phenomena behave as they do. In the previous example, while description would emphasize the types and distributions of land use in a region, explanation would seek to account for the observed patterns. In pursuit of explanation, the researcher would determine what influence variables ranging from climate, terrain and soil, to markets and technology, to culture and beliefs, have upon land use.

For *prediction*, the investigator strives to show what events, distributions or behaviour will occur in the future given certain conditions. Thus, he would attempt to indicate what changes in land use could be expected if factors of production, distribution or consumption were altered. Explanation is not always a necessary prerequisite for prediction, as in some instances it is possible to forecast future changes without understanding why these changes occur. Hare (1985; 132) has observed that the public demand is for prediction, as the decision makers and general public want to know what the outcome will be if we go on as we have been, and what will happen if we intervene and make changes. Hare also notes that prediction is extremely difficult due to the enormous number of unknowns in any system.

Description, explanation and prediction are usually accepted as the major concerns of analysts. Effort may be devoted to one or more of these levels when tackling a research problem. Development of theory, however, requires work beyond the level of description into the realms of explanation–prediction. Another concept is *prescription*, implying statements concerned with what *should be* rather than with what *is* or *will be*. As attention is given to applied work, prescriptive or *normative* research is encountered with greater frequency. Before prescribing, however, the analyst has an obligation to be able to describe and explain the problem under attention.

2.2 PHILOSOPHIES, IDEOLOGIES AND THEORY

Research philosophy is interpreted here as the set of principles or guidelines used to direct research activity. Various philosophies co-exist, and they lead researchers to pose different questions, accept different evidence, and even to identify different ultimate goals for research. Ideology represents a set of doctrines which reflect values and strongly influence the way in which individuals perceive the world and therefore in turn how they identify problems. To illustrate, a combination of doctrines, assertions and intentions can be used to differentiate capitalist and communist ideologies. The importance given to theory depends very much upon the research philosophy which is adopted. Even then, disagreements may arise as to what constitutes adequate theory. These various aspects are examined more thoroughly in the following subsections. Unless these matters are understood, it is difficult to judge the adequacy of research activity, or to determine appropriate directions for future research effort.

2.2.1 PHILOSOPHICAL AND IDEOLOGICAL FOUNDATIONS

Numerous research philosophies exist (Christenson, 1982; Johnston, 1983a). The attributes of three of them - positivism, phenomenology and idealism - are considered here in order to illustrate how choice of research problem, research strategy and research standards are governed substantially by choice of philosophy.

Positivism represents a broad school of philosophy, and generalizations about it are difficult. Nevertheless, this term is often used interchangeably with 'scientific method' and has been a dominant force in structuring what is judged as acceptable research. This approach is characterized by such concepts as order, regularities, hypotheses, theories, laws, explanation, prediction, models and systems. Walmsley (1974; 97) has given another perspective when commenting that positivism is associated with a belief in empirical truth and logical consistency.

In terms of actual procedure, Ackerman (1963; 433) provided a good description of what is involved. The investigator proceeds through several well-defined phases after identifying a problem: observation and description; construction of hypotheses; testing of these hypotheses either through conduct of an experiment or further observation; replication and verification of experiment and observation; and finally, 'the building of a body of theory from verified hypotheses which in turn becomes the basis for new hypotheses, and new observations and experiment'.

The ultimate purpose of positivism is the generation of theories to explain and predict the relationships between phenomena. The procedure used is one that is amenable to replication by other investigators in order that the results from experiments or observations may be verified. By building upon previous research, investigations are designed to extend knowledge of basic processes and result in a steady accumulation of knowledge. This philosophy has been particularly significant for research conducted in spatial analysis (Ch. 4).

The positivist's approach is not without problems. Geographers are often unable to isolate and measure each of the factors that might affect a particular relationship. Without being able to identify the nature of the cause-effect relationships, it becomes difficult to establish theories upon which to base explanation and prediction. As Blalock (1970) has observed, due to the highly inter-related nature of the variables there may be almost as many theories or explanations as there are investigators. These and other considerations have led people such as Guelke (1971; 45) to conclude that '... there is a strong possibility that those geographers who are searching for laws of human spatial behaviour are involved in a futile search'.

A reaction against positivism led to the development of an alternative approach which has come to be known as humanism (Zelinsky, 1975; Davgun, 1980; Smith, 1984; Guelke, 1986). Within humanism there has been identified a range of alternative philosophies, including existentialism, phenomenology, idealism and realism. Phenomenology and idealism are reviewed here.

One alternative which has received considerable attention is phenomenology. A number of geographers have outlined the attributes of this philosophy (Relph, 1970; Tuan, 1971a, 1971b; Mercer and Powell, 1972; Walmsley, 1974; King, 1976; Billinge, 1977). All of those individuals agree that an appeal of phenomenology is its rejection of hypothesis testing and lack of emphasis upon development of theory.

Relph (1970) provided a succinct overview of this philosophy. The phenomenologist studies man–environment relationships by focusing upon human experiences, including actions, memories, fantasies and perceptions. Whereas the positivist assumes that there is an objective world independent of man, the phenomenologist believes that all knowledge stems from the world of experience and cannot be isolated from that world. As a consequence, any perception or behaviour is not governed simply by an object or event seen in the world but rather by a larger 'thematic field' incorporating all the possible intentions, meanings and former experiences related to that object or event. The phenomenologist seeks to understand the 'essences' of the thematic field associated with given phenomena.

Man is thus viewed as the source of acts and intention, and it is only through their study that meaning can be given to behaviour. The major implication of this posture is that there is no single, objective world. Instead, there is a variety of worlds, the range determined by the number and type of attitudes and intentions of man. From this position, it is easy to appreciate why the concept of a single, rational and objective world held by the positivist is rejected, and why the establishment of theory is given little importance. This viewpoint holds considerable intuitive appeal. Thus, the discussion in section 1.2 was essentially phenomenological in assuming that 'resources are not; they become' based upon the given culture, knowledge and skills of a society. And, if it is accepted that the world can only be understood in terms of man's attitudes and intentions, then the research theme of ecological analysis or man–environment relations takes on new significance. Much of this viewpoint underlies research on perceptions and attitudes (Ch. 5), landscape evaluation (Ch. 6), behavioural carrying capacity (Ch. 7), natural hazards (Ch. 8) and evaluation (Ch. 10).

Not surprisingly, the positivists are not impressed by the research procedure generated by phenomenology. If the world is defined by the changing experiences, attitudes and intentions of mankind, then the positivists despair at ever seeing the phenomenologists establish a cumulative fund of knowledge. This consideration reveals a fundamental conflict between the two philosophies. At the same time, however, it emphasizes the importance of the individual researcher determining which philosophy will provide the underpinning for his work.

Idealism is another humanist approach which has been developed. Guelke (1974; 1982a, b), the main advocate of idealism, has offered idealism as a way to maintain analytical rigour but to deny the need to develop theory. He views an idealist human geography as an alternative to the positivist view.

Guelke has argued that the objective of the researcher subscribing to idealism is to understand the development of cultural landscapes by uncovering the thought process lying behind them. To achieve what he calls rational explanation, the investigator proceeds in two stages. First, the researcher ascertains the intention of the person in the action to be explained. Second, the researcher tries to understand the ideas used by the person in interpreting the situation being handled. The purpose is to discover what the person believed, not why he believed it.

Guelke has maintained that rethinking the thoughts of people in another time and place does not involve some mysterious form of mind reading. Rather, it requires the investigator to set aside his own values and cultural context and strive to reconstruct the thoughts behind actions which were taken. As an example, he suggests that to explain the increase in soybean acreage in the American Midwest the researcher must analyse the thought process of the farmers who planted the crop.

The idealist approach nurtures an appreciation for the cultural context and time frame within which events occur (Hufferd, 1980). In that manner, it emphasizes the importance of diverse backgrounds, cultures, values, motivations and intentions, aspects which are critical in resource management. The idealist approach leads to insight and understanding of problems and human responses in specific situations.

The conflict with positivism, which stresses generalizations and theories, is obvious. Nevertheless, the existence of phenomenology and idealism also emphasizes the importance of being aware of alternative research philosophies. Different philosophies have different ultimate goals, and also imply different types of evidence and argument as being acceptable. If one resource manager views a problem as a positivist and another resource manager views the same problem as a phenomenologist or idealist, it is highly likely that there will be disagreements, as each will perceive different situations, ask different questions, and apply different methods.

If a research *philosophy* may be defined as the body of principles adopted for the conduct of research, then *ideology* may be differentiated as the combined doctrines, values, and intentions that guide an individual's outlook on life (Sandbach, 1980). This distinction is made because in addition to the conflict over positivist–phenomenological–idealistic approaches to research another basic conflict has emerged having implications for research questions and research strategies. This conflict is termed ideological since it arises from the emergence of geographers who are arguing that the writings of Marx provide a desirable perspective to guide geographical research.

Harvey (1972, 1973, 1983, 1984), has been the most prominent and articulate advocate of a Marxist approach to geographical research, although others have argued for its acceptance (Blaut, 1975; Giri, 1983; Peet, 1975; 1977; 1985; Slater, 1975; 1977; Young and Sukhwal, 1984). Marx's basic arguments are not reviewed here. Instead, attention is directed towards the main implications of the Marxist perspective for research in resource analysis.

Much of the Marxist-based research has concentrated upon urban processes. Urbanization and many of its facets such as ghetto formation, highway development and slum clearance are seen as symptoms of rather than as substantial problems in themselves. The fundamental processes underlying urbanization are considered to be capital formation, foreign and domestic trade, and international money flows, all reflecting concerns with economic growth and capital accumulation (Harvey, 1975; 102). These processes are viewed as relevant to resource management and development as well, suggesting that resource problems should be defined in terms of the activities of capitalist institutions.

Harvey (1974) has argued convincingly that different scientific persuasions inevitably reach different conclusions. This argument emerges from his examination of the studies of Malthus, Ricardo and Marx relative to population–resources relationships. As a result, the Marxists do not accept the emphasis placed upon value-free inquiries stressed by the positivists. They argue that each individual has a personal ideology which governs the choice of problem, variables deemed important, and inferences to be drawn. The Marxists are alarmed that most researchers are not aware of the pervasive influence their 'capitalist' or 'establishment' education has upon their outlook. At the same time, the Marxists urge investigators to participate actively in modifying social processes which they study. This stance runs counter to much of the neutrality stressed by positivists.

Not everyone subscribes to the Marxist outlook (Berry, 1974; 343–5). An overriding and legitimate issue is whether this ideology is in any way superior or more desirable than any other. The answer to this question is, of course, determined by personal values or beliefs. And, to the extent that the controversy regarding different ideologies makes geographers become aware that each person has an ideological framework, implicit or explicit, it can only be healthy (Duncan and Ley, 1982; Chouinard and Fincher, 1983). Too many people in the past have assumed their ideology without systematically examining its assumptions and goals.

2.2.2 THEORY

Many commentators have noted attempts to develop theory as one of the significant developments within geography (Kohn, 1970, 212; Moss, 1970, 14; Gokhman and Saushkin, 1972; Guelke, 1974; Taafe, 1974). At the same time, it has been noted that theory has remained poorly articulated for the discipline in general (Hewitt and Hare, 1973; 36; Guelke, 1971; 43) and for resource management in particular (Burton and Kates, 1965; viii). It is thus appropriate to inquire as to what is meant by theory, and what are its advantages and disadvantages.

Numerous definitions have been offered for 'theory'. Kerlinger (1964; 11) has stated that a theory presents a systematic view of phenomena by specifying relationships among variables. The ultimate purpose of theory is to explain and predict these phenomena. Campbell and Wood (1969; 82) argued that theory is a set of statements about relationships that has been established with some degree of confidence. Like Kerlinger, they insisted that a theory must be able to explain relationships, and to have predictive value. The key concepts associated with theory are thus specification of relationships among variables, plus explanatory and predictive power. In contrast, 'hypothesis' is viewed as much more tentative. Kerlinger (1964; 20) viewed an hypothesis as 'a conjectural statement' concerning the relationship between two or more variables. Newman (1974; 22) saw an hypothesis as a statement of a relationship between two or more phenomena, worded so that the direction and strength of the relationship can be tested. At the risk of oversimplifying, hypotheses, theories and laws

Table 2.1 Relationship among hypotheses, theories, and laws

1. Hypothesis:
A proposition tentatively assumed in order to test its accord with facts or relationships that are known or may be determined. It specifies the direction and strength of relationship between two or more variables, and is amenable to empirical testing.

2. Theory:
A plausible statement accounting for the relationship between two or more phenomena. It is used as a basis for explanation and prediction. A theory implies a greater range of supporting evidence and a higher likelihood than a hypothesis, but has not been conclusively established as with a law.

3. Law:
A statement concerning a relationship among phenomena that so far as is known is invariable under given conditions (example: a law of thermodynamics). It implies an assertion based upon conclusive evidence or tests and having universal validity.

Hypotheses, theories, and laws may be generated either by speculation or deduction, or by abstraction or induction from evidence.

may be considered as a continuum in which the degree of certainty about specified relationships steadily increases (Table 2.1).

If theory is the ultimate goal for research, at least for those subscribing to positivism, it is desirable to have standards by which potential theories may be judged. Bunge (1962; 2–3) offered four standards which must be met before statements of relationships may be considered to be theories. *Clarity* requires explicitness and freedom from contradiction. *Simplicity* demands minimizing the number of variables involved. *Generality* is gained when the scope of the statement is broadened beyond the information used to establish it. *Accuracy* is achieved by becoming specific. These standards, as Bunge recognized, create tension since they are conflicting. Simplicity and generality lead to inaccuracy. As Levins (1968; 7) observed, it is not possible to maximize simultaneously generality, realism and precision. Nevertheless, these standards may be used to determine the adequacy of current theories even though it is not usually possible to satisfy them all.

Despite these difficulties, development of theory offers significant potential benefits to the researcher. Theories facilitate the identification of regularities in a complex world (Chojnicki, 1970; 214) and permit research results to become cumulative, building upon and extending previous investigations (Kohn, 1970; 213). Furthermore, theories systematize or logically interconnect a great deal of initially isolated knowledge, explain relationships, and generate additional research hypotheses. Burton (1963; 156) summarized the benefits from development of theory. As he commented,

> Theory provides the sieve through which myriads of facts are sorted, and without it the facts remain a meaningless jumble. Theory provides the measure against which exceptional and unusual events can be recognized. In a world without theory there are no exceptions; everything is unique. That is why theory is so important.

Others have been less enthusiastic about the pursuit of theory. Harris (1971; 162) has argued that development of theory necessitates abstraction and simplification in order to eliminate complexities and reveal common characteristics. But he believed that geographers are characterized by their ability to see the complex of variables creating the character of places, regions or landscapes. Such a synthetic viewpoint is necessarily lost when simplifying and abstracting in the search for generalizations and theory. Countering this argument are Campbell and Wood (1969; 84), who argued that simplification is the basis for analytical thought. In their view, '... the value of resulting theories lies in the insights they provide into certain aspects of reality, rather than into the whole of it'.

Other objections have arisen. Broek (1965; 63) criticized theoretically-inclined geographers for letting the search for theories become an end in itself rather than a means to understanding the variety of the earth. Similar sentiments are expressed by King (1976; 302) who concluded that the quest for theory often goes beyond the point of diminishing returns and begins to feed upon itself rather than upon observations from the real world. Guelke (1974; 193) expressed another, and probably more fundamental, concern. He believed that the wide acceptance of the desirability of theory is based upon acceptance of a specific research philosophy, that of positivism. If other research philosophies are adopted, theory assumes a less significant role.

It is important that students have a good understanding as to what is understood by the concept of theory. Otherwise, it will be difficult to determine how adequate a proposed theory is, and in which direction further work should proceed to refine or strengthen theoretical development. At a more basic level, awareness of the characteristics of theory may help to determine which research philosophy should provide the foundation for investigations. If theory is perceived as neither attractive nor feasible in a given field of endeavour, then questions should be generated about the appropriateness of applying the 'scientific method' in such instances.

2.3 BASIC CONSIDERATIONS

The preceding discussion has considered the nature of the research process as well as alternative types of research. The following pages cover some of the particular considerations demanding attention when either designing or assessing research. The initial considerations include conceptualization, research design, measurement and analysis, all of which must be addressed if research is to be technically efficient.

2.3.1 CONCEPTUALIZATION

Conceptualization refers to defining the nature of a problem as well as identifying its parts and their relationships. This aspect requires that attention be directed towards operational definitions, assumptions, variables and relationships. Each of these is discussed below.

Resource analysis problems may be defined at very general or more specific levels. Firey (1960) provided a broad-scale conceptualization when stating that three broad groupings of knowledge must be considered when studying resource allocation processes. He defined these as physical habitat, human culture and economic scarcity. In more conventional terms, these parts may be identified as ecological, ethnological and economic. In other words, Firey defined resource problems as consisting of three interrelated parts. His framework emphasizes that all three must be studied in order to understand the impact of allocating natural resources. A more refined framework incorporating similar ideas has been developed by Nelson (1973; 1978) to guide studies of national parks and other resource developments. He identified four components in his framework: (1) ecology, (2) strategies and institutional arrangements, (3) perceptions, attitudes and values, and (4) technology. This framework served as the basis for comparative inquiries about park management in Europe, North and South America, Africa, Asia and the Soviet Union (Nelson, Needham and Mann, 1978), as well as to analyse large-scale resource-based industrial development in southern Ontario (Nelson, Day and Jessen, 1981; Nelson and Fenge, 1982) and conflict between fisheries and petroleum interests (Val and Nelson, 1983).

Whitney and Dufournaud (1982; 138–40) have developed a more detailed conceptual framework for a study of the flows of energy, food, nutrients and water between urban centres and rural hinterlands in Third World nations (Fig. 2.1). In the rural component of the framework, various linkages which connect demand for commodities to resources are presented. These linkages ultimately depict the impact on the biophysical environment through depletion of the resources. The figure illustrates how impact can be modified through substitution of extra-regional imports of food, energy and nutrients for ones produced in the hinterland.

The conceptual framework also suggests how changes in use of one resource may have impacts upon other resources. The destruction of forests for wood and charcoal leads to soil deterioration which in turn may adversely affect water supplies, result in decreased crop yields, cause reductions in carrying capacity of grazing lands, and trigger siltation of power-generating dams and reservoirs. Similar linkages are shown for the urban component regarding the pathways of some waste flows of water, energy and food. These wastes or residuals may become either positive or negative resources, depending upon the manner in which they are handled. The conceptual framework highlights links and relationships, and suggests points for analysis.

These conceptual frameworks demonstrate that no one framework is better or more desirable than others. Frameworks have to be devised that are relevant to the problem, process, resource sector, issue or topic being studied. Nevertheless, all of the frameworks have common features. Each defines a problem, and indicates the component parts. Each also attempts to indicate the relationships among the component parts. In addition to clarifying the nature of the research problem, these frameworks assist the analyst in examining previous studies directed to the problem. In this manner, it is possible to ascertain where a proposed study may build upon and extend earlier investigations, and where gaps exist in our knowledge.

A distinction may be made between theoretical and conceptual frameworks. As seen in section 2.2.2, theoretical frameworks involve statements having both explanatory and predictive power. These two

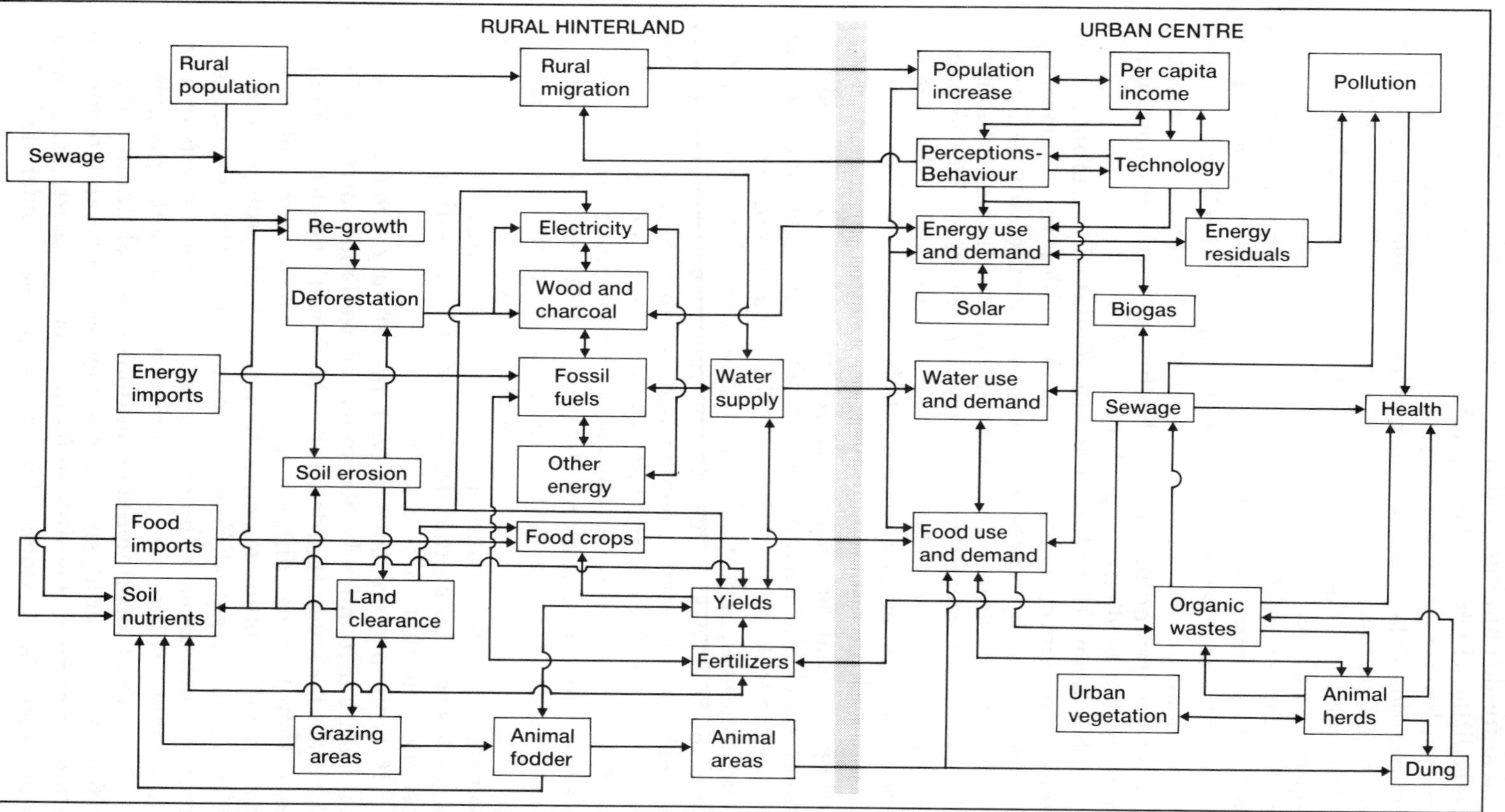

Fig. 2.1 A conceptual framework for food, energy and water use and impacts on the biophysical environment (*after Whitney and Dufournaud, 1982, 139*)

attributes are demanding, and help to explain why there is as yet relatively little which can be identified as geographical theories of resource analysis or management. In contrast, conceptual frameworks are organizational devices, used to structure a problem and to identify its various parts. Conceptual frameworks do not offer explanatory or predictive power. Thus, many conceptual frameworks have been developed. Some have evolved to a stage in which they are used as the departure point for most studies in a given field. In the field of hazards research, for example, a large majority of researchers use Gilbert White's conceptual framework as a starting point (Ch. 8). In such situations, conceptual frameworks contribute to the development of cumulative understanding although by themselves they do not contain explanatory and predictive capability.

Labovitz and Hagedorn (1971; 16–20) state that it is not enough to identify important components or variables in a conceptual framework. The components also must be operationally defined. In this sense, definitions do not comprise any kind of fundamental truths since they are arbitrary. Being arbitrary, definitions can not be judged as right or wrong, true or false. Their role is to indicate the specific manner in which a term or concept is to be used.

Research in resource analysis emphasizes the importance of having operational definitions before embarking upon a study. In hazards research, difficulty has been experienced in defining 'drought' (Lawson and Stockton, 1981; Steila, 1983). Yet a definition of this term is crucial if the adequacy of adjustments to drought is to be judged. The difficulty of this task is revealed by Saarinen (1966; 144–8) who uncovered 39 definitions of drought when studying this phenomenon in the Great Plains of the United States. Many of the definitions were related directly to land-use systems which had varying capabilities for adjusting to drought conditions. Heathcote (1983) experienced similar problems when studying arid lands throughout the world. Similar interpretative problems were encountered by Mohan and Subramanyam (1980) and Naganna and Barai (1982), with the former two investigators concluding that drought refers to a relative rather than an absolute condition.

If problems are encountered in defining drought, similar difficulties are encountered when analysing wetlands, an increasingly popular field for study (Bardecki, 1984b). If wetlands are difficult to define, it then becomes difficult to conduct an inventory of them to determine whether management action is needed to protect or preserve them. Two analysts with different definitions of 'wetlands' could reach different conclusions as to their nature and extent in a given area and therefore could disagree over appropriate management strategies.

As a result, operational definitions have substantial implications for resource analysis. Unless key concepts and terms are operationally defined, it is difficult for the user of a report to know what relevance assembled evidence has for the problem under study. The discussion of reliability and validity in section 2.3.2 elaborates upon this aspect. Second, if a fund of cumulative knowledge is to be realized, study results must be comparable. When the basic terms are not defined, efforts at comparing studies can be frustrated. And third, different interpretations of terms can lead to diverging perceptions of stated or intended policies in resource management. Legislation and regulations frequently are deliberately vague, to allow officials some discretion in applying them to specific cases. Over time, precedents establish definitions for key concepts and notions.

If assumptions are to be made, they should be clearly stated when conceptualizing the problem. Assumptions, designed to simplify the complexity of the real world, represent a common strategy especially in attempts at construction of theory. Making assumptions involves taking for granted, without proof, selected aspects in order to keep problems simple and manageable. This benefit is gained at the expense of sacrificing detail and realism. At later stages assumptions may be relaxed, modified or discarded depending upon the progress of the research (Stynes, Spotts and Strunk, 1985). As Blalock (1970; 63) has remarked,

> The development of a science consists of substituting increasingly realistic and more useful assumptions, so that the resulting theoretical explanation accounts for an increasing variety of facts and yields more and more precise predictions that can be tested in terms of the data.

Assumptions have been used in various types of geographical and resource analysis studies. Studies of land use have often made broad assumptions. Notable in this regard was von Thunen's theory to account for the types of agricultural activity that would evolve around an urban market. Von Thunen made assumptions regarding the nature of terrain, marketing conditions, transportation facilities, motivations of farmers, and costs. None of these was 'realistic', but it allowed him to postulate a pattern of agricultural activity around the city. Then, this simplified model could be compared to existing agricultural patterns around cities. Where deviations occurred, as they inevitably did, the assumptions could be examined and varied to explore the different processes operating upon the rural economy.

In resource analysis, assumptions have played an important role in studies attempting to place a value on recreational activities. One approach has calculated the value of a recreational experience based on indirect evidence associated with observed recreationist behaviour, especially willingness to incur travel costs to reach recreation sites (Hotelling, 1947; Clawson, 1959; Clawson and Knetsch, 1966). The approach first involved dividing the total population from which recreationists originate into distance zones. Travelling costs within each zone to the recreation site are roughly similar. Such a procedure allows participation rates at the recreation site to be expressed relative to travel costs. This information provides a basis for constructing a demand schedule for the recreation site. Numerous assumptions are made in such an approach. Costs of travel are considered to be incurred solely for reaching the site. If travelling to the site provided other benefits along the way then not all costs should be attributed to the draw of the site being valued. All recreationists are assumed to encounter the same alternatives while travelling to the site. Further, all recreationists are deemed to have similar preferences and incomes. These and other assumptions are not realistic, but allowed problems to be defined in such a way that analysis could be started. Other researchers have attempted to modify the assumptions in order to make the value estimates more closely reflect reality (Pearse, 1968).

Forecasts of natural resource supply and demand are also characterized by assumptions (section 3.3). In the early 1970s, Meadows *et al.* (1972) generated considerable debate after their examination of five factors - population, agricultural production, natural resources, industrial production, pollution - which they believed ultimately limit growth on the planet earth. Their study drew attention because of its conclusions suggesting imminent global disaster. However, too many people focused upon the output of the modelling exercise, and did not scrutinize the key assumptions used in the forecast; even though the assumptions were presented for inspection and criticism (Meadows *et al.*, 1972; 27). Discussion of three of the 100 or so causal links involved in the model - per capita resource use, desired birth rate, pollution effect on life expectancy - emphasized how sensitive forecasts or projections can be to underlying assumptions (Meadows *et al.*, 1972; 109–26).

Blunden (1985) has reminded us that both short- and long-term variables affect supply and demand of resources, and that these must be incorporated through assumptions. Regarding minerals, he noted that supply and demand are influenced by instability in the minerals market, political nationalism, environmental costs, taxation levels, economic cycles, investment decisions in the face of uncertainty and international aid programmes. Also referring to minerals but using more general terms, Rees (1985) suggested that proven reserve levels are a function of technological knowledge and skills, demand levels, production and processing costs, price of the resource product, plus availability and price of substitutes. Since all of these may vary, the analyst must make assumptions about each of them.

Given the use of assumptions to make complex problems manageable, the student of resource analysis should watch for them in any study he uses. Obviously a forecast will only be as accurate as the assumptions upon which it was based. On a different note, analysts should consider where in their own studies assumptions might be introduced. The ecological and regional analysis research themes in geography make the investigator so aware of the need for an holistic view that many find it difficult to make assumptions of any kind. Only the spatial analysis theme puts emphasis upon assumption-making. If greater progress is to be made in developing theory, geographers will have to become more adept at making assumptions explicit. Such a venture can be profitable as long as it is remembered that the long-term effort should be directed towards modifying the assumptions to more closely reflect conditions in the real world.

Operational definitions and assumptions presuppose the investigator has been able to identify variables and relationships. However, for much research, the main payoff may be identification of variables. Schaefer (1953; 243) has reinforced the significance of such exploratory types of inquiry by commenting that 'it is only too true that social scientists, and geographers among them, are often still in the dark as to which variables are the relevant ones in any given situation'. Even when variables are identified, they are frequently difficult to operationalize and measure. In studies of institutional arrangements (Ch. 11), Mitchell (1975; 263) has shown that such concepts as values, customs, ideologies, leadership, public interest, power structure, communication patterns, pressure, influence and coordination often become the centre of research effort. Operationalizing these concepts in a way that will facilitate comparison of results between studies as well as accumulation of knowledge is a necessary but challenging task.

In brief, conceptualization involves defining the nature of the problem to be investigated, as well as its component parts and their relationships. This statement recognizes, however, that the objective of research may be to identify variables. In such cases, conceptualization will have to be much more general in scope, similar to the framework outlined by Firey (1960). In building a conceptual framework, the investigator should pay close attention to establishing operational definitions, and outlining assumptions. With this work accomplished, attention may be directed towards deriving research designs and measurement procedures.

2.3.2 RESEARCH DESIGN

A research design represents a strategy or procedure for collecting evidence about variables identified in the conceptual framework. Ackoff (1953; 49) urged investigators to begin by identifying an ideal research design. That is, we should decide how evidence should be assembled as if no restrictions existed concerning time, expense, personnel or ethical considerations. He maintained that recognizing the ideal design is not simply wishful thinking or dreaming. The ideal procedures establish a *standard* against which we can compare the actual procedures used. In this manner, the shortcomings of the research procedure are made explicit and it is then possible to consider their implications for the adequacy of evidence collected.

Campbell and Stanley (1966) divided research designs into

three types (pre-experimental, experimental, and quasi-experimental) and evaluated them against twelve commonly encountered obstacles. The characteristics of some of their designs are considered here in order to illustrate that designs offer different advantages. The analyst therefore must exercise judgement and have considerable appreciation of his problem prior to data collection if maximum advantage is to be gained during data gathering.

Much research in resource analysis has been based upon one-shot case studies (Table 2.2), the first research design included under the category of pre-experimental designs. Observations are made on individuals, groups, phenomena or distributions after the occurrence of a policy, programme, project or natural process. Observations are made only once, subsequent to the agent which is presumed to have caused change. No baseline data are available against which to compare the post-agent experience. No comparison is made with a control group of people or phenomena. As a result of this total lack of control, Campbell and Stanley concluded that case studies '... have almost no scientific value' because they believed that 'securing scientific evidence involves making at least one comparison'.

A contrasting view is provided by Salter (1967; 71–2) who

Table 2.2 Research designs for resource analysis *(from Campbell and Stanley, 1966)*

Pre-experimental designs								
1. One-shot case study					X		0	
2. One-group pretest–posttest			0_1		X		0_2	
3. Static group comparison					X		0_1	
							0_2	
Experimental designs								
4. Pretest–posttest control group	*R*		0_1		X		0_2	
	R		0_3				0_4	
5. Solomon four-group	*R*		0_1		X		0_2	
	R		0_3				0_4	
	R				X		0_5	
	R						0_6	
6. Posttest-only control group	*R*				X		0_1	
	R						0_2	
Quasi-experimental designs								
7. Non-equivalent comparison group			0_1		X		0_2	
			0_3				0_4	
8. Time-series or longitudinal design		0_1	0_2	0_3	X	0_4	0_5	0_6
9. Multiple time-series		0_1	0_2	0_3	X	0_4	0_5	0_6
		0_7	0_8	0_9		0_{10}	0_{11}	0_{12}

Notes:

1. X: indicates the exposure of individuals/phenomena to an activity or process.
2. 0: indicates the observation or measurement of effects.
3. *R:* indicates individuals/phenomena assigned to groups on a random basis.
4. Time is interpreted from left to right.

argued that case studies can be valuable, particularly when the investigator is starting to explore a problem and is not sure which are the significant variables and relationships. Although analysis of a single case will rarely be sufficient for a full inquiry, a large number of case studies can suggest fundamental relationships (Kennedy, 1979; Yin, 1981).

The second pre-experimental design represents an improvement over the first by incorporating baseline information. Such data may be collected by historical research or by making observations before the occurrence of the change agent. This procedure facilitates one comparison over time but does not isolate the impact of the agent causing change. Variables other than the agent may influence the observed results at the second time period. Without a control group, it becomes impossible to ascertain the influence of other intervening variables. The final design attempts to reduce the 'conditioning' which can be created by repeated observations over time. Conditioning is particularly critical when observing people, as repeated interviews over time may have an influence on attitudes or behaviour. However, by eliminating the observations prior to the agent of change the investigator loses information about the situation prior to the programme or phenomena being studied. In such instances, the analyst must rely upon the recall of respondents, and/or upon using historical evidence if such exists.

The next three designs (numbers 4, 5 and 6 in Table 2.2) are based upon experimental principles, with the fourth one representing the classical experimental design, the fifth one intended to eliminate the 'conditioning' effect from before and after observations, and the sixth one also intended to reduce 'conditioning' when participants cannot be split into four groups. By making comparisons over time as well as between a control and a 'treatment' group, the researcher should be able to determine the impact upon the dependent variable. This type of design is well suited for studies in resource analysis emphasizing the biophysical environment. When studying ecological carrying capacity (Ch. 7), paired sites can be used. One site could be a campground in a park, whereas the other could be an environmentally similar site removed from human activity. Observations of soil and vegetation could be taken prior to the opening of the camping season, and then a second set could be made at the end of the season. By comparing the results from the two sites, inferences could be made about the impact of human activity on changes in the biophysical characteristics of camping sites.

As soon as research begins to focus upon changes in human behaviour and attitudes, however, substantial problems are found with the experimental method. Perhaps the major obstacle relates to ethical problems surrounding the need for manipulation and control. Individuals usually are self-selected into groups, creating problems for randomly assigning them to different categories. The independent variable (a policy, programme or project, or natural process) can not be manipulated to suit the wishes of the investigator. To illustrate, a researcher would have problems justifying the exclusion of some individuals from a new management programme intended to increase incomes simply because he wished to find out how much incomes changed as a result of the management programme (Mitchell, 1977b; 166). Simultaneously, many other variables will be operating upon changes in income, and it is usually impossible for the investigator to control them. This becomes even more evident when the time between observations is in terms of months or years as is often the case in resource analysis.

While the experimental designs frequently are inapplicable to socially-oriented resource analyses, they still serve a valuable purpose by providing a standard against which the study procedure may be contrasted. Pragmatic considerations may lead to use of a pre-experimental or quasi-experimental design. However, the researcher should be in a better position to assess the soundness of evidence by being aware of the attributes of experimental procedures.

Quasi-experimental designs have been created for research situations in which manipulation of the independent variables and control of respondents or phenomena are not possible (Caporaso, 1973; Cook and Campbell, 1979). Weiss and Rein (1970; 97) have commented that when experimental designs are not applicable then '... a more historically oriented, more qualitative evaluation has greater value'.

Of the quasi-experimental designs, the eighth offers the greatest range of applicability to both biophysical and socio-economic investigations (Table 2.2). Known as a longitudinal or time-series design, this approach attempts to monitor change over an extended period of time (Wall and Williams, 1970). It recognizes that distributions, attitudes and behaviour may alter over time after the introduction of a policy, programme or project, and that it may be necessary to make a series of observations to catch such alterations. The same reasoning applies to physical phenomena. When studying ecological carrying capacity of campgrounds or hiking trails, the nature and *rate* of biophysical change may only be attained by making a series of observations, either throughout one season and/or across several seasons.

In general, experimental designs have the greatest applicability for problems associated with the natural environment. In such studies it is often possible to manipulate and control variables, or at least to attempt control without becoming enmeshed in ethical issues. Pre-experimental and quasi-experimental designs appear to be most practical for socio-economic research, with the second and eighth designs having the greatest applicability (Table 2.2). There can be little doubt, however, that if the research goal is ultimately to be able to predict then the fourth design is the ideal. Those who decide to strive for theoretical development should therefore always be considering how their studies can be brought closer to the standards established by this design.

When comparing research designs, the analyst should bear several things in mind. If concerned with accumulation of knowledge, he should seek procedures which can be verified by other investigators (Olsson, 1968). This concern with *replication* and *verification*, often viewed as one of the main concerns of the positivist philosophy, is essential if knowledge is to be cumulative. Another concern should be with *generalization*, or a capability going beyond the specific information represented by one study. Generalization is interrelated with verification and replication, as it is usually through the latter that the former is realized. It is for this reason that many hold the one-shot case study in low regard – such a study is difficult to replicate and verify, and hence is not always conducive to the production of generalizations.

2.3.3 MEASUREMENT

Measurement concentrates attention upon types of data, data collection methods, plus reliability and validity. Measurement represents a substantial concern in research, and yet it also has generated considerable conflict. One of the most pronounced conflicts in geography has been the qualitative–quantitative dispute. In this instance, strong disagreement has arisen over the feasibility of

Table 2.3 Levels of measurement *(modified after Siegel, 1956)*

1. Nominal	– mutually exclusive categories – all observations within each category are treated the same	Example 1: Respondent's sex: (1) Male, (2) Female Example 2: Question: What are your feelings about fluoridating the public water supply system for this community? (1) Support, (2) Oppose
2. Ordinal	– direction and relative position on scale are known – distances between any two points on the scale are not measured by a common unit of measurement	*Question:* What are your feelings about fluoridating the public water supply system for this community? *Answer:* (1) Strongly support, (2) Support, (3) Neutral, (4) Oppose, (5) Strongly oppose
3. Interval	– direction and magnitude of position on scale known. That is, distances between any two numbers on the scale are known but there is an arbitrary zero point and a unit of measurement.	– temperatures in degrees centigrade or Fahrenheit – because of an arbitrary zero point, we cannot state that 20°C is twice as warm as 10°C – 0°C ≠ 0°F
4. Ratio	– all characteristics of an interval scale plus a true zero point	– distance or weight – the zero point is identical whether using yards or metres or ounces or grams respectively

measuring certain phenomena, especially those associated with social variables. The point often overlooked by the critics of quantification is that while everything can be measured, some things cannot be measured with the same degree of refinement as others. This point underlines the existence of four different levels of measurement commonly applied in research: nominal, ordinal, interval and ratio (Table 2.3).

The existence of different measurement levels reveals that all phenomena may be measured 'quantitatively'. However, each level has varying restrictions on how the data can be subsequently handled. The researcher should always strive to obtain the highest level of measurement since such a procedure ensures the broadest choice of analytical techniques. Generally, social and behavioural variables are difficult to measure at higher than an ordinal scale whereas biophysical data can usually be obtained at either an interval or ratio scale.

Having decided upon the level of measurement at which data can be gathered, the analyst must select one or more data collection techniques. Runkel and McGrath (1972; 81–118) have assessed the merits of several data collection strategies (Fig. 2.2). Although their discussion is oriented towards studies of user(actor)-activity(behaviour)-facility(context) systems, their range of strategies has general relevance for resource analysis. Studies of the biophysical environment will tend to rely upon field experiments, experimental simulations and laboratory experiments whereas socio-economic research will more often use sample surveys, and judgement tasks. Both types of inquiry draw upon field studies, theory and simulation.

Webb *et al.* (1966) make an important point in describing methods (physical traces, archival, observation) for obtaining data on human respondents *without* using interviews or questionnaire surveys. Their criticism that the dominant mass of social science research is based upon interviews and questionnaires is pertinent to resource analysis (Ch. 5). They lament an overdependence by investigators upon a single method. Since all data collection methods have biases, their objection is not directed so much against interviews and questionnaires as it is against their being used alone. Methods must be supplemented by alternatives measuring the same variables but containing different weaknesses. Thus, the issue is not seen as involving a choice among individual methods. On the contrary, the issue '... is the necessity for a multiple operationism, a collection of methods combined to avoid sharing the same weaknesses'. (Webb *et al.* (1966); 1–2). This argument deserves close attention by resource analysts, as evidence based upon a variety of cross-checking methods has a higher probability of representing the reality of a problem than evidence based upon a single method.

The concern expressed by Webb *et al.* leads to the concepts of *validity* and *reliability*, Although many types of validity exist, in this

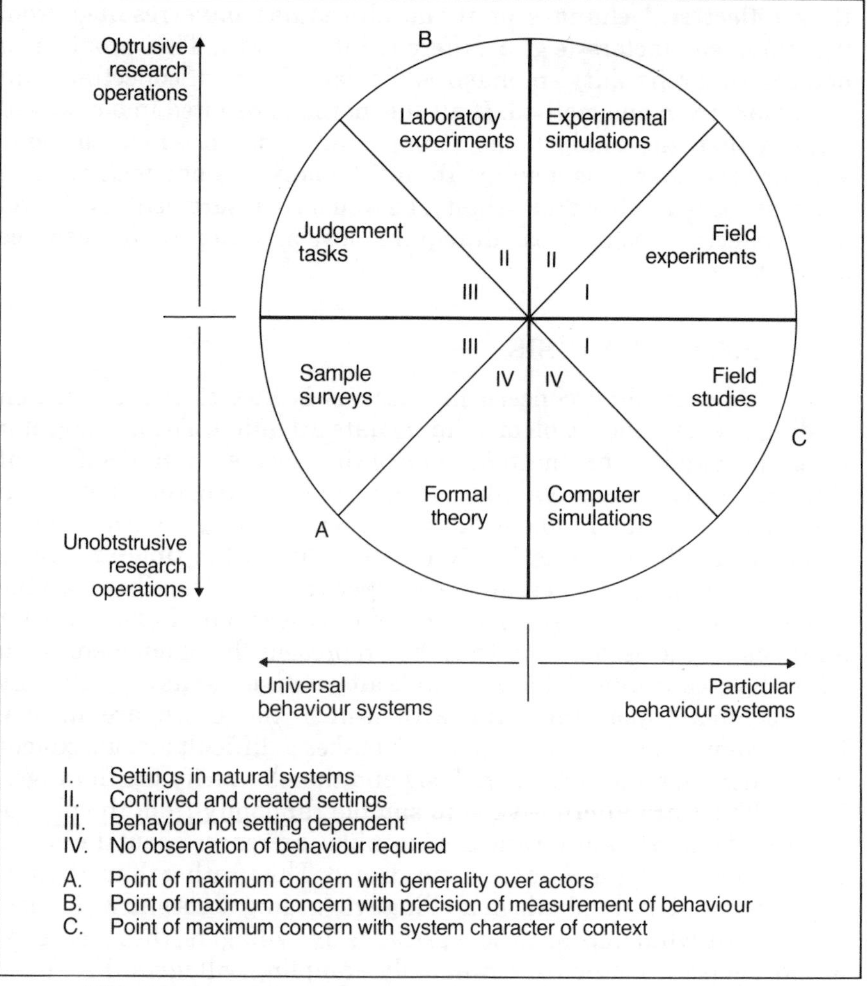

Fig. 2.2 Research strategies for data collection (*from Runkel and McGrath, 1972*)

instance it refers to whether an observation chosen to reflect a characteristic actually measures the characteristic. Validity clearly becomes a function of the soundness of operational definitions, measurement levels and data collection methods. Validity is an important criterion for judging research. If a measurement or variable is not valid the associated evidence will have little value.

Reliability relates to consistency of measurement. This concept requires that repeated measures of the same phenomena produce basically similar findings. In resource analysis, because we are dealing with a dynamic system, reliability is sometimes difficult to judge, especially if actual change has occurred with the passage of time. If interviews conducted at four-month intervals with the same set of respondents reveal different responses, it has to be determined whether they reflect real changes or if the alterations have resulted from measurement factors (e.g. a different interviewer). This problem in determining reliability emphasizes the desirability of collecting data with more than one method. If all the methods resulted in a changed pattern then the analyst has stronger grounds on which to judge whether the change is genuine than if he only has one method. The concepts of reliability and validity, as well as measurement levels and data collection techniques, all require close scrutiny by the resource analyst.

2.3.4 ANALYSIS

Of overriding concern in analysis is how to relate research findings beyond the problem of immediate attention. The investigator normally handles this matter in one of three ways. First, if sufficient time and resources are available, he may analyse all of the phenomena associated with the problem. Although representing a desirable end result, this alternative is rarely pursued due to the time and costs involved. Second, if the researcher is experienced and familiar with the problem, he may deliberately select a cross-section of examples for analysis on the assumption that they represent the phenomena with which he is concerned. This is a viable alternative, but its effectiveness is dependent upon the skill with which the cases are drawn. Furthermore, the case study approach makes it difficult for subsequent researchers to replicate the analysis and thereby verify the findings.

The third alternative is to sample randomly from the phenomena under investigation and then to make inferences about the larger group from which the interview was drawn. Thus, rather than attempt to interview all individuals in a village regarding domestic water use, or to choose what appear to be representative villagers, the researcher would devise a method for randomly sampling villagers. From the sample, the researcher would then generalize as to the needs and behaviour of all villagers.

A major difficulty is to determine how representative the sample is of the entire group. It is for this purpose that inferential statistics were devised. They allow the researcher to estimate the characteristics of phenomena or to examine relationships with a predetermined level of probability. In the study of rural villagers, it facilitates the following types of statements. The sample results suggest with a level of confidence of 95 per cent that 80 per cent + or – 6 per cent of the campers collect their own drinking water within a journey of a two-hour walk. Or, with a probability of 5 per cent that we are incorrect, there appears to be a significant difference in attitudes about a village biogas unit between people under 30 years and those over 50 years of age.

Despite advantages, statistical and other quantitative analytical techniques are not without drawbacks. Perhaps the most serious is the fact that most techniques have a number of assumptions that the data must meet. And, unfortunately, the more powerful techniques usually have the most severe limitations. The statistical techniques usually applicable to interval or ratio level data are termed 'parametric' statistics. These techniques usually assume that the data being analysed are normally distributed, have equal variances, and are based upon independent observations. A fourth assumption often encountered is linearity. These assumptions enter because of the mathematical requirements of the statistical estimating or testing procedures. Consequently, before using quantitative techniques, the analyst must check his data to see whether or not they satisfy the requirements.

If the data do not satisfy assumptions, the investigator has a number of alternatives (Mitchell, 1974a). He may consider transformations, nonparametric techniques or the concept of robustness. Transformations involve changing the data into other forms in order to approximate more closely the assumptions, especially that of normality. A danger exists, however, that in transforming the data the investigator may lose sight of his original objectives. As Gould (1970; 442) has remarked, 'too often we end up relating the value of one variable to the log of another, with the square root of the third, the arc sine of the fourth, and the log of the log of a fifth. Everything is normal, statistically significant at the one percent level – except we have not the faintest idea what it means'.

If transformations are not considered to be satisfactory, the analyst may turn to nonparametric techniques which have less restrictive assumptions (Siegel, 1956; Kraft and Van Eden, 1968; Bradley, 1968; Conover, 1971; Gibbons, 1971). As well as having less restrictive assumptions, nonparametric statistics frequently are the only ones appropriate for data at nominal or ordinal levels of measurement. The concept of robustness, or the ability of a technique not to be sensitive to assumption violations, is a third alternative deserving more attention from geographers. Unfortunately, while many parametric techniques have been proven to be remarkably insensitive to violation of assumptions, this concept usually has been used incorrectly by geographers (Mitchell, 1974a; 511–14).

This discussion has not touched upon all aspects relevant to analysis of evidence. The two covered here were selected because of the frequent misunderstanding that has been encountered in the minds of resource analysts. The issue of level of measurement stresses that the quantitative–qualitative dichotomy is an artificial one since all data can be collected in a quantitative form (section 2.3.3). The more important issue is what level the measurement can reach in order to increase the range of analytical techniques. The second issue, drawing inferences from samples, emphasizes that if statistical inferential techniques are rejected then an obligation exists for the investigator to show how sample findings are extended to the larger population from which they were drawn. Too often quantitative techniques are ignored or rejected without an appreciation for what they were designed to do. Simultaneously, the investigator is cautioned that such techniques usually have numerous assumptions that must be satisfied.

2.3.5 ETHICAL ASPECTS

Sections 2.3.1 to 2.3.4 examined various considerations (conceptualization, research design, measurement, analysis) which must be addressed to ensure that research contributes to improved explanation, understanding and knowledge. However, as intimated in section 2.3.2, the analyst also has obligations as a member of society to respect the dignity and integrity of those people or animals under study. This obligation requires that ethical considerations must be addressed as well as those relating to technical efficiency (Manheim, 1981; Mitchell and Draper, 1982; 1983; Morrill, 1984). Tension may arise because of the desire to improve understanding and the concurrent need to respect integrity of respondents. In developing a research strategy, the analyst should be aware as to the possible trade-offs.

Several conventions have been developed regarding ethical matters. The concept of 'harm–benefit' has emerged to remind investigators to examine the collective benefits to society or a group against potential harm to individuals. The guideline is that research should not proceed unless the benefits outweigh the harm. This guideline is intuitively sensible. There are practical problems in applying it, however, as results of research are not always predictable. Even if outcomes can be estimated, their implications may be perceived in different ways.

Many societies give significant value to individual privacy, and the right of individuals to decide which aspects of their lives they will reveal to outsiders. The search for knowledge may intrude upon individual or collective privacy, and this potential dilemma needs to be addressed. This dilemma increases in complexity when investigators pursue research in a region with a culture different from their own, or when they become involved in comparative research which includes cultures with differing values. Guidelines for appropriate ethical behaviour applicable in one culture may not apply in another culture. As a result, generalizations about desirable ethical behaviour are difficult to develop. Nevertheless, sensitivity to personal integrity of respondents normally should be a central concern for researchers.

One convention is that people should only participate in a study on the basis of 'informed consent'. This aspect raises questions as to how much needs to be known for a person to be informed. As well, there is an increasing chance for a reactive effect as the respondents in a study become aware of the analysts' objectives. Other conventions to guard against intrusion of personal privacy include the use of anonymity or confidentiality. Pseudonyms are sometimes used for this purpose. However, use of anonymity or confidentiality makes it difficult for other investigators to replicate or verify findings, so once again technical and ethical considerations come into conflict.

Deception is used to avoid reactive effects, and to allow observation of 'normal' behaviour. Deception may occur through omission or commission, and often takes the form of covert observation through participant observation. Those opposing the use of deception argue that it violates the principle of informed consent, and that it also hinders replication and verification. If deception is used, investigators run the risk of antagonizing respondents, making further work by themselves or subsequent investigators difficult to pursue. Once more, tension arises due to the dual commitments to improving knowledge and to respecting integrity of respondents.

These comments regarding harm–benefit calculation, privacy and deception stress the need for the analyst to consider the trade-offs which might be made in balancing concerns with technical efficiency and ethical considerations. In a given situation, various options will exist, and there usually will be no one obvious correct or proper path to follow.

2.3.6 PRACTICAL CONSIDERATIONS

Just as the analyst must consider trade-offs among technical efficiency and ethical aspects, so must attention be given to practical matters (McLellan, 1983). For example, from the viewpoint of technical efficiency, an investigator might decide that a longitudinal research design was most appropriate for an environmental impact assessment. Through such a design, baseline conditions could be established, and the change associated with succession in a natural system could be determined over time. Such an approach would require collection of data over at least several seasons, and perhaps over several years. However, if a client requires the assessment within six months, then the research design which is ideal from the point of view of technical efficiency will have to be set aside in favour of a design which will provide more limited understanding.

In the pursuit of improved knowledge and understanding, the resource analyst would favour research strategies that stress validity, accuracy and precision, even if these characteristics necessitate prolonged periods for data collection, use of sophisticated measurement techniques and reliance upon complex analytical tools. In contrast, the analyst confronted with the need to provide advice within a shorter time frame may well rely upon readily available information, and analytical methods which do not make substantial demands upon equipment or time. In such situations, it is important for the analyst to be aware of the ideal strategy regarding technical efficiency and ethical aspects. Such awareness will help to sensitize the investigator about limitations of the more constrained approach and help in deciding which of the more constrained alternatives will provide the best evidence (McLellan, 1983).

2.4 GENERAL CONSIDERATIONS

Conceptualization, research design, measurement and analysis, harm–benefit ratios, privacy, deception and time constraints are specific considerations requiring attention in resource analysis. More general considerations also exist and demand reflection. Some of the more important of these include the need for compromise, the presence of subjectivity, the possibility of serendipity results, and the tension between lateral and vertical ways of thinking.

2.4.1 COMPROMISE

The resource analyst must choose from a variety of alternatives when conducting research. The comments of Webb *et al.* (1966) about questionnaires and interviews have general applicability to all approaches, methods and techniques. Each has strengths and weaknesses. None is perfect. The investigator must assemble a combination that seems best suited to a given research problem.

As Blalock (1970; 33) commented, this situation results in the research process becoming a continuous series of compromises. At each point where a decision is made some things are sacrificed in order to gain others. Runkel and McGrath (1972; v) described the situation well when commenting that

> Each alternative offers advantages and disadvantages; there is no magical path to 'good' research. There is never an unquestionably best method. Choices must be made to suit the investigator's purpose – the questions he is trying to answer.

In other words, the investigator is continuously forced to make compromises. Whatever approach or procedure is adopted will have drawbacks. The researcher must attempt to maximize the strengths and minimize the weaknesses relative to his problem. To do this, it is essential that the investigator be aware of alternatives and their relative merits. In this manner he can better assess other studies as well as improve his own work. We shall attempt to determine how well geographers working in resource analysis have chosen among the alternative approaches and techniques during their inquiries.

2.4.2 SUBJECTIVITY

On a superficial level, the conflict between different research philosophies and different ideologies appears to centre upon the role of objectivity in research. The positivists are often seen as advocating objectivity with its implications of being without bias or being impersonal. Such a stance is untenable. As Beck (1959; 76) has argued and as earlier sections have illustrated, the research process requires the analyst to make value judgements, starting with the choice of problem for study and then extending over the variety of decisions needed in assembling a research strategy. In addition, when selecting variables and making other decisions, the researcher must often rely heavily on his own insights and intuition without having well accepted scientific principles for guidelines (Blalock, 1970; 40). Indeed, in the social sciences there are often strong differences of opinion as to what is established fact, what are reasonably satisfactory explanations and what are valid procedures (Nagel, 1961; 448).

The only conclusion to be drawn is that research will always contain a strong element of subjectivity. Rather than stressing the need for objectivity, it is more productive to emphasize the desirability of investigators being *systematic*. That is, whether they subscribe to positivism or phenomenology, researchers should provide a clear description of their research problem and method of attack. In this way, the reader can determine the adequacy of the approach used. Furthermore, if others wish to replicate the study, they then have enough details as to how the original researcher proceeded. The main point is that being objective and systematic should not be treated as synonymous. Subjectivity, an ever-present and desirable element in research, does not preclude being systematic.

2.4.3 SERENDIPITY RESULTS

'Serendipity' is usually defined as the ability to find, by accident, interesting items of information or knowledge when searching for something else (Cannon, 1945; 68–78). A disturbing aspect in research reports can be an over-emphasis upon the rationale and logic associated with the findings. When this occurs in extreme form, a component of the research process often left out is the element of unforeseen development, of happy or lucky chance, otherwise termed as serendipitous findings. Barber and Fox (1958; 128) urged researchers to be aware of the possibility of discovering important serendipitous findings when observing that

> By its very nature, scientific research is a voyage into the unknown by routes that are in some measure unpredictable and unplannable. Chance or luck is therefore as inevitable in scientific research as are logic and what Pasteur called 'the prepared mind'.

In establishing a research framework and plan, it is usually desirable to have the problem well structured and to have specific questions for which answers are being sought. A highly unstructured approach has a strong likelihood of diffusing effort over such a broad scale that the chance of indepth understanding becomes slight. Yet a preoccupation with a structured problem can run counter to being able to identify and then follow up unexpected and apparently irrelevant findings. Some major scientific findings have resulted through investigators having the creative imagination to see an unexpected finding not as irrelevant to the planned programme of research but as representing a significant piece of knowledge in itself. Pasteur's discovery is perhaps the most often cited example of a serendipitous finding. Cultures being used for another problem became contaminated. Rather than immediately throwing away these cultures, Pasteur noted the changes in them, made further studies, and was on the way to discovering the process of pasteurization. A combination of a serendipitous finding plus a prepared and creative mind led to valuable new knowledge.

For resource analysis, the implications are that investigators should not be so blinded by preconceptions, expectations and convictions that unexpected results are overlooked. The methods and assumptions associated with a systematic investigation have a tendency to focus selectively the researcher's attention. Focusing of attention is necessary and acceptable as long as it does not constrict the imagination. A balance between structure and serendipity is needed in resource analysis studies.

2.4.4 VERTICAL AND LATERAL THINKING

De Bono (1967) has made a distinction between vertical and lateral thinking that is significant for resource analysis research. He described the difference between the two by drawing an analogy with digging a hole. The orientation of the vertical thinker is to dig existing holes deeper and bigger, and in that way build upon and expand previous work. In contrast, lateral thinking involves starting to dig a hole somewhere else. In this process, the researcher rejects the existing hole or knowledge, takes up a position elsewhere, and explores its potential.

De Bono acknowledged that vertical thinking has been the source of some of mankind's greatest breakthroughs as the steady accumulation of knowledge leads up to a significant discovery. He also believed that the greatest amount of research effort is directed towards the logical enlargement of accepted holes. On the other hand, he observed that if the hole is in the wrong place, no amount of further digging or improvement will put the hole in the correct place. And yet, because it is easier to dig in an established hole than break new ground, many diggers persist at old holes rather than starting elsewhere. In his words (1967; 23),

> A half-dug hole offers a direction in which to expand effort. Effort needs a direction and there are few more frustrating things than eager

> effort looking for a direction. Effort must be rewarded by some tangible result; the more immediate the results, the more encouraged is the effort. Enlarging the hole that is being dug offers real progress and an assurance of future achievement. Finally, there is a comfortable, earned familiarity with a well-worked hole.

This preoccupation with existing holes can be unfortunate. As de Bono notes, some of the great new ideas and advances have resulted from people ignoring existing holes and starting a new one.

In the following chapters concerned with resource analysis research, we will endeavour to determine how deep some of the familiar holes have been dug, and where there is need to start looking for new holes. Progress in research will result from a concurrent expansion of existing holes and a continuing search for new ones.

CHAPTER 3
RESOURCE APPRAISAL

3.1 INTRODUCTION

In the spatial research tradition, a basic concern is with the location, distribution and areal extent of phenomena. In resource analysis, this tradition manifests itself with regard to the appraisal of resource supply and demand. In a word, such work focuses upon *inventory*. A host of pertinent questions arise. Where are the resources? How much is there? What is their condition? How available are they? What are the demands for them? How will changing prices, technologies and values affect future demand? How will different resource uses interact to influence future supplies? What opportunities exist to improve productivity? Other questions occur. In conducting appraisals, which resources should be inventoried first? What parts of a country or region should be inventoried first? What inventory methods should be used? (Herfindahl, 1969; 1). While not covering all of these questions, this chapter seeks to outline the way in which geographers and others have approached the problem of inventorying resource supply and demand.

Section 3.2 addresses the issue of resource supply. Geographical research regarding *land use* is reviewed in detail, ranging from traditional mapping based upon field observation and conventional air photograph interpretation to application of infrared, thermal infrared and radar imagery as well as computer displays. Work concerning *land capability* also is covered, with experiences from several countries being described. While geographers have devoted substantial effort to land use and land capability, other aspects of resource supply also have been studied. Selected examples are briefly discussed. Estimating demand is reviewed in section 3.3, with attention given to analyses of water and energy demand as well as the application of futuristic forecasting techniques. The final sections consider the implications of this work for resource management (section 3.4) and the conduct of research (section 3.5).

3.2 DETERMINING SUPPLY

Estimation of available resources is difficult. Substantial differences may emerge depending upon analysts' interpretations of what constitutes a 'resource'. Indeed, various concepts have been developed to differentiate among alternative types of resource supply. With regard to mineral resources, the following categories have been used (Blunden, 1985, 21–8; Rees, 1985, 15–25):

1. *Resource base.*The total quantity of a substance or property within the geosystem.
2. *Hypothetical or speculative resources.* Due to favourable geological conditions believed to be present, deposits which might be found in previously unexplored or little-explored areas.
3. *Conditional or subeconomic reserves.* Deposits which have been discovered but which are uneconomical due to current prices and technology.
4. *Proven or known reserves.* Deposits which have been discovered and are economical to extract with reference to prevailing demand, prices and technology.

Depending upon which of the four categories is used, and which assumptions are made, different estimates may be provided regarding the resource supply in a region or country.

Studies concerned with resource supply may focus upon actual or potential supply. As a result, this section is divided into two parts. The first (3.2.1), concentrating upon actual supply or use, considers the geographical contribution toward land use inventory. While land use is only one aspect of concern in resource inventory, similar research issues and problems arise when inventorying other resources such as water, forests or minerals. The second part (3.2.2) deals with resource capability or potential. Land capability studies are reviewed initially, followed by studies concerned with other aspects of resource supply.

3.2.1 LAND USE

Many land use inventory methods exist, and geographers have had a long-standing interest in them (Whitaker, 1954, 231; Armand *et al.*, 1960; Board, 1968; Lopatina, 1971). One of the most influential workers in this area of research was a British geographer, Dudley Stamp. He devised a land use classification system for Britain during the 1930s, and later was a driving force in developing a system to be used for a world land use survey.

To use land or other resources to best advantage, Stamp (1960; 37–8) believed a number of steps were required: (1) *survey*, in which the present condition was recorded, (2) *analysis*, in which the reasons for patterns were sought and existing trends were identified, and (3) *planning*, in which the future was designed. In his view, the essential first step was a survey of present conditions. It was in this spirit that he organized the First Land Utilization Survey of Britain during 1930, with 'the primary purpose ... to make a complete record over the whole of Britain of the uses to which the land is put at the present time' (Stamp, 1931; 41).

As in all resource surveys, an initial task was to develop a classification system. The ideal system is based upon categories which are exhaustive (do not omit any phenomena) and mutually exclusive (do not have any categories which overlap). For Stamp, a third concern was that his system should be simple and easily understood, since the field work was to be conducted by volunteers including university geography faculty and students, school teachers and their students, as well as members of geographical associations. After a number of experiments in different parts of Britain, Stamp developed a system with six categories: (1) forests and woodlands, (2) meadowland and permanent grass, (3) arable or tilled land including rotation grass and fallow land, (4) heathland, moorland and rough hill pasture, (5) gardens, allotments, orchards, nurseries, and (6) agriculturally unproductive land (buildings, mines, cemeteries, derelict land).

Using Ordnance Survey maps at a scale of 1 : 10,560, volunteers recorded the existing land use on a field-by-field basis. These field observations were completed between 1931 and 1933, with Stamp estimating that about a quarter of a million school children participated in the mapping. Maps were published at a scale of 1 : 63,360. The first two sheets became available early in 1933; the last not until after the Second World War. The maps were complemented by monographs prepared for each county. Each monograph drew upon the inventory data and related them to other historical, economic, climatic, terrain and soil information in order to facilitate interpretation of the maps. Stamp (1948) later synthesized the county monographs into a book entitled *The Land of Britain: Its Use and Misuse*.

A Second Land Use Survey was inaugurated during 1960 under the direction of Alice Coleman, another geographer. During 1958–9, a pilot area was mapped in East Kent (Coleman, 1961). This experience was then extended to the nation. As with the first survey, field observations were completed by volunteers from schools, local geographical societies, training colleges, university departments, rural studies groups, county branches of the National Farmers' Union and other such groups. The scale for the published maps was 1 : 25,000, and the land use categories adhered as closely as possible to those recommended by the World Land Use Survey. Thirteen general land use classes were identified which included one major deviation from and four additions to the World Land Use Survey scheme. The first maps were published during 1961, with others becoming available throughout the rest of the 1960s.

At the International Geographical Union Congress in Lisbon

during 1949, Van Valkenburg had proposed that a commission should be established for the purpose of developing a land use inventory procedure for all countries in the world. This idea received support, and the United Nations Educational, Scientific and Cultural Organization provided a grant to enable a meeting to be held by a smaller committee later that year. The five-man committee, chaired by Van Valkenburg from the United States, included four other geographers: Stamp (Britain), Boesch (Switzerland), Gourou (France) and Waibel (Brazil).

The committee concluded that a World Land Use Survey, based upon factual knowledge, would be 'a necessary and proper foundation for plans of improvement and development, especially in those areas commonly regarded as underdeveloped' (Van Valkenburg, 1950; 1). A survey would have two objectives. The first would be 'to record the present use of land in all parts of the world on a uniform system of classification and notation with such amplification as may be necessary locally' (Van Valkenburg, 1950; 2). The second would be to secure publication of the results at a scale of 1 : 1,000,000. This scale was chosen because it was the only one on which maps were available for all parts of the world.

The committee recognized that one of its major tasks was to develop a world land use classification appropriate for a 1 : 1,000,000 scale. This job was a difficult one since a vast range of land uses and human activities existed throughout the world under differing natural and cultural conditions. The committee agreed upon a classification system similar to that used in the First Land Utilization Survey in Britain. Nine categories were identified, including: (1) settlements and associated non-agricultural lands, (2) horticulture, (3) trees and other perennial crops, (4) cropland, (5) improved permanent pasture, (6) unimproved grazing, (7) woodlands (8) swamps and marshes, and (9) unproductive land. It was hoped that while more detailed information could be assembled during surveys, all information could be aggregated into these categories for mapping at a scale of 1 : 1,000,000.

Stamp became director of the World Land Use Survey during 1951 and progress reports were given to the International Geographical Union Congresses in Washington (1952) and Rio de Janiero (1956). During this period, Stamp (1960; 47–8) was able to describe land use surveys which had been started in Eastern Pakistan (Bangladesh), Canada, Tanganyika, Tanzania, Nyasaland (Malawi), Cyprus and Japan. Despite such progress, however, Board (1968; 35–6) later cautioned that different needs of countries and variation in standards of topographical base mapping resulted in there being no world survey in any strict sense.

In 1956, the Commission on World Land Use Survey was reorganized. Stamp became its chairman, and its goal was to stimulate comparable land use surveys throughout the world. Two types of activities resulted. In a small number of countries (Cyprus, Sudan, Iraq) surveys were completed on the basis of the World Land Use

Survey classification. The greatest effort, however, resulted from national organizations or research workers such as those in Greece (Nakos, 1983) who built upon the World Land Use Survey ideas but 'ultimately went their own way' (Board, 1968; 36).

Experience from Canada illustrates the far-reaching impact of the World Land Use Survey. Land use mapping in Canada had been started during 1950 by the Geographical Branch of the federal Department of Mines and Technical Surveys. The early work was done at different scales and levels of classification intensity. Nicholson *et al.* (1961; 2) have described how, after the World Land Use Commission presented its report to the 1952 International Geographical Union Congress, the Geographical Branch began to experiment with pilot land use surveys in several parts of Canada using the Commission's ideas. In 1959, a Standing Committee of the House of Commons recommended that land use survey work should be accelerated on a country-wide basis. It stressed that such a programme would be valuable to Canada as well to 'those who are concerned with the total world picture and are endeavouring to encourage the individual countries to produce such records' (Canada, House of Commons, 1959; 721).

In implementing the land use mapping programme, the Geographical Branch made 'every effort to follow the recommendation of the World Land Use Commission and yet, at the same time, ensure that the resulting maps and reports would be of maximum benefit to the Canadian people' (Nicholson *et al.*, 1961; 3). Five scales, ranging from 1 : 1,000,000 to 1 : 50,000, were selected depending upon the intensity of land use and area to be depicted. These maps were prepared on the basis of field observations and air photo interpretation completed by government employees or consultants. All land use categories corresponded to those in the World Land Use Survey (Table 3.1). Within each of the major categories, subcategories were identified. For example, the urban category was subdivided into industrial, commercial, residential, recreational and associated non-agricultural land subgroups.

Numerous problems arose in attempting to use the World Land Use categories for pasture and grazing land (Nicholson *et al.*, 1961; 8–9). Improved permanent pasture as found in Britain and Western Europe rarely occurred in Eastern Canada. In Canada, hay fields were commonly used for pasturing livestock after cutting of the first hay crop. Consequently, a problem arose as to whether such fields should be mapped as cropland or improved pasture. For the unimproved grazing land category, other problems arose. One occurred because this category was designed to identify the natural grasslands in the world. In the Western Canadian prairies, large areas of natural grassland fitted this category and could be mapped. On the other hand, areas of natural grassland were scarce in Eastern Canada. Often stony or steeply sloping fields were cleared and used for rough grazing. These

Table 3.1 Land-use survey classification systems and scales (*after Stamp, 1931; Van Valkenburg, 1950; Stamp, 1960; Coleman, 1961; Nicholson, Cornwall, and Raymond, 1961; McClellan, 1965*)

First Land Utilization Survey in Britain (1931–)	World Land-Use Survey (1949–)	Second Land-Use Survey in Britain (1960–)	Canadian Land-Use Inventory (1960–)
1. Land agriculturally unproductive (red)	1. Settlements and associated non-agricultural lands (red)	1. Settlement (grey)	1. Urban (red)
2. Gardens, nurseries, orchards, allotments (purple)	2. Horticulture (deep purple)	2. Market gardening (purple)	2. Horticulture (dark purple)
	3. Tree and other perennial crops (light purple)	3. Orchards (purple stripes)	3. Orchards and vineyards (light and medium purple)
3. Arable land (brown)	4. Cropland (brown)	4. Arable (brown)	4. Cropland (brown)
4. Meadowland and permanent grass (light green)	5. Improved permanent pasture (light green)	5. Grass (light green)	5. Improved pasture and forage crops (light green)
5. Heath and moorland (yellow)	6. Unimproved grazing land (orange and yellow)	6. Heath, moorland, and roughland (yellow)	6. Rough grazing land (orange and yellow)
6. Forests and woodlands (dark green)	7. Woodlands (different shades of green)	7. Woodlands (dark green)	7. Woodland (different shades of green)
	8. Swamps and marshes (blue)	8. Water and marsh (blue)	8. Swamp, marsh, or bog (light blue)
	9. Unproductive land (grey)	9. Derelict land (black stripple)	9. Unproductive (grey)
		10. Industry (red)	10. Water (blue)
		11. Transport (orange)	
		12. Open spaces (lime green)	
		13. Unvegetated land (white)	
Scale of published maps 1 : 63,360	Scale of published maps 1 : 1,000,000	Scale of published maps 1 : 25,000	Scales of published maps 1 : 1,000,000; 1 : 500,000; 1 : 250,000; 1 : 126,720; 1 : 50,000

were mapped as unimproved grazing land, even though they would revert to tree growth if left untended.

The particular problems which arose in adapting the World Land Use Survey to the Canadian environment indicate why Board was able to argue that no uniform world land use survey has been completed. Nevertheless, while countries often modified the classification system to meet local needs, general adaption of World Land Use Survey ideas did mark a significant step towards facilitating collection of data which subsequently could be analysed on a comparative basis.

The World Land Use Survey had its roots in the 1930s from Stamp's initiatives to design an inexpensive and relatively simple method to document land use patterns in Britain. Data were collected through direct observation and were recorded directly on large-scale maps. In the 1950s and 1960s, increasing use was made of aerial photographic interpretation with field observation used primarily as a check. Later surveys have relied upon increasingly sophisticated forms of remote sensing for data collection. The data subsequently have been used as input for automated cartographic work or for more inclusive geographic information systems.

Specific applications of remote sensing and geographic information systems in resource inventory are presented in section 3.2.3. At this stage, only a general overview is given. Remote sensing has been defined in various ways, but basically it involves observation of an object from a distance. In this context, conventional vertical aerial photographs were the most familiar form of remote sensor data employed in resource analysis until the mid 1960s.

A number of considerations prompted a search for a term to replace 'airphoto interpretation' as the label used to describe analysis of data generated from non-photographic imagery such as thermal infrared and radar. Standard black and white or colour film records what the human eye can see. As film sensitivity was extended beyond the spectrum visible to the eye, infrared film was developed. This film is sensitive to wavelengths longer than those visible to the human eye, and penetrates haze better than conventional film. Furthermore, because infrared energy reflects differently from vegetation which is healthy rather than diseased, it can be used to monitor the condition of crops.

Other developments not involving photographs occurred. Advances in radar allowed imagery to be developed which depicted surface forms more starkly than by photography. Radiation emitted by components of the environment facilitated application of thermal infrared scanning. Such scanning can operate at night as well as day, and has proven valuable for inventorying nocturnal wildlife and for detecting thermal pollution. The introduction of orbiting satellites provided a new platform from which many of these techniques could operate. The satellites facilitated data collection for larger areas and on a more regular basis compared to conventional airborne photography.

These various techniques – photographic and non-photographic – used singly or in combination, are referred to collectively as remote sensing. Air photo interpretation is still applied to photographic imagery whereas 'image interpretation' is applied to non-photographic imagery such as thermal infrared or radar. As a result, air photo interpretation now forms part of a continuum of image interpretation systems involving different sensors and different wavelengths of electromagnetic energy.

The first satellite specifically designed for studying the earth's resources was the Earth Resources Technology Satellite (ERTS), launched in July 1972. The primary function of this unmanned satellite, orbiting the earth at an altitude of 915 kilometers, was to supply a range of remotely sensed data about the earth. The ERTS satellite completed 14 orbits in 24 hours, and a full scanning sequence of the earth occurred every 18 days. Since any area was viewed repetitively at the same local time every 18 days, opportunity was provided to monitor phenomena over time.

The ERTS satellite carried a multispectral scanner and a three-unit television camera system. The scanner collected imagery on four different bands of the electromagnetic spectrum. The four different images have been used singly or in combination depending upon the problem being investigated. The ERTS imagery, providing information on ecological patterns, geological patterns, physical relationships and land use patterns, has been valuable for numerous resource studies, including the inventorying of hazard and environmentally sensitive areas, monitoring of pollution and crop growth, and enumerating wildlife.

The ERTS satellite functioned for three years. It had been planned as an experimental exercise, and was used mainly by American and Canadian researchers and agencies. Officially, it was referred to as ERTS-I, to distinguish it from ERTS-II, a second satellite launched in January 1975. The imagery from these satellites now is referred to as LANDSAT I and II respectively. Several specific applications are reviewed in section 3.2.2.

The ERTS programme has been the primary source of remote sensing imagery since the early 1970s. However, another programme has been initiated. In 1977, France began the SPOT (System Probatoire d'Observation de la Terre) programme which subsequently was joined by Sweden and Belgium. During 1981, a decision was taken to operate SPOT as a commercial programme that eventually would be self-financing.

SPOT1 was launched on 21 February 1986 as the world's first commercial remote sensing satellite. The satellite is in a quasi polar orbit at an altitude of 832 kilometres. In phase with the rotation of the earth, SPOT1 makes a complete ground track cycle every 26 days.

The two imaging instruments provide data on a 60 kilometre-wide strip for nadir viewing. The instruments can provide either multispectral or high resolution panchromatic information. Either gives highly detailed data. The multispectral mode covers green, red and near infrared spectral bands and provides information for 20 by 20 square metre grids. The panchromatic mode has a resolution of 10 by 10 metres.

The design lifetime of SPOT1 and 2 is about 2 years. SPOT2 was scheduled to be placed in operation during 1988 and with SPOT1 will provide high resolution images until 1990. SPOT3 is scheduled to replace SPOT2 toward the end of 1990 and will last four years. SPOT4 then will be used from 1994 to 1998.

The main applications for the images from the SPOT programme will be land management studies, assessment of renewable resources, exploration of mineral and petroleum resources, and cartography. Given the great amount of detail in the high resolution images, the primary initial use will likely be mostly through visual interpretation. The high resolution and large scale makes the SPOT images a viable alternative to more expensive and not as regular conventional aerial photographs.

The increased amount of data from orbiting satellites has provided impetus for both computer mapping and geographic information systems (GIS) (Monmonier, 1982; Dobson, 1983). The term GIS was created during the development of the Canada Geographic Information System in the early 1960s (Tomlinson, 1984, 31–2; Goodchild, 1985, 35). GIS evolved from automated cartography in response to the needs of resource managers to analyse growing quantities of data in a timely manner. As Tomlinson (1984; 33) remarked, 'The real-world time of institutional decision making was coming up against the interminably long time required to analyse any large volume of map data by manual methods.'

Goodchild (1985; 36) has defined GIS as a system using a spatial data base to provide answers to questions of a geographical nature. A GIS is designed to facilitate sorting, selective retrieval, calculation and spatial analysis and modelling. It is capable of allowing the input and editing of any type of geographic data, and output of information in the format of tables and/or maps. The two major areas of application have been resource management and urban planning, with resource management accounting for the largest number of operating systems (Maher and Wightman, 1985, 43; Walsh, 1985). Most of the developmental work for GIS has originated in government agencies. In parallel, however, the International Geographical Union created a Commission on Geographical Data Sensing and Processing during 1968. It organized the first international GIS conference in 1970 and published the first texts on GIS in 1972 (Tomlinson, 1972).

Tomlinson (1984) provides a good overview of the evolution of GIS from the 1960s to 1980s, and identifies a number of challenges. First, attention is needed regarding the ultimate size of data bases so that they can be organized and managed effectively. Second, methods are required to allow interaction among various types of data and different data bases. Third, more effort is needed to establish dynamic rather than static data bases which in turn should improve modelling capability. And fourth, access, communication, confidentiality and security are all substantial issues involving technical, administrative and political considerations. The issues identified by Tomlinson are increasingly being addressed in general reviews of remote sensing (Kairu, 1982; Townshend, 1981a, b), analyses of specific applications of remote sensing (Jensen, 1983; Johannson and Barney, 1981; Lulla, 1983; Murtha and Harding, 1984; Woodcock, Strahler and Franklin, 1983), and assessments of GIS (Kessell, Good and Hopkins, 1984; Titzer and Moser, 1982).

Substantial progress has occurred in the realm of resource inventory methods. In 1930, Stamp organized a land use survey in Britain which relied upon observation by some 250,000 schoolchildren on a field-by-field basis. As recently as the early 1960s, a second survey was completed in Britain which relied heavily upon field observations by volunteers. By the late 1980s, the resource analyst had access to remotely sensed data, and computer facilities to manipulate and map the data. These technological advances do not mean that the geographer should discard field observation and conventional aerial photography. For many problems, these are still the most effective and efficient. Nevertheless, the resource analyst who does not develop an understanding of the opportunities offered by remote sensing, computer data storage, manipulation, and display, and the application of these procedures in resources inventory, is not making the most effective use of the techniques currently available to him.

3.2.2 LAND CAPABILITY

While it is helpful to have current natural resource information, the resource manager needs to know resource potential or capability before making decisions. However, capability is a function of assumptions which are made. For example, an index of agricultural potential must incorporate a multitude of possibilities for different crops under different technologies, management objectives, and financial arrangements. Nevertheless, knowing the potential, resource managers should be in a better position to determine whether existing activity represents the best use of resources. This reasoning is the rationale for research on resource capability. It is an area of research which has attracted geographical interest for some time (Mabbutt, 1968; Young, 1968; Mints and Kakhanovskaya, 1974; Sharma and Sharma, 1980; Taher, 1980; Smit, 1981; Smit and Brklacich, 1985).

Many countries have developed classification systems for resource capability. The United States has been one of the leaders in this area (United States, Land Committee, 1941). The Department of

Agriculture developed a land-capability classification system to help landowners interpret soil maps and to facilitate management decisions based on soil potential, and limitations in use (Osunade, 1979; 168). Tillmann *et al.* (1975) developed a computer-based technique for evaluating, in terms of physical suitability, the potential of land for specific uses. They applied their capability system in Michigan to demonstrate its utility in locating sites for disposal of solid waste, liquid waste and individual septic waste.

In Britain, the government realized during the 1930s that a national policy to preserve 'good' agricultural land could not be implemented. No definition existed for such land. No attempt had been made to inventory its distribution. At that time, Stamp was still directing the First Land Utilization Survey, and a government Royal Commission requested him to devise a land suitability classification. Drawing upon the land use survey, he started in 1938 to work upon this problem related to land capability. He recognized the difficulty of establishing such a system, since 'what is the "best" land for one purpose is not necessarily the best use for another' (Stamp, 1960; 106). He evolved a system which had three general categories and ten specific classes (Table 3.2). Stamp recognized that the classification was broad and general, and noted that it would be 'idle to pretend that this simple tenfold classification of the land of Britain is the final answer to the problem' (Stamp, 1960; 111).

Table 3.2 Stamp's classification of agricultural land in Britain (*from Stamp, 1960*)

Category I: Good Quality Land

1. First-class land capable of intensive cultivation
2. Good general purpose farmland
3. First-class land with water conditions especially favouring grass
4. Good but heavy land

Category II: Medium quality land

5. Medium quality light land
6. Medium quality general purpose farmland

Category III: Poor quality land

7. Poor quality heavy land
8. Poor quality mountain and moorland
9. Poor quality light land
10. Poorest land

A subsequent classification system, influenced by the United States Department of Agriculture classification, was devised beginning in the 1960s (Mackney, 1974; Morgan, 1974). Its objective was to indicate the *long-term* agricultural value of land, against which the impact of *shorter-term* variables such as standard of management and adequacy of equipment or farm structure could be considered. Prior to this system, however, the one devised by Stamp was the only national capability classification system available. And, while postwar changes in farming practices led to its becoming outdated, one reviewer noted that his system had been of 'outstanding value in land use planning' (Morgan, 1974; 80).

During the 1960s, Canada introduced an inventory procedure which combined information about present land use (section 3.2.1), resource capability, and socio-economic variables (McCormack, 1971; Hoffman, 1976; Rees, 1977). This information, along with that from an agroclimatic classification system, a computer-based information and mapping system, and pilot land use projects, comprise the Canada Land Inventory. The general intent of the inventory is to aid decision making for programmes of land adjustment and regional economic development.

The Canada Land Inventory was designed to produce an inventory of resource potential for agriculture, forestry, recreation and wildlife (ungulates and waterfowl). Seven numerical classes were established for each resource, with class 1 representing the highest capability. To illustrate, class 1 agricultural lands have no significant limitations. Along with classes 2 and 3, such lands are considered capable of sustained production of common field crops. Class 4 land is physically marginal for sustained agriculture. Land in class 5 is unsuitable for annual field crops but appropriate for forage crops or improved pasture. Land in class 6 is limited to rough grazing and class 7 land is unsuited for agricultural use.

As with all assessments of land capability, numerous assumptions were built in. Regarding agriculture capability, the following assumptions were made: (1) soils are well managed and cropping is done with a largely mechanized system, and (2) land improvements considered feasible by the individual farmer (removal of trees) are assumed to have been completed whether or not they are, whereas land improvements beyond the means of a single farmer (irrigation) are assumed not to be in place unless already completed. In contrast, the following aspects were *not* considered: distance to market, size of farm, type of ownership, skill or resources of individual farmer, or hazard of crop damage by storms. For recreation capability, it was assumed that higher frequency of use implied higher recreational value and that uniform demand and access applied to all areas. As such assumptions are varied, different assessments of capability could be expected.

The wide range of uses to which the Canada Land Inventory has been put illustrates the value of resource capability information. The agricultural capability data help in delimiting agricultural lands, identifying submarginal farmland, consolidating farms into viable units, establishing a more equitable assessment base, and indicating where urban and industrial development will least harm agricultural production. The forestry information has proven useful in designating timber leases, determining assessments, and planning for wildlife and recreation. This latter application has tied in closely with the recreation data for identification of potential park and recreation areas, designation of lakeshore cottage lots, reservation of water frontage for public areas, and zoning within large parks. The wildlife data are used to identify habitats requiring protection and to estimate potential returns from trapping or other harvesting activities. As long as the data are used for their intended purposes, resource capability information can serve as a useful input to a variety of resource management decisions. It must always be recognized, however, that the capability estimates are based upon a series of assumptions which may be valid at a national level but less valid in specific regions.

3.2.3 OTHER RESOURCE INVENTORY APPROACHES

Whether focusing upon resource use or resource potential, geographers have used a variety of inventory methods. Aerial photographs continue to be important, especially for large-scale evaluation or when equipment necessary to handle remote sensing imagery is not available. Several studies illustrate this point. Raghavswamy and Vaidyanadhan (1980) utilized air photo interpretation to study land forms, soils, vegetation, land use and land cover capabilities in an area of about 680 square kilometres of the coastal city of Visakhapatnam in Andhra Pradesh in India. Rao and Vaidyanadhan (1981) analysed similar features in the Krishna delta in the same state. Singh, Pofali and Batt (1985) used air photos to study land resource development in a watershed and Tiwari and Singh (1984) utilized them to assess forest biomass.

Remote sensing imagery also can be used with minimal investment in computers and software, and thus can be utilized in areas where such facilities are not readily available. Work by Pratap and Sheda (1983), Biswas (1984), Saxena, Saxena and Vidhyanath (1984) and Deshmukh and Chaturvedi (1984) shows how imagery can be applied in studies ranging from forest cover, watershed planning to land use evaluation. Remote sensing information increasingly is being used in the developed nations. Applications range from monitoring of dumpsites (Ohlhorst, 1981), classification of forest resources (Fox, Mayer and Forbes, 1983), land management and planning (Woodcock, Strahler and Franklin, 1983; Hathout and Smil, 1985), soil surveys (Roudabush *et al.*, 1985) water management (LeDrew and Franklin, 1985), to delineating areas prone to hazards (Yool *et al.*, 1985).

Use of air photographs and remote sensing imagery has not been the only approach to resource inventory. By drawing upon existing statistical information, geographers have mapped resource patterns, ranging from surface and groundwater in southern India (Ganesh, 1984) to coal resources in Canada (Harker, 1984). Reliance upon existing published information has also allowed geographers to assess the adequacy of resources at a global scale (Gerasimov, 1983) or with regard to specific resource sectors within individual nations (Pierce and Furuseth, 1983). Mapping and analytical skills have been combined to produce natural resource-oriented atlases where the intent has been to highlight use patterns, potentials, limitations, and problems (Simpson-Lewis *et al.*, 1979; Ramesh and Tiwari, 1983; Nair *et al.*, 1984). These atlases can be fairly technical and oriented toward professional resource analysts, or can be done in a more popular manner to sensitize the general public to problems and opportunities. Of the latter type, one of the more imaginative has been the Gaian atlas (Lovelock, 1979; Myers, 1984; Zelinsky, 1985).

Research on inventories of current resource use and resource capability is being extended by analysts trying to develop ecological or biophysical inventory systems which will lead to identification of ecozones or regions. Such classifications describe and analyse relatively homogenous units of land at local or regional scales. A hierarchical classification of natural terrestrial ecosystems is developed by using biotic and abiotic criteria (Bailey, 1980; 95). Such inventories usually ignore administrative or political boundaries and emphasize natural units and boundaries in the belief that an ecosystem approach to resource management will better identify potential externalities and other problems. As a result, the classification systems usually focus upon soils, landforms, vegetation, and climate. This approach is being explored in a variety of countries, ranging from the United States (Driscoll *et al.*, 1984; Swanston, 1981), Canada (Thie and Ironside, 1976; Rubec, 1979; Bird and Rapport, 1986), to India (Chattopadhyay and Salim, 1985; Nair *et al.*, 1985).

Bastedo and Theberge (1983) have assessed the ecologically-based resource classification systems, and noted several weaknesses. These include a tendency to emphasize biophysical information and neglect cultural detail, to focus upon ecological structure and overlook process, and to present the results in too complex a form. These conclusions have led them and Nelson to develop what they call the ABC resource survey approach (Bastedo, Nelson and Theberge, 1984; Bastedo, 1986).

The ABC approach incorporates abiotic, biotic and cultural information into a comprehensive survey method devised to identify environmentally sensitive areas. The major thrust is not toward determination of land use capabilities but instead toward conservation of ecological values by identification of (1) areas that require special protection or land use controls, (2) dominant land uses and associated management possibilities, (3) the spatial dimensions required for resource management, (4) immediate management needs, and (5) data gaps and research opportunities (Bastedo, Nelson and Theberge, 1984; 127–9). Through their ABC approach, they believe that a form of resource management can be implemented which reflects the three objectives of the World Conservation Strategy: (1) maintenance of essential ecological processes and life support systems, (2) preservation of genetic diversity, and (3) sustainable utilization of species and ecosystems (Allen, 1980; International Union for the Conservation of Nature and Natural Resources, 1980; 1984). It is this kind of experimental research, building upon and extending previous inventory methods, which is likely to generate new understanding and innovative approaches to resource management problems.

3.3 ESTIMATING DEMAND

The difficulties encountered in such research are revealed by studies of water demand. Sewell and Bower (1968) suggested that identification of relevant variables is one of four problems faced by researchers. The other three include selection of an appropriate time horizon, consideration of uncertainty, and consideration of short-run variability. Concerning variables, they argued that demand for water is a function of five variables: population, nature of the economy, technology, social tastes and policy decisions.

While these variables are relatively easy to identify, they are difficult to measure. Population estimates require information on numbers, age, sex, fertility rates, migration and death rates. Significant assumptions must be frequently made to derive estimates for these aspects. Estimates about the economy require data about personal income, employment and industrial output. These aspects also require assumptions.

Technological changes may influence water demand in at least four ways, including development of new products, new processes, new or different raw materials, and improved methods for handling water. Unfortunately, it is difficult to forecast what breakthroughs may occur and when they will be implemented. Changes in social tastes and policy decisions are equally difficult. What societal preferences will prevail 10, 20 or 30 years in the future? What decisions will be made concerning pricing, extent of metering, subsidies, and water quality standards? Knowing that such considerations are potentially significant is one thing. Being able to operationalize them in forecasts is another.

A number of approaches have been adopted regarding the impact of such variables. One has been to hold them constant. In estimating energy demand and supply between 1966 and 1990, the National Energy Board of Canada (1969; 75–8) made the following political, economic and technological assumptions. There would be no major war; overseas petroleum supplies would be available to North America over the long term; no important changes would occur in national or international trading patterns. Canada would experience a high level of economic activity; the economy would depend increasingly on manufacturing and service industries; existing inter-fuel prices would prevail. No new energy form would come into general use; there would be no new means of energy transportation but intensified pressure to reduce air and water pollution. With these and other assumptions made, estimates of future energy supply and demand were developed.

Resources for the Future, in forecasting resource needs between 1960 and 2000 for the United States, estimated future changes in technology. This was done in the belief that 'assumptions, broad or narrow, daring or cautious, always determine the result' (Landsberg, 1964; 6). Advances in technology were taken into account whenever their form and consequences could be envisaged. As the report noted,

> This is not common practice; in many projections, because of the multitude of uncertainties, no allowance is made for technological change. But in striving for the closest possible appreciation of the future, it has seemed better to guess, even on slender evidence, than to ignore. A footloose speculation four decades ago about dieselization of the railroads would have yielded a better projection of future coal and oil demand than one based on the assumption that locomotives would forever carry boilers (Landsberg, 1964; 10).

In contrast, Resources for the Future consciously ignored any major changes in future price relationships. In other words, estimates of future supplies were not allowed to influence projections of requirements. This procedure was recognized as being unrealistic. As a product becomes more or less scarce, changes in relative price normally occur and lead to restraint on production or to substitution. The reason for this procedure was to enable the study to test adequacy of resource supplies to meet demands without substantial changes in price relationships. If prices were allowed to adjust themselves, it was thought that possible trouble areas would be masked.

In the context of these concerns, geographers have pursued several lines of research. One has focused upon estimating future demand for resources and exploring the impact of policy decisions on future demand. Grima (1972; 1973) used multivariate analysis to explore the relationship between residential water demand and such independent variables as housing density, household size, lot size, precipitation, temperature, water balance and water retaining characteristics of the soil for several communities in southern Ontario. Having created a multiple regression equation which described the relationship, he then considered the impact of pricing (metering, increasing marginal charges) and non-pricing (capacity of plumbing fixtures, lawn sprinkling regulations) policy alternatives on water demand. Similar work using multiple regression has been done for communities in British Columbia (Sewell and Roueche, 1974), Illinois (Wong, 1972), England (Rees, J.A., 1972; 1973; 1974), and India (Lee, 1969). In contrast, Mitchell and Leighton (1977) developed a multivariate but non-statistical procedure designed to help smaller municipalities to improve their water forecasts.

Another line of research has considered the potential of 'futuristic' procedures to improve forecasts (Maruyama and Dator, 1971). As a group, such techniques provide means by which the occurrence and significance of future events can be incorporated into forecasts and resource management. Many futuristic procedures have been developed (Jantsch, 1967). Only two – the Delphi and Scenario – are reviewed here.

The Delphi technique was developed by the RAND Corporation during research whose objective was to identify the timing and significance of future developments concerning scientific breakthroughs, population growth, automation, space progress, future weapons systems, and probability and prevention of war. Brainstorming sessions in which a group of experts was gathered to discuss a problem were viewed as having two weaknesses. It was often expensive and difficult to bring experts to one place. Furthermore, once a group was assembled, some people inevitably dominated because of personalities or other attributes having little bearing on the problem. The Delphi technique was designed to realize the advantage of brainstorming (stimulation of group interaction) while avoiding the disadvantages (expense; group psychology effects).

RAND proceeded in the following manner. Experts around the world were identified and invited to serve on a panel for one of the topics. For scientific breakthroughs, each panel member was invited by letter to name inventions which were urgently needed and realizable in the next 50 years. Forty-nine items were identified. In a second round, panel members were given the list of 49 items and asked to indicate the date on which there was a 50–50 probability of the breakthrough occurring. These estimates were combined and displayed as quartiles and medians.

Reasonable consensus emerged for 10 items. In a third round, the consensus for 10 items was presented, and dissenters were asked to elaborate upon why they disagreed. At the same time, 17 items for which agreement had not been reached were presented. Panel members were invited to elaborate upon reasons for the timing they had identified. This exercise was repeated in a fourth round. At each stage, the number of items for which consensus was reached went up.

In jargonistic terms, the Delphi technique may be described as a 'succession of iterative brainstorming rounds' (Jantsch, 1967; 137). In simpler terms, the Delphi technique replaces direct discussion among experts with a series of questionnaires sent to selected experts. Successive questionnaires provide feedback from previous responses, allowing experts to be stimulated by other viewpoints (Linstone and Turoff, 1975).

In such a procedure, however, at least two concerns arise. As with any brainstorming exercise, the forecasts will be influenced by the selection of experts. In addition, the usual experience has been that many respondents stop participating after two or three rounds. Thus, while a series of rounds is desirable to reach consensus, using too many rounds results in participants dropping out. On the positive side, the Delphi technique offers a means to identify the occurrence and consequences of events in the future. Such estimates could then be used when forecasting demands for or supplies of natural resources, or in anticipating future resource management problems.

The Delphi technique has been applied to a variety of resource management situations. It has been used to identify community beliefs concerning soil conservation (Earle, Brownlea and Rose, 1981) and to determine the ranking of environmental and natural resource policy issues (Leitch and Leistritz, 1984). Bardecki (1984a; 1985) utilized it when studying wetlands, and Peace (1985) adapted it to a study of land use. The Delphi technique also has been applied in a study of the quality of elk habitat in western Montana (Schuster *et al.*, 1985). This mix of applications suggests that resource analysts and managers are finding that the Delphi technique is a useful aid for identifying the probability of future conditions and for then assessing the implications for resource allocation decisions.

The scenario is another technique for exploring the future. In a scenario, the writer describes a logical sequence of events which evolve from specified assumptions (Jantsch, 1967; 180–1). It is well suited for incorporating many aspects of a problem, and to allow the analyst to gain a 'feel' for likely future events as well as key decision points. The scenario focuses the investigator's attention on the dynamics and interaction of events. Frequently, several scenarios are prepared. While it is accepted that none will come true as outlined, the general patterns described are viewed as the most likely if certain assumptions and decisions are made.

Scenarios often have been used to dramatize the nature of possible problems in the future. In *Silent Spring*, Rachel Carson's (1962) first chapter was a scenario. Its purpose was to draw attention to the future consequences of indiscriminate use of chemicals to combat insects and weeds. The chapter describes a hypothetical town in the rural United States which at one time was a prosperous agricultural centre and enjoyed an abundance of wildlife, flowers and other vegetation. Carson then described how the situation changed. Livestock started to die for unexplained reasons. Adults and children became ill, with several sudden and unexplained deaths. The flocks of birds disappeared. Vegetation became withered and brown. Having caught the reader's attention, Carson then went on to explain what had silenced the voices of spring in many American towns.

Others have used the scenario in similar ways. Ehrlich (1968; 72–80) used three different scenarios to illustrate the possible consequences of different policies concerning population control. Two of the scenarios portray grim sequences of events resulting from an exploding global population. Starvation, wars, and natural disasters overwhelm the earth as mankind moves into the 'famine decades'. In contrast, a third scenario sketches events associated with a world in which population control, agricultural development and limited industrialization are used. Ehrlich invited his readers to create other scenarios by way of examing the future. In a similar manner, Ericksen (1975) used the scenario technique to explore implications of different flood adjustment policies for a community in South Dakota while Haas, Kates and Bowden (1977) used it in a comparative analysis of hazardous events in four cities. In a somewhat related manner, Martinson (1980) has examined science fiction literature to see what alternative ecologies are presented and to consider the likelihood of such scenarios becoming reality in the future.

Scenarios can be made more ‘realistic’ by basing them upon Delphi exercises. Two geographers combined these techniques to examine the implications of different energy policies in Canada (Sewell and Foster, 1976). The modified Delphi technique used ideas provided by university and government researchers at a workshop. Sewell and Foster then prepared two scenarios based upon differing assumptions about prevailing political philosophies over the next 25 years. In one scenario, a philosophy which promotes technological growth dominates. In the other, conservation and recycling are dominant. In each scenario, the role of energy is critical. The two scenarios consider different combinations of variables which could affect energy extraction, generation, transportation, and use. The actual scenarios are presented as hypothetical debates in the Canadian House of Commons on 14 May 2000. This strategy facilitated examination of the implications of a variety of energy policies.

Forecasts of either supply or demand have often been inaccurate due to the many assumptions and other problems. In Canada, the history of energy supply and demand forecasting illustrates this point dramatically (Helliwell, MacGregor and Plourde, 1983; Robinson, 1983). Regarding supplies of natural gas, in 1969 and 1970 it was estimated that a substantial surplus of supply over domestic demand would exist by 1990. However, by 1975 the situation had reversed with a significant deficit being forecast. By the late 1970s another reverse occurred in the forecasts, and by 1981 a large surplus was being predicted for 1990. As Robinson (1983; 302) observed, this pattern represents a double reversal over a 12-year period, moving from optimism, to pessimism and back to optimism. The magnitudes of the changes were not minor, with the supply forecasts varying by a factor of two over six years and the forecast for domestic demand changing by 32 per cent in a four-year period.

Given these problems, Robinson (1982a) has questioned the merit of believing that forecasts can be improved by increasing the sophistication of the techniques. He suggested that the problems would not be solved by increasing sophistication because the difficulties were not due to unsophistication but rather to the process of forecasting itself, a view shared by Midttun and Baumgartner (1986). In the field of energy, he argued that forecasts had been based on the extrapolation of past trends and the assumptions made by forecasters. Such an approach is inherently conservative and is biased toward producing images of the future which are derivatives of the status quo. These considerations led Robinson (1982a; 232) to conclude that '... attempting to improve the quality of forecasting by increasing the sophistication of analysis is a bit like adding new wings to your car because it wouldn't fly with the first pair: the fault lies not with the accessories but with the vehicle itself'.

This type of criticism led Robinson to offer two specific suggestions to improve forecasts, especially those dealing with demand. First, he noted that the traditional 'top down' approach in estimating energy demand involved forecasting the values of macroeconomic and demographic variables such as GNP and population, determining historical links between these variables and consumption, and deriving future levels of energy demand by applying these relationships to the demographic and macroeconomic forecasts (Robinson, 1982b; 627). This approach worked well when economic growth was relatively steady and the real price of energy was constant or even declined. In the more turbulent 1970s and 1980s, however, this approach became increasingly inadequate.

As an alternative, Robinson (1982b) has argued that a 'bottom up' approach should be adopted. Such an approach recognizes that demand for energy is a derived demand in which energy is not valued for itself but rather for the work or service which it provides. Thus, people do not want petroleum or electricity, but transportation, heat and light. From this viewpoint, it is sensible to focus on a 'bottom up' or 'end use' approach, in which attention is directed upon the tasks or end uses for which energy is consumed. The demand for energy is determined by estimating these services, analysing the efficiency of use, and then deriving tertiary, secondary and finally primary energy consumption. By having a sharper understanding of the uses to which energy is put, Robinson believed there is greater opportunity to analyse alternative efficiencies, and fuel substitutabilities. This approach requires information which many countries do not yet systematically collect, but it does emphasize that there is more than one way of digging a hole.

In a further demonstration of lateral thinking, Robinson (1982c) has argued for the use of backcasting rather than forecasting. Good forecasts attempt to converge upon the most likely future under specified conditions and try to indicate the likelihood of that future. In contrast, good backcasts would be expected to diverge, as they reveal the policy implications of alternative futures. In other words, in backcasting the analyst does not try to forecast the future. Instead, a number of future end points are identified, and then the conditions necessary to reach each end point are examined. These alternatives can then be provided to the policy maker who can see which actions will have to be taken to reach a preferred future end point. To conduct backcasting, Robinson (1982c) suggested that six steps would have to be followed: (1) specification of goals and constraints, (2) description of present resource consumption and production, (3) outline of the future economy, (4) demand analysis, (5) supply analysis, and (6) determination of the implications of the analysis. The manner in which backcasting could be applied in the energy field is shown in Table 3.3.

Table 3.3 Outline of proposed backcasting method (*after Robinson, 1982C, 339*)

1. **Specify goals and constraints**
2. **Describe current energy consumption and production**
   Develop a detailed description of present energy consumption and production, by source, fuel, sector, type and end-use and specify primary and secondary production and consumption, and, as far as possible, tertiary consumption.
3. **Develop outline of future economy**
   - Choose end-point date;
   - construct a model of the end-point economy;
   - choose mid-point dates; and
   - derive a demand scenario (list of end-use demands) that corresponds to the results of the model.
4. **Undertake demand analysis**
   - Derive tertiary and secondary consumption profiles for the end-point from the end-use demand scenario, ie specify the type of energy used and the efficiency of use.
   - Determine demand management measures necessary over time to attain these secondary profiles.
   - Specify the costs of the measures outlined in the demand scenarios.
5. **Undertake supply analysis**
   - Develop an inventory of available supply sources.
   - Match available supply sources to secondary consumption profile.
   - Derive energy supply industry requirements to supply the energy required.
   - Develop a primary energy requirements profile by adding together the results of the above two steps.
   - Determine those supply policy measures necessary over time to attain the primary consumption profiles.
   - Specify the costs of the measures outlined.
6. **Determine implications of the analysis**
   Analyse the social, environmental, economic, political and technological implications of the supply and demand analyses.

The analyst has many difficult methodological and institutional problems with which to deal in handling the issue of resource demand. In this section, it has been shown that strategies have ranged from extrapolation of past experience, use of multivariate methods, experimentation with futuristic methods, and attempts to discover either new holes in which to dig or else to dig in a different manner in existing holes. By definition, the future is uncertain and therefore will always be difficult for us to predict or anticipate. However, since so many resource allocation decisions have implications for the future, it is important that geographical resource analysts devote their talent and skill to exploring ways in which we can improve our ability to anticipate the future, or to improve our ability to achieve desired societal futures.

3.4 IMPLICATIONS FOR RESOURCE MANAGEMENT

Inventorying of resource use or capability, whether based upon field observation or remote sensing, has obvious value for the resource manager. Before making decisions concerning future allocation of resources, it is helpful to know their amount, quality and distribution as well as the way they are being utilized. Land use and other resource inventories are thus a fundamental tool for resource managers. Through the work of Stamp, Van Valkenburg and others with the International Geographical Union, geographers have influenced the design of land use surveys around the world. Indeed, along with hazards research (Ch. 8), it is possible that these research activities by geographers are the ones which have had the greatest international impact on resource policy.

Resource capability or potential studies are closely related to investigations of present use. It is only by knowing the potential of a resource that managers can decide whether existing uses or practices should be altered to realize more benefits. This work has a close relationship with research regarding carrying capacities (Ch. 7). Both are concerned with identifying thresholds or constraints for resource use. To this end, at least two considerations arise. Technical or research-based information is necessary for understanding the nature of the physical system. Simultaneously, value-based judgements must be made concerning feasible levels of output or acceptable levels of use.

Another application of resource capability data is in environmental impact assessments (Ch. 9). Knowing the potential or sensitivity of an environment, managers should be in a better position to judge the impact of new developments or activity. Capability information in itself is not sufficient for estimating impacts, but it is a necessary component for such work.

3.5 IMPLICATIONS FOR RESEARCH

Determining the distribution and availability of resources, and the demand for them, involves extensive use of the spatial research tradition in geography. Such studies also relate closely to the ecological and regional analysis themes since inventory information is useful for planning resource and regional development. As a result, relative to de Bono's (1967) ideas about lateral and vertical thinking, ongoing inventory research represents extension of a well-developed hole by the discipline. At the same time, the application of new technologies, especially computer cartography, remote sensing, and geographic information systems, is permitting exploration of new holes which previously were inaccessible to the geographer.

Inventory research has not yet provided theoretical breakthroughs in geography. On the other hand, it has contributed towards demonstrating the value of geographical concepts and techniques for tackling significant problems (section 3.4). In designing a resource inventory, classification systems and scale are important factors to be considered. The characteristics of an ideal classification system would include simplicity, mutually-exclusive and exhaustive categories, universal applicability, and ease of recording. These attributes tend to conflict. For example, universal applicability may require so many categories that the system becomes complex and cumbersome rather than simple. Scale is a second major problem, particularly at a global level. The variety of physical terrains, cultures, technological capacity and economic development at a world scale makes it difficult to devise a classification which will depict meaningful patterns at scales such as 1 : 1,000,000.

In devising resource inventory systems, the need for unambiguous operational definitions is apparent. Resource use or resource capability categories must be made explicit. Definitions are also needed to incorporate independent variables into demand forecasts. The implementation of concepts and classifications has been a major obstacle. In Britain, Coppock and Duffield (1975; 97) have argued that in recreation surveys, 'capacity' has not been adequately defined nor satisfactorily measured. A similar experience was reported from Canada. In commenting upon the Canada Land Inventory, Taylor (1965; 84) noted that 'recreational resources' were to be inventoried. Although this concept was part of the conventional wisdom of resource planners, Taylor observed that no one had ever defined it. The outcome was 'a flurry of activity during which a classification has been attempted before the phenomena to be classified have been identified'. As a result, development of acceptable operational definitions represents an area for more attention by resource analysts.

Assumptions play an important role in inventory work. For surveys of resource capability, assumptions normally are made about management objectives, technological capacity and available capital. Depending upon the assumptions made, quite different estimates of capacity can emerge. Forecasts of resource demand also make assumptions ranging over political, social, economic and technological conditions in the future. It was concern about assumptions in forecasts being used in a normative manner that partially prompted Robinson to argue for more attention to the development of backcasting.

Various data sources and measurement techniques generate issues demanding attention. The use of several data sources which cross check each other is desirable. The advent of satellite-generated imagery has emphasized the need for conventional aerial photographs to bridge the gap between the broad regional view with its attendant problems of resolution and interpretation, and 'ground truth' as obtained by field checking. Time should be taken to choose the combination of data sources and data collection techniques which offer the best mix of accuracy, expense, time, and reliability. In the future, it seems probable that increasing use will be made of new forms of remotely sensed data. At the same time, surveys may find that field observation and conventional air photo interpretation are most appropriate.

When data are processed and manipulated, several considerations arise. The assumptions of statistical techniques must be met. This aspect is important in studies of resource demand, where multiple regression equations are often used (section 3.3). The analyst must be satisfied that assumptions such as normality are met or that transformations have been used. Another aspect of concern is the extent to which independent variables are selected primarily because they are amenable to statistical manipulation. In the demand studies, variables are often used which appear to be conceptually less satisfying than others not used. It often appears that those chosen were used because they could be measured at interval or ratio levels. There should be concern that continuing effort to develop or adapt sophisticated techniques may sometimes overlook the poor or inadequate data which are being input to them.

Inventory research reflects the need for compromise and subjectivity found in all investigations. Comprehensive but complex classification systems often are rejected in favour of imperfect ones which are simple and easily applicable in the field. The search for comparability is compromised when modified classifications are devised to respond to the needs and problems of specific places. Generalizations are sacrificed to satisfy local, regional, or even national problems. However, in spite of the many problems not yet overcome in such research, considerable accomplishments have been realized. From individual research efforts to collaborative programmes such as the World Land Use Survey, geographers have made substantial contributions. Indeed, because of their disciplinary background, geographers usually are well prepared to carry out resource inventory programmes.

CHAPTER 4
RESOURCE ALLOCATION

4.1 INTRODUCTION

The two research traditions of spatial and regional analysis are foundations for the studies in this chapter, with many based in economic geography. A fundamental concern has been to understand the spatial patterns and processes associated with the production, consumption and distribution of resource-based commodities, products and services. Geographers have sought to identify the variables which account for observed patterns, explore relationships among these variables, and establish generalizations.

Several ideas have formed the basis for such research. The concept of *spatial interaction* has involved two types of inquiry (section 4.2). One, concentrating upon analysing the actual flow of commodities, products and services among communities, regions or nations, is frequently referred to as 'commodity flow' analysis. The second has focused upon possible flows of goods, people and ideas. In practice, these studies have drawn upon simulation models, especially those based upon diffusion. *Spatial organization* represents a second core idea (section 4.3). Such work concentrates upon describing the spatial patterns associated with given phenomena, and then exploring the processes beneath these patterns. As with work in spatial interaction, this research also considers alternative forms of spatial organization which would confer greater benefits to society.

A third idea is embodied by the concept of *regional planning and development* (section 4.4). Research questions centre upon the impact of resource development on local or regional economies, the nature of regionalization in resource use or management, and conflicting uses relative to different activities in a specified regional environment. In addition to outlining studies emerging from these core ideas, this chapter considers their implications for resource management (section 4.5) and research (section 4.6).

4.2 SPATIAL INTERACTIONS

Analysis of the movement of commodities, products, services, people and ideas among places represents a long-standing interest by geographers (Ullman, 1957; Leinbach, 1976) and has been applied to resource problems over a long period (Whitaker, 1954; 231–2). In this section attention is first directed to studies which analyse the actual movement of resource commodities and resource users against alternative patterns. Subsequently, attention turns to studies which simulate the movement of products, ideas and people.

A study of the movement and marketing of bituminous coal in eastern Australia has the characteristics of many commodity flow studies. Wilson (1967) sought to compare the theoretical market area of coal mines in New South Wales and Queensland against the actual commodity movements from separate production points. The extent of the theoretical market area was delimited by using commodity price and freight rates as reflected in costs to consumers. Wilson was aware that discrepancies might arise between the theoretical and actual market areas, but felt this approach was useful in that it tested initial assumptions about commodity flow (rational economic man striving to minimize assembly costs) as well as drew attention to anomalies. The study itself was based upon origin–destination statistics supplied by the railroad systems plus a questionnaire survey of coal producers and consumers.

Wilson had to make several assumptions. First, he assumed for each production coal *field* that an average f.o.b.-mine price could be determined, thereby eliminating major differences arising from size, grade, degree of preparation or other similar variables within a coal field while maintaining inter-field differences resulting from inherent quality, extraction methods or location. Second, since coal either was shipped under confidential rates in Queensland or under five rates in New South Wales, he had to approximate rates from responses to the questionnaire survey. And third, since each major coal field contained numerous collieries and since an average f.o.b.-mine price was assumed for each field, Wilson had to assume an average location of production for each field from which all distances were calculated.

After making these assumptions, he addressed the issue of measurement. Ideally, a combination of f.o.b. and freight rates provides sufficient information to calculate ‘indifference’ or ‘break-even’ points which determine the area over which each coal field has a cost advantage. However, market areas delimited on the basis of cost per unit would overstate the competitive position of low-grade coal areas. As an alternative, Wilson decided to calculate distribution costs on the basis of a cost/heat delivered ratio, expressed as a ratio of cost per million BTU. For gas coals, this procedure led to a cost/volume of gas measure.

Graphical methods were used to calculate coal market areas

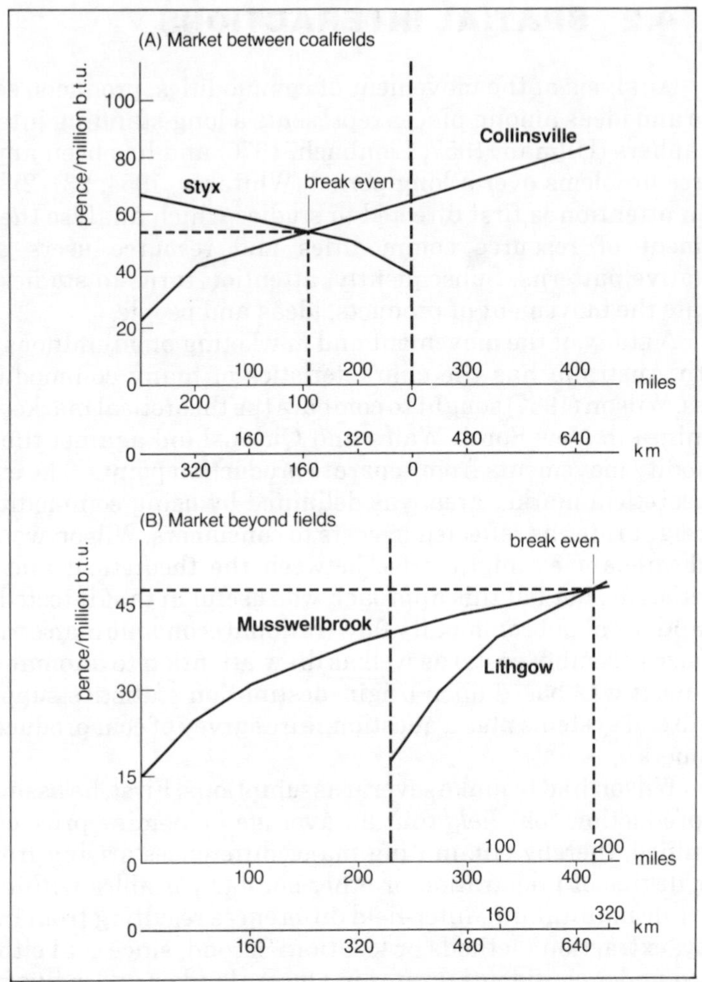

Fig. 4.1 Determination of the 'break-even' point (*from Wilson, 1967*)

(Fig. 4.1). The delivered cost curves for two coal fields were superimposed on a graph. The origins were separated by a distance representing the rail distance between the two fields. The intersection of the lines marked the location (distance from either origin) as well as the value of the break-even point. By joining the break-even points around each field, a system of theoretical market areas for fuel coal was defined (Fig. 4.2). A comparable map for gas coal was prepared. These market areas reflected two further assumptions: (1) all rail routes were equally accessible; (2) all hauls used the shortest route between producer and consumer.

In comparing the marketing areas based on theoretical and actual flows, Wilson found that the use and distribution of coal verified the assumption of rational economic behaviour. It also confirmed the assumption that spatial variation in consumption was related mainly

Fig. 4.2 Theoretical market areas for fields producing coal, New South Wales and Queensland (*from Wilson, 1967*)

to the ratio of delivered cost to unit of heat or gas. Simultaneously, the mapping exercise drew attention to other significant variables requiring analysis. These included the effects of a regulatory agency (the Queensland Coal Board), the specialized requirements of consumers (brick kilns and locomotives) and variations in initial costs and/or transportation charges associated with a multiplicity of factors. Thus, by using commodity flow data, Wilson was able to contrast existing patterns against alternative patterns of use and distribution, and to suggest variables needing further study in order to account for the allocation of bituminous coal in eastern Australia.

The type of analysis used by Wilson has been applied by other investigators. Wadley (1981) has examined cost, price and revenue differentials involved in the supply of electricity in Queensland. At a different scale, Bradbury (1985) has used the example if INCO, a multinational corporation, to study international flows associated with production of nickel. In a different context altogether, Fesenmaier and Lieber (1985) have used the concept of *distance decay* which underlies all of these inquiries to assess the linkage between spatial structure and participant behaviour in outdoor recreation. An illustration of an application of *distance decay* is provided in the investigation by Williams and Zelinsky (1971) described below.

At an international scale, Williams and Zelinsky (1970) studied the flows of tourists among a selected group of countries which dominate the international tourist market. In addition to reporting upon spatial patterns of tourist flows, they hoped that their inquiry would

> arouse some interest in investigating and modeling the dynamics of tourist flows as an interesting problem in its own right and also as a possible means for gaining insights into other population movements and into the general questions of diffusion of knowledge and attitudes (Williams and Zelinsky, 1970; 549).

As in Wilson's study in Australia, Williams and Zelinsky encountered significant data problems. The major source for international tourist movement data was the International Union of Official Tourist Organizations in Geneva. Due to different national reporting procedures, comparability of figures was often frustrated. This aspect led to a study of flows among 14 countries for which data were reasonably consistent over a five-year period.

Data analysis proceeded in several phases. First, inter-nation flow tables were constructed for each of the five years. Second, to identify spatial patterns, cartograms for each country were prepared using aggregated flows over the five-year period (Fig. 4.3). The schematic drawings highlighted the absolute volume and directions of flows of tourists among regions.

Having tabulated and mapped the flow data, the investigators

Fig. 4.3 Cartogram to show aggregate tourist flows from three selected countries to thirteen foreign lands for 1958, 1959, 1964, 1965, and 1966. All thirteen countries are in the same relative position for each country as indicated in the top left section: the top figure beside each square is the absolute number of tourists (in millions) accounted for in the flow indicated by the dashed line: the lower figure expresses this number as a percentage of the total tourists sent by the country in question to the other thirteen. In the case of W. Germany the third figure gives the total number of tourists received in millions. (*From Williams and Zelinsky, 1970. Reprinted by permission of* Economic Geography.)

Key (for flows between countries)

- (stippled) total number of tourists received by each country from the other thirteen
- (hatched) total number of tourists sent by each country to the other thirteen
- (black) distribution of tourists from the indicated countries to each of other thirteen
- – – connecting link

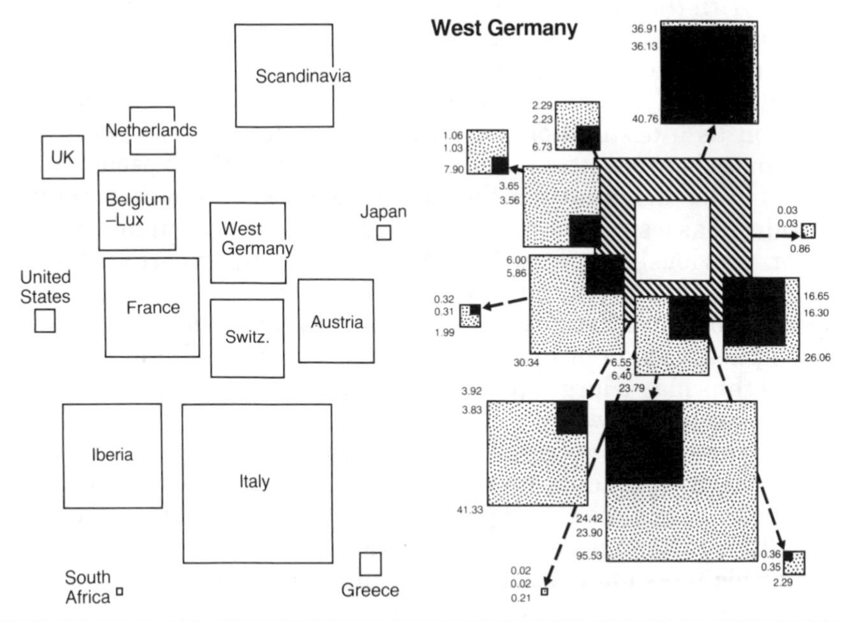

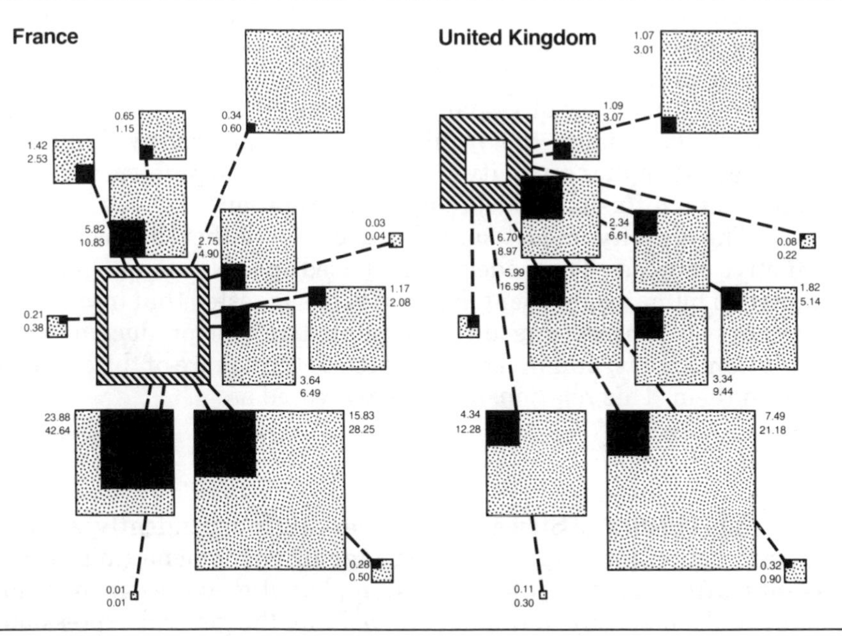

attempted to develop a flow assignment model. Tourists were assigned to destinations under an hypothesis of indifference. In other words, the expected flow to a given country from other countries was expressed as a function of the percentage of the overall tourist traffic received by that country. To illustrate, if a country received 20 per cent of all the tourists in the system, under the indifference hypothesis that country should receive 20 per cent of the tourists from each source country.

With this model, two indices were derived. One demonstrated the difference between actual and expected flows for each pair of countries. Any deviations from the expected patterns were identified for further analysis. The other index, indicating the relative success of a nation as a destination for tourists, was derived by dividing the differences between actual and expected flows by the expected flow.

From their analysis, the authors believed that tourism could be considered as a single or multi-destination impermanent migration, a notion previously expressed by Wolfe (1966) and subsequently articulated by Matley (1976; 6). In the latter's words, 'the movement of persons from one location to another forms the most important element of the phenomenon of international tourism. Spatial and locational factors thus play a large part in explaining the development of tourist movements and flows'.

The studies reviewed to this point have focused upon actual flows and interactions. In many situations, the resource manager would like to explore the implications of a locational decision before actually making a decision. Since a decision must be made without being able to examine consequences of alternative choices in a real context, the manager often will turn to simulation, '... a method for experimenting with a real system in an artificial environment by studying the behaviour of a model of the real system under a variety of different conditions' (Cesario, 1975; 39). While simulation has been applied to a broad set of resource problems (Buhyoff, Williams and Kemperer, 1981; Elmes, 1985), only two studies are reviewed in detail here. The first applies a gravity model to a recreation problem while the second uses a diffusion model relative to irrigation.

The gravity model may be used for either descriptive or predictive purposes. The model itself is based upon Newtonian physics, adapted to human movement. Reilly (1929) suggested that interaction between two centres was directly related to the product of their populations (mass) and inversely related to the square of the distance between them. This relationship was expressed as

$$I_{ij} = \frac{P_i P_j}{d_{ij}^2}$$

Zipf (1949) and Stewart (1950), working independently, applied this interaction formula to a wide range of phenomena (migration, freight traffic, exchange of information), but altered the exponent for distance. Their specific formulae evolved into the general expression

$$I_{ij} = G\frac{P_i P_j}{d_{ij}^b}$$

I_{ij} = interaction between two centres, P_i and P_j

$P_i P_j$ = a measure of the mass of the two centres

d_{ij} = distance between the two centres

G = gravitational constant

b = exponent

Such an expression may be used to describe existing interactions between two centres and places, as well as to predict or simulate interaction for centres with given characteristics and a specified distance. The evolution and characteristics of the model have been reviewed by Carrothers (1956), Isard *et al.* (1960; 493–568), Lukermann and Porter (1960), Olsson (1965) and Smith (1983).

Several issues have to be addressed in using gravity models. These include the measurement of mass and distance as well as determination of the constant and exponent. Another consideration is whether all interactions should be treated as linear relationships or whether some are better accounted for through curvilinear expressions.

Mass has been measured in several ways (Isard *et al.*, 1960; 505–6). Population numbers for the two centres are frequently used. Depending upon the problem, however, measurements might use income, total value of retail or wholesale trade, commodity output, value added through manufacture, total investment in facilities, and number of facilities, families or car registrations. A further concern is whether measurements of mass should be weighted. To illustrate, when studying the volume of first-class or luxury travel between two places, it might be reasonable to weight population numbers by average per capita incomes of each place on the assumption that areas with higher per capita incomes will generate more volume of such travel. Again, depending upon the problem, a variety of weights could be applied (average education, family size).

Distance is often measured as straight line distance between two places, but alternatives such as actual route distance, transportation costs, time and intervening opportunities have also been used. Determining the gravitational constant and exponent is difficult, since these are employed to 'calibrate' or adjust the interaction figure to correspond with observed behaviour. No simple guidelines exist. While early research used distance exponents of 1 or 2, Isard *et al.* (1960; 508–9) show that values from 0.68 to 3 have been used. Similar variety has occurred with gravitational constants. These considerations reveal that descriptions, predictions or simulations based upon gravity models will only be as good as decisions regarding the measurement of mass and distance and assumptions concerning constants and exponents.

Gravity models have been used to study recreational demand. Crevo, (1963) used a gravity model to describe trips from southeastern Connecticut to two coastal parks while Ullman and Volk (1962) used a different model to predict attendance at reservoirs in the Meramec Basin. At a different scale, Bell (1977) adapted a modified gravity model to analyse the distribution of summer homes. All of these studies were based upon an awareness that recreational demand involves two aspects (Ellis and Van Doren, 1966; 57). One involves determining levels of demand for various activities. The second focuses upon *where* the demand will emerge, since the 'recreational system for a given activity presents a spatial pattern resulting from a complex interaction between people, facilities, resources and space' (Ellis and Van Doren, 1966; 57). Since any change in one of these components may distort interaction patterns, the resource manager should know in advance the implications of deciding to provide new facilities. Gravity models provide a useful tool for such analysis since once interaction patterns based on historical data have been modelled, future patterns may be simulated.

A study by Ellis and Van Doren (1966) demonstrates how the gravity model may be applied. They sought to create a model which would replicate the flows for 1964 among the 55 parks in the Michigan state system. Origins and destinations of campers for that year were compiled from 296,000 camper permits issued in the state during 1964. With this data base, they developed two models. One was based upon the gravity model.

The investigators used two gravity model formulae. The first was

$$I_{ij} = \frac{GP_i\,A_j}{TD_{ij}^{b}}$$

where G = the gravitational constant

A_j = attraction index for each of the 55 parks

P_i = origin populations of camper-days by county

TD_{ij} = minimum time-distance (hours) of route from i to j

b = exponent

while the second was

$$I_{ij} = G\ \frac{P_i\,A_j}{TD_{ij}^{b}}\ \text{x}\ \Sigma_n \frac{TD_{in}^{b}}{A_n}$$

The outcome from these formulae appear in Table 4.1. A first exponent (1.4), derived from a sample of 1962 data for 25 parks and 186 origin places, proved to be unacceptable for the 1964 attendance data since parks in close proximity to urbanized counties were being over-predicted. A second exponent (0.97) was derived from the 1962 data

Table 4.1 Error measures for gravity model runs in Michigan parks (*from Ellis and Van Doren, 1965*)

Run Number	Value of Exponent	Standard deviation of prediction (%)	Number of Errors	
			≤20%	≥50%
1	1.4	120.0	7	38
2	1.4	61.5	13	32
3	1.4	75.0	12	25
4	1.4	87.2	11	30
5	0.97	55.4	19	16
6	0.97	88.1	11	32
7	0.36	44.1	20	14

using only Michigan origins. This improved the simulation, but a third exponent (0.36) was even more satisfying. It was derived from regression on actual 1964 data for campers from Wayne County, which included Detroit. Better fits were obtained with the low exponent in the first formula, so the more complex second formula was discarded. Nevertheless, the standard deviation of prediction was still substantial, and suggested further adjustments were desirable for the gravitational constant, attraction index and distance exponent. Once the model was able to replicate the actual flow of campers, it could be used to simulate future patterns resulting from introduction of additional state parks.

Diffusion models provide another means to analyse the spatial distribution of phenomena, with explicit attention being given to change over time. This work was originated in Sweden during the early 1950s by Hägerstrand (1952, 1967). Diffusion studies seek to describe or predict the spread of an innovation in a region through the use of probability models. Hägerstrand suggested that a key independent variable in the diffusion of an idea, good or service was information and its communication. Subsequent diffusion models have thus sought to identify communications linkages which exist at local, regional and international scales. Based upon understanding the spread of information in an area, researchers seek to simulate the spatial diffusion of a specific innovation.

The basic diffusion model assumes that there are *tellers* and *receivers* of the innovation who are distributed evenly over the landscape. It is also assumed that a message, information or an innovation can move in any direction. Information about an innovation is assumed to spread through person-to-person exchanges. The probability of a person with knowledge about the innovation coming into contact with a potential receiver is treated as a function of distance, the probability of a message being passed declining with distance between two individuals. It is upon this premise that a mean information field is determined. Random numbers are then used to simulate the distribution of the innovation over time across the mean information field.

The northern high plains of Colorado, east of Denver, have experienced a sequential development of agricultural activity. Open range grazing was established in the 1860s, to be replaced by general farming during the 1890s. Following the depression in the 1930s, a one-crop wheat economy evolved in the 1940s to be followed by dryland farming and cattle farming in the 1950s. Starting about 1945, pump irrigation in the Colorado northern high plains became a part of the landscape. The introduction, adaption and diffusion of pump irrigation in the Colorado northern high plains became the concern of a study by Bowden (1965) using a modification of Hägerstrand's simulation method.

By 1940, only 10 irrigation wells existed. In 1948, following development of irrigation technology, the rate of installation jumped up. In that year, 19 wells were installed whereas previously the maximum number installed in any one year had been four. Between 1948 and 1962, 410 wells were installed. Bowden's objective was to replicate the diffusion of irrigation wells between 1948 and 1962. Since his simulated total by 1962 fell within 10 per cent of the actual figure and conformed to the observed spatial pattern, he then used the 1962 pattern as a new base and simulated further development to 1975 and 1990 (Figs 4.4 to 4.6). The ultimate goal was to use the simulation to appraise the physical, legal, economic and social implications of pump irrigation development. The Colorado resource managers subsequently reviewed Bowden's report, and based on its findings legislated a maximum of 16 wells per township and established minimum distances between wells to avoid over-mining of the ground water resource.

Diffusion studies have been applied to a variety of resource management situations in various countries. Learmonth and Akhtar (1984) used a diffusion model to examine the resurgence of malaria in India between 1965 and 1976, with particular regard to its relationship to water development projects. For Nigeria, Oyeleye (1982) analysed the diffusion of agricultural cooperatives. In India, Mohammad (1978) studied the diffusion of four agricultural innovations - chemical fertilizers, improved agricultural implements and equipment, improved variations of seeds for rice, wheat, sugar cane, maize and potato, and plant protection measures (insecticides and pesticides) - with regard to size of farm holdings, tenurial status, irrigation facilities, and availability of input and credit.

Diffusion studies were developed initially in the context of developed countries. As they have been applied in Third World countries, investigators have found that special conditions in those countries often demand modifications to the basic assumptions. For example, Yapa (1977; 1979) has studied the implementation of the Green Revolution in India, in which new varieties of high-yielding rice and wheat were introduced in conjunction with chemical fertilizers, pesticides and irrigation. He concluded that as a result of the managers

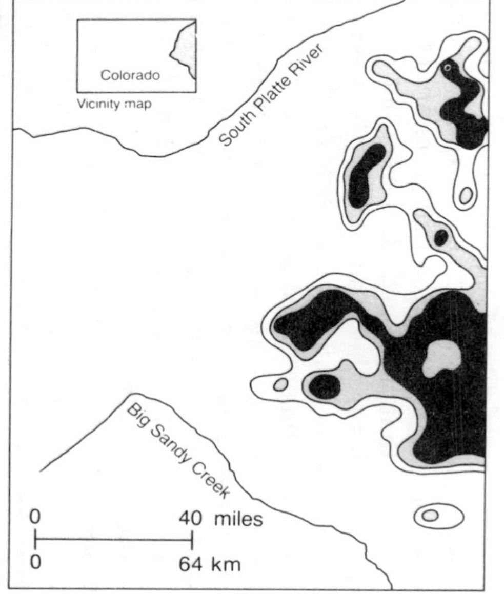

Fig. 4.4 Simulated pattern of 410 wells, 1962 (*adapted from Bowden, 1965, after Gould, 1969c*)

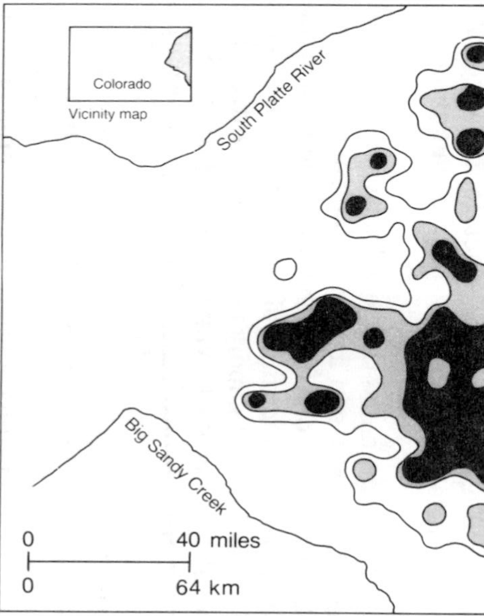

Fig. 4.5 Actual pattern of 410 wells, 1962 (*adapted from Bowden, 1965, after Gould, 1969c*)

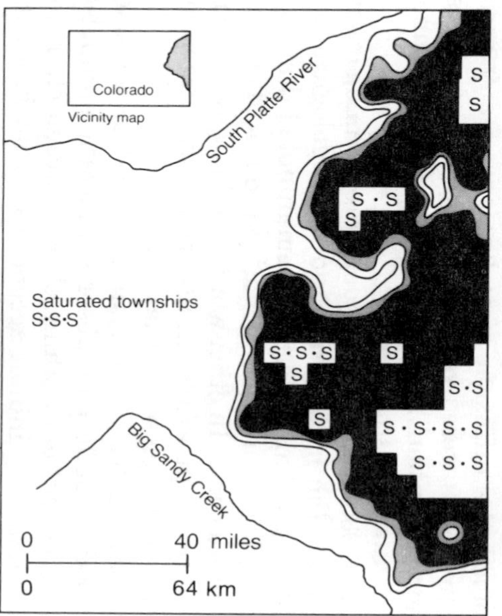

Fig. 4.6 Simulated pattern of pump irrigation wells, 1990 (*adapted from Bowden, 1965, after Gould, 1969c*)

concentrating upon the diffusion of technology, many social and environmental problems were overlooked or ignored. As a result, he argued that more attention should be given to non-technological considerations in diffusion studies.

Freeman's (1985) study of early adopters of farming innovations in Kenya illustrates the managerial and methodological problems which may arise in the Third World. Freeman noted that as a time-dependent process, diffusion of an innovation is normally described by a logistic or S-shaped curve. In other words, a relatively small number of farmers initially adopt a new innovation, then larger numbers adopt, and finally the laggards or latecomers adopt. The diffusion process may be slowed by cultural, institutional or physiographic barriers which resist, deflect or absorb innovation impulses. For example, religious, educational, ethnic, class or income characteristics of potential adopters may inhibit acceptance of an innovation. Or institutional obstacles such as weak central place hierarchies, poor communications media, inadequate educational opportunities or inequitable land tenure systems may prevent adoption of labour-saving devices.

However, Freeman noted the possibility of another inhibiting factor. He asked what if elites in a country took action to prevent the spread of profitable innovations from the early adopters to the masses of potential adopters? Pre-empting of innovations for economic or political gain is possible if oligopoly power is concentrated in certain groups with privileged access to valuable innovations due to availability of capital, appreciation of research findings, or resources to wait for larger, longer-term profits. Manoeuvres such as forcing the legislation of quotas or prohibiting the distribution of a new crop or technology can pre-empt the benefits to an elite minority.

Freeman showed how the patterns of coffee, pyrethrum (a basic ingredient in insecticides), and commercial dairy production in Kenya illustrate the conscious restriction of activities to selected groups in a country. These restrictions, started in the early years of colonialism in Kenya, have been perpetuated more than 20 years after the colonial era. Freeman indicated that these activities were not isolated ones since the diffusion histories of other innovations in Kenya such as tea, passionfruit and sugar show similar characteristics. He concluded by arguing that resource managers need to give more attention to the concept of 'pre-emption rent'. In addition, he argued that the conventional constraining barriers in diffusion models (attributes of potential adopters, enabling institutions, exogenous environmental factors) needed modification to incorporate the idea of barriers from restrictive legislation instigated by elite oligopolies.

Whether using descriptive commodity flow analysis, gravity models or diffusion models, the geographer has a variety of techniques to investigate interaction patterns and processes. These offer scholarly challenge, as they demand creative approaches to problems of conceptualization, research design, and measurement. At the same time, they have considerable practical value in providing insights for resource allocation decisions.

4.3 SPATIAL ORGANIZATION

Studies of spatial organization have focused upon the evaluation of spatial patterns, or upon locational decisions for particular services, facilities or activities (Privalouskaya, 1984a). In the resource management field, most research has concentrated upon activities and facilities. Concerning activities and facilities, representative studies are presented incorporating recreation and deforestation.

Regarding recreation, numerous studies have focused upon spatial organization of activities and facilities. Murphy and Rosenblood (1974), adapting concepts from the consumer behaviour literature, studied the search behaviour of first-time tourists to Vancouver Island in British Columbia. In Quebec, Brière (1961–2) developed a general framework for analysing the spatial aspects of tourism, and Rajotte (1975) examined the location of recreational facilities relative to market demand, zones of supply, and transportation networks. In Kentucky, Wall (1978) assessed the validity of intervening opportunity and stepping stone assumptions in studying visitor hinterlands at a national and state park. At a different scale, Aldskogius (1967) studied the relationship of vacation house settlement patterns in Sweden to site and situation variables, as well as investigating recreational day trip behaviour (Aldskogius, 1977). Aldskogius' earlier study is the one examined in detail below.

The study by Aldskogius considers the theme of vacation house settlement in the Siljan Region of Sweden, northwest of Stockholm. Vacation homes, defined as dwellings not permanently inhabited and used primarily for recreational purposes, first appeared in that region during the early 1890s. A slow but steady growth occurred until the 1930s, followed by accelerated development after 1945. As Aldskogius defined the problem, the spatial distribution of vacation house settlement represents the cumulation of many individual location decisions. In making a decision, each individual weighs the site and relative positional characteristics of a vacation home. Together, these characteristics define the recreational place utility of an area. The research problem then becomes one of determining the variables accounting for recreational place utility.

In reviewing the literature, Aldskogius found two general characteristics influencing recreational utility. The first are ones closely associated with recreational utility, and include such variables as land forms, climatic characteristics, scenery, vegetation, land use types, hunting and fishing opportunities, accessibility, and proximity to amenities and service establishments. The second relates to factors which operate as restrictions or controls on locational decisions, and include land ownership patterns, alternative land uses, and public planning.

Due to financial constraints, he did not use a questionnaire survey nor an examination of landscape writing to identify attitudes toward landscape features (Ch. 6). With regard to the Siljan Region, he relied upon the following variables to measure recreational place utility: relief, water bodies and shorelines, proximity to Lake Siljan, open land, seter settlement (partially used settlements), and accessibility to major roads and to retail trade outlets. These factors were used as independent variables in regression analysis. The dependent variables were vacation house settlement (Y_t), vacation homes owned by people with their permanent residences outside (Y_u) and inside (Y_i) the study area and the total of homes owned by external or internal residents (Y_s). The variables, operational definitions, and transformations used to satisfy the normality assumption are shown in Table 4.2.

Stepwise multiple regression was used to test the relationships among the independent variables and each of the dependent variables. Open land, seter settlement and length of shoreline were statistically significant variables in all of the models. In the first model (Y_t), these variables plus distance to higher order service centres accounted for 66 per cent of the variation in the spatial distribution of vacation homes in the Siljan Region. Comparable figures for the other models were 70 per cent (Y_u), 51 per cent (Y_i) and 70 per cent (Y_s). Except for the intraregional ownership model (Y_i), the reasonably high level of statistical explanation suggests that significant variables were identified.

Aldskogius considered the first model, (Y_t), to be most important. The 34 per cent of the variation left unexplained was considered to be a function of several aspects: variables not included in the analysis, faulty or unsatisfactory operational definitions of variables included, measurement errors, and random variation. In an effort to identify other variables, Aldskogius calculated the residuals for the Y_t model and found that the largest positive residuals usually were found in areas with substantial vacation house settlement. This was especially the case where the area of open land was small but where lakeside concentrations of settlement were found. In his view, this indicated that the attractive effect of lakes was being underestimated. As a result, the operational measure used by him, length of shoreline, needs improvement. While plotting of residuals indicated one variable already used which could be improved upon, Aldskogius did not find any other obvious locational variables by this exercise.

In concluding, he was pleased that the model proved itself to be operational and showed a fairly high level of explanation. On the other hand, Aldskogius (1967; 92) cautioned that his work was only a start. The regression technique described, but provided no insights into, the process of vacation house settlement growth. The time element was

Table 4.2 Variables used in the analysis of recreational place utility (*from Aldskogius, 1967*)

Variable	Operational definition	Transformation	Hypothesis
Yt all vacation house settlement	Number of houses	$\log_{10}(y+1)$	
Yu vacation houses owned by extraregional owners	Value of buildings in 1000's Skr	$\log_{10}(y+1)$	
Yi vacation houses owned by intraregional owners	Value of buildings in 1000's Skr	$\log_{10}(y+1)$	
Ys sum of *Yu* and *Yi*	Value of buildings in 1000's Skr	$\log_{10}(y+1)$	
X_1 relief	Relative relief in metres	—	Positively related to *Y*
X_2 water bodies and shorelines	Length of shoreline in kilometres	$\sqrt{(x+1)}$	Positively related to *Y*
X_3 proximity to Lake Siljan	Air distance in kilometres	—	Negatively related to *Y*
X_4 open land	Area of open land in square kilometres	$\sqrt{(x+1)}$	Positively related to *Y*
X_5 seter settlement	Number of seter cottages	$\sqrt{(x+1)}$	Positively related to *Y*
X_6 accessibility	Road length in kilometres	$\sqrt{(x+1)}$	Positively related to *Y*
X_7 access to grocery store	Area within 3 km from grocery store	$\sqrt{(x+1)}$	Positively related to *Y*
X_8 distance to higher order service centre	Road distance in kilometres	$\sqrt{(x+1)}$	Negatively related to *Y*

also omitted, as all of the data were based upon events in a single year. He suggested that circumstantial evidence indicated the presence of private information fields and social networks among the early visitors to the area in the late nineteenth and early twentieth centuries. In this context, he suggested that the development of Swedish vacation house settlement may be viewed as a social diffusion process. One implication is that to incorporate development through time an investigator could create a diffusion model similar to Bowden's in order to analyse the development process.

Recreation activities and facilities have not been the only focus for studies of spatial organization. Production and distribution facilities have also been studied. Examples are Hamilton's (1964) investigation of location factors in the Yugoslav iron and steel industry and Elliot's (1968) analysis of the Tyne coal trade in England. The forest industry has also attracted attention, as in Hardwick's (1964) research of the forest industry's spatial structure in coastal British Columbia and Dinsdale's (1965) work in northern New York.

Evolution of spatial patterns also may be approached in a qualitative manner, as shown by a study by Digernes (1979). He noted that during 1977 the United Nations held a conference on desertification in Nairobi. A major conclusion at that time was that human pressure rather than climatic factors was more important in the desertification process. With regard to the Sahel region, the main human factors leading to severe deforestation, erosion and soil deterioration were overcultivation, overgrazing and overcutting of vegetation for fuel. The cutting of wood for fuel has received considerable attention, as it is believed that this activity is one that should be able to be modified.

Digernes (1979) conducted a study in Bara, the Sudan, regarding the impact of fuelwood collection on deforestation and aggravation of desertification. He calculated the amounts of firewood and charcoal consumed in Bara and then estimated the consequences for local tree cover and regeneration ratios. He became aware that significant changes had occurred in the pattern of wood and charcoal consumption over a period of a decade, and depicted those shifts with conceptual diagrams (Fig. 4.7).

Digernes concluded that the shift involved several stages. In the first stage, the women collected wood from the adjacent countryside. During the next stage, men would supply charcoal obtained from greater distances. At this point, an important change occurred from the attainment of fuel free of charge to that of a purchase of fuel. Subsequent stages increased the reliance of the community on external sources of energy supply. Figure 4.7 is useful as it serves the same purpose as a scenario (Ch. 3). The exact details of the conceptual diagrams may not be accurate, but general patterns are indicated. The analyst and manager then can consider the implications. They also can consider possible actions if different spatial structures are desired.

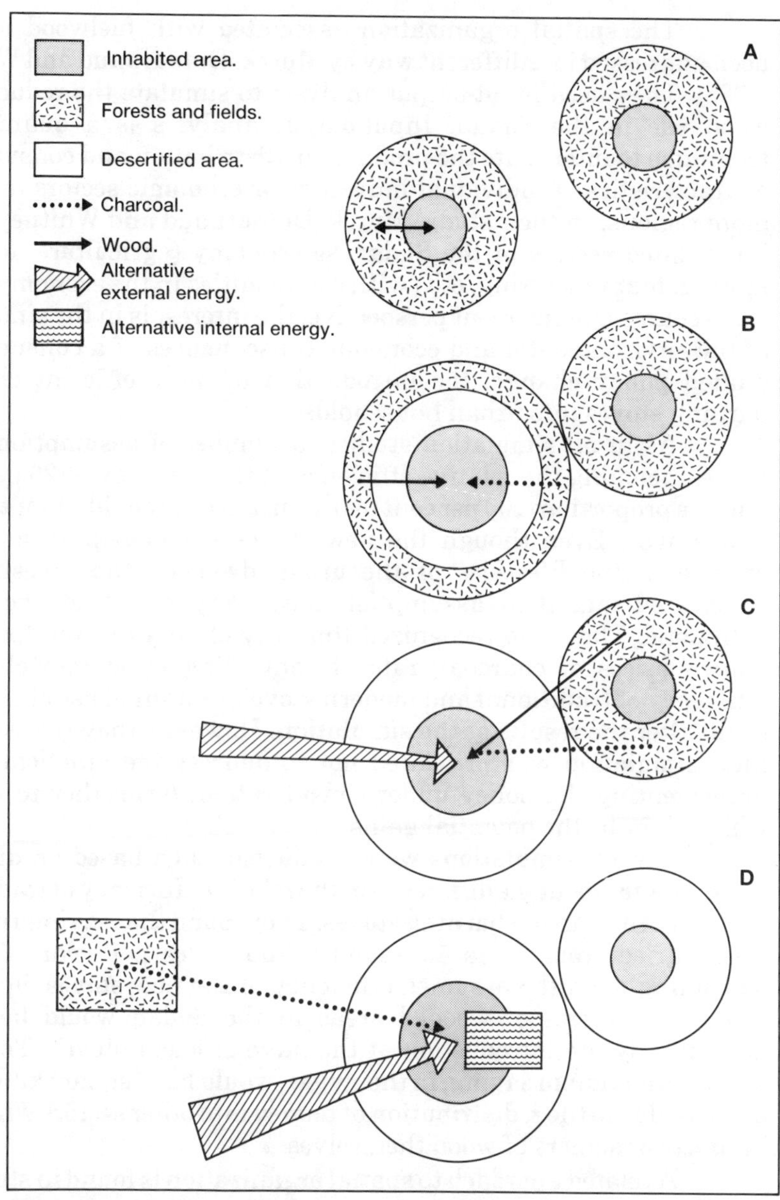

Fig. 4.7 Model for fuel-supply for domestic use in dryland population centres. Stage A: Wood is obtained from fields and forests by the users themselves. Stage B: Wood and charcoal are supplied by professionals from distant parts of the centre perimeter. Stage C: Professionals provide wood and charcoal from other population centres. Alternative energy sources are imported. The centre is totally dependent upon external energy. Stage D: Professionals bring charcoal from fuel-producing forest reserves. The amount of external alternative energy sources increases. Alternative energy is produced locally. (*after Digernes, 1979, 31*)

The spatial organization associated with fuelwood use has been addressed in a different way by Murck, Dufournaud and Whitney (1985). They used input-output analysis to simulate the reduction of wood use in the Sudan. Input-output analysis is a quantitative technique to interrelate the production, distribution and consumption characteristics of individual industries or economic sectors in one or more regions. In their study, Murck, Dufournaud and Whitney (1985) interrelated sectors of the Sudanese economy (agriculture, forestry, mining, manufacturing, etc.) with commodities in the economy. From the resource management perspective, the interest is in the simulation of the environmental and economic consequences of a consumption-related policy change, the introduction of more efficient charcoal burning stoves into urban households.

As in all simulation studies, a number of assumptions were made, including the relative efficiency of the new stoves (26 per cent) and the proportion (100 per cent) of the urban households adopting the new stoves. Even though the new stoves would require no major change in the lifestyles of the urban dwellers, the investigators recognized that their assumption that everyone would adopt was optimistic. They also recognized that any changes in the fixed and known prices of charcoal, rate of converting wood into charcoal, efficiency of traditional and modern stoves, or annual use of charcoal could alter the results of the simulation. However, they stressed that their simulation was presented not to address the practicalities of implementing the policy under consideration, but rather to explore what might be the potential gains.

Several simulations were conducted, each based on different assumptions about the difference in the relative efficiency of traditional and modern charcoal burning stoves. They found that savings in wood used varied from 45 to 193 square kilometres per year. That is, depending upon the assumed efficiency of the new stoves, up to 193 square kilometres of wooded areas in the Sudan would be saved annually by the introduction of the more efficient stoves. The most realistic maximum saving, in their view, would be 71 square kilometres per year due to the redistribution of money into other sectors which are indirect consumers of wood themselves.

A related approach to spatial organization is found in studies of the distribution of economic flows and transactions over space. This strategy analyses interactions among production and consumption centres to determine which spatial pattern minimizes the cost of moving products or commodities to consumers. This approach, designated at the *transportation problem*, involves development of a model which minimizes the total cost of transportation within a system (Scott, 1971, 1; Cox, 1965). The technique of linear programming is often used to determine this optimum arrangement of production, distribution and consumption activity (Isard *et al.*, 1960; 413–92). The solution of the transportation problem '... provides a theoretical norm with which actual flows can be compared. Actual deviations from the norm of perfect competition can be analysed ... as a further step in the study of flow problems and the elaboration of explanatory models' (Cox, 1965; 235).

Numerous studies based upon the transportation problem have been completed. Sheskin (1978) applied a modelling algorithm to identify a preferred natural gas pipeline route from Alaska to the conterminous United States. Green and Mitchelson (1981) also used a modelling algorithm to analyse opportunities for greater efficiencies through cooperative effort among electrical utilities in distributing power in the southeastern United States. Similar modelling has been used in the preparation of regional forest management plans to optimize the location and timing of timber harvesting, road construction and other land management activities (Jones, Hyde and Meacham, 1986). At an urban scale, Bronitsky and Wallace (1974) used linear programming to determine the optimal patterns for deliveries of mineral aggregates within the Greater New York Metropolitan Area.

For the Soviet Union, Barr (1970) analysed transport costs as a factor in the location and flow patterns of the wood-processing industry, giving particular attention to the relationship between freight rate structure, weight-loss and the value of a commodity, and the location of a major processing industry. Aware that transportation costs were not the only variable with significance for industrial location, he also examined the role of labour, capital costs, energy, economies of scale, and inertia.

Concentrating upon aggregate location patterns rather than decisions regarding individual plants, Barr contrasted his findings with results from another study of wood processing in the western United States. He found in both the Soviet Union and the United States that actual transportation costs exceeded optimal costs by at least 12 per cent. The same general reasons accounted for this discrepancy in both nations: greater complexity of lumber species in reality than covered in the model; established connections between certain buyers and sellers; product differentiation; urgency of demand in which small price differences were ignored; and seasonal availability of supplies (Barr, 1970; 6–7).

Barr's research indicated other matters requiring further research. Conversion factors were used to make comparable all of the physical output from the wood-processing industry. For example, Barr (1970; 115) assumed that the species in all shipments of both roundwood and lumber were of equal utility, and that any species could be substituted for any other species. Such an assumption is clearly unrealistic, but had to be made to operationalize the model. If greater differentiation of quality could be achieved, the chaotic pattern of small shipment movements might be better accounted for.

Another focus of research related to spatial organization has been the role of environmental guidelines and regulations in industrial location decisions (South, 1986). Singh (1983) has explained how many cities in the national capital region of India have planned industrial sites so as to reduce the effects of air pollution. In Britain, Chapman (1980) has considered the interrelationship between environmental policy and industrial location. Rogerson and Kobben (1982) have examined the locational impact of environmental legislation on the clothing and textile industry in South Africa.

In the United States, Stafford (1985) studied the influence of environmental regulations relative to traditional locational factors such as markets, labour and materials for the location decisions of large, multiplant manufacturing firms. He posed a series of questions. Do pollution control regulations influence the present or prospective locations of industrial plants? Are environmental regulations of sufficient importance to be included in industrial location models? At what scales – temporal and spatial – of the location search are environmental regulations explicitly considered by firms? Have search spaces become more restricted as a result of environmental regulations? To what extent do manufacturers trade off scale economies for ease of obtaining permits? To what extent does imposition of environmental regulations enhance or diminish the business and political climate of a region?

From his survey of firms, Stafford (1985; 232) concluded that environmental regulations were not a major factor in new manufacturing plant location decisions in the United States. For the majority of firms in his sample, environmental regulations were of minimal importance, and even for those firms for which environmental concerns were important they never were dominant.

At the same time, Stafford discovered that industry representatives had some legitimate concerns and constructive suggestions about environmental regulations. The manufacturers felt that some regulations had been poorly conceived, altered too frequently, and involved costs disproportionate to the public gains. A consequence was inordinate delays and uncertainty for the manufacturers. Stafford concluded that most manufacturers were asking for clarity and fairness rather than a licence to pollute. For them, inconsistency and continually changing rules created an atmosphere of uncertainty which made investment decisions difficult.

As in the discussion of spatial interaction research, it is clear that studies of spatial organization offer a host of concepts, methods and techniques. The multidimensional nature of the research problem makes such investigations amenable to the use of multivariate statistical techniques, such as regression analysis and linear programming. While these techniques are mathematically sophisticated, investigators have to ascertain that their assumptions are met. Aldskogius' (1967) careful transformation of data to satisfy normality requirements is a fine example of such issues being addressed. While quantitative methods may be useful, this area of inquiry does not preclude more qualitative studies. The study by Digernes (1979) is a good example of this latter type. Application of such a diversity of approaches is healthy if it allows fundamental problems (spatial-interaction; spatial organization) to be analysed and cross-verified through different procedures.

4.4 REGIONAL PLANNING AND DEVELOPMENT

Numerous types of research may be related to 'regional planning and development'. Common themes in such work include appraising conflicting demands upon scarce resources, identifying future patterns of resource allocation, or assessing the impact of resource allocation decisions. Geographers have actively pursued research in all of these.

In analysis of resource conflicts, studies have focused upon an array of scales and resource problems. Numerous investigators have considered the conflicts associated with development of energy resources. Dalland (1983) explored development and conservation interests regarding hydro power and minerals in Norway. Hydro-electric projects often generate conflict, especially when megaprojects are proposed for areas with high wilderness value. Dragun (1983) and Mercer (1983) have studied such conflicts in Australia. Offshore extraction of oil and natural gas can pose difficulties for other resource users, and Rudzitis (1982) has explored this with regard to oil and shrimp interests along the Texas Gulf coast. Forests and woodlands may be used for multiple purposes, which in turn can create differences of opinion as to whose rights should prevail (Wood and Kirkpatrick, 1984). Agricultural lands may also come under pressure for development by users with other interests in both developed (Platt, 1981; Krueger and Maguire, 1985) or developing (Cooke, 1985) countries. Geographers have applied a number of techniques in analysing such conflicts. One of the more promising of these appears to be metagame analysis (Hipel, 1981; Dufournaud, 1982).

In studying future possible patterns of resource allocation, geographers have concentrated upon the role of natural resources in regional economic development. Thus, Kayastha and Singh (1982) have examined the linkages among resources, industrial development and planning in Uttar Pradesh in India. Shift-share analysis was used by Cowley (1983) in a study of the role of energy consumption in industrial and regional growth. And, Hansen (1983) reviewed the evolution of the oil-dominated economy of Norway.

A related theme has been the appropriate spatial units for resource management and regional economic development. This has been a frequently addressed problem in the Soviet Union (Chepurko and Chizhora, 1982; Privalovaskay, 1984b). As with other problems, a variety of techniques has been applied, such as Helleiner's (1981) use of graph theory to delimit regions along a waterway. The impetus for such work is that the boundaries of natural regions, administrative regions and functional regions rarely coincide, so that there is practical incentive to develop management areas that incorporate these different dimensions.

Assessing the impact of resource allocation decisions also has generated interest. It has stimulated a growing field of enquiry known as evaluative research (Ch. 10). An example of such work is the study of Auty (1983) in which the impact of high cost energy upon Third World regional economies was appraised. A more specific type of inquiry has focused upon the impact of either development or termination of resource projects, incorporating the concepts from environmental impact assessment literature (Ch. 9). Relatively little work has been done regarding the termination or abandonment of resource development projects. Some notable exceptions exist, and usually concentrate upon the problems with closure of mines and the consequences for the associated 'one industry' town (Day and Hegadoren, 1981; Bradbury and St Martin, 1983). Much more work of this kind is needed if social and economic dislocation is to be minimized when non-renewable resource extraction activity is phased out.

The previous comments illustrate that a wide variety of issues, topics and spatial scales have triggered geographic research relative to regional planning and development. Only two areas of inquiry are outlined in detail below. They were selected because of their generality and their close ties to the spatial and regional traditions in geographic research.

The first study is based upon the unified field theory developed for political geography by Jones (1954). He developed an idea–area chain consisting of the following: political idea–decision–movement–circulation field–political area (Table 4.3). The purpose of field theory was to provide a framework to interrelate historical, political and geographical data. The investigator could start his inquiry at either end of the chain. Jones (1954; 122) felt that his theory could be used '... to guide analysis, to identify questions, to avoid single-factor explanations, [and] to see where path of inquiry should ultimately reach'.

A study of the evolution of national parks in Kenya has used Jones' theory. De Blij and Capone (1969) found that the decisions which defined and delimited national parks, their frequent revision, interference with traditional migration patterns, and associated spatial adjustments were well accounted for by the idea–area chain.

The first interest in nature reserves for Africa arose in the 1890s from Britain and Germany, but was not based upon ecological considerations. Rather, the intent was to raise revenue through controlled hunting and thereby gain public support for the British East Africa Company. Little attention was given to such questions as the

Table 4.3 Jones' 'Idea–Area' chain (*developed from Jones, 1954*)

Concept	Operational definition	Example
Political idea	Implies more than just a state idea. It means any political idea.	Zionism
Decision	A conscious choice arising from the political idea.	Balfour Declaration
Movement	Viewed to be similar to Gottman's circulation. Some decisions create movement, some change it, some restrict.	Migration
Circulation fields	Movement may not involve large numbers of men or quantities of matter. It may consist only of radio waves – but usually people and things move as a result of political decisions. Such politically induced movements are considered to be circulation fields.	– Field of settlement – Governmental activity – War
Political area	Used inclusively to mean any politically organized area, whether a nation state, a dependent area, a subdivision of a state, or an administrative area or district.	Israel

space requirements of a viable ecological unit or the consequences for the African peoples whose lands might become sanctuary areas. In de Blij and Capone's view, the nature of the original idea was the source of much of the subsequent political trouble which arose over national parks.

Moving from the idea to decision, the colonial powers with African dependencies held a conference in 1900 and declared an intent to establish game reserves. In British East Africa, this declaration led to the establishment of several game reserves between 1900 and 1906. Due to lack of knowledge about local conditions, these decisions made in London interfered with rights on traditional hunting grounds, and interrupted ancient nomadic migration routes. Gradual awareness of these problems led to recognition that while some wildlife needed total protection, others could share the landscape with human activity. This recognition led to the idea of a hierarchy of conservation areas. Six levels of protection and control were established. However, the levels were difficult to implement, and by the late 1960s these had been reduced to three: national parks, game reserves, and game-controlled areas.

The early idea to establish national parks generated movement and circulation fields. Fields of administrative control were established between the central government and people whose involvement with Nairobi would otherwise have been minimal. Areas which might not otherwise have received roads were scheduled for road construction. The decision not only created movement. It also changed or restricted existing patterns. Traditional migration routes were altered, and squatters were removed from designated conservation areas. Furthermore, a circulation field emerged from the tourist industry. Hotels owned by non-Kenyans and outside tour groups affected the aspirations and awareness of local peoples.

De Blij and Capone demonstrated that the idea–area chain provided a useful organizational framework to structure an inquiry whose purpose was to document the evolution of an idea and associated events. In this manner, the idea–area chain provided the three things envisioned by Jones (1954; 111): a compact description, a clue to explanation, and a tool for better work. Further applications of Jones' concept to regional planning and development might provide greater insight into the nature of the resource allocation process. The concept might also be used in conjunction with simulation and diffusion studies in an effort to move from description towards explanation.

The second area of inquiry focuses upon the location of public facilities having 'noxious' characteristics. This work, pioneered by Wolpert and his colleagues, deals with the '... location of a facility which is needed within a region but is not necessarily desired by the residents of any potential site' (Austin, Smith and Wolpert, 1970; 315–16). In the resource management field, such public facilities include waste disposal sites, sewage treatment plants, sand and gravel pits or other mineral extraction sites near urban areas, highways, airports and power generating plants or their associated power corridors. The objective of research has been to see if a better balance can be achieved between efficiency (difference between benefits and costs, or how much?) and equity (distribution of benefits and costs, or who pays?) (Mumphrey and Wolpert, 1973; Wolpert, 1976; Morrill and Symons, 1977).

Teitz (1968) was one of the earliest to identify the need for research on public facility location, and this aspect has been developed by Wolpert. Through numerous case studies, Wolpert's group had emphasized the potential and actual conflict arising from siting decisions. Using a framework based upon confrontation and conflict, Wolpert and others have described the issues in conflict as well as examined the interaction of citizen groups with policy makers and policy implementers (Wolpert, 1970; Mumphrey, Seley and Wolpert, 1971; Seley and Wolpert, 1974; Miller, 1973; Amir, 1972; Lindell and Earle, 1983).

The topic of 'noxious' facilities is attractive to geographers, for although strongly tied to locational and regional analysis, it also has close relationships to study of man–environment relations. Study of the mineral industry is particularly attractive in this regard, especially that part providing aggregate material for construction (sand and gravel industry). Because of high transportation costs, sand and gravel operations are usually located close to urban areas. The outcome is conflict during the stages of conception, development, operation and abandonment. Indeed, in many instances, the 'derelict landscape' left after termination of sand and gravel production is viewed as the most serious geographical externality.

Geographers have shown a long-standing interest in analysing the problems and opportunities of the mineral aggregate industry, especially as they relate to the noxious facilities aspect. Some of the earliest research was completed in Britain (Beaver, 1944; 1955; Wooldridge and Beaver, 1950). Combining the interests of both the geomorphologist and economic geographer, this work demonstrated the great value of physical and human geographers collaborating in resource-related problems. Comparable work has been done in the United States (Green, 1969), Canada (Ross, 1967; McLellan, 1975; 1985), the Soviet Union (Kirillova and Ovchinnikova, 1975) and East Germany (Werner, 1973).

Much of the work by Wolpert and others has concentrated upon conflict generated when a public facility has been proposed, or during the time when the decision was being made. In either situation, the time frame is compressed, and the results do not indicate how individuals adapt to noxious facilities in the longer term. Addressing themselves to this aspect, Mitchell and Priddle (1981) investigated the reality and perception of the impact of an electrical power transmission corridor in Ontario. Some 25 years after the construction of a 230 kV power line, they ran two transects, one incorporating the power corridor and the other paralleling it at a distance of 1.6 kilometres. These two routes, passing through rural land having both farm and non-farm residents, served as treatment and control groups as described by Campbell and Stanley (1966) (Ch. 2).

Sampling and statistical analysis revealed no significant physical differences (physiography, surficial geology, soil associations, land capability, land use) between the two corridors. Economic analysis of assessment records showed no differences existed regarding numbers and types of land sales and land value. A third phase involved a questionnaire survey of residents in each corridor. Those living in the power corridor seemed to be more closely attuned to the reality of the impact than those in the control route. Thus, in the longer term, respondents appear to have adjusted to the 'noxious' facility.

Follow-up studies illustrate, however, why analysis of resource problems is not always sufficient to identify patterns or solutions. In a subsequent study to the one by Mitchell and Priddle (1981), Boyer, Mitchell and Fenton (1978) drew a larger sample of properties and respondents to analyse the long-term social and economic impacts of a 500 kV and 230 kV transmission line. The results suggested that properties along the transmission lines had been depreciated in value by between 16 to 29 per cent, with the largest depreciating effect on small properties.

The power utility responsible for the transmission lines was unsatisfied with the results of the study by Boyer, Mitchell and Fenton (1978), as various land owners were using the study as evidence to argue that greater compensation should have been paid. The power utility thus commissioned a third study of the impact of transmission lines on property values. Not surprisingly, the consultants found that there was no significant impact by the transmission lines on property values (Woods Gordon, 1981).

These findings suggest greater research effort emphasizing the temporal dimension is needed. Such work is of scholarly challenge (do adjustment patterns represent cognitive dissonance (Ch. 5) or genuine adjustment?) as well as of practical value (what compensation should be paid when acquiring land for public projects?). These studies on power corridors and mineral extraction/derelict land represent only some of the aspects of noxious facility location that deserve greater attention by geographers interested in resource analysis. Such work also provides an opportunity to explore the NIMBY (not in my backyard) syndrome which is characteristic in siting of noxious facilities (Matheny and Williams, 1985). The NIMBY concept also has been expressed as LULU (locally unwanted land uses) (Popper, 1983).

4.5 IMPLICATIONS FOR RESOURCE MANAGEMENT

There is little doubt that research concerning spatial interactions, spatial organization and regional planning and development offers considerable potential for assisting resource management. A variety of spatial concepts, methods and techniques can be brought to bear on pressing resource problems. Interaction and organization studies can help to determine locations for facilities by determining critical distance thresholds for travel between places. Analyses can be used to contrast optimum interaction and organization patterns against what actually occurs. This knowledge could provide a foundation for effecting changes to gain greater efficiency or equity in spatial systems. The range of techniques available – commodity flow mapping, gravity models, diffusion models, multivariate statistics, linear programming, input–output analysis, metagaming, shift share analysis, graph theory – provides a useful set of tools to tackle complex problems. At the same time, work related to regional planning and development can provide insights into the basic processes generating allocation conflicts, as well as to assist in determining the impact of resource decisions upon local, regional, national and international environments.

While most of the research reviewed in this chapter has related to public resource management decisions, it can also be applied to the needs of the private sector, something geographers can and should do more of. The entrepreneur, whether an individual campground operator or farmer, or a multifaceted firm or farm organization, encounters numerous spatial decisions. For example, the potential campground operator needs to know the spatial extent of his market, the significance of alternative competing opportunities and the necessary range of facilities and services to attract customers. Farmers have to decide whether to adopt technological innovations, and what combinations of crops to plant. Larger organizations are concerned with how one productive unit will fit into an existing system of production and distribution activities, and are concerned as to how costs of transporting commodities or products can be reduced. The geographer is not the only one who can provide guidance for such decisions. However, the ideas and tools associated with spatial analysis suggest that the geographer could play a much more active role in the private sector than has generally been the case.

4.6 IMPLICATIONS FOR RESEARCH

Spatial and regional analysis as research traditions have a significant role in resources research. The ideas and methods associated with these traditions deserve greater attention by geographers, since the majority of geographic work in resource analysis has been based upon the man–environment research tradition. A better balance of the three traditions will increase the potential of geographic study in resource analysis for management and development problems.

It was stated earlier (section 1.6.1) that research based upon spatial analysis had probably progressed the furthest in developing generalizations and theories in geography. However, with reference to resource analysis, little theoretical development has occurred, even though there has been a continuous search for generalization. Given this state of the art it is to be hoped that future research will follow the suggestions offered by Boyce (1974; 1–2). He believed that man and his activities are distributed in a logical and orderly manner. To develop generalizations, Boyce urged geographers to use a mixture of empirical and theoretical research. In his words

> By observing reality through a conceptual framework, imperfections, peculiarities, and deviations from a general concept can be identified. Conversely, examination of factual reality is necessary if for no other reason than to suggest needed improvement in theory. ... Thus a careful blend of fact and theory is a prerequisite to sound geographical understanding. Theory without facts, or with only a few facts to verify the theory, often leads to blind acceptance of presumed spatial arrangements – arrangements that may exist only in the mind of the theoretician (Boyce, 1974: 2).

In developing such research, both the positivist and phenomonologist viewpoints will be essential. Studies combining a concern with both structure and process also will be needed, as well as a mixture of ideas from such disciplines as geography, regional science, economics, planning and management science.

At the conceptualization stage, work still needs to be done to identify and define critical variables. For example, such research as Aldskogius' (1967) study on recreational place utility needs to improve its understanding of and operational definitions for critical independent variables. Similar problems arise in the application of gravity models, where the problem is to operationalize concepts such as mass and distance. Where good starts have been made in establishing conceptual frameworks, such as Jones' (1954) unified field theory, further work is required to translate these ideas into ones that can be applied in the field. Simultaneously, investigators need to give further attention to the use of assumptions. The spatial analytic work is characterized by explicit assumptions about such aspects as the impact of distance upon transportation costs, the goals of decision makers and the exchange of information. More directly comparable work is required so that the validity of assumptions may be ascertained as a first stage towards their being discarded or modified.

As with much other work in resource analysis, a majority of the investigations concerned with spatial interactions, organization and planning relies upon the one-shot case study. More effort is needed to explore the potential of other research designs identified by Campbell and Stanley (1966). Concern with process has resulted in a number of inquiries explicitly considering change over time. Bowden's (1965) study of diffusion of pump irrigation and Digernes' (1979) study of desertification in the Sudan illustrate distinctly different approaches to incorporating the temporal variable. Although ethical problems may arise when using experimental and control groups, some work has been able to adopt the principles of experimental design without adversely affecting individuals. The research on the impact of power corridors by Mitchell and Priddle (1981) and Boyer, Mitchell and Fenton (1978) is one example of the application of experimental design principles in resource analysis. Ideally, what is needed is a variety of studies applying different research designs in order to determine which are most productive, practical and socially acceptable in various contexts.

Measurement problems abound in spatial analysis, since many variables cannot be measured directly. In gravity models, distance may be measured as linear distance, route distance, time or cost. When studying international tourist flows, Williams and Zelinsky (1970) found that statistical data were often fragmented and not always comparable. In his analysis of the movement and marketing of bituminous coal in eastern Australia, Wilson (1967) discovered that basic cost data were frequently confidential and had to be estimated or obtained from secondary sources. In Aldskogius' (1967) recreational study in Sweden, needed information was not obtained due to time and cost constraints and some variables were chosen because they were ones for which data were available. As a result, these types of difficulty reinforce the need for more comparative work. Only by verifying findings will the validity and reliability of results be ascertained.

The multidimensional aspect of research problems has stimulated the application of multivariate statistical techniques, ranging from multiple regression and correlation to linear programming. The researcher must be aware that such techniques have limiting assumptions, and that the data must satisfy them. In this regard, Aldskogius' (1967) work represents a fine investigation. Before conducting multiple regression analysis, he checked all of the variables to determine whether each was normally distributed. When variables were skewed, he used transformations to alter the distributions to ones more closely approximating normality.

At a more general level, the research reviewed in this chapter, like other work in resource analysis, illustrates that compromise and subjectivity are integral components. Numerous approaches are available for each problem, and investigators select those which satisfy their biases and interests as well as available data. No single approach is best. Each has strengths and weaknesses. At the same time, while some of the work is focusing upon traditional research holes, others are exploring new holes, or else applying new techniques and methods to older holes. If the work continues in this balanced fashion, there are grounds to believe that the research may establish long-standing generalizations as well as contribute to more immediate problems.

CHAPTER 5

PERCEPTIONS, ATTITUDES AND BEHAVIOUR

5.1 INTRODUCTION

Rooted in the man–environment research tradition, and closely tied to the emergence of the behavioural approach to geography, patterns of belief, preference and behaviour have attracted attention as topics having their own inherent interest as well as for their potential contribution for improving environmental decisions (Lowenthal, 1972a; 251). As Burton (1971; 1) has observed, 'the social role of attitude and perception studies is to provide an input into the planning process and to serve as a vehicle for public participation in decision making'.

This emerging area of inquiry has been characterized by interdisciplinary studies, and has been given a variety of labels such as environmental psychology, environmental perception, environmental behaviour, human ecology, sociophysical design, ecological psychology, environmental physiology, human engineering, environmental design, sociological psychology, behavioural geography, and psychogeography (Saarinen, 1976; 2). Numerous reviews (Saarinen 1969; 1984; Mercer, 1971; Sewell and Burton, 1971; Pocock, 1973; Saarinen and Sell, 1980; 1981; Saarinen, Sell and Husband, 1982; Saarinen, Seamon and Sell, 1984; Nag, 1983) are available for a field that Saarinen (1976; 8) described as lacking an agreed upon name, body of theory or well-developed methodology. This assessment was expressed earlier by Lowenthal (1972b; 333) who commented that

> the field as a whole remains essentially unorganized and disjointed. Work in environmental perception and behavior falls short of realizing its full potential because it lacks commonly accepted definitions, objectives, and mechanisms for applying research results to the needs of environmental planning and decision making. Above all, studies in this field now require a more systematically organized theoretical base.

It is in this growing but diffuse field that one psychologist complimented geographers for persistent, vigorous and enterprising research (Craik, 1970a; 50–1) and that a geographer concluded was progressing due to increasing integration of disciplines and more critical assessment of theories and methodologies (Saarinen, 1984). Others have expressed concern that if geographers treat environmental perceptions, attitudes and behaviour as an end in themselves, rather than as a means to understanding spatial processes, man–environment relationships or regional complexity, the research will not make a substantial contribution to the progress of geographical inquiry (Bunting and Guelke, 1979).

It is in this context that investigations in perceptions, attitudes and behaviour by geographers and others in related disciplines are examined in this chapter. Attention is first directed to some basic considerations which analysts confront when working in this field (section 5.2). Subsequently, studies concerning attitudes towards resources and the environment are described, with particular attention to inquiries offering insights as to how environmental strategies are selected (section 5.3). The following section (5.4) considers differences in perceptions and attitudes that occur between and among individuals and groups in the general public and resource management organizations. The fact that substantial differences exist leads the way to studies concerned with citizen involvement or public participation (section 5.5). The final sections consider the implications of the ongoing work for resource management (section 5.5) and the conduct of research (section 5.6).

5.2 BASIC CONSIDERATIONS

As geographers have investigated perceptions, attitudes and behaviour, they have gradually become aware of the necessity to become better informed about basis issues. More specifically, geographers have become conscious that behavioural work will only advance if attention is given to operational definitions, relationships between verbal and overt behaviour, measuring procedures and research paradigms. These aspects are considered below.

Increasing interest in environmental matters and resource management has led to a proliferation of studies. A problem hindering the comparability and verification of findings has been the wide range of definitions of the terms 'perceptions' and 'attitudes'. Schiff (1971; 7) and Saarinen (1976; 7) have drawn attention to the complexity of these concepts, and have urged geographers to be more careful with the way in which such terms are operationalized. Schiff has explained that psychologists consider aspects of perception which range from the neurological to the physical to the social. She suggested that it is only the latter aspect which is of concern to the resource analyst, and defined it as

> the impression one has of a social stimulus or set of stimuli, as that impression is modified by the perceiver's past experience in general, his previous experience with the same or similar stimuli and the individual's state at the moment he is viewing the stimulus of interest (Schiff, 1971; 7).

Since an individual's perception is governed by past experiences plus present outlook conditioned by values, moods, social circumstances and expectations, two people viewing the same stimulus may 'see' different images. This is the whole rationale for the behavioural approach to geography, with its explicit concern for the '... subjective geographical conceptions of the world about them which exist in the minds of countless ordinary folk' (Wright, 1947; 10). However, if these subjective geographical conceptions are to be understood, it is essential that geographers know what it is that they are measuring. A necessary but not sufficient condition for clarity is development of standardized definitions for key concepts.

The concept of 'attitude' also requires clarification if results from investigations are to be capable of confirmation, modification or rejection. Schiff (1971; 8–9), noting that attitudes are perhaps even harder to define than perceptions, suggested that general usage implies an individual's feelings toward and beliefs about an object. More precisely, she defined an attitude as an '... organized set of feelings and beliefs which will influence an individual's behaviour'.

Many psychologists agree that attitudes may be broken into effective, cognitive and behavioural components. The effective component consists of feelings with regard to liking or disliking an object. The cognitive component incorporates the beliefs, which may or may not be true, about the object. The behavioural component covers the way in which a person will react or behave relative to the object. The key aspect to recognize is that individuals will organize their effective and cognitive components into an attitudinal system which will lead to a predisposition to respond to an object consistent with that system. As a result, investigators must seek understanding of both effective and cognitive components rather than some umbrella concept of attitudes which mixes them both.

The reason for dwelling upon operational definitions for these two concepts is that the investigator normally can not measure them directly. He usually has to infer them from either observing behaviour or listening to what people say. Since observation often is not possible, or else raises substantial ethical problems, the analyst normally relies upon interviews or other means to obtain information about stated preferences or beliefs. The major task then is to ascertain how useful such statements are in reflecting actual perceptions and attitudes and in predicting future behaviour.

A major problem is that available evidence indicates little relationship often exists between verbal behaviour (what a person says he feels or will do in a situation) and overt behaviour (what is actually felt or done). The benchmark study drawing this situation to attention was published in 1934 by La Piere. His study dramatically showed that discrepancies may appear between what is stated and what is done. As geographers moved into behavioural research, little awareness or recognition was given to this and other studies, well known by other behavioural and social scientists, although cautionary warnings were given by several geographers regarding the ambiguity and ambivalence associated with attitudes and behaviour (White, 1966, 116; O'Riordan, 1973; Tuan, 1973).

Numerous ideas have been offered to account for the inconsistency between verbal and overt behaviour. One of the most popular has been the theory of cognitive dissonance which states that individuals seek consistency between their cognitions of how they act and their cognitions of how they should act based upon available information and experience (Festinger, 1957). If a person is committed to some behaviour which is inconsistent with information he receives, the resulting dissonance may be reduced or eliminated by altering the behaviour *or* by altering the perception of the meaning, significance or validity of the information. Adams (1973) used this theory in studying how beach trip decisions were influenced by weather forecasts, and Parkes (1973) applied it in a study of how recreationists adapted to changing water quality. The implications are that individuals who appear to be acting irrationally are in fact behaving in a manner which is consistent with a pattern resulting from cognitive dissonance.

Recognition of the presence of hierarchies of attitudes is a closely related notion. For example, representatives of a developing country may agree at an international conference that a given species of fish is in danger, and that fishing effort should be reduced. However, during the next fishing season the same country increases its fishing effort regarding that species. Setting aside the possible interpretation that the nation never intended to subscribe to the agreement, it is possible that its action could be due to another more dominant attitude that overrides concern about preservation of fish stocks.

The resource managers from the developing country may feel that the fisheries resource should be exploited as vigorously as possible in order to transform it into capital which could be used to upgrade education, health and social services. As a result, an attitude about the nature and rate of national development may override a sincere concern about the preservation of a commercial fishery. In this instance, rather than different weight being given to available information and causing dissonance, the explanation is found in a hierarchy of attitudes under which a given attitude triggers action only if it is not dominated by a more pervasive attitude.

For the analyst studying perceptions, attitudes and behaviour, awareness of cognitive dissonance and hierarchies of attitudes does not simplify the identification of a positive relationship between verbal and overt behaviour. Awareness of these ideas should, however, make the investigator more attuned to behavioural processes and thereby less likely to jump to hasty predictions. A further complication is that perceptions and attitudes may evolve over time. Consequently, their valid measurement at one time does not ensure that they will not change in the future.

Ross and Marts (1975) illustrated the implications of changing environmental attitudes during a study of the controversy over a dam to be built in the United States which would inundate land in Canada. They noted that public resource agencies are vulnerable since they have long-term planning horizons and are directly exposed to the political process. Actual implementation of programmes is usually in segments during which societal goals, technologies and attitudes may alter. And, since each step is normally viewed by the agency as part of a sequence in an incremental plan, opposition at any stage poses a threat to the entire programme. Starting in 1927, Seattle City Light constructed three dams and reservoirs for power generation on the Skagit River. Little opposition was raised against these early projects. However, when the High Ross Dam, part of Seattle Light's staged development of the Skagit, was proposed in the late 1960s, considerable opposition arose. This opposition was triggered by several factors, one of which was a heightened concern for environmental quality. Ross and Marts (1975; 222–3) noted that 'groups supporting projects such as Ross Dam fail to appreciate these changed attitudes towards nature and view the particular project as an isolated problem. The result is confrontation'.

The complexity of environmental perceptions, attitudes and behaviour reinforces the argument of Webb *et al.* (1966) that multiple methods are required to ensure reliable and valid data (Ch. 2). During the early 1970s, a psychologist warned geographers against over-relying upon questionnaire surveys (Winkel, 1971). He argued that such measurement techniques '... can create attitudes as well as measure them, may be subject to characteristics of the individual which are irrelevant to the traits being measured, are useful for those who will consent to be interviewed and they can disturb the situation being measured' (Winkel, 1971; 15). This message was repeated several years later by geographers. Tuan (1973; 411) cautioned that '... one-shot surveys of environmental attitudes tend to minimize the component of ambiguity and ambivalence'. In the same year, O'Riordan (1973; 20) argued that the link between environmental words and environmental deeds was poorly understood and that 'the continuance of "paper and pencil" attitude surveys will not overcome this problem, only exacerbate it'. During the same period, Saarinen (1971; 1974) critiqued questionnaires used in natural hazards research.

If the advent of perception and attitude studies accomplishes nothing more than teaching a healthy respect for the limitations of questionnaires, its accomplishments will not be trivial. Nevertheless, it is easy to criticize and more difficult to offer constructive alternatives. Furthermore, questionnaire surveys have numerous strengths, including a rapid and effective way of collecting large amounts of data at relatively low expense. The issue becomes as to what are the most promising alternatives for measurement of perceptions and attitudes? It was left to a psychologist to make the most substantive suggestions about a research paradigm combining a variety of approaches.

Craik (1968; 1970a) has published two versions of his paradigm, the second being only slightly different from the first. The original one is drawn upon here, with some reference to its successor. The paradigm was designed for a problem which Craik (1968; 30) posed in the following terms: 'How do people come to grasp cognitively the everyday physical world in which they live and move?' In order to understand the way in which the everyday physical environment is comprehended, he broke the problem into four components. Whose comprehension was to be studied (Observers)? By what means could the environment be displayed to the observer (Media of Presentation)? What behavioural reactions would be elicited and recorded (Response Formats)? What were the pertinent characteristics of the environmental displays and by what standards would the observer's comprehension be judged (Environmental Dimensions)? These four questions would be addressed concerning comprehension of Environmental Displays or units of the everyday physical environment which could vary from buildings and urban scenes to forest glades (Table 5.1).

Craik suggested that research is required concerning a variety of **Observers.** The general public deserves greater research since their views are needed in public involvement programmes. At the same time, the observations of specific subgroups are required. He recommended attention be given to groups whose members are thought to have special competence in environmental management and design, such as architects, planners and engineers. This type of specialist deserves analysis since Craik (1970b; 89) believed that there '... are plenty of reasons for advancing the hypothesis that environmental decision makers differ from their clients in their perception, interpretation and evaluation of the everyday physical environment'. Other groups identified by him include ones having specific needs (elderly persons, wilderness area campers, flood plain dwellers), and others formed according to personality dimensions (Craik, 1976; Craik and McKechnie, 1977). This latter group has been studied in natural hazards investigations (Ch. 8).

Following selection of a group of observers, a decision has to be made as to how to present the environmental display (**Media of Presentation**). As Craik (1968; 31) observed, 'the practical problem is this: how to present the environmental display to the group of observers within a reasonable and efficient time span, but in such a

Table 5.1 Craik's process model for the comprehension of environmental displays (*adapted from Craik, 1968 and Craik, 1970a*)

(1) Observers	(2) Media of presentation	(3) Response formats	(4) Environmental dimensions
Special competence groups: architects geographers planners and designers real-estate appraisers landscape artists and painters natural resources managers	**Direct presentation** looking at walking around and through driving around and through aerial views living in	**Descriptive responses** free standardized ratings adjective checklists mood and activity checklists Q-sort decks	Measures of objective characteristics of environmental displays Judgements by experts
Special user–client groups: elderly persons migrant workers wilderness area campers floodplain dwellers	**Representation** sketches, drawings, maps models, replicas photography cinema television	**Global responses** thematic potential analysis emphatic interpretation symbolic and multisensory equivalence graphic presentation	Any judgement form in column (3) based upon more extensive acquaintance with the environmental display
Group formed on the basis of relevant personality measures	**Imaginal presentation**	**Inferential responses**	
		Attitudinal responses	
Everyman, general public		**Preferential responses**	

way that the full and complex character of the display is conveyed to them'. Another consideration is to present the environmental display in several different forms to ensure that reactions are prompted by the environmental display rather than the media of presentation. Craik provided a range of alternatives. Direct experience is often the most desirable, since then all five senses are able to react to the display. On the other hand, direct experience contains limitations, notably the logistical problems of assembling and transporting observers. A further problem is the difficulty in controlling other variables which may influence reaction, such as weather, time of day or season.

Representational methods offer an alternative media of presentation which may be attractive due to reduced costs, greater convenience and capability of attaining more standardization. While it might be difficult and expensive to have 50 observers visit 20 sites to assess their 'aesthetic value', it would be relatively convenient to show the same observers slides or cinema views of the sites. The major problem here, of course, is that observers are being asked to react to a simulation of the display which only requires use of one sense (sight) rather than all five senses when encountering the real environment. These relative advantages of alternative media of presentation emphasize that no single media is 'best'. The ideal approach would be to use a number of the media in any study in order that they may serve as checks on one another. We shall attempt to see how analysts have approached this aspect when studying landscape evaluation (Ch. 6), behavioural carrying capacity (Ch. 7) and hazards (Ch. 8).

The way in which observers respond to environmental displays is a basic concern, and requires the analyst to record responses. This necessitates thought about different **Response Formats**. Table 5.1 lists a variety of such formats. Some provide impressions and judgements in everyday language which may be standardized (ratings, adjective check-lists) or unstructured (free responses). Other procedures represent indirect methods of measuring responses to environmental displays. For example, in thematic potential analysis, observers are asked to write or tell a story regarding a number of environmental displays. These stories are then analysed to determine what they reveal about environmental perceptions and attitudes. Observers have also been asked to draw sketches or maps of areas in order to ascertain their views about where wilderness areas are located in national parks. An illustration of this response format is found in Chapter 7 regarding carrying capacity. As with media of presentation, the analyst should seek to use a series of response formats in order to have checks on different methods used.

To understand the observers' comprehension of environmental displays it is necessary to have a coherent system of classification and measurement for the everyday physical environment (**Environmental Dimensions**). Such a system is not presently available, or at least not generally agreed upon by researchers. It therefore represents a research frontier. As Craik indicated, several alternatives exist. Environmental displays may be classified and measured relative to such dimensions as size, shape, tonal variations and other physical parameters. Considerable effort has been directed to such measures in landscape evaluation research (Ch. 6). In other studies, investigators have relied upon the judgement of experts, or observers with special competence or experience. Again, as with media of presentation and response formats, the investigator should look for a mix of validational criteria or environmental dimensions.

5.3 ATTITUDES TOWARDS RESOURCES AND THE ENVIRONMENT

Tuan (1976; 266) has called for a 'humanistic' geography whose purpose would be '... an understanding of the human world by studying people's relations with nature, their geographical behavior as well as their feelings and ideas in regard to space and place'. The function of the geographer in such work was considered to be a clarification of '... the meaning of concepts, symbols, and aspirations as they pertain to space and place'. Tuan (1967; 1968a; 1971b; 1974) has made numerous substantial contributions to this area of inquiry which has special relevance for resource analysis.

In Chapter 1, Zimmermann was quoted as saying that 'resources are not – they become'. Other investigators have since urged researchers to consider explicitly perceptions and attitudes as an influence upon how societies adapt to or use their environment. Sauer (1952; 2–3) maintained that 'natural resources are in fact cultural appraisals'. A similar viewpoint was expressed in Spoehr's (1956; 97) observation that 'what is necessary is an examination, not merely of culturally conditioned attitudes toward natural resources, but of how various peoples have come to regard their relationship with their respective habitats (of which resources are but a part) and indeed with the entire physical universe in which they exist'.

Numerous geographers have addressed their research to the way in which individuals, groups and societies interpret and react to their environment. Glacken (1967) has provided the most comprehensive and in-depth analysis of mankind's attitudes toward nature, while others have focused upon more restricted aspects. For example, Tuan (1968b) has demonstrated that differences between European and Chinese attitudes toward nature are more apparent than real. He showed that the stereotype of the European viewing nature as subordinate to him and the Chinese seeing himself as a part of nature was not verified by actual management practices. Deforestation and erosion induced by human activity has been as common in China as in Mediterranean Europe.

In Australia, Pigram (1972) has shown how two groups of

people with different cultures have used the same habitat in differing ways. In the Namoi Valley in New South Wales, the natural environment is conducive to dryland grain production and the grazing of livestock. An economy based upon these activities became well established prior to the construction of a dam and introduction of irrigation. Following introduction of irrigation, a minor revolution occurred with the spectacular development of cotton growing. However, this new crop mainly resulted from the influx of immigrant cotton growers from California. The original settlers continued to rely primarily upon grain and livestock. These different uses of the environment subsequently generated conflict over the use and allocation of water supplies. As Pigram (1972; 134) concluded,

> Contrasting mental images or cultural interpretations of the resource base explain in great part the anomalous juxtaposition of two different patterns of land use which persist in what is essentially a homogeneous setting in terms of water availability and irrigatible soil.

On a different level, several researchers have analysed the effect of attitudes upon resource management strategies. Allan (1983) has reviewed experiences with reclamation of abandoned land and the cultivation of virgin lands in the Soviet Union, Egypt and Libya. He concluded that the policies and activities to expand agricultural lands were usually carried beyond the point where positive returns could be expected. He suggested that a significant reason for these problematic ventures was an unrealistic perception of the potential of such lands. The overly optimistic perceptions were partly a response to the needs of new political leaders anxious to realize development achievements, and partly the result of the distorting atmosphere in which national governments and external consultants interact. The resulting projects were unviable, but were sustained because they had become 'national fantasies'. Their termination would cause an unacceptable loss of face for the leaders.

An investigation by Wall (1976) compared anti-pollution strategies adopted in the United Kingdom and the United States. He identified distinctly different coping styles, with the United States tending to designate standards enforced by legal sanctions whereas Britain generally avoided standards and relied upon persuasion and cooperation. Wall suggested that these contrasting styles may be accounted for to a significant degree by different cultural values, perceptions and attitudes.

Wall's study indicated that research on environmental perceptions and attitudes may present insights about national character as well as about resource management strategies. Nash (1968) has argued that studies of conservation history deserve more attention for just this reason. He suggested that analysis of the history of resource management allowed opportunity to investigate such fundamental issues as the tension between individual freedom and social purposes;

the relationship between the expert and the people; the conflict between utilitarian and aesthetic interests; and the advantages and limitations of alternative custodianship strategies for the environment (Nash, 1968; x–xii). These and related issues represent a fertile but largely untilled field for further research by geographers.

5.4 PERCEPTIONS, ATTITUDES AND CITIZEN PARTICIPATION

Environmental perceptions and attitudes do not only vary across cultures and through time. They also may differ among various groups within a community, region or country. Research has revealed that significant differences may occur among individuals and groups of the lay public, among resource managers, and between the public and resource managers. This situation has given added strength to those who advocate greater citizen participation or public involvement in resource decisions. Their argument is based upon the premise that in value-laden decisions, the experts are not necessarily the best judges as to what is desirable or necessary. In this section, a variety of studies which demonstrate the nature of differences among and between the lay public and resource managers is discussed. The final subsection considers the actual process of citizen involvement.

5.4.1 PERCEPTIONS OF THE GENERAL PUBLIC

Perception and attitude studies of the general public may be pursued with a number of interests in mind: to identify problems, opportunities or alternative strategies, to determine how well perceptions relate to reality, or to ascertain how stable perceptions and attitudes are. All of these aspects sensitize the resource manager to the concerns of the general public, and also indicate opportunities for information and education programmes.

Numerous studies have attempted to determine the way in which individuals perceive resource management issues or problems, as well as to examine the range of strategies which are recognized by members of the general public. These studies cover a gamut of resource matters, ranging from energy conservation (Jackson, 1980), water conservation (Baumann, 1983), water quality (Ilberry, Foster and Donoghue, 1982), sport fishing (Kreutzwiser and Lee, 1982; Thomas, Gill and Adams, 1984), soil erosion (Mather, 1982), recycling (O'Riordan and Turner, 1979), air pollution (Thovez and Singh, 1984), to agriculture (Kromm and White, 1985; 1987).

Jackson (1980; 115) has argued that the success of energy conservation programmes ultimately depends upon the responsiveness of consumers to governmental incentives and controls as well as on public perception of energy problems. He believed that the role of consumers' perceptions and attitudes can be most influential concerning energy consumption and conservation behaviour. For those reasons, he conducted a survey of residents in Edmonton and Calgary, Alberta in order to describe and explain variations in perceptions of energy problems at provincial, national and global scales as well as to explore variations in the awareness and adoption of conservation measures by individuals and households. He believed that a practical implication of such work would be the identification of obstacles or barriers to conservation, and the opportunity to note appropriate incentives to alleviate their effect.

Jackson found that most respondents dismissed the seriousness of energy problems at the provincial level, probably reflecting the energy-rich situation in Alberta. And, while many urban Albertans had initiated some efforts to conserve energy, their efforts involved little personal sacrifice or minimal changes in habitual behaviour. Reducing thermostat settings and switching off lights and appliances were preferred to the use of insulation, which is costly, or the use of car pools, which is inconvenient.

Studies of perceptions and attitudes also have revealed a wide variation in the ability of the general public to understand the manner in which natural systems or human interventions in such systems function. On one extreme, Karan (1980) analysed public awareness of environmental problems in Calcutta, a city which has intense problems associated with water, air and wastes. Karan studied changes in public awareness of pollution problems between 1974 and 1978, and compared this awareness with the results of official monitoring programmes by the Central Public Health Engineering Institute of India. He found that the level of awareness of air and water pollution among the people of Calcutta had increased. A close association existed between actual pollution and the perception of pollution in the study area. Respondents also had a highly accurate understanding regarding the sources of air and water pollutants.

In contrast, Churchill (1985) found that in New York state the general public had a poor understanding of the impact of an ice boom. This boom had been installed during 1965 to reduce the movement of ice which could disrupt hydroelectric power generation on the Niagara River. The increase in power generation due to the presence of the ice boom was calculated to have saved between $10 and $30 million annually. In addition, flooding due to ice jams and ice damage to shoreline properties in the upper Niagara River have been less extensive since the installation of the boom. No negative environmental consequences have been identified through many studies by independent researchers. Nevertheless, the local inhabitants perceive that the boom has caused climatic cooling, and attribute to the boom such adverse consequences as higher heating bills, shortened growing seasons and rising water levels.

Churchill concluded that much of this misunderstanding arose from a combination of coincidental environmental events and media publicity regarding the concerns. For example, he noted that the winters have generally become colder in the Buffalo area and the surface elevation of Lake Erie has become higher. Both of these phenomena began only a few years prior to the installation of the ice boom. Since a certain amount of climatic change must occur before most individuals notice it, Churchill said that it is easy to appreciate how a perceived correlation between the ice boom and colder winters could develop. As he noted, for most people correlation implies causality.

Studies focused upon visitor attitudes toward wilderness fire management policy illustrate how attitudes may shift over time (Lucas, 1985; McCool and Stankey, 1986). McCool and Stankey (1986) surveyed visitors to the Selway–Bitterroot Wilderness in Montana to analyse changes in attitudes and knowledge about fires in wilderness areas. Conducted in 1984, their study was designed to allow comparisons with an earlier study in 1971 by Stankey (1976) in the same field area. The 330 respondents receiving a mail questionnaire were given a series of 11 statements regarding the role and effects of naturally occurring fire in the northern Rocky Mountains as well as a list of nine different policy statements about wildfire in wilderness.

Between 1971 and 1984, McCool and Stankey found that there was a significant increase in the knowledge concerning the effects of fires. A shift in attitudes also occurred. In 1971 the majority (56 per cent) of the users favoured a fire suppression approach. By 1984, only 17 per cent supported that approach and over 70 per cent favoured a policy of allowing fires to burn in wilderness. The responses also indicated where information programmes could be focused. McCool and Stankey concluded that there was a need for more information about the size of natural fires, wildlife mortality, ecological effects of fire suppression, and the capability of natural fire to create forest openings.

5.4.2 PERCEPTIONS OF THE RESOURCE MANAGERS

Just as perceptions and attitudes may vary among members of the general public, so they may vary among resource managers whether they be elected officials or technical managers. Maggiotto and Bowan (1982), political scientists, have suggested that a major factor in accounting for a legislator's policy position is the way in which he or she perceives and defines issues. They believe that perception and attitudes are basic conditioners of action. Thus they argued that more attention should be given to perceptions, instead of the more traditional focus of political scientists upon party affiliation, constituency pressures, interest groups and colleagues' cues.

Maggiotto and Bowan (1982) conducted a survey of state

legislators in Florida to examine their perceptions towards air pollution. They discovered that the legislators viewed air pollution in two distinct ways. One group perceived pollution to be an economic issue. The other viewed it to be a health and environmental issue. The legislators who scored highly on a health and environmental dimension were less willing to accept environmental deterioration, viewed present controls to be inadequate, advocated an expanded role by government relative to air pollution, and argued their views more vigorously, even in the face of opposition from constituents. The legislators with the economic orientation held polar opposite views. Maggiotto and Bowan also found out, however, that positions taken on air pollution were not readily transferable to other environmental matters such as water pollution or conservation. Nevertheless, their findings emphasize that substantial differences in perceptions may exist among those responsible for developing and introducing legislation, regulations or controls.

A study by Sawyer (1983) in Maryland revealed similar differences among technical planners or managers. Sawyer surveyed water supply planners at the ten key regulatory and advisory organizations in Maryland to identify their attitudes towards water conservation strategies. He also interviewed the water supply managers at 35 utilities in the state to find out the extent to which water conservation strategies were used in conjunction with supply management methods in non-drought situations.

Sawyer's findings revealed that most utility managers dismissed the use of conservation methods except in situations where drought or equipment failure generated shortages. In contrast, many of the planners considered water conservation methods to be valuable tools which should be utilized in non-crisis situations as part of an overall package to provide water to consumers.

Sewell (1971a) has provided further evidence that experts are not always in agreement regarding resource decisions. He analysed the perceptions and attitudes of a sample of engineers and public health officials in British Columbia. Most public health officials ranked environmental quality problems as the major issue facing the province in the late 1960s whereas engineers placed environmental deterioration well down the list. In terms of solutions, public health officials favoured discussing the problem with offenders, trying to find a means of reducing the problem, and resorting to the courts as a final means. Engineers were inclined to support technologically-oriented solutions and desired stricter enforcement of regulations. Neither group was dissatisfied with existing legislation or regulations, nor considered possible solutions outside of the realm of their standard professional practices. Concerning their role in decision making, the engineers perceived themselves primarily as technical advisers. In contrast, only 25 per cent of health officials saw their roles as advisory. Nearly a third of them considered their role to include decision making as well as provision of advice. In their roles, both groups were reluctant to seek views from outside their own professions. Neither group had continuous external contacts. Neither group was overly anxious to establish direct links with the public, although the public health officials were more disposed to involve the public than were the engineers.

In Sewell's (1971a; 40) view, the two professions were characterized in the following terms

> the perceptions and attitudes of the two groups of professionals studied have all the characteristics of a closed system. Their views seem to be highly conditioned by training, adherence to standards and practices of the respective professions, and allegiance to the agency's or firm's goals or mission. Both groups believe they are highly qualified to do their respective jobs and that they act in the public interest. Contact with representatives of other agencies or the general public, however, is considered either unnecessary or potentially harmful.

Other researchers have provided evidence in accord with Sewell's statement. In analysing water management decisions in the United States, Marshall (1966; 301) noted that selectivity in recruitment by agencies plus self-selection into professions tended to ensure that an individual identified with an organization as well as its values and goals. MacIver (1970; 143) also has shown in Canada how identification with the outlook and goals of a particular organization conditioned the range of choice perceived by resource managers. Willhite, Bowlus and Tarbet (1973) indicated that the attitudes of forestry students changed significantly during their course of studies, and suggested that much of the change was attributable to professional 'indoctrination'. And Thomas (1976) demonstrated how different experts disagreed on the relative merits and weaknesses of numerical water quality indices due to professional training, type of employer and occupational responsibility. Aspects of professional and agency indoctrination are detailed more fully in section 11.3.3. These studies all suggest that experts bring different professional biases to bear when analysing resource problems. Their viewpoints, especially for value-laden issues, are not sacrosanct.

5.4.3 DIFFERENCES BETWEEN THE GENERAL PUBLIC AND RESOURCE MANAGERS

The general public and the resource managers do not always have different perceptions concerning issues, problems and appropriate solutions. More commonly, there will be areas of convergence and divergence. It is useful for the resource manager to be aware of common and different viewpoints, and perception and attitude studies often can help to pinpoint these (Kamieniecki, 1982; Staudt and Harris, 1985).

Eastern North Carolina is a relatively undeveloped rural

region with a low population density. Consequently, resource allocation problems and pressures have not been overly severe. At the same time, allocation decisions must be made. Lowery *et al.* (1983) have examined the attitudes of commercial fishermen and policy makers concerning fishing operations and their regulation by government. Their interest was to determine the extent of conflict between the preferred fisheries management strategies of fishermen and policy makers.

Lowery *et al.* used two methods. Ethnographic field work was carried out on Harkers Island, North Carolina for one and a half years in order to better understand the fishing community and its culture. Subsequently, attitude surveys were completed with fishermen from Harkers Island as well as with personnel from the state Division of Marine Fisheries responsible for regulating the fisheries adjacent to Harkers Island.

In the survey, six questions were explored. By what means do agencies best communicate regulatory information? Which interest groups are most influential in shaping fisheries management policy? What restrictions are most acceptable to commercial fishermen? What effects do current policies have upon fish abundance? What future effects are anticipated? What should be the future balance of local, state, and federal fisheries management efforts?

Areas of agreement and disagreement emerged. The fishermen and policy makers agreed that the most effective forms of communication were word of mouth in the fishing community, posting of proclamation sheets, and radio and television announcements. Many of the regulations already in effect received the support of the majority of fishermen, including restricted seasons for shrimp, restricted access for oysters and clams, and catch limits for striped bass, flounder and channel bass.

Disagreements arose over the relative influence of the marine interest groups. While both the managers and fishermen agreed that the seafood dealers were most influential, the managers ranked the commercial fishermen as second and the commercial fishermen ranked themselves last behind sport fishermen, state fisheries biologists and private conservation groups. Differences also appeared concerning the expected effects of the Fishing Conservation and Management Act on future fish abundance and of the proper balance of federal, state and local fisheries management efforts.

Sawyer and Feldman (1981) were interested in the impact of specific barriers and incentive policies for residential solar use. They conducted surveys to compare the planners' assessments of the barriers and incentives to those of homeowners who had personally experienced the entire sequence of solar equipment purchase, installation and operation.

The planning respondents were selected from those individuals who represented the initial designers and directors of the US solar energy programme for domestic water and space heating systems.

They were asked to rank the significance of 18 barriers identified in the literature as most influential in restricting adopting of solar systems in the residential sector. Three general barriers were viewed as most significant: initial high cost, consumer insecurity and the lack of clear, reliable information. Regarding incentives, income tax credits were evaluated as the most helpful, followed by information on other solar experiences, and training programmes for installation and repair personnel.

The citizen survey concentrated upon non-subsidized solar owners in New England and the Southwest. The goal was to determine the perceptions and attitudes of actual end-users who were neither participants in research/demonstration projects nor established solar 'pioneers'. The citizens selected the same two barriers as the planners as being most significant: high initial cost and lack of clear, reliable information. Differences also appeared. The owners' third-ranked variable, technical malfunctions, was ranked eighth by the planning community. The planners viewed obsolete solar equipment and unproven payback experience more seriously than the owners, while the owners were more concerned about adverse utility pricing policies. Regarding incentives, the owners viewed tax incentives and information programmes as the most helpful.

Sawyer and Feldman (1981; 470) note that such findings must be used with caution, particularly in extending them beyond the scope of the initial data. As an example, they noted that income tax credits were ranked far above low interest loans by both policy makers and owners. While the owners were not participants in solar research/demonstration projects, they still represent innovators. Such a group adopts new technology quickly, and may be influenced by reasons such as status, curiosity or inventiveness which may not be applicable to later adopters. Furthermore, the sample of owners was in a high income group. For such people, a tax credit might be worth one-third to one-half of the purchase price. Later adopters would probably be closer to the national income mean. For them, tax credits would bring fewer benefits. For low-income groups, solar heat might be unfeasible without low interest loans or some form of instalment payment. Such a cautionary note is appropriate as sometimes people apply their findings much too generally.

5.4.4 CITIZEN INVOLVEMENT

The emergence of varying perceptions and attitudes suggests that citizen involvement or public participation has the potential to make the resource allocation process more effective and equitable. Lowenthal (1966; 132–3) offered pragmatic reasons for assessing public views – they can be used in reaching actual decisions, smoothing the managerial path and altering public opinion. White (1966; 105) presented more basic reasons. Like Zimmermann (1951), Sauer (1952) and Spoehr (1956), he believed that resources are culturally defined. Any managerial choice therefore 'presumes a view of the resource together with preferences in outcome and methods'. He went on to suggest that attitudes affect decisions in three ways. First, there are the beliefs of the people sharing the decision. Second, there are their views as to what others want. Third, there are their views as to what others should want. In that context, this section examines both the nature of the public participation process and methods to evaluate it.

The nature of public participation has received considerable attention (Connor, 1978; Erickson, 1980; Nelson, 1982; Sadler, 1978, 1981; Smith, 1982). Six basic questions arise, and each is addressed here in turn.

First, what degree of public involvement is desirable and feasible? The response is conditioned by the particular situation in question. However, some general comments can be offered. Arnstein (1969) argued that citizen involvement represents a redistribution of power from the managers to the public. On that basis, she believed that different degrees of involvement could be identified, ranging from nonparticipation to tokenism to actual sharing of power (Table 5.2). Traditional managers often are hesitant to go beyond non-participation or tokenism on the belief that the general public is usually ignorant or apathetic, that the time required is disproportionate to the benefits and that the managers have a responsibility to exert professional judgement (Sewell, 1974). Citizens, in contrast, are increasingly seeking what they view to be 'meaningful participation'

Table 5.2 Arnstein's eight rungs on the ladder of citizen participation (*from Arnstein, 1969*)

Rungs on the ladder of citizen participation	Nature of involvement	Degree of power sharing
1. Manipulation	Rubberstamp committees	
2. Therapy	Powerholders educate or cure citizens	Non-participation
3. Informing	Citizens' rights and options are identified	
4. Consultation	Citizens are heard but not necessarily heeded	Degrees of tokenism
5. Placation	Advice is received from citizens but not acted upon	
6. Partnership	Trade-offs are negotiated	
7. Delegated power	Citizens are given management power for selected or all parts of programmes	Degrees of citizen power
8. Citizen control		

and wish to share some of the power involved. In that regard, it is important to consider who or which group is accountable for the consequences of any decisions, as it is there that authority for decisions should rest.

Second, which segments of the public should be consulted? A distinction often is drawn between the active and inactive publics (section 12.4.2.1). Ideally, a good cross-section of the affected public should have the opportunity to participate. However, the reality is that some individuals or groups make it their business to become involved, whether or not they are formally invited. The question then is to determine whether these members of the active public are representative of the interests which might be affected. It is because there has been concern that the members of the active public do not always represent society at large that resource managers have made the effort to canvas the views of those associated with the inactive public, also known as the 'silent majority'. Contacting the inactive public often involves the holding of open houses, and using questionnaire surveys. The time and expense required to incorporate the inactive public is usually much higher than to obtain the views of the active public.

Third, at which points in the planning and policy processes should public input be sought? Smith (1982; 561–3) has suggested that resource planning involves three levels: *normative*, in which decisions are made to determine what ought to be done; *strategic*, in which decisions are made to determine what can be done; and *operational*, in which decisions are made to determine what will be done. In that context, he concluded that most public participation programmes arise at the operational stage.

In Smith's judgement, the absence of public participation at the normative and strategic levels has led to a tendency for public hearings at the operational level to become greatly expanded in scope and to develop into protracted debates over a variety of issues. Such situations lead to criticism of public participation, with the critics pointing to excessive costs and time delays as a result of irresponsible participation. In his view, however, there is another explanation. For example, in trying to determine where best to site the next power plant, utility managers may decide to consult the public regarding social and environmental impacts at three possible sites. For them, the public participation is addressing operational questions. However, the public might wish to discuss whether the power plant is even needed, and challenge the validity of projections of energy demand. They are more interested in normative issues. A resultant lack of communication ensues because the different parties are addressing different levels of the problem. And both sides become disillusioned. The utility managers view the public as irresponsible and the public charges the utility as offering only token participation. Thus it is important to recognize different stages, and to utilize appropriate mechanisms.

Fourth, what are the components of a good public participation programme? Usually, three components must be provided. Initially, information must be distributed to those whose views are sought so that they understand the intent and goals of the allocation problem. Following the 'information out' phase, provision must be made to receive reactions from the general public and interest groups. This second stage represents 'information in'. Most planning exercises occur over a period of time, so a third provision is needed to facilitate continuous exchange or dialogue between the resource managers and the affected public.

If there are three components to a public participation programme, then the fifth question is, which public participation mechanisms are most effective in given situations? This question emphasizes that there is a range of strategies available, and that it is unlikely that a set procedure will fit every situation. Table 5.3 presents some of the mechanisms available for public participation along with a qualitative assessment of their strengths and weaknesses. Lobbying often is not recognized as a form of public participation, but it is definitely a method for interest groups to present their views to decision makers. Advisory bodies may take many forms, involving a group of politicians established to investigate a problem and report, or perhaps involving a group of scientific experts asked to examine an issue such as the 'greenhouse effect'. Environmental mediation has become a recent tool to try to identify different interests and to find a satisfactory solution. It is discussed in more detail in Chapter 12.

A sixth question asks how the time needed for public

Table 5.3 Public participation mechanisms

	Representativeness	**Information in**	**Information out**	**Continuous exchange**	**Ability to make decisions**
Public meetings	Poor	Poor	Good	Poor	Poor–Fair
Task force	Poor	Good	Good	Good	Fair–Good
Advisory groups	Poor–Good	Poor–Good	Poor–Good	Good	Fair
Social surveys	Good	Poor	Fair	Poor	Poor
Individual/group submissions	Poor	Good	Poor	Poor	Poor
Litigation	Poor–Fair	Good	Good	Poor	Good
Arbitration	Poor–Fair	Good	Good	Poor	Good
Environmental mediation	Poor–Fair	Good	Good	Fair	Good
Lobbying	Poor–Fair	Good	Fair	Good	Fair

Source: Modified after Shrubsole (1986, 20).

participation programmes can be balanced against the desire to reduce the time and cost to make decisions (Anand and Scott, 1982). Public participation programmes do require substantial commitments of time for the information out, information in, and dialogue phases. At the same time, decision makers are faced with problems that often do not go away and frequently become worse, so that pressure exists to take action or at least to appear to be taking action. Most of the conventional mechanisms for participation assume a lengthy time period for resource planning (Mitchell, 1983). If pressure grows to accelerate the resource allocation process, then new mechanisms will have to be developed. The alternative is for public participation to be sharply curtailed.

The above six questions provide guidelines for the development of a public participation programme. At the same time, geographers and others have been active in assessing experience with public participation (Ch. 10). General evaluative frameworks have been developed (Homenuck, Durlak and Morgenstern, 1978; Sewell and Phillips, 1979; Smith, 1983b). Alternatively, specific mechanisms have been reviewed, with public inquiries drawing considerable attention (Lysyk, 1978; Kemp, O'Riordan and Purdue, 1984, 1986; O'Riordan, 1984; Purdue, Kemp and O'Riordan, 1984). Assessments also have focused upon the role of interest groups (Lowe and Goyder, 1983) or upon experiences in substantive areas such as air pollution (Stewart, Dennis and Ely, 1984), hazardous wastes (Kraft and Kraut, 1985), energy planning (Smith, 1983a; Webb Edmunds, 1984) or park planning (Hoole, 1978; Priddle, 1979–1980). Here attention is directed toward description of one evaluative framework.

Smith (1983b) has argued that evaluation of public participation should include three aspects: *context, process,* and *outcome* (Table 5.4). Smith believed that since public participation programmes occur within a specific context, it is important to understand the significance of that context for the process. He suggested that the context includes the historical background behind the establishment of a particular programme to involve the public, the institutional arrangements which create opportunities and barriers, and the agency features of the specific organizations conducting the participatory programme.

Most of the evaluations of public participation programmes have keyed upon the process through which participation occurs. This focus upon the procedural aspects draws attention to the goals and objectives for participation, the number and type of the public(s) involved, as well as the methods employed.

The third aspect for evaluation is the outcome, in which the results of the participation programme are described and its effectiveness is assessed. Smith defined effectiveness with reference to six criteria:

1. Focus on issues: the extent to which the participatory mandate

Table 5.4 A Schema for the Evaluation of Public Participation (*source: Smith, 1983b, 242*)

Context
1. historical background
2. institutional arrangements
   — political structure and processes
   — legislation and regulations
   — administrative structures
3. agency features
   — status
   — function
   — terms of reference
   — financial arrangements

Process
1. goals and objectives for participation
   — mandate given participation by agency
   — objectives of participants
2. number and nature of public(s) involved
   — who are they?
   — how representative are they?
   — how organized are they?
3. methodology employed
   — techniques
   — information access
   — resources

Outcome
1. results of participatory exercise
2. effectiveness
   — focus on issues
   — representativeness of participants
   — appropriateness of process
   — degree of awareness achieved
   — impact and influence of participation
   — time and cost

agrees with the goals and objectives of the participants.

2. Representativeness of participants: the extent to which all the interests pertinent to the issue under consideration are included.
3. Appropriateness of the process: the degree to which the methods used are suitable relative to the mandate of the exercise and the involved public(s).
4. Degree of awareness achieved: the awareness and education created by participation about the issues being studied.
5. Impact and influence of participation: the effects of participation on the eventual decisions made and its influence upon later issues and concerns.
6. Time and cost: the efficiency of the programme when balanced against its characteristics of equity and accountability.

Smith stressed that these criteria do not lead to an objective or quantitative assessment. However, he believed that these criteria can be used as a filter to discern the credibility and significance of a public participation programme. While not quantitative, his approach is systematic, and does allow anyone to know the basis upon which judgements would be drawn.

5.5 IMPLICATIONS FOR RESOURCE MANAGEMENT

Perception and attitude studies may make several contributions to resource management (White, 1984). Images, or perceptions of reality, are important and should be appreciated by resource managers (Vallentyne, 1984). By understanding the effects of 'cultural filters' upon how the environment and resources are seen, managers can better judge the transferability of experiences from one region to another. In many instances, different attitudes toward nature in one region will thwart a strategy which has proven successful in another.

On a different level, investigations of perceptions and attitudes can facilitate public involvement. Such research has demonstrated that experts do not always sense what the general public desires, especially in situations involving fundamental values. Surveys of public viewpoints can also provide basic information which the managers can consider when making decisions. Furthermore, such information can assist managers in structuring public education and information programmes.

Several cautions are in order, however. Neither public participation nor perception and attitude studies represent a panacea for resource problems. Information from the former should represent only one of numerous aspects to be considered when making decisions. The latter also encounter difficulties, some of which have been identified by Sewell (1971b; 129): the possibility of introducing bias into responses, the variations in meanings of various terms to different people, the tendency of information to quickly get out of date, the impact of continuous sampling of a given population on responses, and the scarcity of competent personnel to conduct studies. Each of these barriers has to be overcome if perception and attitude studies are to be useful to resource managers.

5.6 IMPLICATIONS FOR RESEARCH

Perception and attitude studies are strongly based in the man-environment research tradition in geography. The work itself has had a strongly applied orientation, as investigators have sought to contribute to improving resource decisions. The result is that much of the research has attempted to identify the key variables and relationships associated with perceptions and attitudes which influence environmental behaviour. Attempts have been made at explaining behavioural patterns, and suggestions have been offered concerning what behaviour should be. Relatively little success has been achieved in predicting behaviour.

This situation is partially accounted for by the lack of theoretical development in the field (Saarinen, 1976; 8). While psychological theories are available, these basic aspects of attitude theory 'appear to play little role in either conceptualization or measurement' (Heberlein, 1973; 25). Or, where psychological theories have been drawn upon in resource studies, little success has been realized in incorporating them into an 'accepted theoretical base to perception studies in geography' (Wood, 1970; 136). Concurrently, a theoretical vacuum exists concerning the process of citizen involvement. The search for a firm theoretical foundation for such research represents a pressing need for future work.

While the research has not developed a theoretical base, it has integrated concepts and approaches from several disciplines, especially those of geography, psychology, sociology and anthropology (Saarinen, 1984). This coming together of several disciplines, so necessary for progress in this area, has perhaps also contributed to the slowness of theoretical development. Concepts from different disciplines have made conceptualization of problems difficult and this has been further hampered by difficulty in operationalizing terms (Schiff, 1971). Unanalysed premises and assumptions have provided another impediment for research (Wengert, 1976; 24).

It would be those subscribing to positivism who would pursue the development of theory. Investigators operating from a phenomenological or idealistic perspective would not emphasize theoretical aspects. Instead, the latter will stress the political and historical context for key resource management events and decisions (Biswas, 1981; 9). On the belief that contextual elements will support, inhibit or mould the perceptions and motivations of individuals and socio-economic groups, they will strive to understand the way in which people viewed their problems and opportunities at a given time and place, and not be as concerned about development of generalizations or theories.

A limited range of research designs has been applied. Because of ethical and practical problems of controlling variables, the experimental approach has rarely been used (Saarinen, 1976; 9). Instead, researchers try to abstract or generalize from analysing total behaviour in real life situations. Cause-and-effect relationships are almost impossible to isolate in such an approach because of the numerous other factors which influence environmental behaviour. This difficulty is compounded by a heavy reliance upon the 'one-shot case study' which is not capable of identifying changes over time (Tuan, 1973; 411). More imaginative use of alternate research designs will be necessary in the future.

Measurement represents another concern. In many instances

the variables under study cannot be measured directly. Instead, they are inferred from observation of other variables. For example, attitudes are not measured directly but are inferred from what people say or do. Such a situation necessitates use of a variety of measurement techniques that can cross check each other. Unfortunately, research to date has over-relied upon the personal interview or mailed questionnaire. Other techniques such as direct observation, participant observation, analysis of written material and simulation need to be experimented with. As Craik (1968; 1970a) argued, we need to employ as many *media of presentation* and *response formats* as possible.

A related concern is that much of the required information concerning public participation is difficult to document. Dawson (1960; 145) has explained that most of the contact between interest group representatives and government officials is informal and therefore almost impossible to substantiate. Her experience has been confirmed by others. Anderson (1973; 98) expressed frustration at trying to study procedures characterized by secret information and informal consultations. Additional problems in describing, explaining or predicting the process arise due to the complexity of the interaction process. In his view

> Any one civil servant or pressure group official moves in a web of relationships between people, parties, pressure groups, political leaders and civil servants. The individual is probably aware to some extent of these inter-relationships and acts in part at least in anticipation of the reaction of others; in part too, he may have very private and even idiosyncratic motives. (Anderson, 1973; 98.)

These research problems are substantial, and may even seem overwhelming. However, they should attract rather than deter imaginative scholarship. Referring to de Bono's notion of lateral thinking, perception and attitude studies represent a fertile hole for digging. We must discover new approaches for extending this hole.

CHAPTER 6
LANDSCAPE EVALUATION

6.1 INTRODUCTION

Concern with delimiting landscapes with high amenity or heritage value has resulted in numerous investigators developing alternative methods to apply in a variety of settings. The applications have ranged from Britain and North America (Penning-Rowsell, 1981a, b), to Belgium (Tips, 1984), Australia (Seddon and Pike, 1979), international (Buhyoff *et al.*, 1983) and cross cultural comparisons (Zube and Pitt, 1981). The outcome has been a field of research characterized by major differences of opinion regarding the most appropriate research philosophies (Dearden, 1985a; Hamilton, 1982, 73), objectivity and subjectivity (Jacques, 1980; 1981; Shuttleworth, 1979–1980; Powell, 1981), relevant methods or techniques (Clamp, 1981), as well as a host of difficult methodological issues (Daniel and Vining, 1983). While investigators are all digging in the same hole whether they refer to it as environmental aesthetics (Sadler and Carlson, 1982) or valued environments (Gold and Burgess, 1982), they are using many different kinds of shovels.

Many reasons underlie the lack of agreement in the field of landscape evaluation. Lowenthal (1978; 3) has noted that some of the differences are due to a variety of premises being used in the studies, ranging from explanations based on a priori judgements, professional expertise and the public pulse. Some of the differences also are attributable to the lack of definite boundaries and the presence of numerous forms and features which make landscapes difficult to classify and measure (Relph, 1984–1985; 102). As Shoard (1981; 91) has observed, most landscapes appear as seamless webs which merge into one another and change depending upon the time of day or season and over the years. How to capture the indeterminacy, subtlety and intangible qualities of the landscape is a major dilemma. This is further compounded if it is accepted that qualities of a good method for assessing landscape quality include reliability, validity and utility (Dearden, 1980c; 52).

Part of the confusion arises from a theoretical vacuum associated with research on landscape evaluation (Appleton, 1975). Furthermore, many are pessimistic that a theoretical foundation will ever be established. As Kates (1966–1967; 22) has argued

> Except within the vaguest limits, beauty cannot be described: therefore, it cannot be defined. It cannot be measured in quantity or quality: therefore, it cannot be made into the basis of a science. It has always proved impregnable to the frontal attacks of aestheticians.

Others believe that effort should be devoted to landscape evaluation even if the prospects for development of theory are poor. Leopold (1969a; 37) was pragmatic. He argued that many resource disputes arise over conflicting concerns for the environment where development proposals are made. Those pressing for technical development (building of a dam, oil pipeline, nuclear power plant) usually employ numerical arguments which demonstrate the economic gains to be realized through development. Those favouring protection of the environment usually make emotional appeals about the landscape without numerical information and detailed computations. In Leopold's view, it was time that the environmentalists supported arguments with numbers. Hence the necessity for developing methods to measure the attractiveness of landscapes.

This chapter outlines various approaches and techniques which have been used in landscape evaluation. Three general approaches exist. The first is an informal process through which experts strive for a consensus about the landscape attributes of an area (section 6.2). The second approach attempts to describe the landscape in terms of its different components or in its totality. Such approaches have drawn the interest of landscape architects, foresters, planners and geographers (section 6.3). Emphasis is given to identifying and measuring critical landscape variables, determining their inter-relationships, and assessing their relative importance. The third approach, termed landscape preferences, seeks to discover which aspects of the environment are seen as attractive and unattractive (section 6.4). At least two distinct strategies are applied. One is indirect, inferring preferences from evidence such as literature, art and comparable sources. The other is direct, involving interviews with individuals.

The relative merits of the three general approaches and their associated techniques are outlined in the following sections. Although the ongoing work in landscape evaluation is often contradictory, it is important for several reasons. Its basic rationale, that of providing means by which to compare scenery or amenity values against other resource considerations, is a valid one. At the same time, work on landscape evaluation has potential for improving resource inventories (Ch. 3), carrying capacity decisions (Ch. 7) and environmental impact assessments (Ch. 9). Strongly rooted in a man–environment tradition, landscape evaluation represents a research problem amenable to analysis from a geographical perspective.

6.2 LANDSCAPE CONSENSUS STUDIES

The consensus approach is perhaps the oldest way of deriving evaluations (Turner, 1975; 157). It usually involves a team of experts who designate areas of high value based upon field reconnaissance and/or analysis of maps, aerial photographs and other available material. Two major drawbacks arise. The first is that the evaluators rarely make any definite measurements. Without a systematic data base, the experts have little of substance from which to explain or defend their choices. The second is that the values and interests of a professional elite need to be reconciled with those of the general public (Lowenthal, 1981; 225).

The consensus approach has been the basis of management decisions in many countries even though it is frequently held in low esteem for its lack of an 'objective' method. Turner (1975; 157) commented that the consensus approach has been used extensively in Britain, and that 'few of us can argue that consensus methods which produced the designations of the National Parks and Areas of Outstanding Natural Beauty (A.O.N.B.) were in error'. Blacksell and Gilg (1975; 135) reiterated this view, and noted that National Parks, Areas of Outstanding Beauty and Areas of Great Landscape Value cover more than 40 per cent of England and Wales. On the other hand, while they agreed that there is general support for the areas designated, major disagreements have arisen over the details of boundaries. In such situations, they thought that a method for determining boundaries in a more systematic manner would reduce conflicts. Furthermore, they argued that such a method could be used to identify smaller but more critical tracts of land for even more rigorous control. For example, it has been suggested that small areas of exceptional landscape value within National Parks should be designated as National Heritage Areas, and given greater protection. Unfortunately, no guidance has been given concerning the rationale for specifying such areas.

In the United States, Knudson (1976; 282) showed that the consensus approach has also been used. Regarding a programme to designate outstanding streams, a National Wild and Scenic Rivers programme was established during 1968. The Bureau of Outdoor Recreation as well as comparable state agencies sought to identify scenic rivers. The federal system for evaluating scenic rivers placed 'great reliance ... upon professional judgement and opinion from an interdisciplinary, inter-agency team'. Criteria have been established to guide the selection of scenic rivers, but they are very general and require each evaluator thoroughly to understand the intent of Congress.

The United States Forest Service also has relied upon professionals in planning visual quality objectives for timber harvest areas. As Benson, McCool and Schlieter (1985; 1) have remarked, landscape architects act on behalf of the viewing public because 'it is assumed that the visual quality perceptions of the landscape architect correspond to those of the general public'. In their research, Benson, McCool, and Schlieter (1985) found that landscape architects readily differentiated among areas with varying degrees of visual impact from harvesting. The results also revealed that the landscape architects preferred less disturbed areas to those with more substantial visual impact.

The consensus approach thus has strengths and weaknesses. It is flexible, and usually minimizes time and expense. Furthermore, some believe that 'the simple intuitive committee approach would be more easily defended under cross examination by unsympathetic counsel than the quasi objectivity and dubious statistics of some recent techniques' (Turner, 1975; 157). On the other hand, this approach lacks a theoretical foundation, does not usually provide systematic evidence to support decisions, and is often not amenable to replication by other groups. In addition, many feel in times of highly charged rhetoric about lands and waters that 'there is a clear advantage in adopting more objective and specific criteria and then applying them uniformly' (Knudson, 1976; 283). The following sections (6.3 and 6.4) consider some attempts to develop more 'objective' and 'systematic' approaches to landscape evaluation.

6.3 LANDSCAPE DESCRIPTION STUDIES

Descriptive studies may incorporate one or two considerations. One concern is to identify and measure the attributes of specific landscapes. The other involves assessing the relative quality of landscapes against some standards or criteria. These concerns contrast with the 'landscape preference' studies (section 6.4) in which the emphasis is upon obtaining personal appreciation of landscapes (Craik, 1972a; 292).

The descriptive studies represent a specialized type of resource inventory (Ch. 3). The basic objective is to produce a map of a given region which locates the presence and nature of scenic resources. Craik (1972b; 255) argued that systematic landscape appraisals of this kind produce several advantages:

1. They focus attention on important criteria in decisions involving landscape preservation, the development of outdoor recreational activities and the routeing of roads and power lines in open country.
2. The comparative evaluation of a region provides a context for making choices among specific sites within it.
3. The numerical information, quantitative indices and detailed computations help to give environmental variables parity with economic and social variables.

4. Periodic appraisal of a region facilitates monitoring the rate of change of landscape quality.
5. Before-and-after studies indicate the impact of specific development projects.

Landscape architects have devoted considerable effort to landscape evaluation research. Litton (1968; 1972; 1974; Litton and Tetlow, 1978) has been one of the pioneers in this field. His work is based on the premise that in both general or detailed land-use planning, and in preparing environmental impact assessments, resource managers need to anticipate the visual impact of projected changes. By being able to anticipate the impact, Litton believes the resource manager will be able to modify actions to meet environmental considerations.

Litton sought to identify generalized attributes of landscapes. This approach was based on the assumption that consciousness of landscape components is a prerequisite to making visually appropriate decisions. His work suggested two major considerations for such decisions. 'Factors of recognition' identified the dominant characteristics which determine the nature of landscapes. Principal recognition factors are *form, space* and *time*, and *variability*. These factors, although beyond the capacity of an observer to change, are subject to degradation. Secondary recognition factors, *observer position, distance* and *sequence*, describe relationships between the observer and landscape and are subject to manipulation. These recognition factors were used in defining six different landscape or 'compositional types': panoramic, feature, enclosed, focal, forest, and detailed (Table 6.1).

Litton (1972; 266) stressed that the 'entire emphasis here is on the question of objectivity concerning visual dimensions of the landscape, not in the matter of 'like-dislike' preferences, nor, at this point, on other matters dealing with human responsiveness to landscape'. However, he was conscious that evaluation of aesthetic quality assumes criteria. In his approach, such criteria were not defined by recreational opportunities, development needs or personal opinions. Instead, he used three generally recognized criteria - *unity, vividness* and *variety* - which may be applied to a painting, to music or to a landscape. He believed that use of these criteria, in conjunction with the compositional types, would generate greater landscape consciousness by resource managers. However, being conscious was not enough. Evidence was needed as well, and Litton thought that evidence could be obtained relative to his framework.

Litton noted that since the special lines, surfaces and proportions of landscape types are most vulnerable, it is possible to identify the most sensitive landscapes: feature, enclosed and focal (Litton, 1974). The feature landscape is built upon dominant and obvious elements: a land form, a water display, a vegetation complex.

Table 6.1 Litton's compositional types for landscape appraisal (*after Litton, 1972*)

Compositional type	Characteristics
1. Panoramic landscape Subdivisions: 1. Water bodies 2. Plains 3. Ranges	Absence of enclosure is implied. Less abstractly, an angular limitation closer to 180°, a response to peripheral vision, seems more typical. Dominant line quality is that of horizontality. The panoramic landscape is expanding, reaching out without bounds. It is not a horizontal composition contained by screening edges nor is it one of restricted distances. It is a placid arrangement of great stability, a simple foil against which subordinate forms, edges, or minor enclosures at foreground or middleground distances are seen. The outside limits appear static while close-in elements appear to move in response to the travelling viewer.
2. Feature landscape 1. Landform dominated 2. Water expression 3. Ranges	A single thing or a cohesive set of related elements dominates their surroundings. These convex elements of landform are one key to this type, but tree forms and vivid expressions of water are also included. Features are easy to identify as concrete and specific things which have distinction. The attributes of contrast apply: isolation, conspicuous size, distinct silhouette, and obvious surface patterns.
3. Enclosed landscape Subdivisions: 1. Slope-face enclosure 2. Cliff-face enclosure 3. Vegetation-face enclosure	Marked by its concavity, becoming an integrated unit because of basin-like containment of floor by surrounding walls. Space or spatial definition is to the enclosed landscape what individual projecting forms and dominating elements are to the feature landscape. Even though enclosed landscapes tend to be more passive compositions than do feature landscapes, the more vivid examples indicate higher quality and easier recognition.
4. Focal Landscape Subdivisions: 1. Convergence point or area 2.Terminal feature 3. Open portal 4. Screened closure	Is a composition of nearly parallel lines or a series of aligned objects which appear to converge upon a point. Most often associated with river and stream courses, drainage defiles, or elongated strips of riparian vegetation, the type can also be based upon faults, scarps, or other linear expressions of geological structure.
5. Forest or canopied landscape	That arrangement within the forest itself, under the envelopment of leaf canopy, and upon the ground plane. In addition to the overhead limitation, it is further defined by tree stem scale, their character and density, and by the nature of the forest floor with its undergrowth complex.
6. Detail landscapes	Are a small world of visual compositions that accompany each of the larger landscape types. They are local but regional clues to surroundings — the building units from which the larger landscape is finally constructed. A detail is a visual fragment that can, in turn, be identified as belonging to a specific and larger landscape which is its source.

With high contrast and vivid characteristics, visual vulnerability is high. The same situation occurs for an enclosed landscape (e.g. a valley with well-defined encircling walls) and a focal landscape (e.g. straight segment of a riverscape). By focusing upon form and variability, it is possible to recognize parts of the landscape which are more sensitive than others. For example, *edges* (where dissimilar materials come together) are vulnerable to disruptions. Common edges are skylines, land and water junctures and ridgelines. Their high vulnerability is immediately apparent. Litton systematically identified a range of such variables that resource managers should consider.

Litton is not the only landscape architect who has attempted to develop methods for assessing the visual value of the environment. Zube (1970) developed a descriptive technique as his contribution to the North Atlantic Regional Water Resources Study while Vaughan (1973–1974) and Haggerty (1974–1975) developed techniques for assessing the visual impact of power transmission corridors in Ontario. An encouraging feature of such work is that it has proven to be reliable across a range of observers. Craik (1972a) tested Litton's procedure to determine whether it yielded reproducible data. He showed 100 colour slides of different landscapes to panels of observers representing foresters, landscape architects, general arts university students and university students taking a geography course in conservation. Each respondent was asked to indicate for each landscape which compositional type it represented and which rating they would give it relative to specified criteria. Although some differences in interpretation occurred, Craik found the results encouraging as substantial consensus occurred.

In a more general study, Zube (1974) asked whether individuals from different backgrounds use similar evaluative and descriptive terms concerning landscapes. He used individuals selected from environmental designers (landscape architects, planners, architects) and resource managers (foresters, wildlife managers, hydrologists, soil scientists). Some of the respondents were taken to different landscapes in central Massachusetts whereas others examined aerial photographs and topographic maps of the same landscapes. Each group was asked to describe and evaluate the landscapes using a set of 25 semantic differential scales, to write an unstructured description of a part of the landscape, and to rank order by scenic quality six aerial photographs. Like Craik, Zube's results suggest that there is a reasonable level of agreement concerning descriptive and evaluative terms employed by different professionals. These findings, which require further confirmation before being considered conclusive, are encouraging. They suggest that the goal of developing landscape appraisal techniques which yield comparable results may be a realistic one (Zube, 1976).

The field of landscape appraisal has not been restricted to architects. A major contribution in this research has been made by a geologist, Leopold (1969a, b; Leopold and Marchant, 1968). His purpose was to describe objectively landscapes in a quantitative fashion in order to aid decisions regarding alternative uses for the environment. The event that stimulated his work was an application to the Federal Power Commission to build a hydropower dam in the Hell's Canyon area of the Snake River in Idaho. The problem was to determine the aesthetic value of Hell's Canyon relative to other river valleys in

Table 6.2 Leopold's factors and criteria for measuring landscape aesthetics (*from Leopold, 1969a*)

Factor number	Descriptive categories	Evaluation numbers 1	2	3	4	5
	Physical factors					
1	River width (ft) (at low flow)	<3.0	3–10	10–30	30–100	>100
2	Depth (ft) (at low flow)	<0.5	0.5–1	1–2	2–5	>5
3	Velocity (ft per sec.) (at low flow)	<0.5	0.5–1	1–2	3–5	>5
4	Stream depth (ft)	<1	1–2	2–4	4–8	>8
5	Flow variability	Little variation		Normal	Ephemeral or	large variation
6	River pattern	Torrent	Pool and riffle	Without riffles	Meander	Braided
7	Valley height/width	≤1	2–5	5–10	11–14	≥15
8	Stream bed material	Clay or silt	Sand	Sand and gravel	Gravel	Cobbles or larger
9	Bed slope (ft/ft)	<0.0005	0.0005–0.001	0.001–0.0005	0.0005–0.01	>0.01
10	Drainage area (sq. mile)	<1	1–10	10–100	100–1,000	>1,000
11	Stream order	≤2	3	4	5	≥6
12	Erosion of banks	Stable		Slumping		Eroding large-
13	Sediment deposition in bed	Stable				scale deposition
14	Width of valley flat (ft)	<100	100–300	300–500	500–1,000	>1,000
	Biologic and water quality factors					
15	Water colour	Clear colourless		Green tints		Brown
16	Turbidity (parts per million)	<25	25–150	150–1,000	1,000–5,000	>5,000
17	Floating material	None	Vegetation	Foamy	Oily	Variety
18	Water condition (general)	Poor		Good		Excellent
	Algae					
19	Amount	Absent				Infested
20	Type	Green	Blue-green	Diatom	Floating green	None
	Larger plants					
21	Amount	Absent				Infested
22	Kind	None	Unknown rooted	*Elodea*, duck weed	Water lily	Cattail
23	River fauna	None				Large variety
24	Pollution Evidence	None				Evident
	Land flora					Evident
25	Valley	Open	Open w. grass, trees	Brushy	Wooded	Trees and brush

26	Hillside	Open	Open w. grass, trees	Brushy	Wooded	Trees and brush
27	Diversity	Small				Great
28	Condition	Good				Over-used
	Human use and interest factors					
	Trash and litter					
29	Metal (no. per 100 ft of river)	<2	2–5	5–10	10–50	>50
30	Paper	<2	2–5	5–10	10–50	>50
31	Other	<2	2–5	5–10	10–50	>50
32	Material removable	Easily removed				Difficult removal
33	Artificial controls (dams, etc.)	Free and natural				Controlled
	Accessibility					
34	Individual	Wilderness				Urban or paved access
35	Mass use	Wilderness				Urban or paved access
36	Local scene	Diverse views and scenes				Closed or without diversity
37	Vistas	Vistas of far places				Closed or no vistas
38	View confinement	Open or no obstructions				Closed by hills, cliffs or trees
39	Land use	Wilderness	Grazed	Lumbering	Forest, mixed recreation	Urbanized
40	Utilities	Scene unobstructed by power lines				Scene obstructed by utilities
41	Degree of change	Original				Materially altered
42	Recovery potential	Natural recovery				Natural recovery unlikely
43	Urbanization	No buildings				Many buildings
44	Special views	None				Unusual interest
45	Historic features	None				Many
46	Misfits	None				Many

Key: < less than, > greater than, ≤ less than or equal to, / divided by central Idaho and relative to other well-known valleys in existing national parks.

Leopold considered three factors to be relevant to landscape aesthetics: physical features, biological attributes, human use factors. To operationalize these factors, he developed a total of 46 criteria to describe the aesthetic character of a landscape (Table 6.2). These factors and criteria were then applied to 12 river valleys in central Idaho (one of which was Hell's Canyon) and to four river valleys in national parks. Table 6.2 shows that some of the criteria could be directly measured (river width, depth, velocity) whereas others had to be estimated in terms of categories (presence of trash and litter, accessibility). To achieve a common measurement scale, all observations were expressed as ordinal values ranging between 1 and 5. Leopold stressed that the ordinal values did not imply evaluation. In other words, a '5' is not meant to indicate a quality 'superior' to a '2'. The numbers simply indicate the presence or absence of different features, with no judgement being made that a river wider than 30.4 m (100 ft) is aesthetically more desirable than a river between 0.9 m (3 ft) and 3.04 m (10 ft) (Table 6.2).

The philosophy underlying this approach was expressed by Leopold (1969a; 40) in the following way: 'Landscape that is unique either in a positive or negative way is of more significance to society than one that is common.' The data from the 12 sites were used to determine the 'relative uniqueness' of each site. The calculations involved determining for each criterion how many of the 12 sites fell into each of the 5 categories. Concerning river width for example, it might be found that only one river fell into the fifth category (width greater than 30.4 m (100 ft)). A uniqueness ratio would then be computed which was the reciprocal of the number of sites sharing the category value. One river in a category would create a uniqueness ratio of 1/1 or 1, two rivers in a category a ratio of 1/2 or 0.50 and so on. If all 12 rivers fell into the same category, the ratio would be 1/12 or 0.08.

Following this procedure, a uniqueness ratio for each of the 46 criteria at the 12 sites was calculated. Adding the ratios for all 46 criteria produced a total uniqueness ratio (Table 6.3). The higher the ratio, the 'more unique' the site. The uniqueness ratios can also be broken down into the three basic components (physical, biological, human interest) to see which factors are most influential in determining the status of a site (Table 6.4).

Leopold and Marchand (1968) subsequently applied this procedure to 24 minor valleys in the vicinity of Berkeley, California, but reduced the number of criteria from 46 to 28. His work has generated considerable thought, ranging from Hamill's (1975; 1985) critiques of the approach to other attempts to assess the scenic value of river valleys. Knudson's (1976) evaluation of Indiana rivers and Chubb and Bauman's (1977) work in Michigan are representative of assessment procedures stimulated by Leopold's ideas. Each of the in-

Table 6.3 Total uniqueness values for Leopold's 12 sites (*from Leopold, 1969a*)

Site No.	Location	Total uniqueness ratio
1.	Wood River, 6 miles above Ketchum	**11.07**
2.	Salmon River, ¼ mile above Stanley	**11.00**
3.	Middle Fork Salmon River at Dagger Falls	**11.87**
4.	South Fork Salmon River, near Warm Lake	**13.93**
5.	Hell's Canyon, below Hell's Canyon Dam	**16.09**
6.	Weiser River at Evergreen Forest Camp on Highway 95	**11.17**
7.	Little Salmon River, 6 miles north of New Meadows	**23.10**
8.	Little Salmon River, 4 miles south of Pollock	**13.78**
9.	Salmon River, 2 miles below Riggins	**10.25**
10.	Salmon River, at Carey Falls, 20 miles above Riggins	**14.31**
11.	French Creek, 1 mile above junction with Salmon River	**11.95**
12.	North Fork Payette River, near Smiths Ferry	**10.21**

Note: 'Total uniqueness value' is an objective measure of how different each site is from other sites studied, without regard to 'positive' or 'negative' aesthetic values.
River pollution at site 7, for example, makes this area relatively unusual and gives it the highest 'uniqueness ratio'.

vestigators sought to reduce the number of criteria or variables. Knudson included eight factors (naturalness of bank vegetation, vegetation depth-length, physical modifications, human development, special natural features, aesthetic quality of water, paralleling roads, crossings) while Chubb and Bauman combined 16 recreation activities with eight inventory variables (basic physical features, special physical features, water quality, soil conditions, biological features, land use, aesthetic features, accessibility).

The above studies have used Leopold's technique as a departure point in trying to resolve some of the difficulties associated with his procedure. Leopold (with Marchand, 1968, 714–17), conscious of the problems inherent in his approach, identified the following aspects for consideration.

1. A uniqueness score is just a measure of uniqueness and not an indication of attractiveness or unattractiveness of a site.
2. The uniqueness score does not differentiate between the significance of different factors. All factors are given equal weight. Adding unweighted uniqueness factors may average out significant differences.
3. Uniqueness is only one of the characteristics of an environment deserving attention. Equal attention should be given to such aspects as intensity, novelty, complexity, variation and incongruity.
4. The three over-all factors – physical, biological and human interest –

Table 6.4 Uniqueness ratios for physical, biological and human interest factors

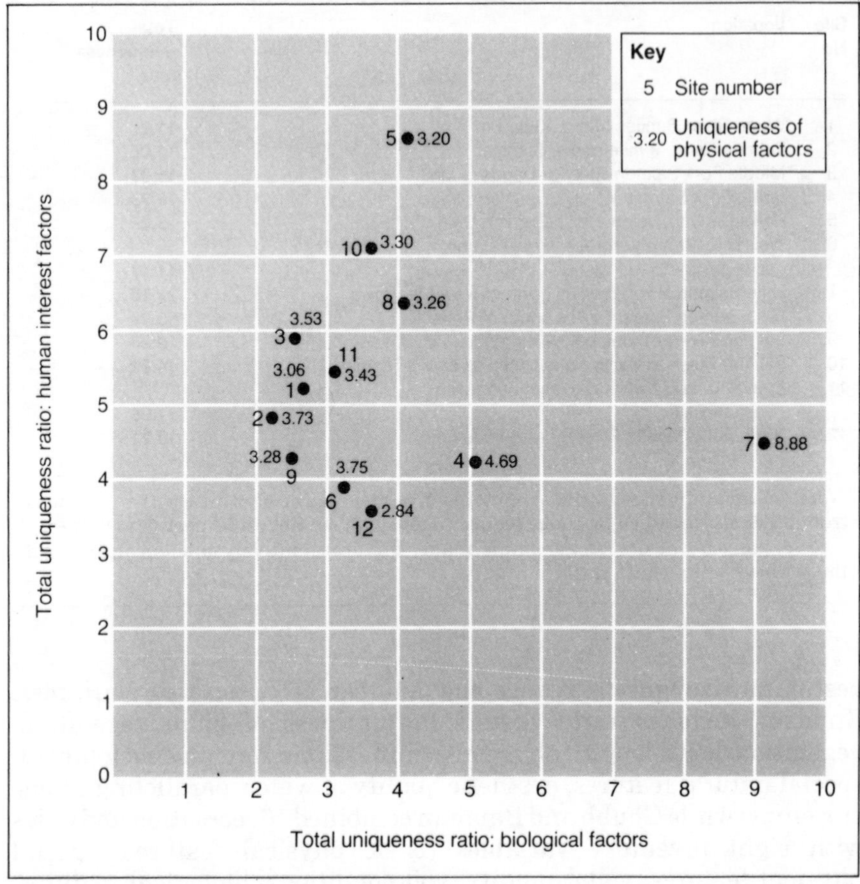

are not directly comparable and are not necessarily valid indicators of landscape aesthetics.

5. The uniqueness of a site is a function of the sampling in space and time. The number and variety of sites could appreciably affect the uniqueness ratio of a site. Some variables are highly changeable over different seasons.

Although these points represent potential weaknesses in Leopold's system, they also indicate future research directions. Those who are critical of Leopold's technique have an obligation to indicate how they would overcome such difficulties. Resolution of these weaknesses will come only after more research, and each individual will have to judge whether further digging in this hole (vertical thinking) or exploring other holes (lateral thinking) will be more productive.

Leopold's focus was upon river valleys. Other researchers have concentrated upon regions or areas. Notable in this respect is work by

Fines (1968), a planner, and Linton (1968), a geographer. Fines' research has been based on southeastern England, whereas Linton's has derived from study in Scotland.

Fines' approach was developed as part of a review of a development plan for East Sussex. He established a scale of landscape values, and then appraised the East Sussex landscape on the basis of that scale. The scale itself was devised by having a 'representative group' of 45 persons view and rank 20 colour photographs. One of the photographs was designated as a 'control view' and given a numerical value of 1. The respondents were asked to score each of the other photographs relative to the control view. The respondents had varying backgrounds with design experience. No significant differences arose in the ranking of the photographs by three groups differentiated on the basis of whether individuals had considerable, limited or no design experience. On the other hand, a significant difference did appear in the ranges of values given to the photographs.

A final scale was devised from the mean values from the group with considerable design experience. Fines' (1968) rationale for this decision was that

> first, such people are most likely to seek and to obtain the greatest enjoyment from the landscape; secondly, the extended scale of values associated with this group approximates to an absolute scale which, it is hoped, may eventually represent the experience of the majority as the standard of education and the amount of leisure time increases.

The actual scale is a continuous series from 0 to 32 arranged in six descriptive categories: unsightly (0 to under 1.0), undistinguished (1.0 to under 2.0), pleasant (2.0 to under 4.0), distinguished (4.0 to under 8.0), superb (8.0 to under 16.0) and spectacular (16.0 to 32.0) (Fig. 6.1). A value of 18.0 was taken to represent the highest score that could be attained by a view in Great Britain and 12.0 represented the highest score from a view in Lowland Britain.

This scale was applied to East Sussex by the author. The evaluation of landscapes was based on the overall beauty of a view rather than giving points to different components. This procedure thus contrasts with Leopold's which scored separate components. Fines adopted this approach on the rationale that 'the value of a landscape composition is certainly greater than the aggregate value of its component parts'.

The actual procedure involved field observation from a car or on foot. He recommended that the surveyor should obtain two viewpoints for each kilometer square. At each viewpoint, the values of viewers in all directions are recorded. For each tract of land the highest and lowest score are established. This information is recorded on 1 : 25,000 topographic maps. Isolines would join points with identical scores, resulting in a map depicting areas of different landscape value.

Fines estimated that his procedure, when applied to the

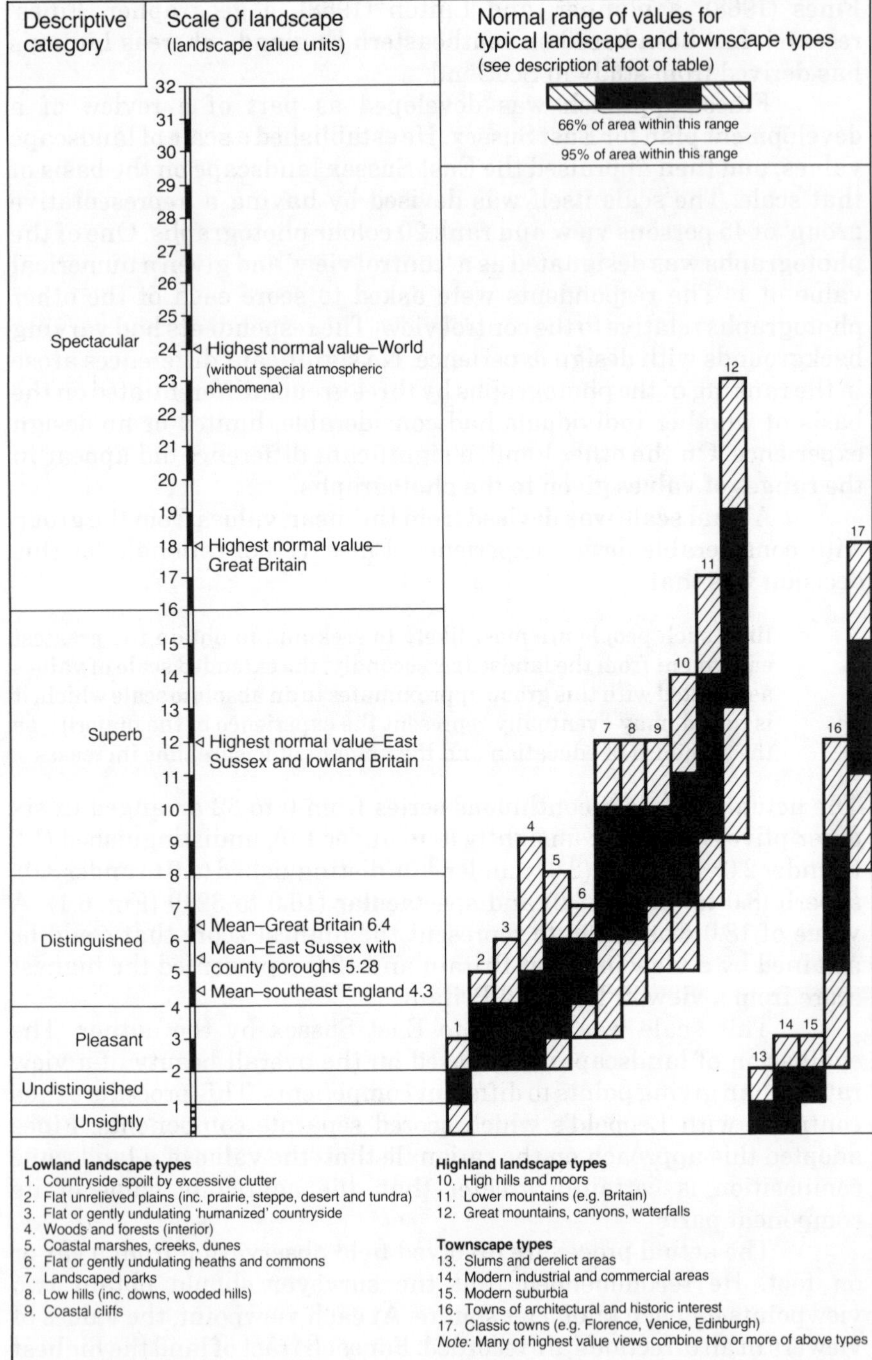

Descriptive category
Scale of landscape (landscape value units)
Normal range of values for typical landscape and townscape types (see description at foot of table)
66% of area within this range
95% of area within this range
Spectacular
Superb
Distinguished
Pleasant
Undistinguished
Unsightly
Highest normal value–World (without special atmospheric phenomena)
Highest normal value–Great Britain
Highest normal value–East Sussex and lowland Britain
Mean–Great Britain 6.4
Mean–East Sussex with county boroughs 5.28
Mean–southeast England 4.3
Lowland landscape types
1. Countryside spoilt by excessive clutter
2. Flat unrelieved plains (inc. prairie, steppe, desert and tundra)
3. Flat or gently undulating 'humanized' countryside
4. Woods and forests (interior)
5. Coastal marshes, creeks, dunes
6. Flat or gently undulating heaths and commons
7. Landscaped parks
8. Low hills (inc. downs, wooded hills)
9. Coastal cliffs
Highland landscape types
10. High hills and moors
11. Lower mountains (e.g. Britain)
12. Great mountains, canyons, waterfalls
Townscape types
13. Slums and derelict areas
14. Modern industrial and commercial areas
15. Modern suburbia
16. Towns of architectural and historic interest
17. Classic towns (e.g. Florence, Venice, Edinburgh)
Note: Many of highest value views combine two or more of above types

Fig. 6.1 Fines' scale of landscape values (*from Fines, 1968*)

2003 km^2 of East Sussex, required 90 days for field work by a team consisting of a surveyor and a driver. This rate of work would represent evaluation of about 22 km^2 per day in areas of Lowland Britain. Field work in the Highlands would require more time because of relative inaccessibility, even though fewer observations would be needed.

Like Leopold's procedure, that by Fines triggered criticism and further inquiries. Brancher (1969) has drawn attention to several problems. He questioned the creation of a scale based on scores by a 'representative' group of 45 people without any explanation being given about how or why the group is representative. More seriously, Brancher questioned development of the final scale on the rankings of the group with greatest design experience. He was not convinced that the rankings of such a group were the ones upon which landscape standards should be measured. Other criticisms have been made. Linton (1968) argued that more experimentation was needed to establish a ranking scale, and it was not clear why the six categories were based on a geometric progression. Of greater concern to him, however, was the fact that Fines' method required experienced and skilled personnel and an extensive programme of field work. These aspects made him concerned that such a procedure could only be afforded by relatively wealthy planning agencies.

Linton's landscape appraisal technique was offered as an alternative to Fines'. The latter was seen as overly complicated and time-consuming, as well as being based upon an unverified measurement scale. These aspects led Linton to devise an appraisal system based upon two variables – landforms and land use. He constructed six types of 'landform landscapes' appropriate to Scotland: (1) lowlands, (2) hill country, (3) bold hills, (4) mountains, (5) plateau uplands and (6) low uplands. The criteria used in defining these categories included relative relief as the primary criterion in conjunction with steepness of slopes, abruptness of accidentation, frequency and depth of dissecting valleys and isolation of hill masses from their neighbours.

Having established six categories of landform landscapes, Linton assigned numerical values to each. The scoring was arbitrary. For example, he argued that the second, third and fourth categories represented an ascending sequence of land forms which are 'at least interesting and may be highly exciting'. He then proposed scores of 5, 6 and 8 points, respectively. The other three were considered to be 'intrinsically tame', resulting in 0 points for lowlands, 2 for low uplands and 3 for plateau uplands. The presence of water was judged to increase the scenic quality of a landscape. Linton conferred 2 bonus points to areas with water in the foreground and middle distance, and 1 point for uplands containing a significant water component.

Linton argued that scenic quality is not determined by landforms alone. Land-use is also important. Therefore, he devised a classification of land uses including categories for: (1) urbanized and industrialized landscapes, (2) continuous forest, (3) treeless farmland,

(4) moorland, (5) varied forest and moorland, (6) richly varied farming, (7) wild landscapes. Numerical ratings were also given to these categories. The arbitrary nature by which ratings were decided is obvious with regard to the continuous forest category. In Linton's (1968; 231) words:

> Continuous forest on lowland or low upland extinguishes the scenic effects of relief completely, so the score must be at least -2. Hill country which scores 5 does not have its scenic effects wholly obliterated, so the negative points for continuous forest should not be so many as -5. Probably the right score is -3, but in fact, a more conservative view has been taken here and the points actually awarded are -2.

From this procedure, maps were prepared based upon landforms and land-use. These two maps were combined to form a composite assessment. Six landform categories and seven land-use categories make a potential of 42 combinations. In Scotland, only four categories did not appear. Specific examples of the other 38 alternatives were identified (Table 6.5). These large number of possible categories prompted Linton to group the results into broader categories separated by point values in steps of three (-6, -3, 0, 3, 6, 9, 12). The composite map (Fig. 6.2) was offered as 'the first analytical representation of the scenic resources of Scotland'.

Linton argued that his procedure satisfied his purpose of identifying how much of the Scottish scenery was better than a prescribed standard and indicating where such scenery was located. He believed that his technique was objective in the sense that other researchers could repeat the exercise and would obtain essentially the same results. On the other hand, he cautioned that refinement of the measurement scale might be required. Furthermore, he warned that the map itself was incapable of making decisions for resource managers. 'It offers nothing but information about the extent and location of our scenic resources. Decisions must still be made as to what action should be taken regarding these resources, and when' (Linton, 1968; 238).

Although Linton was stimulated by the inadequacy of Fines' measurement scale to devise an assessment technique, his procedure is open to criticism regarding the numerical ratings assigned to landscapes (Lowenthal, 1978, 29; Dearden, 1980b, 320; Dearden, 1980c, 52). Fines' scale was based upon the preferences of individuals with design experience; Linton's upon his own vast field experience in Scotland. It is apparent, then, that establishment of standards or measurement scales is a primary research need in landscape evaluation.

Another problem with methods such as Linton's is that they assume it is reasonable to disaggregate a landscape into finite components or parts, score each of them, and then sum the individual scores to obtain a measure of scenic value (Dearden, 1980b; 320). This

Table 6.5 Linton's composite assessment categories (*from Linton, 1968*)

Category and Rating	**Urbanised and Industrialised** −5	**Continuous Forest** −2	**Treeless Farmland** +1	**Moorland** +3	**Varied Forest and Moorland** +4	**Richly Varied Farmland** +5	**Wild Landscape** +6
Lowland 0	Ayrshire coast −5	Culbin Forest −2	Machars of Wigtown +1	Moors of Wigtown +3	Cromar +4	Strathearn +5	Colonsay +6
Low uplands 2	NE Lanarkshire −3	Darnaway Forest 0	NE Berwickshire +3	Loch Shin +5	Methven and Glenalmond +6	Gifford (East Lothian) +7	Gruinard Bay +8
Plateau Uplands 3	*(No example)* −2	Kielder Forest +1	Falahill (Midlothian) +4	Monadhliath +6	Potrail Water +7	*(No example)* +8	Mid Argyll +9
Hill country 5	Bathgate Hills 0	Nethy Forest +3	Gala Valley +6	Crawick Water +8	Speyside +9	Middle Tweed +10	Loch Moidart +11
Bold hills 6	Leadhills–Wanlockhead +1	Strathyre Forest +4	Loch Chon +7	Dalveen Pass +9	Bennachie +10	*(No example)* +11	Morvern and Sunart +12
Mountains 8	Kinlochleven +3	Loch Lubnaig +6	Glen Elchaig +9	Glen Clova +11	Achnashellach +12	*(No example)* +13	Coigach +14

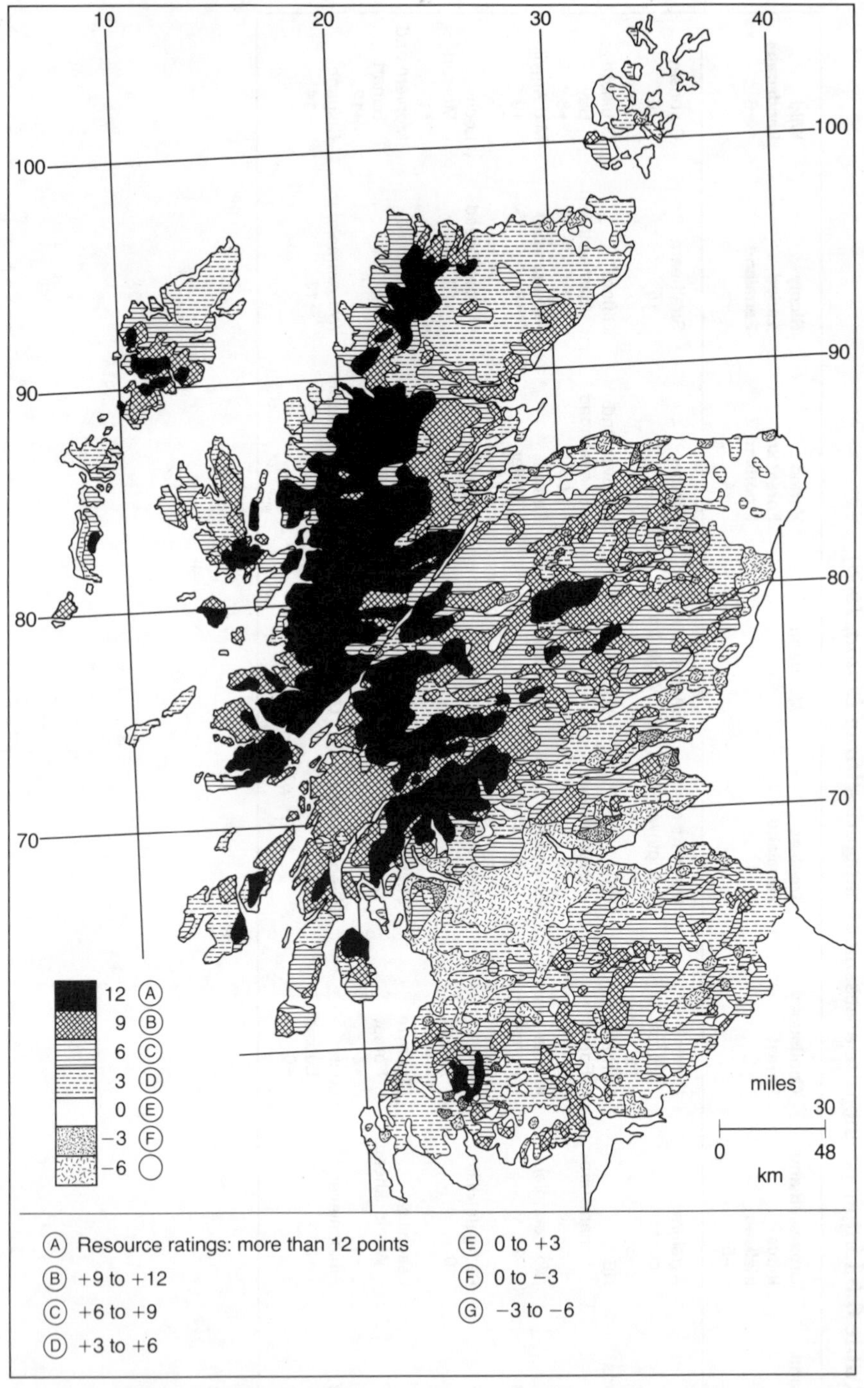

Fig. 6.2 Linton's composite scenic assessment for Scotland (*from Linton, 1968*)

procedure does not incorporate the interactive or synergistic effects between and among various components. It also poses problems regarding the appropriate number of components to use in such assessments.

On the positive side, however, Linton's explicit attention to the influence of *land use* on landscape appeal was a step forward. To illustrate, Anderson (1981) has shown that observers' judgements about scenic value are sensitive to land use. She conducted a study using scenery from northern Arizona ponderosa pine forests. Her results revealed that when observers believed a landscape was designated for different types of land use then their assessments of its scenic value changed.

Linton's approach was designed to obtain a scenic inventory at minimum expense, and to ensure reliability of results. In these concerns he was highly successful. Gilg applied Linton's method in two separate studies of Scotland. First, he had a class of first-year geography students survey 200 km^2 in the Lomond Hills area (Gilg, 1974). Ten groups (four students per group) surveyed about 30 squares, giving a score to each. Sixty-four squares were surveyed independently by two groups of students. The vast majority of scores, 55 out of 64, differed by only two points or less. A second exercise was conducted several years later using another class of first-year geography students (Gilg, 1976). These students also worked in the Lomond Hills area and scored kilometer squares regarding land use, landform and composite scenic value. Again, Gilg found that the method produced reliable results without a great deal of field labour, laboratory analysis or statistical analysis. His major reservation in both instances was that the procedure gave undue weight to land forms.

In a third study, Gilg (1975) tackled the difficult issue of a measurement scale. Since his other studies demonstrated that the procedure was workable and easy to apply, he felt that the scale of values and applicability of the technique outside of Scotland needed exploration. He used a colour slide experiment, in which second and third year geography students were asked to assess the visual quality of 38 slides over a range of 0–95 points. The slides, selected to match the 38 categories established by Linton, depicted landscapes from throughout Britain and continental Europe. The results indicated that landform scores were generally agreed upon but that land-use scores were much more variable. Based upon this evidence, he suggested a new measurement system which allocated points to different categories in the following manner: lowlands (5), hill country (20), bold hills (30), mountains (50), plateau uplands and low uplands (15); urbanized and industrialized landscapes (-6), continuous forest (24), treeless farmland (-3), varied forest and moorland (10), richly varied farming (18), wild landscapes (5). These scores were subsequently confirmed by further experiments with school teachers associated with environmental courses. The work by Gilg and others such as Wallace (1974) to test reliability, measurement scales and general applicability of existing or new techniques represents a healthy trend in landscape research. This type of activity represents progress towards a culmination of knowledge and understanding about landscape quality. Necessary checks and modifications are made relative to preceding work. In this way, the cutting edge of research effort gradually moves ahead.

6.4 LANDSCAPE PREFERENCE STUDIES

Preference studies may utilize indirect or direct strategies. The indirect strategy infers attitudes about landscape quality through examination of available information. Lowenthal (1968; 88) cogently explained the rationale for such research when stating

> To be effective ... planning and design should be grounded on intimate knowledge of the ways people think and feel about the environment; this calls for a substantial familiarity with social and intellectual history, with psychology and philosophy, with art and anthropology. All these fields contribute to our knowledge of how we see the world we live in, how vision and value affect action, and how action alters institutions.

Lowenthal has applied this approach when studying attitudes toward the landscape in England and the United States. The major data sources have been literature, speeches, notes from public hearings, newspaper articles, letters, travel guides and art (Lowenthal, 1978; 16–26).

Lowenthal and Prince (1964; 1965) posed a series of questions regarding England. They sought to determine the visual qualities of the English landscape, how people perceived the landscape, and what they wanted to see as opposed to what actually existed. This latter point has important resource management implications, for as they argued 'Landscapes are formed by landscape tastes. People in any country see their terrain through preferred and accustomed spectacles, and tend to make it over as they see it. The English landscape, as much as any other, mirrors a long succession of such idealized images and visual prejudices' (Lowenthal and Prince, 1965; 186). Such a viewpoint reflects Zimmermann's functional definition of resources (Ch. 1).

Their first inquiry identified common aspects – variety and openness – associated with recurring landscape features: hedged and walled fields, villages and council estates, suburban and semi-detached houses, seaside resorts, coalfield industrial districts, parklands (Lowenthal and Prince, 1964). They found that private and public interests as well as local and national values were usually accommodated in a manner that made England 'a settled and comfortable land'. In a subsequent study, they attempted to identify prominent and well-loved aspects of the countryside. They suggested that the following attributes were preferred by the English: the bucolic, the picturesque based on an intimate lived-in appearance as opposed to natural grandeur, the deciduous over the coniferous scene, neatness and tidiness, antiquarianism over the present, and individualism. From these attributes, two conflicting tendencies were seen to arise concerning English landscape taste. One accepted what the authorities stated was good, and judged not on the basis of immediate feeling but from historical and other associations. The other shunned 'good' taste and external standards in favour of a commitment to the 'old, the tried, the worn, and at times, the ugly – in short, to whatever is, as long as it is uniquely and unyieldingly itself' (Lowenthal and Prince, 1965; 222).

Comparable research has been done for the United States but with different results. Lowenthal (1968) judged that in their landscape tastes Americans emphasized size, wildness, extremes and formlessness. Other preference patterns emphasized the future over the past or present, individual features over aggregates, the remote and spectacular over the nearby and typical. By the mid 1970s, however, Lowenthal (1975; 1977) noted 'changing attitudes toward American artifacts and landscapes ... ' Pessimism about the present and future had drawn attention to a 'nostalgia for the past and rural areas'.

Changing attitudes and preferences create a dilemma for the resource manager attempting to incorporate public viewpoints into decisions since as Lowenthal (1978; 26) has remarked, 'each epoch, each people, ignores or shuns certain landscapes, adores and venerates others'. If his interpretation is correct, American landscape tastes travelled full circle in less than a decade. If public preferences are to be important in designating landscapes to preserve or protect, it is clear that changing and frequently conflicting public views provide an incomplete guide. Undoubtedly, preferences should be one consideration in management decisions about the landscape, but they should not be the overriding factor.

The research by Lowenthal and Prince has been based mainly upon the views expressed in literature, letters and newspapers (Lowenthal and Prince, 1976). The views examined are not based upon a systematic sample, nor are they representative in any statistical sense. Nevertheless, Lowenthal and Prince have sought to identify the viewpoints which appeared again and again in the comments of statesmen and men of letters on the assumption that such views reappear in the schoolroom, the press and the pulpit. Not only would such ideas and feelings influence a wide cross-section of public opinion, but their spokesmen were often among the most active in making decisions which affected the landscape (Salter and Lloyd, 1977). For similar reasons, R. Rees (1973, 1976) has urged geographers to give greater attention to landscape painting as not only a record of historical landscapes but also 'as an expression of the man–nature relationship; and as a determinant of our perception and appreciation of the environment' (Rees, R., 1973; 147). In this context, Zaring (1977) has demonstrated how paintings reveal attitudes towards the landscape in Wales, and Marsh (1985) has examined how landscapes depicted on tourists' post cards can be used to understand landscape preferences at different time periods.

The direct approach normally involves asking respondents to indicate their preference for actual landscapes or for landscapes depicted upon photographs. The logistical problem of transporting respondents to a variety of sites, and the difficulties in controlling other variables (weather, time of viewing), have made the use of photographs popular even though it is not yet firmly established whether photographs validly simulate the real world.

Shafer, Hamilton and Schmidt (1969) used photographs in attempting to determine why some landscapes are preferred over others. The specific objective was to identify quantitative variables in a landscape that were significantly correlated to public preference. They believed if a resource manager knew what features determined the aesthetic appeal of a landscape he would make better decisions about purchasing, developing or preserving such features.

One hundred black and white photographs of landscapes were taken of wildlands in the United States. Half were of eastern scenes and half were of western scenes. Landscapes were classified into 10 categories based upon presence of vegetation, non-vegetation, water and sky. Each photograph then had a plastic grid overlay placed upon it. Each square was assigned to one of the 10 categories depending upon the dominant feature in the square. For every photograph, four variables were used to describe each of the 10 categories (Fig. 6.3).

Six further variables were included. Three measured the variation of sky, land and water. A grid was placed over a photograph. In the centre of each square, a circular area was scored as 1, 2, or 3 depending on whether the circular area was composed of sky, land, or water. Tonal variation for each circle was measured with a photometer and scored on a three-point ordinal scale.

Preference scores for each photograph were obtained through interviewing Adirondack campers. The 100 photographs were given identification numbers and then randomly assigned into 20 packages with 5 pictures in each. Each respondent examined 4 packages, and ranked the photographs from 1 to 5 in each package. A score of 1 indicated first preference. The first respondent looked at the first 4 packages, the second respondent used the second 4 and so on until all 20 packages had been examined by 5 different people. At that point, the 100 photographs were randomly sorted into 20 new packages and interviewing continued. This procedure was used until 250 respondents were interviewed.

The interviews resulted in each photograph being ranked 50 times. The 50 separate scores for each photograph were added, with the total score being treated as its preference value. The preference scores had a theoretical range of 50 to 250, with 50 representing the most

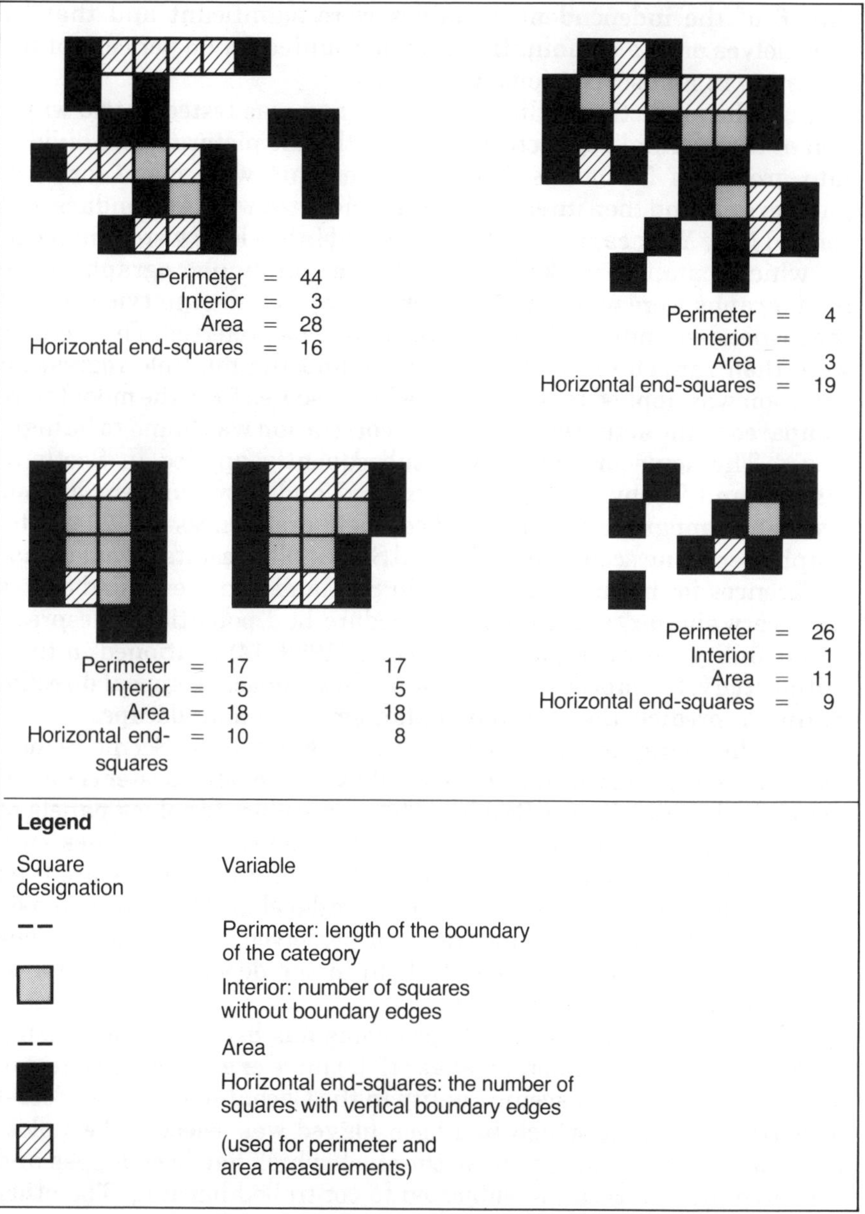

Fig. 6.3 Shafer's system of landscape zone configurations (*from Shafer, Hamilton and Schmidt, 1969*)

preferred scene. The actual scores ranged from 71 to 228 with a mean of 150 and a standard deviation of 37.75. These scores were then considered as dependent variables, and a model was formulated to link them to the 46 independent variables based on the measurements taken from the photographs. A multiple regression equation indicated that 6 of the independent variables were significant and that by themselves or in a combination they accounted for 66 per cent of the variation in landscape preference scores.

The predictive ability of the equation was tested in two ways. Ten of the original 100 pictures and another 20 pictures were divided into groups of 5 pictures. The measurements were made for each photograph, and then interviews were conducted with Adirondack and central New York campers. Three hundred interviews were completed in which campers looked at 1 package of 5 photographs. The photographs were paired in 10 different ways by the interviewer, and the respondent indicated which landscape was preferred. The pictures were then ranked on a scale of 1 to 5, and the multiple regression equation was applied to the data. Predicted scores from the model were compared to the actual scores and the correlation was found to be high.

The same procedure was subsequently applied in Scotland (Shafer and Tooby, 1973). Two hundred and fifty campers at four Scottish campgrounds each ranked their preferences for 20 photographs depicting scenes in the United States. The results revealed that preferences for natural landscapes in Scotland and the United States were very similar, and that the procedure had potential widespread applicability. However, as Shafer *et al.* (1969; 14) cautioned in their initial study, the procedure does not predict landscape appeal directly. Rather, it predicts the appeal of a photograph of a landscape.

Photographs have been a central feature of the Scenic Beauty Estimation (SBE) technique developed by Daniel and Boster (1976) of the United States Forest Service. Their procedure involves panels of viewers numerically rating a series of randomly chosen slides on a scale between 0 (dislike) and 9 (like). These ordinal ratings are then transformed following a scaling procedure developed by psychologists to produce an 'interval' scale index of perceived scenic quality. The purpose of this work has been to help in the development of forest management policy and practice.

A range of management problems has been addressed using the SBE technique. Anderson *et al.* (1982) have examined the effect of prescribed burning on scenic quality in the Coconino National Forest in Arizona. An area which had been logged was selected. Two plots were identified. One was to have the slash which had been lopped and scattered after harvesting subjected to controlled burning. The other was to be a control. The plots were photographed prior to the burn, within a month after the burn, and periodically during the next five years. The slides then were shown to university student volunteers who were divided into nine panels of 21 to 34 people.

The results suggested that the scenic effects of prescribed burning may be short term. Immediately following burning, the scenic values were significantly lower on the treatment plot. However, within one year the scenic values on the burn site were higher than those on the unburned control plot. In subsequent years there were no significant differences in the perceived scenic quality of the two sites. Anderson *et al.* concluded that such findings could be incorporated into information and education programmes.

The Scenic Beauty Estimation technique has been used in several other situations. Benson and Ullrich (1981) used it in several studies of timber harvesting and roadbuilding. Their motivation was the recognition that managers often have several management alternatives which may differ in their visual impact. If public preferences could be predicted, then they believed that the manager would have a basis for incorporating aesthetic costs and benefits when evaluating alternative actions. Brown and Daniel (1984) took a more general approach, and developed statistical models relating public perception of scenic beauty to forest characteristics. They also used the SBE technique, and then used the data from that to create multiple regression models which could be used to predict scenic quality at both site and stand scales. It should be noted that development of such regression models does not require exclusive reliance on photographs to determine public perception of scenic quality. Dearden (1980c; Dearden and Rosenblood, 1980) has also used multiple regression analysis based on data collected from observers' assessments of actual conditions in the field.

The SBE technique is but one application of the multi-dimensional scaling methods developed by psychologists. Just as the work on perceptions, attitudes and behaviour (Ch. 5) has involved considerable interaction between geographers and psychologists, so has research in landscape evaluation involved interdisciplinary work. For geographers, this type of work has primarily been oriented toward testing the possible utility of measurement techniques devised by psychologists. Examples include studies by Pearce and Waters (1983), Pomeroy *et al.* (1983) and Fitzgibbon *et al.* (1985).

The valuing of landscape quality also has led to the application of concepts developed by economists. In Chapter 4 we saw how gravity models have been used to assess the inherent 'pull' or attractiveness of places. This approach is an indirect way of inferring from actual behaviour what a person is willing to pay to travel to a place. From that information, estimations can be made about the monetary value of the attractiveness of that place.

An alternative approach is to ask travellers directly about the values they give to a place. The economists address this willingness-to-pay by asking respondents to indicate through a bidding exercise what they would be willing to spend to have access to a place. This approach often is referred to as the contingent market valuation approach.

Vaux, Gardner and Mills (1984) recognized that contingent market valuation studies have weaknesses. One concern is that the bidding game is a hypothetical one, so it is difficult to know whether respondents would behave in the same way in a real situation as they do in the hypothetical one. Another concern is that individuals may adopt a bidding strategy that does not reflect their true willingness to pay depending upon how they believe their bids might be used in setting entrance fees or other regulations. Recognizing such problems, however, Vaux, Gardner and Mills (1984) used this procedure in combination with photographs to determine the impact of fire on forest recreation.

The results from their contingent valuation approach indicated that low intensity fires can have beneficial effects for recreation while high intensity fires have adverse effects. However, the impact of fire is not always negative nor unanimous, and furthermore, preferences may vary over time. These types of findings suggest that there is still considerable opportunity for further work to be done whether it be for specific management strategies such as controlled burning or for more general assessments of amenity values of forests (Sorg and Loomis, 1984).

6.5 IMPLICATIONS FOR RESOURCE MANAGEMENT

Lowenthal (1981; 218) has identified three major ways in which work in landscape evaluation may assist resource managers. First, it helps to identify what should be preserved and why. Second, it contributes towards policies regarding the way in which preserved landscapes should be used. Third, it stimulates rather than hinders alternative uses of sensitive environments.

In the context of resource management, Shoard (1981; 104) has reminded us that too often landscape evaluation research is justified for its use in identifying and helping to preserve areas of outstanding natural beauty. While natural beauty is not unimportant, emphasis upon that aspect alone overlooks the many other activities which occur in areas of great natural beauty - hunting, fishing, canoeing, hiking, birdwatching, horseriding, walking and driving. The collective value of such diverse activities stresses that landscape aesthetics have substantial value even if they often are extremely difficult to express in monetary terms.

Landscape evaluation research has numerous management implications. Research can lead to *inventories* of scenic attributes, which can then be considered along with other information normally available to the decision makers (Ch. 3). Landscape assessments may also serve as a significant input to *environmental impact assessments* since an overriding concern in such work is to determine the impact of human intervention in natural systems (Ch. 9). Another application is in *land use planning*, especially when deciding whether a specific site, corridor or area deserves to be preserved, protected, maintained or improved (Penning-Rowsell, 1975; 149–51).

Use of landscape evaluation research findings in land use planning is particularly relevant in a variety of situations, ranging from recreation to siting public facilities such as roads, pipelines or power transmission lines. Fines (1968; 51) applied his method to the routeing of power lines. Evans and Wood (1980), Goodall and Whitlow (1980) and Schroeder and Daniel (1980) have all studied aspects of scenic quality regarding siting of highway routes. Call *et al* (1981) have incorporated visitor impact on scenic view areas into environmental assessment work. And studies of landscape evaluation increasingly have been applied to planning for coastal zone areas (Blanco *et al.*, 1982; Nassauer, 1983; Nassauer and Benner, 1984; Nieman, 1980, Ris, 1982; Smardon and Fellman, 1982; and Wohlwill, 1982).

By using landscape assessment in resource decisions, many investigators are hopeful that conflict will be reduced (Leopold, 1969a, 37; Knudson, 1976, 282; Chubb and Bauman, 1977, 97). Comparative, quantitative assessments of landscape values are viewed as essential if landscape amenities are to receive equal consideration in decisions. In addition, by indirectly or directly obtaining public preferences, it is believed that decisions more in harmony with societal values will be reached. In this manner, landscape assessments become a means to facilitate public involvement in resource decisions.

Landscape research must give greater attention to several other aspects, however, to increase its utility in resource management. Researchers continuously seek to improve the reliability and validity of their techniques. Such effort usually involves the use of ever-more complex and sophisticated concepts and methods. Yet, if assessment techniques are to be of practical use, methods must be developed which can be easily applied and readily interpreted. Turner (1975; 157) has pinpointed the paradox when commenting that 'there is probably a range of applicable methods of varying theoretical validity, in which the simpler cheaper techniques may be more practical than more complex ones, even when these may be more desirable and intellectually respectable'. Researchers must give more thought to the necessary tradeoffs among theoretical soundness, elegance, ease of interpretation and expense (Dearden, 1981a; 104). Penning-Rowsell (1975; 152) also urged that ease of updating information from assessments deserves more attention. This concern is becoming increasingly important with the need to monitor the effects of policies, programmes and projects (Fig. 6.4).

A further consideration is the role which landscape preferences should have in land use planning. Many would argue that in an era of citizen involvement such preferences should be incorporated in decisions (Bromley, 1981; Dearden, 1981b). Others have noted that many individuals have difficulty in articulating their preferences. Furthermore, it has been shown that preferences change over time (Ross and Marts, 1975). If preferences are to be used to establish standards or norms to guide land use decisions, the changeable nature

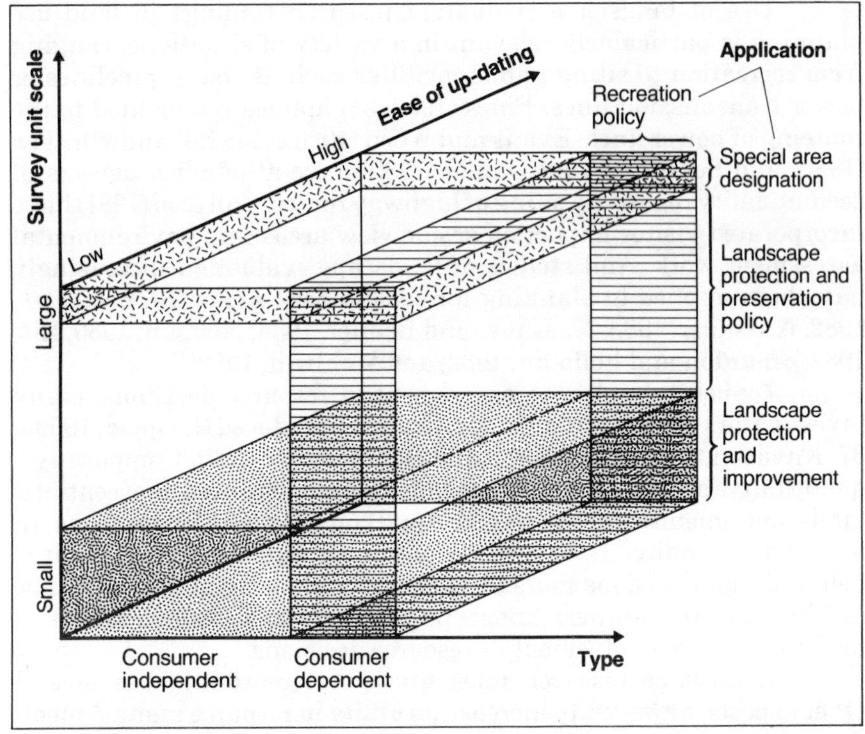

Fig. 6.4 Penning-Rowsell's constraints on the application of landscape evaluation (*from Penning-Rowsell, 1975*)

of preferences represents a serious dilemma that demands further attention.

6.6 IMPLICATIONS FOR RESEARCH

Landscape evaluation has close ties to the man–environment research theme in geography, particularly when seeking to determine which aspects of a landscape are viewed as desirable. The research relates to practical resource problems, ranging from inventories, to impact assessment and land use planning. Various individuals have offered assessments of the ongoing research activity (Dearden, 1980b; Penning-Rowsell, 1981a; 1981b; Haase and Richter, 1983). However, Lowenthal (1978; 63) has identified a series of questions which define a research agenda. He argued that improved knowledge is needed regarding: (1) how landscapes are identified and thought about, (2) which landscape components are admired, (3) which physical attributes and symbolic meanings are highlighted by various cultures at different times, (4) how purpose, intensity, immediacy, duration, novelty and sense of crisis affect experiences with landscape, and (5) how individuals and groups differ in awareness toward, selection of, and preference for favoured landscapes. Research focused upon these five aspects would make both basic and applied contributions. Relating to all of these points is a pressing need for work oriented to improving theoretical and conceptual frameworks (Zube, Sell and Taylor, 1982; Sell, Taylor and Zube, 1984).

Like many of the other open resource questions, landscape evaluation illustrates the artificiality of the dichotomy between positivist and phenomenological research philosophies (Dearden, 1985a; 264). The nature of landscape research requires recognition of the notion that individuals 'see' different environments. In this sense, the views of phenomenology are basic (Hamilton, 1982; 73). Yet, at the same time, considerable effort has been devoted to replicating and verifying techniques and findings, a concern usually attributed to the positivists. These aspects emphasize that the concerns of both viewpoints can, and often must, be interwoven during investigations. If the legitimate plurality of approaches were accepted, then unproductive debates on the relative merits of 'objectivity' (Shuttleworth, 1979–1980); Powell, 1981) and 'subjectivity' (Jacques, 1980) and 'quantification' (Carlson, 1977; Ribe, 1982; Baggs, 1983) could be ended.

Just as different research philosophies seem appropriate, so do the perspectives of different disciplines. Input from landscape architects, foresters, engineers, earth scientists, psychologists and geographers are all required, and are represented in the work reviewed in this chapter. As in research on perceptions, attitudes and behaviour (Ch. 5) and on hazards (Ch. 8), landscape evaluation studies have drawn geographers and psychologists into productive partnerships which must continue if further progress is to be realized.

Concerning conceptualization, several needs exist. Appleton (1975; 121) has argued persuasively that many assumptions have been made without adequate consideration. When carving up landscapes into component parts, investigators have used different divisions and scales. In some instances, landscape units which have proven their worth in geomorphological studies have been adopted directly for landscape evaluation. Appleton urged investigators to examine assumptions more carefully with a view to rationalizing explicity their use. This viewpoint also has been reiterated by Lowenthal (1978; 28–30).

Research strategies have drawn on a combination of field observation, simulation and surveys with respondents. Experimental design principles have been difficult to integrate into strategies, since control groups frequently are awkward to define. Respondents must view the real or simulated landscape before being able to express preferences, giving a control group little meaning. However, although choice of research designs has been restricted, substantial effort has been directed towards replication and verification. Linton's technique has been replicated several times by Gilg (1974; 1975; 1976). Shafer *et al.* (1969; Shafer and Tooby, 1973) has replicated his procedure in two countries. In both instances such work confirmed the reliability of the respective procedures. Other researchers have applied several techniques in one area, and then contrasted the results relative to reliability, ease of use and expense (Penning-Rowsell and Hardy, 1973; Blacksell and Gilg, 1975). This awareness of the value in using a variety of methods (Dearden, 1981a; 104) and the effort to compare effectiveness of methods (Feimer *et al.* 1981; Kane, 1981) is a praiseworthy characteristic of research in landscape evaluation. Still others have sought to establish whether professionals with different training view the landscape in similar terms (Craik, 1972a; Zube, 1974). This attention to replication is probably rivalled only by the work in carrying capacity (Ch. 7) and hazards (Ch. 8). It also represents a positive feature of the research. Although progress has been slow, the findings are being checked which provides a base for the establishment of cumulative knowledge.

Measurement of preferences has also been an active research concern. Investigators have continuously sought to move measurement from nominal and ordinal to ratio scales (Dearden, 1980a, 172; Law and Zube, 1983). This has involved some arbitrary definitions of scales and weighting of variables but has been balanced by the replication checks, such as Gilg's (1976) attempt to improve Linton's original scale. More work in this area will be essential if further insights are to be gained.

More general considerations have also been encountered. Researchers have had to make trade-offs between the desirability of seeking reactions to actual landscapes and the convenience of using simulated ones. Evaluation on-site is most desirable, but logistical problems have resulted in most researchers using simulated landscapes, notably through photographs. This represents a conscious compromise. It also suggests a future research activity which would examine relationships between perceptions of real and simulated landscapes (Dearden, 1980b; 320–1).

Future work will undoubtedly experience as many negative as positive findings. As Appleton (1975; 123) has argued, however, publication of details about negative results and inadequately tested hypotheses must occur. In brief, more researchers will have to adopt Linton's attitude. After describing his procedure, which he recognized as imperfect, he observed that 'it was necessary for someone to risk mistakes in order to make a beginning' (Linton, 1968; 232).

CHAPTER 7
CARRYING CAPACITY

7.1 INTRODUCTION

Carrying capacity, with close ties to the man–environment theme in geography, has attracted research effort for a considerable time. Although the concept has generated research for both theoretical and practical purposes, it has proven difficult to operationalize (section 7.2). Despite this fundamental problem, research has developed in a number of areas. Some of the earliest work focused upon attempts to determine appropriate man–land ratios (section 7.3). Another cluster of research effort has centred upon the biophysical capacity of the environment (section 7.4). Such work is closely tied to environmental impact assessment studies (Ch. 9). Another thrust has been social or behavioural carrying capacity, especially related to wilderness management (section 7.5). This behaviourally oriented work has linkages with the perception and attitude research reviewed in Chapter 5. These various specific research activities raise implications for resource management (section 7.6) and future research activity (section 7.7).

7.2 THE NATURE OF CARRYING CAPACITY

Carrying capacity has been used in many situations. These include estimates of sustainable levels of population on the globe (Hare, 1980; Westing, 1981; Ehrlich, 1982; Brown, 1986), studies of achievable agricultural production (Bjøness, 1980; Singh and Pande, 1982; Ramanaiah and Reddy, 1983; Harrington, Wilson and Young, 1984), analysis of environmental change from hiking (Coleman, 1981; Hoffman and Alliende, 1982; McDonnell, 1981), determination of use levels for parks and campsites (Smith, 1981; Kuss and Morgan, 1984;

Price, 1985), as well as research for protection of the natural environment (Isakov, 1984). Despite this widespread use, carrying capacity has received sharp criticism (Burch, 1981).

Several remarks by Hare (1980; 380–4) illustrate some of the concerns. He suggested that one of the most important problems for geographers is the carrying capacity of the earth. Specifically, he stated that we need to know what human population can be sustained and how near we are to that limit. He concluded that every attempt to answer these questions has been found inadequate by critics and that in turn the views of the critics have been found inadequate by the next generation of critics. Hare concluded that the carrying capacity of the earth is a meaningless concept unless the future course of technology can be predicted regarding such things as brackish water cultivation, self-nitrogenating cereals and various techniques of gene transfer. Compounding the technological dimension, he also concluded that the political future must be anticipated before carrying capacity estimates could be meaningful.

The observations by Hare highlight the difficulties in dealing with carrying capacity at the global scale. However, there are other aspects which create problems. One of the most basic is that investigators have experienced great difficulty in defining the term (Wall, 1982; 181). Indeed, this situation led Jaakson, Buszwnski and Botting (1976; 359) to conclude that 'there is no generally accepted definition of it and no standard approach of how it should be calculated'. This situation has hampered the comparability of results from different inquiries, which in turn has checked the growth of accumulated knowledge.

Efforts to establish generalizations about carrying capacity have been hindered by the problem-specific nature of studies. Even for a specific area, substantial problems arise. In the view of Lime and Stankey (1971; 175),

> carrying capacity is not a simple, single absolute value. There is no fixed figure we can point to for a particular ... area and say 'This is the carrying capacity.' The ... manager is faced with a complex set of conditions. He must consider a wide range of activities, ... users ... and values, many of which are incompatible with one another.

Comments such as the above stress that carrying capacity should not be viewed as producing an absolute number to guide managers. Different guidelines for carrying capacity will emerge depending upon managerial goals, and also depending upon assumptions made about future or desired technology. As Barkham (1973; 218) has noted, carrying capacity is 'a phrase delightful in its simplicity, complex in its meaning, and difficult to define, as in different situations and to different people it is understood in different ways'. This view was echoed by Bouchard's (1974; 19) remark that carrying capacity was not a magic tool. Information can be provided by investigations, but he was pessimistic that it will ever result in 'numbers or a formula dictating the decisions'.

7.3 MAN-LAND RATIO

During his presidential address in 1956 to the International Geographical Congress at Rio de Janeiro, Stamp addressed the concept of carrying capacity. He argued that no problem was more significant than the rapidly increasing population pressure on material resources (Stamp, 1958; 1). He proposed to develop a series of calculations based on nutrition and land which would address several questions. How much food is required to support an average human being in health and full activity? How much land is needed to produce that amount of food, relative to the type of farming and the quality of the land?

His approach was to focus upon defining a 'standard nutrition unit' or the daily caloric intake needed to maintain both good health and full activity. He concluded that the standard should be 1 million calories per person per year. This standard unit then could be used in several ways. First, by measuring actual production and consumption it is possible to show how far the food intake in a community falls below the standard. Second, by considering total food outputs, the area of land used to support a given population under varying farming conditions can be compared independently of the crops raised. Third, a measure of farming efficiency could be derived. And fourth, by relating actual to potential use, the capability of the land to support the population (in his words, its carrying capacity) could be measured.

Stamp determined the caloric values for wheat, rice, potatoes, milk and meat, and applied his standard nutritional unit to Japan, northern India and the United Kingdom, and then subsequently went on to assess the adequacy of the world's land to support future populations. Hare (1980; 382) later reported that regarding the issue of carrying capacity in this context, Stamp concluded 'To this there is no answer: the unknown factors are too numerous.'

Despite Stamp's pessimistic conclusion, various researchers have addressed the question of carrying capacity of land, especially land under traditional agricultural systems. This work has dealt with such basic questions as what is the critical population density at which immigration is likely to begin, at what stage and to which extent will pressure on the land act as a determinant of population growth, and at what stage and by which criteria can a rural area be judged to be overpopulated (Hunter, 1966; 151). Studies have explored these questions in Ghana (Hunter, 1966), Kenya (Thom and Martin, 1983; Bernard, 1985), Iran (Ehlers, 1982), India (Singh, 1971; Singh and Pande, 1982; Prasad, 1985), and Mexico (Marten and Sancholuz, 1982). Two studies are considered here.

Ramanaiah and Reddy (1983) examined the carrying capacity

of land in Andhra Pradesh, a state in central India. They defined carrying capacity as the number of people that a unit area of land can support. They recognized that the carrying capacity is a function of the quality of the land, the optimum use of the land, cropping patterns, technological factors and socio-economic conditions. Their interest was to see whether the carrying capacity of the land in Andhra Pradesh could be increased.

Their procedure was similar to that proposed by Stamp (1958). Districts were used as the basic analytical unit, and carrying capacity was measured in terms of the caloric output of foodgrain crops which occupied about three quarters of the cropped area in the state. The production of each foodgrain crop was multiplied by its caloric value for 1961, 1971 and 1979. The aggregate caloric value of all of the crops was determined for each year after making adjustments for wastage, assumed to be 20 per cent of total production. Then, the total caloric output was divided by the area under foodgrain crops to obtain the per hectare foodgrain output in calories. This per hectare caloric output was then compared with the weighted average standard nutrition for ingestion in calories per person per year. The optimum carrying capacity was calculated by dividing the calories available for consumption per hectare with the weighted standard nutrition unit for ingestion in calories per person per year.

Ramanaiah and Reddy found that in the 18-year period between 1961 and 1979 there had been a substantial increase in the carrying capacity of land in Andhra Pradesh. The average carrying capacity had increased from 2.35 persons per hectare to 3.77 persons per hectare. The maximum had increased from 4.07 to 7.39 persons/hectare and the minimum from 2.24 to 2.77 persons/hectare. However, seven districts were still categorized as having a low carrying capacity. Since much of the increase in capacity had occurred in the deltaic districts and in the newly irrigated areas, they suggested that the cornerstone of development in the undercapacity districts should be extension of irrigation.

Marten and Sancholuz (1982) examined how many people could be supported in the Jalapa region of Mexico. From the outset, they recognized that the answer could not be a single number. The number of people that could be sustained on the land was viewed to be dependent upon the level of technology for agricultural production, the life style of the inhabitants of the region, especially their patterns of consumption, and environmental standards.

As a result, Marten and Sancholuz presented several scenarios. If there were no limit on the supply of irrigation and agricultural services in support of agriculture, and if all land were allocated to agricultural use, then the Jalapa region could feed eight times its current population. Such production could not be sustained in the long term, however, without special erosion control measures on the steep slopes. If only land suitable for sustained agricultural production without special erosion control measures were developed and if there still were no limit on the availability of agricultural services, then the region theoretically could provide food for 5.5 times the current population. If the presently available services were maintained and the excessively erosive lands were kept out of agricultural use, then the carrying capacity would be 1.5 times the present population. Finally, if the erosive lands were not developed but the present level of agricultural services were doubled, then 2.2 times the present population could be supported.

All of these scenarios regarding carrying capacity for the Jalapa region assumed that the consumption habits of the population do not change. However, Marten and Sancholuz noted that the population in the region was rapidly urbanizing and its habits were changing. They concluded that if the entire population in the region had the same dietary habits as the present urban residents in the region then the carrying capacity in each scenario would have to be reduced by 30 per cent. The different estimates by Marten and Sancholuz emphasize the uncertainty associated with many calculations of carrying capacity. A large number of factors can vary, making precision and accuracy difficult to realize (Street, 1969).

7.4 BIOPHYSICAL CAPACITY

Research on biophysical carrying capacity has covered a range of aspects. Investigators have sought to determine critical thresholds beyond which physical (soils, water) and biological (vegetation, wildlife) phenomena are altered by human activity. The work has been split among inquiries about the trampling effect of hiking on trails or skiing on mountain slopes, user impact on parks, campgrounds and picnic areas, and consequences of transportation or industrial activity on fragile ecosystems. Research designs have ranged from one-shot case studies, experimental designs, to longitudinal inquiries (section 2.3.2).

Studies concerning the effects of trampling and other manifestations of public pressure on trails have been pursued in numerous places. Studies have included investigations of trampling effects in the English Lake District (Coleman, 1981), in the Andean areas of central Chile (Hoffman and Alliende, 1982), and in backcountry areas in the United States (McDonnell, 1981; Cole, 1981; 1983a; 1983b; 1985; Leonard, McMahon and Kehoe, 1985).

A pioneering study on the effects of trampling on vegetation and soils was conducted by Bates (1935) in England. Surveys of footpaths as well as of the adjacent terrain were done during both the summer and winter. Data were collected concerning the frequency of occurrence and areal extent of vegetation species. Bates discovered that many species of plant on trails were damaged or even completely destroyed by treading action. On the other hand, new species which were more resistant to trampling gradually became established along the trails. Concerning the soil, he noted a significant difference for density and moisture content between the trails and adjacent terrain although no differences occurred regarding chemical composition.

Bates supplemented his observation of trampling effects on trails and control areas with other data based on simulation. In one experiment, certain grasses were grown in separate and repeated strips. Some strips were trodden upon daily, and comparisons were made with untrodden strips. In a different experiment, Bates imitated the trampling action of a hoof in wet weather by frequently cutting the grass with a disc harrow. This procedure and the one based on trampling provided guidelines as to which species were hardy and which would fail.

Bates' study, although simple in many ways, established the principles upon which much subsequent research has been based. The use of experimental designs became common. Observations were taken for areas subjected to human activity or for areas in which such activity was simulated. The results from these 'treatment' areas were then compared with results from areas which did not experience any activity. Subsequently, treatment areas have been given different attributes in order to determine alternative methods to combat deterioration. Bates' approach was to cultivate different types of grasses. This procedure is now known as *cultural treatment*, and includes intensive vegetation management. A second procedure focuses upon *surfacing*, using gravel or asphalt on heavily used trails or sites. A third is based upon *design*. Movement patterns are anticipated and then channelled away from fragile ecosystems through the use of barriers (curbs, rocks, shrubbery) (Beardsley, Herrington and Wagar, 1974; 281).

Cole (1985) has argued that in wilderness and similar areas the most pronounced impact of recreational use occurs on trails and at campsites. While some disturbance can be eliminated or minimized, he concluded that much of the vegetation and soil change on trails and campsites is inevitable. Wherever trampling happens, vegetation and soil are disturbed. Cole concluded that the magnitude of change is influenced by the amount and frequency of trampling, type of use, season of use, and site conditions. In most areas, magnitude and frequency of use cause the greatest impact. Fortunately, these variables are the most amenable to control by the resource manager.

In Cole's view, the best way to determine the effect of amount and frequency of trampling is through experimental applications of controlled amounts of trampling on previously undisturbed sites. Furthermore, realistic simulation requires controlled trampling to be applied over several years. A study of the impacts of hiker trampling on forest trails illustrates the research guidelines suggested by Cole.

Leonard, McMahon and Kehoe (1985) conducted a trampling

study which was intended to relate given intensities of use to observed changes in the vegetation and soils of two previously undisturbed forest systems. The study was conducted in the White Mountain National Forest in New Hampshire using simulated trails and study plots on two sites. One site was in a mixed hardwood–softwood stand at about 590 m elevation. The second site was in a coniferous forest at approximately 900 m elevation.

The procedure used an experimental design. Three 30-m long, 1-m wide trails were established at each site. Two were trampled a specified number of times and one remained as a control. Trampling occurred once a week, over a 10-week period from June to August 1978. One trail at each site was designated as 'high use' and received more trampling than the other trail categorized as 'low use'. The trampling was done by four field assistants, ranging from 55 to 73 kg.

To monitor changes in ground cover over time, 10 1-m by 0.5-m study plots were randomly located on each trail. Each plot was photographed at nine different times. During 1978, photographs were taken before trampling began and then at five, two-week intervals as trampling was conducted over the summer. Each plot was photographed again in each of June 1979, 1980 and 1981. The purposes of the photoplot analysis were to monitor the survival and eventual recovery of plant species, to determine what level of trampling caused plant mortality and to determine trail width and soil compaction.

A soil test penetrometer was used to monitor soil compaction. Measurements were taken at the conclusion of the trampling period as well as the following spring. The purposes were to determine the levels of compaction relative to the amount of trampling, the levels of compaction across the width of the trail and the recovery of soils by the following spring.

The findings revealed that the greatest increase in plant mortality occurred at a low intensity of trampling, with very slow increases in mortality at higher intensities. This finding was in agreement with the results from other studies. Revegetation of the trails was rapid. For many species, the percentage of recovery was nearly 100 per cent. The soil also showed compaction after the initial trampling, with compaction changing only slightly as the amount of use continued. Recovery of the soil could not be ascertained from the follow-up observations the next spring, as a longer time for observation was deemed necessary.

Biophysical impacts may be dispersed over a larger area as well, such as when water quality is altered as a result of human use. Werner, Leonard and Crevelling (1985) studied the effects of recreational use on water quality in the St Regis Canoe Area in the Adirondack Mountains of New York. From the more than 50 lakes which are found in the St Regis Canoe Area, the investigators studied one lake which had received moderately heavy camping use at about 35 sites and another lake that had been closed to camping since 1968.

Eight water sampling sites were established on the first lake and one on the second lake which served as a control.

Surface water samples were taken in 1976 and 1977 at all stations on a biweekly basis throughout the summer and on a monthly basis during the balance of the year. The amount of recreational use (overnight and day use) at the treatment lake was recorded by use of sign-in registers and direct head counts when water samples were being taken.

Water quality samples were taken for variables that might be altered by either the discharge of human waste products directly or indirectly as leachate from the soils into the lake or by soil runoff from bare campgrounds into the lake. The variables for which data were assembled were: transparency, pH, conductivity, total dissolved solids, total alkalinity, dissolved oxygen, nitrate, phosphate, calcium, magnesium, sodium, potassium, temperature and fecal coliforms. The data were collected to facilitate three types of comparisons: comparison of sites undergoing different levels of use at approximately the same time, comparison of a site before the busy season with that same site during and after the heavy-use season, and comparison between the treatment and control lakes.

The findings showed little statistical relationship between use and any of the water quality parameters. Variations in levels of nutrients over the study period were small. Their variation appeared to be due to normal climatic influences as well as lake mixing during spring and autumn turnover rather than recreational use patterns.

The previous examples provide an indication of the approaches which are being used to analyse biophysical carrying capacity of natural environments. In these studies, trade-offs have to be made. As Cole (1983, 1–2) has noted, a good monitoring system should have several characteristics: meaningful measures of impacts; reliable and sensitive measurement techniques; manageable costs; and replicable sampling procedure. Cole observed that trade-offs are often made between reliability/sensitivity and cost. Increasingly precise techniques demand more time, particularly if sample sites are numerous. This requires a decision as to whether it is best to obtain more precise data at a smaller number of sites or else less precise data spread over a larger number of sites. The examples used here indicate how these problems have been addressed in studies of trampling and water quality. The same issues are encountered in studies of impacts on campgrounds (Bratton, Strombergh and Harmon, 1982; Cole, 1981; 1983b; Cole and Fichtler, 1983) or from industrial development (Babb and Bliss, 1974).

7.5 SOCIAL CARRYING CAPACITY

Geographers have had an active role in studies of social

carrying capacity. In this section, attention is given to work centred upon recreation-oriented problems. In such research, geographers have had several objectives. One has been to identify the variables which influence the satisfaction of recreationists. Attention has been directed towards an array of biophysical, economic, social and behavioural variables, with special emphasis given to the role of crowding and congestion as determinants of satisfaction. The practical rationale for this type of research has been expressed by Davis (1963; 248) who commented that

> The question of carrying capacity too often sounds like a physical problem when its heart is really a matter of interpersonal quality effects ... we must have more information about the recreationist's thresholds of sensitivity to each other's actions.

The other objective has related to determining alternative ways by which user reactions can be incorporated into management programmes. This relates to the topic of public involvement covered in Chapters 5 and 12.

La Page (1963) drew attention to the need for studies of social carrying capacity for recreational planning, but it was Lucas (1964) who provided one of the first empirical studies on this topic. This study, by a geographer, is generally acknowledged as a benchmark by investigators in many disciplines. Lucas was interested in determining whether boundaries of officially designated wilderness areas corresponded to the wilderness image held by recreationists using the Boundary Waters Canoe Area (BWCA) in Minnesota. He examined three elements of environmental perception of the BWCA for both resource managers and visitors: (1) the importance of wilderness qualities relative to other potential uses; (2) the area considered to be wilderness; and (3) the essential characteristics of wilderness and acceptable types of use. The third element came to grips with such issues as what degree of crowding and types of activity had positive or negative effects on the recreation experience.

Recreational visitors to the BWCA were interviewed in 1960 and 1961. A random sample was selected during both seasons, and almost 300 groups of recreationists were questioned with a formal questionnaire. Respondents were chosen from random checks at all access points to the BWCA, and by visits to campgrounds. The resource manager respondents were drawn from the staff of the Superior National Forest in which the BWCA is located, regional and national forest officers, as well as some state and county officials.

Lucas' analysis of resource managers' perceptions showed that the area viewed as wilderness had changed with alterations to the official boundary. Views also changed concerning appropriate uses. In contrast, the users differed among themselves and with the resource managers on all three points: importance of wilderness, area of wilderness, and essential wilderness qualities.

Wilderness was a major attraction for canoeists, was important to roadside campers and was secondary for all other users. Of the canoeists, differences arose as to what constituted the main attraction. Paddlers saw travelling and camping in wilderness as the main feature of the area whereas motorized canoeists were attracted by the opportunity for fishing.

The area perceived as wilderness was determined through direct questions and a map exercise. Each group was asked at the place where the interview took place whether they felt that they were in the wilderness there and where the wilderness had started. Wilderness was not defined for the respondents in these questions – they were allowed to apply their own interpretations when answering. During the interview, the route of each group was mapped. The respondents then indicated for each lake or road segment whether it was wilderness or non-wilderness. By aggregating the mapped data, Lucas produced wilderness-perception maps for each type of group (paddle and motorized canoeists; day users; auto campers; boat campers; resort guests; private cabin users). Isolines were drawn to indicate the proportion of visitors perceiving a given place as wilderness (Fig. 7.1).

The paddling canoeists emerged as the most demanding group, with a perceived wilderness area smaller than the officially designated area. All other groups were similar to each other, and perceived the wilderness as much larger than the official area. The paddlers were also more bothered by meeting other groups. Sixty-one per cent disliked meeting motor boats while only one group of paddlers disliked meeting other paddlers. Paddlers also disliked heavily used areas, but were less bothered by logging activity if it were screened from their routes. In contrast, motor boaters did not distinguish between different types of encounters and accepted high recreation levels and presence of roads.

In drawing conclusions, Lucas echoed Zimmermann (Ch. 1) by observing that 'all resources are defined by human perception'. He argued that his results indicated rethinking about wilderness was needed, since two principal wildernesses (paddling canoeists' and motorboaters') existed as well as an intermediate wilderness perceived by motor canoeists. None of these wildernesses correlated with the official wilderness designated by management policies.

Lucas suggested that such differences could be a key to increasing carrying capacity. The canoeists' wilderness was easily destroyed by heavy use, especially boat use, while the boaters accepted heavier levels of use and valued fishing more highly than wilderness. The motorboaters also entered their wilderness before reaching areas favoured by canoeists. Using this evidence, Lucas felt that canoeists' satisfaction could be raised, without hurting motorboaters' enjoyment, by concentrating new access points and campgrounds inside the motorboaters' perceived wilderness but away from that of the canoeists. Thus, by his research, Lucas was able to identify, in a

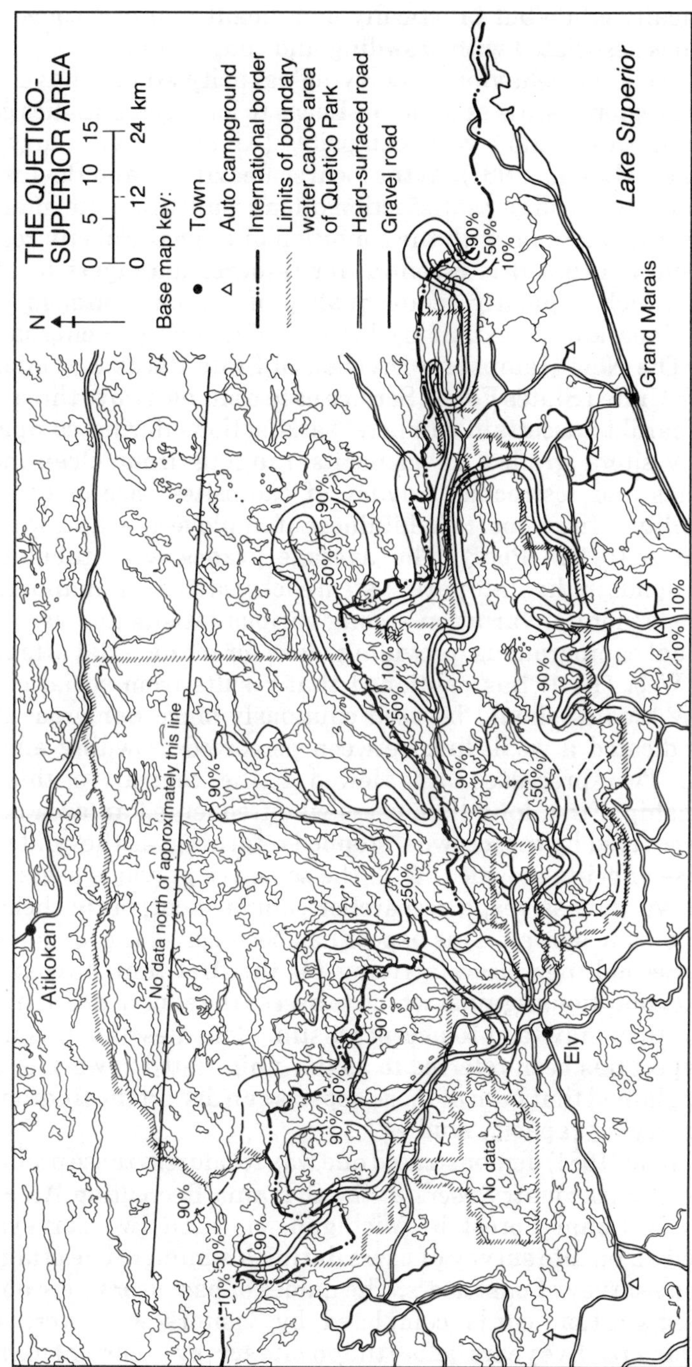

Fig. 7.1 Wilderness perception of the Boundary Waters Canoe Area (*from Lucas, 1964*)

theoretically crude but practically significant manner, some critical user zones associated with crowding and congestion.

Social or behavioural carrying capacity studies have ranged from the regional scale analysis of Lucas to local scale studies centred upon user satisfaction with campsites (Knudson and Curry, 1981; LaPage and Bevins, 1981). At the local scale LaPage and Bevins (1981) have noted that camper satisfaction often results from the interaction of users' expectations with the condition of the natural environment. They believed that it is essential for resource managers to conduct studies which explicitly relate quality of the environment, visitor expectations, and the extent to which satisfactions are being satisfied.

The New Hampshire Division of State Parks in conjunction with the United States Forest Service used a simple two to three minute 'report card' to ascertain campers' satisfactions during campground visits. Visitors graded 14 elements ranging from cleanliness of campsites and restrooms, privacy of campsites, size of campsites, availability of fire wood, to helpfulness of employees on a scale from 'A' (Excellent) to 'E' (Poor). The average grades were tabulated for campgrounds in the state park system each year. In this manner, it was possible to monitor variation among various satisfaction variables at individual campgrounds, providing ideas for managerial attention.

West (1981) has cautioned that results from social carrying capacity studies should be used cautiously since numerous studies have indicated a weak link between perceived crowding and satisfaction. Two processes are viewed to be central to this weak relationship. First, long-time users who frequented an area before it was discovered by the 'crowds' stopped returning, as they did not like the sense of being crowded. With the sensitive previous users having withdrawn themselves, a researcher cannot incorporate their views into an on-site survey. This aspect has been called the 'displacement effect'. Second, new users arriving for the first time have no other baseline conditions against which to assess the experience at a site. As a result, they may tend to accept existing densities of use as normal. This aspect has been referred to as the 'uninitiated newcomer effect'. West explained that both of these aspects can distort the findings from social carrying capacity studies.

West (1981) demonstrated one way to address these problems in a study of backcountry users at the Sylvania Recreation Area in the Ottawa National Forest in Michigan. He used two surveys. One involved an on-site survey of users during a summer. The other was a telephone survey of past users. The names of past users were obtained from registration cards completed by visitors who were at the recreation area five years before the on-site survey of current users. One difficulty with this procedure was that people were being asked to remember experiences from five years previously, creating possible problems of recall. The findings showed that there were no sharp differences between previous users who had stopped visiting the area and uninitiated new visitors regarding their perception of crowding. Furthermore, crowding was not a significant factor in leading to previous users deciding not to return.

These findings, as West stressed, should be used cautiously. Use levels at the two study intervals could be quite different. West explained that one disadvantage of the first year used was that the use levels in that year were quite low and thus the proportion of persons feeling crowded also was low. He noted that the displacement phenomena might not occur until higher densities are reached, suggesting the existence of critical thresholds before the displacement effect comes into play. In this regard, Stankey (1980; 25) has suggested that the most appropriate research design for addressing such issues would be a longitudinal design in which the behaviour of specific individuals and groups would be followed over time. Because of the cost and difficulty of achieving this, however, we often resort to two alternatives. One uses the same site at two different time periods, drawing random sample of users at each period. The other uses two comparable sites at the same time period, again drawing a random sample from each.

Wilderness recreational use often is distributed unevenly. A few access points receive the majority of use, and a small proportion of the trail system is utilized. The resulting pattern generates crowding and congestion, which may reduce the satisfaction of many visitors. The manager's task is to redistribute some of the use.

Lucas (1981) explained that managers have two main types of methods to influence use patterns. Direct methods include rationing of use, either for an entire area, for access points, or for campsites. This approach is viewed to be heavy handed, authoritarian and administratively costly. Indirect methods are less obtrusive, and can range from making selected access points more or less accessible to providing information to visitors to influence their choice of route or campground.

Lucas viewed the use of information as appealing since it is non-authoritarian and is usually viewed as positive rather than as negative control. A key question then becomes to determine the effectiveness of information as a tool to redistribute use. Using registration records, Lucas (1981) surveyed backcountry visitors to the Selway-Bitteroot Wilderness in Montana to find out how influential were the brochures made available at the trail register stations in the area. The finding was that the brochures had little impact in reducing the concentration of use on a few popular trails. Lucas concluded that the ineffectiveness was due to a too narrow focus in the brochure, too limited information about the overused trails and campsites, and user doubt regarding the accuracy of the information provided.

Another problem regarding the effectiveness of information is the effectiveness of unstaffed registration stations. If people do not stop at the registration stations they will not pick up the information.

No matter how attractive or persuasive the information is, if it is not seen it is not likely to influence decisions. Recognition of this potential problem has generated a number of studies about volunteer visitor registration or self-issued permits (Leatherberry and Lime, 1981; Lucas, 1981; 1983; Lucas and Kovalicky, 1981; Krumpe and Brown, 1982; Petersen, 1985).

The questions pursued in such studies are straightforward. Are unstaffed registration stations effective in obtaining information from users? Are some types of users more likely to register than others? Do different designs and locations generate different responses?

Most of the studies use a similar procedure. An electric traffic counter and a synchronized camera are located out of sight and are camouflaged as well as possible. The US Forest Service has explicitly addressed the legality of such a procedure for data collection, and determined that it is acceptable. In addition, to respect the privacy of visitors, the camera was located at a sufficient distance that individuals could not be identified beyond being able to count the number in a party and being able to determine whether people were travelling by foot or by horse. Once the necessary information was taken from the film, it was destroyed. In the various studies, the compliance rate at the registration stations varied from 20 to 88 per cent. These findings have stimulated further efforts to improve the siting and design of registration stations and information displays (Petersen, 1985).

The research on carrying capacity has generated two recent conceptual approaches for wilderness recreation planning. Both the United States Forest Service and the Bureau of Land Management have developed a system for inventorying, planning and managing their recreation resources. This first system is based upon the concept of a recreation opportunity spectrum (Buist and Hoots, 1982; Clark, 1982; Driver, Brown, Stankey and Gregoire, 1987).

The recreation opportunity spectrum defines a range or spectrum of opportunities to meet a mix of visitor activities, settings and experience preferences. The rationale behind the spectrum approach is that people participate in preferred recreation activities, within selected environmental settings, to realize satisfactory experiences. The diversity of activities, settings and experiences has been combined into six classes along a spectrum from primitive, semi-primitive non-motorized, semi-primitive motorized, roaded natural, rural, to urban. Each hectare of land and water in a planning region is allocated into one of these classes as is done in other resource inventory systems (Ch. 3).

Planners do not inventory experiences directly. Instead, five indicator criteria relating to experience are applied to the setting and activity-based categories. The criteria are remoteness, size of area, evidence of humans, use density and managerial noticeability.

Each recreational opportunity spectrum category thus provides a set of experience opportunities which are a product of the types of settings available. Furthermore, each setting provides for appropriate recreation activities, where 'appropriate' is defined as activities which the resource can physically sustain on the basis of the experience outcome.

As Clark (1982) has commented, the spectrum approach helps to clarify relationships among recreational settings, activities and experiences. It accepts that opportunities sought by recreationists range from readily accessible and highly developed areas to undeveloped primitive areas in remote locations. The system by itself does not make decisions. However, it is a tool to help recreationists to make choices about where to go and what to do in harmony with their expectations and preferences. For the managers, the system helps to avoid polarization and strategies that overlook the legitimate value of 'middle ground' options. The recreation opportunity spectrum is not viewed as a cookbook with a specific set of rules, numerical standards or coefficients. In this manner, it reflects the conclusions from carrying capacity research that it is unrealistic and even undesirable to search for a single standard or number to determine the number and mix of users in an area.

The Limits of Acceptable Change (LAC) system is the second approach which has emerged for determining acceptable and appropriate resource and social conditions in recreation settings. It is viewed as 'a reformulation of the recreational carrying capacity concept, with the primary emphasis now on the conditions desired in the area rather than on how much use an area can tolerate' (Stankey *et al.*, 1985; i). It represents a shift from trying to prevent human-induced change to deciding how much change will be allowed to occur, where, and actions needed to control it.

As described by Stankey *et al.* (1985; 3), the LAC system involves four basic components: (1) the specification of acceptable and achievable resource and social conditions, defined by a series of measurable parameters, (2) an analysis of the relationship between existing conditions and those judged acceptable, (3) identification of management actions necessary to achieve those conditions, and (4) a programme of monitoring and evaluation of management effectiveness. These four components are operationalized through nine stages (Fig. 7.2). The definition and description of opportunity classes in the second stage follows the recreation opportunity spectrum system outlined previously. Stankey *et al.* (1985) stated that the LAC approach is not a new idea but is derived from a management-by-objectives approach to planning.

7.6 IMPLICATIONS FOR RESOURCE MANAGEMENT

The research has several implications for management and

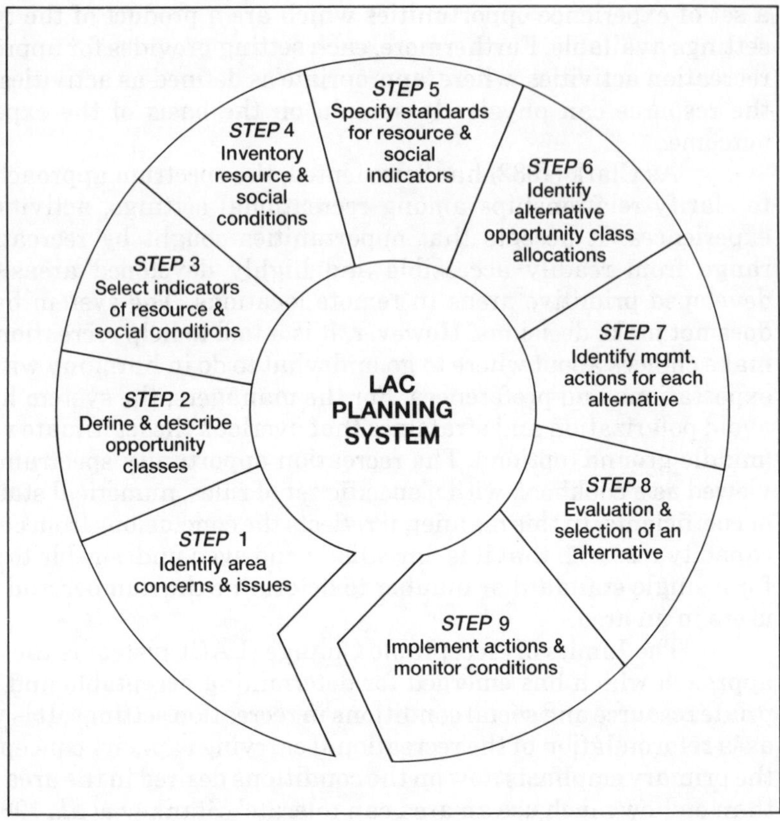

Fig. 7.2 The Limits of Acceptable Change (LAC) planning system (*after Stankey et al.*)

policy. The concept of carrying capacity has an intuitive appeal, suggesting the existence of critical thresholds beyond which serious problems are encountered. However, the research has shown that such thresholds are elusive to identify, primarily because the thresholds shift depending upon assumptions made regarding future technological innovations, social values and other variables.

Thus, while on the surface the concept of carrying capacity appears to be of direct managerial value, the research experience and results should impress upon policy makers the considerable uncertainty associated with any carrying capacity estimates. If that message were received and understood, then policy makers might be more cautious in using the output of capacity studies to substantiate policy choices.

Notwithstanding these somewhat pessimistic observations, carrying capacity research can be very helpful for resource managers. While any given estimate may be subject to error, if a range of estimates reflecting different assumptions is provided then the decision makers have alternatives to consider. And again, while the specific details may not be accurate, the general patterns revealed should help the managers to visualize the range of options. By using the carrying capacity estimates as scenarios rather than as predictions, managers could use them to identify possible futures. Decisions then could be taken to try to ensure that the most preferred 'future' was achieved.

The ongoing research has shown that the concept of carrying capacity may be used in a variety of management situations. Calculations about the productivity of the land lead to estimations as to the population which can be supported in given regions. In areas where shortages of foreign currency make importation of food a costly strategy, the results of carrying capacity research are pertinent to policies ranging from population control to agricultural production.

In a different context, calculations of both biophysical and social capacity may be used in management of general recreation to wilderness areas. During the 1980s in the United States, a significant shift occurred. Rather than trying to eliminate or minimize human-induced change in natural systems as a result of recreational activities, the managers decided to focus upon what change should be viewed as appropriate relative to different settings, activities and opportunities. In this regard, alternative capacity scenarios help to highlight alternatives for the managers. After selecting a scenario, then the managers can assess specific actions such as zoning to help realize the desired end results (Downie, 1984).

7.7 IMPLICATIONS FOR RESEARCH

Carrying capacity research has been approached mainly through the ecological or man–environment tradition by geographers. The nature of the problem suggests, however, that more work based in the spatial analysis tradition needs to be pursued, especially involving spatial distributions and spatial interactions. The ongoing work has drawn both upon the positivist and phenomenological research philosophies. Those studying biophysical capacity usually apply the positivist viewpoint. It is perhaps for this reason that work on the biophysical side of the problem shows the greatest accumulation of knowledge. The phenomenological perspective has proven particularly valuable when studying perception of crowding and congestion in recreation as well as when investigating the role of differing cultural values in agriculture. The application of both research philosophies to these problems suggests that they do not always have to conflict. Indeed, the insights produced from research using the different vantage points may be complementary and supportive.

Research also reveals the necessity of interdisciplinary studies. Biologists, foresters and soil scientists have made substantial contributions in biophysical capacity studies. In social carrying capacity studies, geographers have been most active. In some instances geographers have completed pioneering or benchmark studies. Continuing progress will undoubtedly require combined research efforts from geographers, economists, sociologists, psychologists, anthropologists, biologists, soil scientists and foresters.

Regarding types of studies, emphasis has been upon description and explanation of processes accounting for varying carrying capacities in different areas. Numerous investigators have indicated that their ultimate goal is prediction, but that level is not yet within grasp and may never be attained given all of the assumptions which must be made. A 'theory of carrying capacity' appears to be some distance away. Nevertheless, most researchers offer prescriptions concerning alternative measures which might be taken. Although lacking a theoretical base, many of these prescriptions offer potential for enhancing carrying capacity. This aspect is encouraging, since resource managers are unable to wait for development of theory in this area before making decisions about how resources are to be allocated.

Basic research considerations have been confronted, and several instructive lessons are available to the analyst. Perhaps the most important is the amenability of this problem to the application of experimental research designs. Investigators have shown imagination in developing designs which are both manipulative and non-manipulative. As well, research in both biophysical and social capacity demonstrates the way in which multiple measurement techniques can and should be used in data collection. Biophysical studies have effectively combined field studies with simulation, and social inquiries have drawn upon direct observation, social surveys and simulation. Another measurement feature which arises is the recognition of thresholds, standards and indicators (Ch. 10). In biophysical analyses, investigators have often been able to measure these at interval and ratio levels. The social studies generally reach the ordinal level when trying to identify these critical points.

The overriding consideration in carrying capacity research is the need for subjectivity, whether the approach be positivist or phenomenological. As most writers testify, the final decision about carrying capacity is always an arbitrary one. Someone, somewhere, sometime, must decide what constitutes an undesirable change in vegetation and soils, or an unacceptable level of crowding or congestion. To date, resource analysis studies have provided useful insights to assist managers in reaching such decisions in specific regions. However, variations from place to place and time to time inhibit the development of universally applicable guidelines or predictive skills. If this proves to be true, then the outlook for development of theory is not bright.

Ethical issues also come to the fore in carrying capacity studies, especially those of the perceptual nature. If the researcher wishes to obtain data from visitors to a wilderness area, he runs the risk of infringing upon an aspect that attracted the visitors – isolation from other people. Once the data are collected, the analyst then must confront the ethical issues associated with attempts to influence or control people's attitudes and behaviour. These are tasks that cannot be undertaken lightly, given their potential for affecting other lives and aspirations.

CHAPTER 8

HAZARDS AND RISK ASSESSMENT

8.1 INTRODUCTION

Hazards and risk assessment research is based firmly in the man–environment or ecological tradition. Many investigators relate their inquiries to Barrows' (1923) interpretation of geography as the science of human ecology, with emphasis upon the 'relationships existing between natural environments and the distribution and activities of man'. Barrows' overriding concern was study of 'man's adjustment to the environment', from which he was optimistic that generalizations and principles could be derived.

In the field of resource analysis, the study of hazards has achieved substantial cumulative knowledge concerning the significance of variables and relationships in man's adjustment to the environment (Rossi *et al.*, 1983). A research paradigm, simple yet broad in scope, has been used around the world in the search for the generalizations and principles to which Barrows alluded. At the same time, research on this problem has led to one of the most visible and significant impacts by the geographical profession on resource management policies and practices.

The next section (8.2) describes the research paradigm, and outlines how it evolved from the work and commitment of one scholar's concern for flood-related problems. Attention is then directed to the way in which the paradigm has been applied to a selected range of individual natural hazards (section 8.3). Not all research has focused upon single, natural hazards in one place or region. Some investigators have attempted to identify the 'hazardousness of a place' by examining a variety of hazards (natural and man-made) associated with an area (section 8.4). Another type of research has involved collaborative studies in which investigators have assessed how adjustment patterns have developed relative to specific hazards among different cultures throughout the world (section 8.5). Others have concentrated upon the impact and adjustments resulting from man-made hazards, notably pollution (section 8.6). Research activity has evolved to consider technological hazards such as pesticides, transport of dangerous chemicals and nuclear power (section 8.7) as well as the general field of risk assessment (section 8.8). After reviewing these different research activities, attention is turned to considering the significance of their results for resource management (section 8.9) and for the conduct of research itself (section 8.10).

8.2 EVOLUTION OF A RESEARCH PARADIGM

Numerous investigators have outlined the characteristics of and trends in hazards research (Burton and Kates, 1964a; White, 1973; 1974a; Mitchell, J.K., 1974a; White and Haas, 1975; Burton, Kates and White, 1968; 1978; O'Riordan, 1986; Whyte, 1986). These reviews all confirm that the research originated from concern with a specific resource problem. From such a practical concern, subsequent research led to development of a research paradigm and a model of how man confronts risk and uncertainty.

The research originated from observation of flood plain management in the United States. In 1936, the Flood Control Act was passed and generated substantial expenditures on dams, dykes, levees and other structural measures to reduce flood damage. Interest in this process prompted White (1942) to examine the range of alternatives for flood loss reduction. White later initiated another study with the objective of documenting changes in the urban occupance of flood-plains in the United States since the enactment of the Flood Control Act of 1936. When the report was published, the evidence was startling (White *et al.*, 1958). The principal finding was that although more than 5 billion dollars had been spent in flood reduction measures, damages from floods had been steadily increasing. These findings prompted White to pose a series of questions. What alternative measures could be applied to flood reduction programmes? What would be their social and economic impact? What would be the efficiency and equity of different approaches at national, regional and local scales? As White (1973; 194) later wrote, these questions defined a general research, problem: 'How does man adjust to risk and uncertainty in natural systems, and what does understanding of that process imply for public policy?' This basic question, relating closely to Barrows' concept of human ecology, remains the underpinning of most hazards research.

The basic research paradigm used in the 1958 report and in many subsequent studies has not changed significantly. Restated by White (1974a; 4), the paradigm includes five objectives:

1. Estimate the extent of human occupance in areas subject to extreme events in nature.

2. Determine the range of possible adjustments by social groups to these extreme events.
3. Examine how people perceive the extreme events and resultant hazard.
4. Examine the process of choosing damage-reducing adjustments.
5. Estimate what would be the effects of varying public policy upon that set of responses.

Table 8.1 Natural hazards by principal causal agents (*from Burton and Kates, 1964a*)

Geophysical		Biological	
Climatic and meteorological	Geological and geomorphic	Floral	Faunal
Blizzards and snow	Avalanches	Fungal diseases *For example:* Athlete's foot Dutch elm Wheat stem rust Blister rust	Bacterial and Viral diseases *For example:* Influenza Malaria Typhus Bubonic plague Venereal disease Rabies Hoof and mouth disease Tobacco mosaic
Droughts	Earthquakes		
Floods	Erosion (including soil erosion and shore and beach erosion)		
Fog		Infestations *For example:* Weeds Phreatophytes Water hyacinth	
Frost	Landslides		
Hailstorms	Shifting sand		
Heat waves	Tsunamis	Hay fever	
Hurricanes	Volcanic eruptions	Poison ivy	Infestations *For example:* Rabbits Termites Locusts Grasshoppers
Lightning strokes and fires			
Tornadoes			Venomous animal bites

These five objectives, initially applied to flooding, have served to guide research in a wide array of hazards (Table 8.1). The initial findings that damage was increasing despite increased levels of expenditures on preventive measures, has led researchers to examine systematically the ideal range of possible adjustments (Table 8.2).

White and other researchers stated that a hazard could not exist apart from a human response to it. Human initiative and choice were an essential component of a hazard. That is, floods would not be hazardous if people were not occupying floodplains. Droughts would not be as devastating if individuals did not attempt to farm drought-prone areas. This observation led to questions as to the reasons why man persisted in occupying areas that were hazardous. The traditional

Table 8.2 Theoretical range of adjustments to geophysical events (*from Burton, Kates, and White, 1968*)

Class of Adjustment	**Event**		
	Earthquakes	Floods	Snow
Affect the cause	No known way of altering the earthquake mechanism	Reduce flood flows by: land-use treatment cloud seeding	Change geographical distribution by cloud seeding
Modify the hazard	Stable site selection: soil and slope stabilization; sea wave barriers; fire protection	Control flood flows by: reservoir storage; levees; channel improvement; flood fighting	Reduce impact by snow fences; snow removal; salting and sanding of highways
Modify loss potential	Warning systems; emergency evacuation and preparation; building design; land-use change; permanent evacuation	Warning systems; emergency evacuation and preparation; building design; land-use change; permanent evacuation	Forecasting; rescheduling; inventory control; building design; seasonal adjustments (snow tyres, chains); seasonal migration; designation of snow emergency routes
Adjust to losses			
Spread the losses	Public relief; subsidized insurance	Public relief; subsidized insurance	Public relief; subsidized insurance
Plan for losses	Insurance and reserve funds	Insurance and reserve funds	Insurance and reserve funds
Bear the losses	Individual loss bearing	Individual loss bearing	Individual loss bearing

assumption of 'Economic Man' used in location models did not appear applicable since individuals often did not seem to have a good understanding of the environment in which they were settling or functioning. The outcome was an exploration of alternative decision models that might account for human behaviour in hazardous places. A major innovation came when Simon's (1959) model of 'bounded rationality' and 'satisficing' was used in place of economic optimization models to describe and explain behaviour. This model, used by Kates (1962) in studying the perception and behaviour of floodplain residents in La Follette, Tennessee, helped to account for how individuals perceived a hazard, and how they perceived alternative adjustments. As White (1973, 200–1) commented later, the concept of bounded rationality and associated empirical work indicated that

> a resource-management decision may be hypothesized to involve the interaction of human systems and physical systems in terms of adjustment to a particular hazard. The interaction is represented as a choice-searching process as affected by personality, information, decision situation and managerial role.

The importance of how people perceive hazards and the range of adjustments led to greater attention being given to psychological concepts and techniques as well as to interdisciplinary investigations between geographers and psychologists. Concepts such as perceptions, attitudes, motivations and personality were addressed. This fusing of behavioural concepts and techniques represented some of the earliest empirical work in what has become recognized as the behavioural approach in geography.

After nearly a decade of hazards research, the principal innovator, White, and two colleagues, Burton and Kates, launched a collaborative study of cross-cultural adjustments to natural hazards. A common research strategy and questionnaire were designed (Natural Hazards Research Working Paper No. 16, 1970) and applied to a variety of hazards throughout the world. This work, conducted under the auspices of the International Geographical Union Commission on Man and Environment, is covered in more detail in section 8.5.

Natural hazards continue to create major problems for mankind. The great devastation and loss of life which can be caused are emphasized by dramatic extreme events such as the earthquake in Mexico City in 1985 or by the volcanic eruption in Columbia and the escape of toxic natural gas from a volcanic lake in Cameroon both during 1986. Thus, natural hazards do and should receive considerable attention. However, other research thrusts have been initiated. In parallel with the international collaborative research on natural hazards, some investigators began to focus upon man-made hazards, such as air and water pollution. This work is described in section 8.6. Evolving from the investigations of man-made hazards has been recognition of a more general research and management issue, that of technological hazards. The hazardous nature of technology is epitomized by events ranging from use of herbicides and pesticides on thousands of individual farms to the malfunction of nuclear power plants (Three Mile Island, 1979; Chernobyl, 1986) or chemical plants (Bhopal, 1984). The ultimate hazard from technology is probably the anticipated 'nuclear winter' following widespread use of nuclear weapons in military conflicts. Examples of work focused upon technological hazards are contained in section 8.7.

Awareness of the consequences of natural hazards, man-made

pollution and technological hazards has prompted some investigators to view all such phenomena as coming under the general umbrella of the assessment of 'risk'. This interest has generated research activity in numerous professions and disciplines. Considerable work has been completed by geographers, and this is examined in section 8.8. This change of focus over time illustrates that while the initial problem triggering research (natural hazards) in this field remains important, the general approach has proven adaptable to other related issues and problems.

8.3 INDIVIDUAL NATURAL HAZARDS

Individual natural hazards may be classified in many different ways. Burton and Kates' (1964a; 414–17) classification is organized on the basis of the principal causal agent and shows what a variety of natural hazards occur (Table 8.1). It is not possible to discuss the research on each of the hazards here. Instead, the early study by White *et al.*, (1958) is used to illustrate the manner in which the research began.

Since concern with increasing flood damages led to the first natural hazard studies, it is appropriate to consider the study by White *et al.* (1958) which documented the paradox of increased damage accompanying increasing expenditures for flood control. The study had two objectives. One was to classify the urban flood situations to facilitate generalizations about them. The other was to measure actual changes which occurred in the use of selected floodplains in the two decades following establishment of the flood control legislation during 1936.

White frankly acknowledged that neither the classification nor the study of selected areas was anything but tentative. Ideally, the classification should have been completed before field work in communities was begun to ensure that the selected communities constituted a representative sample. However, without the benefit of detailed field work it was not known what attributes should be included in the classification system. As a result, both phases of the research proceeded simultaneously rather than the first creating the base for the second.

Based on available information, White's research group discovered that over 1,020 communities in the United States with populations greater than 1,000 had significant flood problems. From these communities, 17 were chosen for detailed field work. The selection process tried to ensure a variety of floodplain situations incorporating a cross-section of population size, rate of population change, size of drainage area, frequency and magnitude of flooding, physiographic setting, width of flood plain, functions performed by the city, types of land uses in the floodplain and types of adjustment to the hazard.

The field research used a number of methods. The flood plain was delimited and present land use was mapped. Occupancy changes were estimated from counting the number of structures and facilities from air photographs taken about 1936 compared to numbers observed during field work in the summer of 1956. Interviews were conducted with local planning and engineering officials as well as with realtors and property owners. The interviewers collected data on the estimated severity of the flood hazard, the status of protective adjustments and the influence of the hazard on land use. Numerous generalizations emerged from the study. In all of the study communities, a net increase in the number of structures in the floodplain was documented, even in cities for which total population had dropped. Both highway and flood protection construction triggered occupation of flood-prone areas. The major reliance upon engineering construction supplemented by other practices encouraged encroachment upon floodplains as people viewed the protected areas as 'safe'. Other practices encouraged encroachment, including underestimation of residual flood hazards, overly optimistic views concerning future adjustments, financial arrangements that reimbursed those relocating on floodplains, and building of highways which stimulated further activity in hazardous locations. With these factors identified, the evidence for steadily increasing damages from flooding in the United States became credible despite White's (1958; 19) caution that 'both sectors of the work were provisional and were intended to lay the groundwork for more precise investigations'.

Two of White's students (Ian Burton, and Robert Kates) extended the work started in the 1950s. As an example, Kates' (1962) inquiry involved detailed analysis of several small communities in the United States. A major study was done at La Follette, Tennessee, with a series of smaller inquiries in five other communities in Indiana (1), Wisconsin (1), California (2) and New York (1). The purpose was to consider alternative adjustments to the flood hazards and to examine the role of attitudes, knowledge and experience in conditioning adjustment strategies. A major intention was to compare the attitudes of residents with those of scientists and technicians concerning the nature of the hazard and alternative adjustments.

Kates paid particular attention to the way in which individuals viewed risks and how they reached decisions to reside in flood-prone areas. As noted earlier, Kates rejected the frequently used model of economic optimization and replaced it with Simon's (1959) notion of bounded rationality. The implication was that man was not viewed as a creature enjoying perfect knowledge, systematically weighing all alternatives and seeking to maximize opportunities but rather as one who had incomplete knowledge, was often unable to compare alternatives, and did not necessarily strive for optimum solutions. The boundedly rational person usually 'satisfied', or accepted alternatives that met minimum goals. Kates also broke decision processes into three categories (conscious, habitual, and unconscious and/or trivial) to explore how individuals approached the risk in an uncertain environment.

Kates followed the general research paradigm mentioned earlier. The extent of the floodplain was delimited. Structures, services and facilities were mapped. Business-owners and residents were interviewed to ascertain their perceptions of the hazard and different adjustments. The way in which adjustments (individual and community) were chosen received attention. A variety of alternative adjustments was identified.

After 241 damage observations and 110 interviews, Kates found that the expectancy of future flooding was related to past flooding experiences but not to age, income or education. He also discovered that those working or residing on the floodplain could be broken into a number of groups. Some did not know about the hazard and expressed no concern. Others knew about the flood hazard, but rationalized that they would not be flooded again. Others expected to experience a flood, but anticipated no loss or minor damages and were not concerned. Still others expected future floods and serious damage. Some were undertaking action to minimize damage, while others were fatalistic. These findings confirmed the prior assumption of boundedly rational beings, and suggested that the most common choice mechanisms were conscious ones.

Following their studies of river floodplain occupancy, Burton and Kates applied the research paradigm to coastal flooding (Burton, Kates and Snead, 1968). They also compared the riverine results with those from coastal areas (Burton and Kates, 1964b). In this comparative work they demonstrated the flexibility of the research paradigm, and illustrated how results from one type of hazard could be related to other hazard situations.

The research approach developed by White and his associates at the University of Chicago has been applied to a variety of individual natural hazards. On a global scale, both floods and droughts cause serious damage, disruption and loss of life. Geographers continue to analyse these two natural hazards. Regarding flooding, research in North America has ranged from assessment of the national flood insurance programme in the United States (Arnell, 1984) to analysis of regional management of metropolitan floodplains (Platt, 1987) and the economic consequences of using non-structural adjustments in communities (Babcock and Mitchell, 1980; Muckleston, Turner and Brainerd, 1981; Bennett and Mitchell, 1983). Work in other developed countries has covered flood risk in Britain (Parker and Penning-Rowsell 1982; Penning-Rowsell *et al.*, 1986; Handmer, J., 1987) as well as property and health damage in Australia (Smith, 1981; Handmer and Smith, 1983; Smith and Handmer, 1986). In the developing nations, flooding often has a serious impact upon food production, and as a result investigators have emphasized studies on agricultural responses and adjustments (Islam, 1980; Churchill and Hutchinson, 1984; Paul, 1984; Banerji, 1985). While the damages from flooding are often immediate and visible, those arising from droughts take longer to appear. Nevertheless, the approach developed by White has been applied in countries as diverse as Kenya (Bernard, 1985), Nigeria (Watts, 1983), Upper Volta (Ofori-Sarpong, 1983) and India (Krishna and Sastri, 1980; Malini, 1981; Naganna and Barai, 1982).

Natural hazards triggered by geological or geomorphological causes create major problems in many world regions. Avalanches and landslides have been the focus for research in New Zealand (Prowse *et al.*, 1981), Poland (Pécsi, 1979), Nepal (Johnson *et al.*, 1982) and Japan (Aniya, 1985). Volcanic eruptions also create a hazard, and the most thoroughly analysed contemporary eruption has been that at Mount St Helens in the United States (Perry and Greene, 1982; Saarinen and Sell, 1985). Earthquakes often cause large-scale damage due to the difficulty in providing advanced warning to inhabitants. This phenomenon has attracted general interest (Hewitt, 1983b; 1984) as well as special interest in the process of reconstruction following a quake. The latter type of research utilizes some type of longitudinal research design, as illustrated by studies in Italy (Geipel, 1982; Alexander, 1984) and Guatemala (Bates *et al.*, 1984). Erosion may also be a hazard, in its own right or in association with flooding, droughts, avalanches, landslides or earthquakes (Moore, 1983; Haigh, 1984).

As suggested by Table 8.1, a primary cause of natural hazards may be biological. Such hazards are exemplified by the Dutch elm disease which killed thousands of trees in Britain and North America (Jones, 1981) as well as by the spread of noxious weeds on freshwater lakes which impair both the fishery and recreational use of the water (Dearden, 1983; Johnstone *et al.*, 1985) or in urban areas which are not maintained (Swaminathan *et al.*, 1985). In responding to the problems created by undesirable weeds, resource managers often turn to herbicides which in turn create technological hazards by introducing persistent and toxic chemicals into the environment (section 8.7). The mix of hazards illustrated by these studies indicates that the framework developed by White for his early studies on flooding is applicable to the analysis of many different individual hazards.

8.4 MULTIPLE HAZARDS IN A PLACE

A review of the hazard literature shows that the majority of research has focused upon single hazards. Hewitt and Burton (1971) introduced an innovation by designing a study which considered 'all-hazards-at-a-place'. This shift of emphasis from single hazards to a variety of geophysical and man-made events reflected a continuing search for more generalized frameworks. As a result, they sought to define the conditions which establish the 'hazardousness' of a regional environment. To achieve this goal, they focused upon the whole spectrum of damaging events in one area and explored their aggregate impact. Data were collected for the part of southwestern Ontario centred upon London. Details were assembled about the magnitude and frequency of damaging events as revealed from available records as well as concerning the types of human adjustments. As in many of the hazard studies, however, Hewitt and Burton had to define what was to be included as a 'hazard'. Their main concern was with infrequent events of substantial magnitude that affected large numbers of people. To operationalize this concept, they used four arbitrary criteria for selecting hazard events.

1. Property damage extended to more than 20 families, or economic losses (including loss of income, a halt to production, and costs of emergency measures), exceeded $50,000.
2. Major disruption to social services occurred, including communications failure and closure of essential facilities or economically important establishments.
3. Sudden 'unscheduled' events which put excessive strain on basic services (police, fire departments, hospitals, public utilities) and/or required calling for men, equipment or funds from other jurisdictions.
4. An event killing 10 or more people or injuring 50 or more people.

Using these criteria, the investigators identified 31 hazards in the London area varying from those which were natural (floods, blizzards, tornadoes, hurricanes), quasi-natural (air and water pollution, illness from chemical spraying or exposure to radiation), to those which were of a financial (unemployment, theft, forced moving), accidental (fire, building collapse, home, airplane, boating or car accidents), or health (major surgery, hospitalization, broken bones) nature. A set of 71 possible adjustments was compiled relative to the variety of hazards.

The strategy of examining a variety of hazards in one area was a significant departure from previous work. As Hewitt and Burton (1971; 146–7 observed, this shifted focus was 'conducive to the search for generality in measurement and in explanatory framework'. They thought that interpreting measures of damage for a range of hazard-generating processes led more directly to understanding adjustment patterns than did concentrating upon a single hazard.

Other analysts have considered the diversity of hazards at a place whether the scale be national or local. At a national scale, Heathcote and Thom (1979) coordinated an assessment of natural hazards in Australia. However, the majority of this type of research has been at the local scale. Thus, Cooke (1984) examined a number of geomorphological hazards (slope failure, soil erosion, sediment transfer) in Los Angeles County. His study is not, and was not intended to be, an evaluation of all hazards in the Los Angeles area, and thus did not consider all geomorphological hazards (earthquakes, coastal erosion) let alone other hazards such as air pollution or fire (Radtke, 1983). However, it does integrate a number of hazards. Preston *et al.* (1983) included a broader range of hazards (flooding, storms, air and water pollution, noise) in their analysis of natural and technological hazards in Hamilton, Ontario. In a similar manner, Gruntfest and Huber (1986) examined the hazards created by floods, several geological phenomena, weather patterns, hazardous wastes and air pollution in the Colorado Springs area. In addition to being oriented to scholars, it also was prepared as a guide to planners and developers when determining how to utilize any given location.

A psychologist who participated in the initial London study subsequently analysed the role of personality variables in affecting the propensity to adjust to hazards. Schiff (1977) noted previous hazard research revealed that although propensity to adjust was strongly correlated with experience with hazards, this variable still did not account for all variation in adjustments. Other variables - age, sex, income, education - had been proven to be even less satisfactory explanatory variables and so she followed other researchers who had considered personality dimensions.

Two dimensions of personality were analysed. The first was 'locus of control' (LOC), a measure of the degree to which people accept responsibility for controlling events which affect them. Persons are classified into two categories. One group represents individuals (internals) who feel that they are responsible for their successes or failures while the other incorporates those (externals) who believe that forces beyond their control - chance, fate, God - determine their lives.

Several studies had produced conflicting results concerning the significance of LOC for predicting adjustment patterns. Sims and Baumann (1972), in studying why tornado death rates are higher in the southern United States than in the Midwest, used LOC in analysing adjustments by respondents in Alabama and Illinois. During interviews, respondents were given a set of sentence-completion stems. For example, a person would be asked to complete the following sentences: 'If a tornado is predicted, I ... '; 'During a tornado, I ... '; 'When a tornado is over, I ... '. The responses would then be classified as to whether the respondent expressed ideas consistent with those of an 'internal' or an 'external'. These responses were contrasted with choices made between a series of paired statements designed by psychologists to tap internal and external personalities. Sims and Baumann discovered that the respondents from Illinois were significantly more internally oriented than their Alabama counterparts, and suggested that this might account for differences in tornado-related death rates. They obtained similar results when comparing responses to hurricanes by residents in Florida, Mississippi and Texas against those of people in Puerto Rico (Baumann and Sims, 1974). In contrast, Kirkby (1972) found no evidence to support the idea that LOC was related to adjustment responses to air pollution based on completion of sentence stems in three British cities. Another study by Fischer (1972) also revealed no relationship between LOC and attitudes toward overpopulation or preferred numbers of children.

The second personality dimension was sensation seeking (SS). Psychologists have proposed that each individual has a preferred level of arousal, and that individuals will change behaviour in order to maintain their arousal level at its preferred state. Several scales have been designed to obtain data concerning sensation seeking. Schiff thought that this aspect deserved attention since it seemed logical that respondents with high arousal levels might be less likely to adopt adjustments to hazards than those with lower levels. This would follow from high-level arousal seekers finding satisfaction in unexpected or unusual events.

During the all-hazards-in-a-place study in London, a sample of residents was interviewed. In addition to obtaining data on socioeconomic characteristics, past experience with hazards, and types of adjustments adopted, information was collected about respondents' locus of control and sensation seeking characteristics. Analysis of the results revealed little if any relationship between the tendency to adopt adjustments and either LOC or SS. Such results, in accordance with those of Kirkby and Fischer, conflicted with the results of the two studies by Sims and Baumann.

Schiff considered in some detail why the results of her study and those of Sim and Baumann differed. She noted that LOC was measured by different techniques in the studies which might account for differences in findings. Also, she identified some potential weaknesses in the work of Sims and Baumann. Despite the negative findings of her results, she concluded that personality variables should not be discarded. Instead, she suggested the major implication was that personality variables other than LOC and SS should be studied since those two seem inadequate as explanatory variables. Her approach, systematically relating ongoing work to previous research, represents the procedure through which hazards investigations have slowly but steadily identified the variables having a bearing on adjustment behaviour.

8.5 COLLABORATIVE RESEARCH

During 1967, a collaborative investigation was initiated by White, Burton and Kates with the objective to 'understand the ways in which man perceives extreme natural events and adjusts to the hazard; to apply this knowledge towards reducing the social cost of these events, and to extend such undertakings to the new complex of largely man-made environmental risks' (Collaborative Research on Natural Hazards, 1971; 1). The intent was to determine the utility of findings from the flood studies for other hazards as well as to extend the range of studies to environments and cultural areas outside of North America, particularly to developing nations. Two major publications have emerged from this work. One presents the results from comparative field observations (White, 1974b) and the other contains the findings from analyses of policies at regional, national and international levels (Burton, Kates and White, 1978).

One goal was to stimulate investigations of a variety of hazards in different countries using a similar approach and questionnaire (Natural Hazards Research Working Paper No. 16, 1970). The actual selection of study areas and collaborators was to a large extent fortuitous. Areas were chosen because of their inherent interest and by the availability of competent personnel to pursue research there (White, 1973: 209). It was hoped that from such studies would 'come a more rigorous and searching testing of a number of hypotheses that slowly have emerged over the years since the first office analysis was made of the range of adjustments to floods' (White, 1973; 209).

The principal investigators summarized the results of earlier research in the form of six hypotheses (Natural Hazards Research Working Paper No. 16, 1970). These were:

1. Human occupance that persists in areas of recurrent hazard is justified in the view of the occupants for the following reasons: superior economic opportunity, lack of alternative opportunities, short-term time horizons, and high ratios of reserves to potential loss.
2. Three types of response may be characterized as:
   (1) *Folk or preindustrial*, involving a wide range of adjustments which require more modifications in behaviour in harmony with nature than control of nature, are flexible and easily abandoned, are low in capital requirements, require action only by individuals or small groups, and can vary drastically over short distances;
   (2) *Modern technological or industrial*, involving a more limited range of technological actions which emphasize control over nature, are inflexible and difficult to change, are high in capital requirements, require interdependent social organization, and tend to be uniform;
   (3) *Comprehensive or post industrial*, combining features of both earlier stages so as to incorporate a larger range of adjustments, greater flexibility, and a variety of capital and organizational requirements.
3. Variation in hazard perception and estimation is a function of a combination of the magnitude and frequency of the hazard, recovery and frequency of experience, importance of the hazard to earning or

locational interests and personality factors.
4. The choice of adjustment for individuals is a function of the perception of the hazard, perception of the range of choice, command of technology, relative economic efficiency of alternatives and perceived linkages with other people.
5. The process of estimating economic efficiency for individuals is related to the perceived time horizon, ratio of reserves to anticipated losses, and degree to which choice is required.
6. For communities, the choice of adjustment is a function of perception of hazard, choice, and economic efficiency as influenced by the stability and the power structure of government.

With these hypotheses for guidance, collaborators were encouraged to apply the original research paradigm to different hazards. For each study, the nature and extent of the hazardous area was to be delimited and data were to be collected on land forms, soil and vegetation types, land use and population. The settlement history was to be documented, and the local economy was to be described. During the interviews, data would be obtained for socio-economic characteristics of the household, perception of the hazard, range of possible adjustments, and actual adjustments. Personality traits were to be sought through a story for which respondents selected an outcome, and through a sentence completion test (section 8.4). The entire questionnaire may be found in White (1974a; 6–10). Field studies were completed by collaborators regarding avalanches (Peru), coastal erosion (California), drought (Australia, Brazil, Kenya, Mexico, Nigeria, Tanzania), earthquakes (California, Ontario), flooding (Sri Lanka, India, Malawi, Illinois, England), snow (Michigan), hurricanes or tropical cyclones (United States, Puerto Rico, Bangladesh), volcanoes (Costa Rica, Hawaii) and wind (Colorado). Other studies on man-made hazards were completed in England, Hungary and Yugoslavia (section 8.6). Many of the reports based on this collaborative work are found in White (1974b).

The collaborative work represents a bold step in research. The logistical problems of co-ordinating such large-scale research are not insignificant. In addition, difficulties arise in using a standardized questionnaire, developed in North America, in other culture areas with specific local problems (Torry, 1979; 371–2). Not the least of the problems is translating the questions into other languages (Saarinen, 1974). This latter problem is particularly significant for tests of personality, where tests based on sentence-stems draw on material which assumes North American values. On the other hand, this research effort represents a major attempt to verify findings at a broad scale, something geographers have rarely attempted. It also combines a concern for identifying variables, testing relationships and establishing generalizations while simultaneously addressing pressing practical problems.

8.6 POLLUTION

The five-stage research paradigm originally designed for natural hazards has proven equally applicable for man-made hazards, particularly pollution. Carter (1985) has studied pollution problems associated with air, water, soils and vegetation in Czechoslovakia. Greenland and Yorty (1985) have examined urban air pollution in Denver, while Kumra (1980) has studied the relationships between environmental pollution and human health in the Indian city of Kanpur. In this section, detailed reviews of a comparative study of urban air pollution as well as a study in Australia are presented.

Before pollution can be controlled, hazard researchers believe that improved understanding is needed for the sources, extent and response to contamination in affected areas. Determining the perception of pollution is viewed as a basic component of research directed towards effective social control of environmental disruption. If awareness of the hazard, means of coping with its existence, and feeling of the community about what should be done are ascertained, managers should be better able to select strategies which will be accepted by the affected communities. This belief led Kromm, Probald and Wall (1973) to conduct a comparative study of perceptions towards air pollution in Budapest (Hungary), Ljubljana (Yugoslavia), and Sheffield (England). Surveys were conducted in 1971 using the research paradigm created by White and a modified version of the questionnaire designed for collaborative hazards research (section 8.5). A sample of 120 people were interviewed in Budapest and Sheffield; 160 interviews were completed in Ljubljana. Respondents were stratified in order to obtain interviews in areas of each city with different pollution levels.

In terms of awareness, noise and air pollution were cited frequently as disadvantages in Budapest, the city with the greatest air pollution levels relative to Sheffield and Ljubljana. Within each city, territorial variations in awareness were prominent. People residing in a neighbourhood experiencing pollution were highly aware of the extent and magnitude of the problem. Those living in areas relatively free of pollution tended to ignore or dismiss the problem entirely. At the same time, when specifically asked to identify areas of high and low pollution, residents of all three cities were remarkably accurate. Respondents also had a good appreciation for the sources and types of pollution, with two notable exceptions. The contribution of domestic sources was strongly underestimated. Furthermore, while residents were highly aware of visible pollutants (black or coloured smoke), they ignored or were unaware of the invisible and usually much more dangerous gaseous pollutants in the atmosphere.

Adjustment responses contained some significant managerial implications. Respondents generally expressed a widespread feeling of helplessness as to what an individual could do to influence the magnitude of air pollution. Almost all Ljubljana residents offered no positive suggestions, and 53 per cent of those in Budapest and 27 per cent of Sheffield respondents answered either 'nothing' or 'don't know' when asked the question 'When air pollution is particularly bad what can a person do?' Where suggestions were made, sharp differences appeared. While few people in Budapest or Ljubljana said that they would remain indoors, 28 per cent of those in Sheffield saw such action as appropriate. In contrast, movement away from the affected area, either permanently or temporarily, was not considered feasible for most residents in Ljubljana or Sheffield whereas 29 per cent of Budapest respondents indicated they would seek temporary refuge in the Buda hills. At the same time, no respondents from any of the cities indicated major changes in their own behaviour (curtail use of car, limit domestic fires, change domestic fuels) as possible actions to reduce levels of pollution.

Respondents in all three cities were pessimistic that filing a complaint would stimulate official action, although a significantly greater number in Sheffield felt complaints might work. However, nearly all of the residents of the three cities were unsure as to who should be contacted. With doubts about the effectiveness of individual action, most people depended upon group protection through the government. And, in all three cities, legislation had been passed to reduce the volume of emissions.

A study of complaints resulting from air pollution in Brisbane, Australia, by Auliciems and Dick (1976) revealed somewhat different attitudes about the role of the individual regarding air pollution. Sensitivity of politicians and government officials to complaints was reflected by the activity of the Queensland Air Pollution Control Council. A major task of the Council has been to record and investigate complaints from citizens. To determine the role of citizen involvement in air pollution management, Auliciems and Dick analysed the pattern of complaints over a five year period.

The Council's record includes names and addresses of all complainers, as well as the date and reason for the complaint. Complaints over the five years were plotted on a map. Starting with the most recent complaints and working backwards, plotting was done until 400 complaints had been recorded and then interviews were sought with each household. In addition, a linked interview was completed with the occupant of the house two removed from the complainer. The objective was to compare the attitudes of a complainer and a non-complainer who were in similar proximity to each other and presumably experienced the same levels of pollution. This procedure resulted in 93 interviews with complainers and 110 with non-complainers. The discrepancy in linked interviews resulted from people having moved since the complaint was filed or else the person actually interviewed was not the complainer.

Two unexpected results are significant for resource management and public participation. First, complaints increased with the length of residence in an area. In newer areas, or those with relatively large transient populations, fewer complaints may be expected. These results are significant for decision makers, especially if government action is partially guided by citizen complaints. If this pattern is valid, Auliciems and Dick recommended that authorities devote more attention to the environmental quality of more recently created neighbourhoods. Otherwise, the Brisbane data indicate that older and more established areas will show a disproportionate share of complaints relative to their population and the incidence of pollution.

Second, attitudes of complainers did not correlate highly with either socio-economic characteristics or with dissemination of information by the media. This suggests that programmes aimed at informing citizens about environmental quality in their community cannot rely on media sources. On a different level, the inability of socio-economic variables to predict behaviour regarding complaints led the analysts to conclude that a propensity to complain 'may be explicable by factors of personality'. While their data did not touch upon personality traits, their comment adds force to Schiff's contention that personality variables require further research.

8.7 TECHNOLOGICAL HAZARDS

The problem of air pollution discussed in section 8.6 is only one example of the many types of hazard which can be created through the application of technology (Baum, Fleming and Davidson, 1983; Zeigler, Johnson and Brunn, 1983; Kates, Hohenemser and Kasperson, 1984). After nuclear weapons, nuclear power plants are probably the most widely recognized form of technology which can create hazards (Pasqualetti and Pijawka, 1984). The well publicized problems at Three Mile Island in the United States during 1979 (MacLeod, 1981) and at Chernobyl in the Soviet Union during 1986 (Hohenemser, 1986) highlighted the possible catastrophic consequences of technology out of control. Indeed, nuclear power plants may be viewed as a very special type of the 'noxious facilities' examined in Chapter 4 both because of the potential danger of malfunction at the site and due to the problem of disposing of the spent radioactive wastes (Pushchak and Burton, 1983; Kirby and Jacob, 1986). The possibility of malfunctions at nuclear power plants have attracted research interest from geographers, especially regarding the development of warning and education programmes (Zeigler, Brunn and Johnson, 1981; Johnson, 1985). Of comparable interest has been the hazards associated with operating problems of large chemical or other industrial plants such as the Union Carbide facility at Bhopal in India where thousands of people died when toxic gas escaped from the plant (Banerjee, 1986). Many other technologically-generated hazards exist, ranging from asbestos in the work place (Sandbach, 1982; 124–54), power shortages in metropolitan areas (Nag, 1980) and chemical and road traffic hazards (Smith and Irwin, 1984). Several examples of research focused upon technological hazards are described below.

An ubiquitous technological hazard arises from chemicals applied to control both weeds and pests (Dési *et al.*, 1983; Dearden, 1983; 1985b). The irony often is that the chemicals are selected as a means to control one of the biological natural hazards shown in Table 8.1 but then subsequently create a second-generation hazard. Dearden (1984; 325) explained that resource managers wanted to use 2,4-D to control the Eurasian milfoil weed in Okanagan Lake in British Columbia, Canada because the benefits would be immediate, specific and visible while the costs would be long term, diffuse and difficult to link directly to the 2,4-D. Since Okanagan Lake was a key component in the tourism-oriented regional economy, considerable pressure existed to 'solve' the problem of a rapidly spreading weed which inhibited water-based recreation. In contrast to the resource managers, elected officials and businessmen in the region, public health officials, environmentalists and the general public argued for control measures involving harvesting, biological or dredging techniques. This issue illustrates that although consensus may exist concerning the nature of a problem, varying perceptions can result in quite different strategies being advocated regarding the solution. Society does appear to be recognizing and becoming aware that technology may bring problems as well as benefits.

Production of sufficient food is a preoccupation in many parts of the world, particularly in developing nations. In attempts to increase the output of food, many nations are relying on expansion of irrigation systems as well as upon utilization of chemical fertilizers and improved seeds. However, in solving one problem (the need for more food production), sometimes other problems (disease) are being worsened. Thus, in India, researchers have been finding that the introduction of irrigation technology can lead to the resurgence of malaria (Prasad, 1984; Ramesh, Barai and Hyma, 1984). The building of reservoirs, tanks, canals and pits can result in the introduction of slowly moving or stagnant water which is an ideal habitat for the breeding of mosquitos which transmit the malaria vector. In some instances, it was discovered that the construction of hydro-electric projects also led to an increase in malaria in the riverine villages near the damsite. Frequently, the upsurge in malaria would then lead to the use of chemical pesticides to control the mosquitos.

In the situations in which malaria has increased, a lesson becomes clear. The numerous linkages among and between natural and human systems suggest that resource and health management require an approach that has each problem considered in its entirety. Thus each problem should be dealt with as a complete system rather than being broken into isolated components (Sivasubramanian, 1983).

If problems are treated in isolated segments, then it is possible to become caught in a cycle found in India where use of technology to increase needed food production leads to resurgence of malaria which leads to use of chemical controls and so on.

Just before midnight on 10 November 1979 a train derailed in Mississauga, a city immediately west of Toronto. The 106-car train carried a mix of commodities including styrene, toluene, propane and caustic soda. The subsequent explosions and fires from the derailed propane cars and the escape of chlorine led to the evacuation of nearly a quarter of a million people in 24 hours and the closing of the city for almost a week. Except for damage to the train and track, property damage was slight. There were no deaths and only a few minor injuries. However, the dislocation of 226,000 people from their homes and the disruption to business and public sector activity emphasized another dimension of technological hazards as well as the need to understand and prepare for such events (Burton *et al.*, 1981; Burton and Post, 1983).

Burton *et al.* (1981) studied the derailment in Mississauga not to ask how or why the accident happened but rather to suggest ways for society both to prevent and to respond to such emergencies. In addition to documenting the events following the derailment, the analysts (1) studied the response to the emergency by government, voluntary agencies, the public and private sector, (2) examined the social, health and economic costs of the evacuation and (3) investigated the institutional framework related to the emergency involving emergency planning, risk assessment, insurance and compensation. The researchers used a number of cross-checking data sources including first hand observations at the command post and evacuation centre during the emergency itself, a specially designed questionnaire distributed to 1,000 evacuated households within one week of their return home, another questionnaire to 1,000 households nine months after the derailment, questionnaires to other targeted populations (people registered at the evacuation centre, households just outside the evacuation zone, business people), interviews with selected decision makers, officials and householders, media reports on the emergency, and transcripts from meetings.

Despite there being no loss of life nor substantial property damage from the derailment, the researchers estimated that the costs associated with the evacuation were nearly $70 million (Burton *et al.*, 1981; 9–2). Beyond the estimated costs, a number of problems were identified which would be applicable to most low probability–high consequence disasters. These included coordination of different technical expert groups at the derailment site, coordination of the many volunteer and community groups providing food, shelter and nursing, control of the perimeter around the evacuated area, dissemination of information to homeowners and the general public, and determination of compensation. Increased knowledge on such aspects from research on technological hazards should help individuals, communities, regions and countries in developing more effective societal responses when such disasters occur.

8.8 RISK ASSESSMENT

In section 8.2 it was shown how White's interest in floodplain management led to the development of a general set of research questions which could be applied to natural, man-made and technological hazards. The interest in different kinds of hazards has led to a more general type of inquiry labelled as risk assessment. In Kates' (1978; xvii) view, 'identifying those hazards, estimating the threat they pose to humanity and the environment, and evaluating such risk in a comparative perspective is the work of risk assessment'.

Numerous overviews have been written about risk assessment (Kates, 1978; O'Riordan, 1979, 1982; Whyte and Burton, 1980; Macgill, 1983; Macgill and Snowball, 1983; Burton and Pushchak, 1984; Covello and Mumpower, 1985). Only the general characteristics of this field are noted in this section, since the specific examples presented in sections 8.3 to 8.7 also represent examples of risk assessment.

Kates (1978; 12) differentiated between environmental hazard and risk assessment in the following manner. The former is the potential threat posed to people by events originating in or transmitted by natural or built systems. The latter involves the appraisal of the kinds and degrees of threat posed by any environmental hazard. The appraisal exercise includes three components: (1) recognition of a hazard, (2) measurement of the risk and (3) understanding the social implications. Each of these is considered in more detail.

Concerning hazard identification, Kates suggested that the central question centres upon what constitutes a threat. Specifically, the task is to identify the products, processes, phenomena and persons that create environmental hazards and thereby form a threat to people and nature. He believed that identification of hazards is probably the most important but still least studied of the three components of risk assessment.

While hazard identification focuses upon what constitutes a threat, the estimation or measurement of risk attempts to determine both the likelihood of an event of a given magnitude occurring as well as the likelihood and nature of the associated consequences. The third component - social evaluation - then addresses the issue as to the importance of the estimated risk. This aspect generates an array of issues since the social evaluation of risk involves determining the meaning of risk. Meaning can be variable and relative depending upon culture and other contextual aspects. A further complication is that many dimensions are intangible, forcing any evaluation to balance both quantitative and qualitative considerations.

This brief review indicates that three basic components – identification, measurement, evaluation – combine to form the field of risk assessment. It is an area of inquiry which has attracted interest from researchers in a variety of disciplines or professions. Geographers have been and continue to be influential in this area, one which can readily be linked to Barrows' concern with the study of man's adjustment to the environment (section 8.1).

8.9 IMPLICATIONS FOR RESOURCE MANAGEMENT

The research problem identified by Gilbert White has had profound ramifications for resource management policy and practice (Kates and Burton, 1986a, b). His findings caused a rethinking of earlier resource management strategies which had placed almost exclusive reliance upon structural solutions. The outcome has been a recognition of the gains to be realized by using both structural and non-structural adjustments to cope with natural or technological hazards. In this manner, research focused on hazards and risk assessment has contributed toward broadening the range of options to be considered.

Another implication is less tangible, but no less important. The research results have demonstrated that occupants of hazardous places usually perceive the degree of hazard and the range of possible adjustments in a different light from scientists or professional resource managers. At the same time, results have suggested that professional biases tend to restrict the range of choice considered by managers. These conclusions, based on evidence, provided additional credibility for the claims by the public to become more involved in decision making. In brief, the findings validated the view that 'public participation' or 'citizen involvement' was a necessary aspect in resource management. Since the initial research was completed in the early 1960s, the results of the hazard work and recommendations made by investigators (White, 1966) have been in the vanguard concerning the desirability of consulting the public before finalizing decisions.

The findings from the research on hazards and risk assessment have been applied in many situations, varying from considerations as diverse as urban planning (Tobin, 1982), disaster planning and relief (Foster, 1980; Everson, 1985; May and Williams, 1986), to educational programmes (Sims and Baumann, 1983). Despite these direct applications of research findings, individuals such as Havlick (1984) have been urging analysts to continue to consider how their results can be incorporated more quickly and effectively into the management process. This is an appropriate concern. In addition, geographers could devote more attention to determining the possible transfer of findings from one problem area to another. As an example, risk assessment methods and findings should be equally valuable for both hazard adjustment strategies and environmental impact assessment (Grima, Timmerman, Fowle and Byer, 1986).

8.10 IMPLICATIONS FOR RESEARCH

Hazards research has a strong basis in the man–environment tradition. The original impetus came from concern with a practical problem. At the same time, attention was given to testing relationships and searching for generalizations. To date, the bulk of the work has addressed the identification of variables and testing of relationships. As yet, no 'theory of natural hazards' has been developed by geographers (Caviedes, 1982).

In evolving, investigations have drawn upon both positivist and phenomenologist viewpoints. The positivist outlook has been dominant in physically-oriented studies, whereas the phenomenological stance has underlain the perceptual and attitudinal investigations. Both types of study, however, have focused more than most geographical research in resource analysis upon validation and verification. Studies have been closely tied to one another through a commonly used research paradigm, and variables have been systematically explored. This procedure has shown which variables are not significant in accounting for adjustment patterns, and has pointed the direction for further inquiry.

Interdisciplinary cooperation has been high. White (1973; 203) has stated that 'much of the research could not have taken place without strong cooperation with workers in other disciplines' and indicated that engineers, planners, economists and psychologists have made important contributions. At a different level, Sims, a psychologist, wrote about his experiences in working with geographers (Sims and Baumann, 1975). He attempted to pinpoint the problems which may arise in interdisciplinary work, and noted how conflicts can occur at the stages of conceptualization, research design, data collection and analysis. His paper is instructive for the geographer contemplating interdisciplinary work, whether or not in resource analysis.

Concerning basic research considerations, several important points arise. At the stage of conceptualization, problems have been encountered with operationally defining 'hazards', especially such events as droughts. Choice of research designs has been tempered by the reality of gaining access to individuals and by needing them to relate to the problem being studied. The latter aspect has mitigated against experimental approaches since it is difficult to have respondents who have never experienced a hazard serve as a control group and provide meaningful answers to questions about it. For instance, a study of the urban snow hazard might adopt a 'treatment' group in South Dakota and a 'control' group in Florida. However, it is difficult to imagine what use could be made of responses from the Floridans concerning their perception of the hazard or awareness of range of adjustments. Nevertheless, modified experimental designs have been applied. In a study focusing upon coastal erosion, J.K. Mitchell (1974b) selected a sample of coastal residents and contrasted their views toward erosion against the perceptions of a sample of inland residents. Thus, it is apparent that some of the advantages of experimental designs may be gained even though all variables can never be manipulated.

In terms of alternative research strategies, White and Haas (1975: 223–9) have urged that future studies attempt to conduct *postaudits* and *longitudinal investigations*. The former strategy would focus upon how communities and individuals react when a major disaster occurs. This would require predesignated interdisciplinary teams ready to study hazardous events while they actually occur. Such work would facilitate understanding of how communities react under a variety of circumstances, how warning systems function, how some communities recover while others do not, and how immediate post-disaster decisions are made. This approach raises some difficult ethical issues which were discussed in Chapter 2. The later strategy would involve studying how communities prepare for and/or recover from major natural disasters. Communities would have to be observed for many years in such studies, as the interval between major disasters could be long. To date, studies approaching these strategies have been those concerned with post-disaster recovery (Alexander, 1984; Bates *et al.*, 1984; Geipel, 1982).

Collection of data involves some important lessons. Initial research relied almost exclusively on structured interviews for obtaining data about perceptions and attitudes (Mitchell, 1984). The hazards researchers, as well as other geographers, became aware that other measurement techniques should be used to validate the questionnaire results. This realization led to several hazards studies becoming pioneering efforts to incorporate behavioural techniques. Particularly notable in this regard were Saarinen's (1966) use of the Thematic Apperception Test and Sims and Baumann's (1972) application of Sentence-Completion Tests. These and other studies demonstrated that alternative techniques could be adopted to verify questionnaire findings. The use of such techniques, and the adaptations of behavioural concepts such as 'personality' and 'motivation' placed many of the hazard studies in the forefront of the development of the behavioural approach in geography. Indeed, from the studies on perception of floods emerged the Association of American Geographers first symposium on problems of perception (Lowenthal, 1967).

The general research considerations mentioned in Chapter 2 also appear relevant to the hazards research. In many ways, the structural emphasis in hazard adjustment strategies reflected an exercise in vertical thinking. Engineers trained to build structures to control damage from natural hazards continued to build structures even when it was apparent that such responses were not solving the problem. This activity was analagous to digging de Bono's hole deeper, with the hole in the wrong spot. It took the equivalent of lateral thinking by White to recognize that other holes would have to be dug, if damage were to be reduced. This led to efforts to broaden the range of adjustments, analagous to digging other holes. This analogy emphasizes as clearly as any that preoccupation with a narrow range of strategies in resource management can be counterproductive. Often the only thing that can alter such management practices is evidence based upon research.

The work on hazards and risk assessment has led to innovations in both development of research concepts and methods and in resource policy and practice. As in any mature and vigorous field of inquiry, however, consensus often does not emerge. Indeed, informed, critical and constructive debate among analysts is essential if improvements are to occur. Such debate has appeared at several levels. An exchange between Torry (1979) and Burton, Kates and White (1981) focused attention upon the difficulties of actually doing interdisciplinary research, determining reasonable damage thresholds, and conducting cross-cultural study.

Hewitt (1983a, b) has raised another set of questions when expressing concern that the dominant view in hazards research involves a 'technocratic' approach. The outcome has been concentration of effort in three areas: (1) monitoring and analysis of geophysical processes, (2) designing, planning and managerial activities to contain the geophysical processes or to modify human behaviour relative to those processes, and (3) developing emergency measures (warning systems, relief). In Hewitt's view, the technocratic approach leads to emphasis upon natural and technological systems as well as to reliance upon bureaucratically organized institutions, centrally controlled financial arrangements, and specialized professionals. In contrast, Hewitt (1983a; 24–23) believed that if hazards are conceptualized as a normal part of the human ecology of people or communities, then researchers are led to pose a different set of questions and to examine different types of solutions.

Hewitt argues that hazards are not primarily explained by the natural or technical phenomena or processes that initiate damage. Instead, hazards are viewed as being dependent more upon concerns, pressures, goals and social changes which are unrelated to societal–environmental relationships. The ongoing organization and values of society and its institutions become critically significant in developing means to avoid or reduce risk. Attention thus shifts from the natural or technological conditions and processes to the prevailing social order and historical circumstances. Such a perspective makes the mainstream of social science directly pertinent to the study of hazards, and suggests that human geography, human ecology and anthropology can offer fundamental insights.

This challenging of fundamental assumptions or values is necessary. Just as White acted as a lateral thinker in challenging the reliance upon structural adjustments, so Hewitt also is acting as a lateral thinker by questioning what he has defined as a technocratic approach. Through such questioning and debate, the field of hazards and risk assessment will continue to evolve in response to how societies do and might adjust to natural and technological phenomena.

CHAPTER 9
ENVIRONMENTAL IMPACT ASSESSMENT

9.1 INTRODUCTION

Geographers have had a lengthy interest regarding man's impact upon the environment. Marsh (1864) published one of the earliest statements concerning the character and extent of changes to the natural environment due to human action. He stressed that nature could not always rehabilitate herself. Man's activities frequently triggered a chain of events which impoverished the environment. As a result, Marsh urged protective and precautionary measures to ensure that this chain was not initiated by human action, and that development was designed to minimize disturbance to the harmony in nature.

Others developed this concern in later years. During the 1920s, Sauer founded a geography department at the University of California, Berkeley, which emphasized cultural history and landscape change. Much of his work considered the way in which human activity altered the environment to produce a cultural landscape (Sauer, 1938). In 1955, Sauer and other geographers participated in an interdisciplinary symposium at New York entitled 'Man's Role in Changing the Face of the Earth' (Thomas, 1956). At about the same time, Dansereau (1957) examined man's impact upon the landscape from the perspective of a biogeographer. Subsequently, Glacken (1967) analysed basic philosophies and attitudes associated with man–environment relationships. Thus, geographers have devoted considerable attention to environmental impacts associated with human use of resources. The research has sought to identify the nature of a concern as well as to increase understanding of the problems.

The purpose of this chapter is to review the work by geographers and others relative to environmental impact assessment (Clark, Bisset and Wathern, 1980; Chapman, 1981; Lee, 1982; Meredith, 1983; Grima, Timmerman, Fowle and Byer, 1986). Section 9.2 clarifies what is meant by environmental impact assessment. The role of 'pure' research is analysed (section 9.3) as well as research concerning pre-project (section 9.4) and post-project (section 9.5) impact. Attention is also given to studies which have reviewed procedures for impact assessment (section 9.6). As in other chapters, the final sections (9.7 and 9.8) discuss the implications for resource management and research.

9.2 DEFINING ENVIRONMENTAL IMPACT ASSESSMENT

Numerous publications have appeared which present rationales, methods and techniques for assessments (Ditton and Goodale, 1972; Burchell and Listokin, 1975; Corwin *et al.*, 1975; O'Riordan and Sewell, 1981; Lee, 1983). With this proliferation of books and manuals, many definitions have been offered for environmental impact assessment. A synthesis of the many views indicates that it represents a 'legislative or policy-based concern for possible positive/negative, short/long term effects on our total environment attributable to proposed or existing projects, programs or policies of a public or private origin' (Mitchell and Turkheim, 1977; 47). This interpretation indicates that assessments should be broad in scope, a view reiterated by White (1972b; 914). He argued that an ideal study agenda of a resource proposal would consider impacts upon national economic efficiency, income redistribution, preservation and aesthetics, political equity and environmental control.

Numerous ideas have been offered concerning what it is an environmental assessment should do. Dorney (1977; 184) provided a good summary of the main functions of an assessment when noting that it should:

1. Identify and articulate the environmental goals and objectives of the project as related to the overall goals of the project.
2. Identify human concerns.
3. Describe the proposed action or impact.
4. Describe alternatives.
5. Describe what changes will occur without intervention.
6. Describe the nature and magnitudes of environmental effects.
7. In any weighting or aggregating process of various environmental factors, provide a clear statement as to the procedure followed and a clear indication of the values incorporated into the solution or recommended action.
8. Identify remedial action.
9. Identify any positive results that can be developed by direct or indirect spin-off from the project.
10. Identify any trade-offs necessitated.
11. Develop a baseline inventory capable of conversion to a monitoring system.

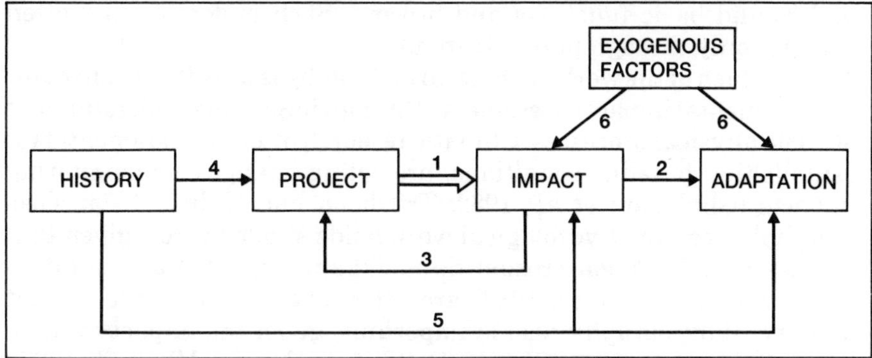

Fig. 9.1 Temporal context for environmental impact assessment (*after Lang and Armour, 1981, The Assessment and Review of Social Impacts, Federal Environmental Assessment and Review Office, Ottawa, p. 61*)

It is important to remember that environmental impact assessment has a temporal context (Fig. 9.1). The direct impacts (1) occur from changes induced by the project on initial conditions in the natural or social environment. However, if analysis only addressed the direct impacts, other important considerations would be overlooked. Thus, the changed conditions lead to adjustment and adaptation (2). Not all people, groups and communities are affected the same nor have equal capability to adapt. The processes of adjustment and adaptation need explicit consideration as part of the assessment exercise.

During the planning phase, the project itself may be modified (3) in response to public comments or other inputs. Any project also extends into the past (4). This history will condition public responsiveness at the stages of direct impact and subsequent adaptation (5). Finally, other external factors (6) may influence the project, and cannot be ignored. Thus, in defining environmental assessment, it is important to recognize both temporal and spatial contexts of projects, programmes or policies.

9.3 'PURE' RESEARCH

In discussing the relationship between 'theory' and 'social relevance' in the first chapter, it was stressed that theoretical or pure research often evolves to have applied value. The field of environmental impact assessment illustrates this aspect very well. If predictions are to be made about the impact of resource development on natural or social systems, the analyst has to understand those systems, especially the way in which they would change over time without any human intervention. Since both natural and social systems are dynamic, if baseline conditions are to be established the investigator has to understand basic functions and process. Such understanding often emerges only through pure research.

Much of the work in physical geography is directly pertinent for environmental impact assessments through improving understanding of basic physical processes. Climatic research often is fundamental for establishing baseline conditions, predicting changes, or monitoring impacts (Chubukov *et al.*, 1982; Trilsbach and Hulme, 1984). Geomorphological and hydrological work holds similar value, given that processes such as soil erosion (Mansikkaniemi, 1982) and siltation (Chettri and Bowonder, 1983) are often triggered by development activity. Biogeography also is important, given the impact of man-induced change on vegetation and wildlife (Veblen and Stewart, 1982).

Studies in the field of economic geography also are pertinent. Gladkevich and Sumina (1982) have measured the environmental impact of industrial centres in the Soviet Union. Impacts on agricultural activity also have been studied, ranging from the effects of land drainage and fertilizer (Wilcock, 1979) to effects of air pollution on crop productivity (Kercher, 1982). The effects of energy development also have been considered, whether these be related to hydro-electricity (Massa, 1985) or oil (Laubier, 1980).

Another area in which basic geographical research is pertinent for impact assessment is recreation and tourism. Mathieson and Wall (1982) have provided an excellent framework for and overview of this work. The research has covered the experiences in developed countries, from impacts on boreal forests in Norway (Bjøness, 1981), to the European Alps (Barker, 1982b; Kariel and Kariel, 1982), to individual towns (Keogh, 1982). For the developing countries, interest has focused upon the impact on regional development (Schuörmann, 1981) as well as on a mix of ecological, economic and social factors (Beekhuis, 1981). Two research projects are reviewed in more detail to indicate the value of basic work for environmental impact assessment.

The impacts of long-range transported air pollution or 'acid precipitation' emerged as a major environmental issue during the 1980s in many countries in the world. Mean annual precipitation with a pH less than 5.6 is widely regarded as containing levels of airborne pollution which exceed natural conditions. One concern has been to delimit the extent of areas subjected to acid rain, and also to determine their susceptibility to damage. Unlike much environmental impact assessment research which is site specific, this type of work can be regional or national in scope.

In Canada, a research programme has been undertaken to provide an overview of the environmental, economic and social impacts of acid rain. Such information is being used in discussions between Canada and the United States regarding control of acid rain, since about 90 per cent of the acid rain which lands on Canada originates from the United States.

As part of the acid rain research, Rubec (1981) examined the attributes of the land across Canada for which the mean levels of precipitation acidity are less than pH 5.6. For such areas, Rubec examined information about the soils, vegetation, surficial geology and annual precipitation levels. To analyse these attributes, Rubec used the computerized, geographic data base of environmental maps covering all of Canada which have been prepared by the federal Department of the Environment. These maps are part of the Canada Land Data System and are at a scale of 1 : 15,000,000. The overlay capabilities and automated computer cartography provided an opportunity to develop preliminary information at a national scale.

Rubec used the maps in the following manner. In general, areas with surficial material including calcareous marine or glacial lake deposits have low sensitivity to acid precipitation. Similarly, luvisolic and organic soils have a higher acid buffering capacity. Vegetation is more difficult to use, but mixed and hardwood forests of southern areas are regarded as being less sensitive.

Using the various maps and having defined the acid buffering capacities of different attributes of the terrestial landscape, Rubec was able to draw a number of conclusions. A total of over 2,565,000 km^2, or about 28 per cent of Canada, was found to receive precipitation with a mean annual acidity of less than pH 5.6. Over 79 per cent of these impinged areas were found to have surficial glaciofluvial or morrainal deposits which provide poor acid buffering capacity. In regional terms, Rubec concluded that the impact of precipitation was probably the greatest in the province of Quebec. This type of information, developed with a geographic information system (Ch. 3), provides a small scale overview of possible environmental impact.

Research in the Yorkshire Dales illustrates the value of hydrological research. McDonald and Kay (1981) became interested in the water quality of reservoir feeder streams. They studied the relationship between coliform bacterial concentration and stream hydrology in two ways. In one study, they took water quality samples from two streams for both normal runoff and then for 11 natural hydrograph events. They found that coliform concentration increased immediately after high flow conditions. They suggested that this pattern was significant for water managers since boating competitions are often held in 'white water' conditions when bacterial concentrations could readily exceed the guidelines of the EEC for direct water contact recreation activities.

In a follow up study, McDonald, Kay and Jenkins (1982) wanted to determine the relative roles of surface fecal sources and instream sources of coliform. During natural high flow conditions, it was not possible to control for these two sources. They therefore devised an experimental design. With the cooperation of the managers responsible for operation of the reservoirs, they arranged for artificial surges to be created through releasing water from the reservoirs. In that manner, surface fecal sources were controlled, and they could determine the role of instream sources. At the outset of the research, they had believed that increase in bacterial numbers during natural high flows was caused by movement of bacteria from surface and near surface fecal sites. They also thought that with artificial surges there might be a diminution of bacterial counts due to dilution effects. However, their research revealed that the bacterial response was characterized by a peak of 10 to 30 times the baseflow concentration during the artificially-induced surge. Since artificial releases are often used in Britain to create 'white water' conditions, they argued that this practice should be reviewed since the participants were being placed in some risk. This basic research is interesting since its findings were counter intuitive. It is likely that only through research would this understanding of the natural system be gained. From that research, the environmental impacts of artificial releases became better understood.

9.4 PRE-PROJECT ANALYSIS

Many techniques have been developed for estimating the environmental impact of proposed activities (Bisset, 1980; Bonnicksen and Lee, 1982; Curtis, 1982; Prasartseree, 1982; Beanlands and Duinker, 1984; Shopley and Fuggle, 1984). In this section, the techniques are discussed under the following categories: checklists, overlays, matrices and networks. It should be stressed, however, that no single technique is perfect. Each has strengths and weaknesses. As a result, it is futile to search for the 'ideal' technique. A more realistic approach is to identify the relative merits of alternatives. In this way, a *combination* of techniques can be chosen to meet the needs of a particular problem.

In evaluating the merits of alternative techniques, it is desirable to make such assessments against an explicit set of criteria. Ideally, an assessment technique should *identify* all of the impacts (primary and secondary) and indicate their timing and duration. Not only should individual impacts be identified. Those arising from the *interaction* of two or more separate impacts should also be noted. Following identification, the technique should *measure* the *magnitude* (high, medium, low) of the impacts. With the magnitude known, the technique should then suggest the *significance* of the impacts. An impact with high magnitude may not automatically have strong significance. Conversely, a low magnitude impact could have serious social significance.

In addition to being comprehensive and accurate, the assessment technique should generate results which are easily understandable. At the same time, the technique should not be so demanding of manpower, money, time, expertise and technological facilities that it is beyond the capacity of agencies to apply it. The discussion of the assessment techniques should be read with these criteria in mind, always remembering that trade-offs must be made. It is unlikely that any one technique will satisfy all of the ideal characteristics. That is, to increase comprehensiveness and accuracy, it may be necessary to commit additional resources and sacrifice simplicity in presentation of results. These are the types of decisions that are continually encountered when conducting environmental impact assessments.

9.4.1 CHECKLISTS

Checklists represent the simplest approach to environmental impact assessment. Checklists normally include a range of items to be considered when preparing an assessment statement. The items on the checklist may be designed for general use, or for a specific project. Two examples illustrate the general approach which has been adopted. The Battelle Institute in the United States developed a checklist of 78 specific environmental considerations which were grouped into four general categories of ecology, environmental pollution, aesthetics and human interest (Dee *et al.*, 1972). Emphasis was upon primary rather than secondary or interaction impacts. The idea of the approach was to ensure that a broad range of considerations would be examined, and that key impacts would be highlighted or 'flagged'. The Battelle Institute subsequently developed a more sophisticated technique combining features of checklists, matrices, and networks (Dee *et al.*, 1973). A technique developed by the US Environmental Protection Agency, Region X (1973), represents another checklist approach. Specific listings were developed for eight different types of project.

Most checklists are used to ensure that important environmental considerations are not overlooked. That is, they focus attention upon specific considerations. In their basic form, they do not consider the interaction, magnitude nor importance of impacts. However, this type of information could be incorporated into a checklist. At their best, they draw attention to significant concerns. At their worst, they generate a voluminous amount of information which is not integrated into an overall plan of analysis.

9.4.2 OVERLAYS

The overlay approach to environmental assessment is usually associated with McHarg (1968; 1969). The overlay approach involves several phases. In the first, the study area is divided into units based either upon a grid system, topographic features or different land uses. Using aerial photography, topographical and resource inventory maps, field observations, public meetings and discussions with local scientific and cultural groups, data are collected for climate, historical geology, physiography, hydrology, soils, plant associations, animals, and land use.

In the second phase, the eight categories of information are examined for their positive, negative or neutral effect on prospective development, or for the effect of development upon them. Once values have been decided upon for the eight categories, they are mapped on transparent overlays. Categories assigned high value are given a dark shading; intermediate values are coloured in grey; low values are lightly shaded or left clear. When the various overlays are superimposed, the cumulative effect of shading highlights those areas where impact would be the greatest and the least.

McHarg (1968) first applied this approach to the location of an interstate highway. Separate overlays were prepared for topography, land values, urbanization, residential quality, historic features, agricultural value, recreational value, wildlife value, water values and susceptibility to erosion. After the ten overlays were superimposed, alternative routes were identified.

The overlay approach has many merits. It is simple, and generates an effective visual display. The resource manager can explore the impact of proposed development by changing the values assigned to different overlay maps, and by varying the number of features included in the analysis. The approach can be adapted for computer analysis, with weighting and mapping done by a computer.

The approach is not without limitations, however. Its application normally requires considerable information which may not always be readily available. Once data are collected, the overlay system can become confusing when large numbers of transparencies are superimposed. The shades of grey on different overlays produce an aggregate pattern which is either black or clear. Intermediate shades are obscured, and difficult to distinguish. The composite map also is a function of the values assigned to different features. This aspect can be a strength, allowing decision makers to identify different consequences when weights are varied. On the other hand, unless the values are made explicit, the investigator can predetermine results by the emphasis placed upon various features.

When these strengths and weaknesses are balanced, it seems as if the overlay method is most useful as a 'first cut' technique to identify major areas of concern. In this manner, it has a function similar to that of checklists. However, unlike checklists, it may incorporate impacts resulting from interaction of activities and environmental variables. On the other hand, overlay methods usually do not provide a 'fine grain' analysis of impacts. Other techniques, such as matrices or networks, become necessary to follow up the concerns flagged by overlays or checklists.

9.4.3 MATRICES

Numerous matrices have been developed for environmental

assessment work (Schlesinger and Daetz, 1973; Aegerter and Messerli 1983). Many of these build upon earlier studies which sought to develop frameworks to incorporate the ecological dimension into environmental planning and management (Hills, 1961; Hills *et al.*, 1970). Matrices differ in sophistication, ranging from extensions of checklists to others involving several stages (Fischer and Davies, 1973), or multiple dimensions (Welch and Lewis, 1976). Regardless of level of complexity, they have several common characteristics: they force consideration of the impact of each aspect of a proposal for a range of environmental concerns; and they consider both the magnitude and importance of impacts.

The pioneering effort with matrices was by Leopold (1971; 1974) and his colleagues in the US Geological Survey. They developed a technique to comply with the requirements of the National Environmental Policy Act of 1969 (section 9.6). The matrix was designed to assess impacts resulting from a range of projects. The matrix itself identified 100 project actions along one axis and 88 environmental 'conditions and characteristics' on the other axis (Table 9.1).

The matrix is used in the following manner (Table 9.1). All actions which are part of the proposed development are identified. A slash is placed in each cell for which an action has a possible impact upon an environmental characteristic or condition. In the upper left-hand corner of each cell with a slash, a number from 1 (least) to 10 (maximum) is inserted to indicate *magnitude* of impact. In the lower right-hand corner, a number from 1 (least) to 10 (greatest) indicates the *importance* of the impact. The numbers are not added, but rather are used to identify concerns arising from the interaction of project activities with the environment.

Leopold's matrix offers several advantages. It serves as a general checklist and identifies first-order interactions. The concept of impact is broken into 'magnitude' and 'importance' components, a valid and important contribution. It was the first effort to relate project actions to environmental alterations. These advantages are balanced by weaknesses. Many interactions are complex and dynamic. Leopold's matrix suggests a direct cause-and-effect relationship which rarely occurs. Immediate and long-term impacts are not differentiated, although separate matrices could be prepared for different time periods. The list is heavily biased toward the physical–biological environment (67 items out of 88). The scoring of magnitude and importance is left to the judgement of the assessor. Different assessors could produce different appraisals.

In brief, this matrix, and others which followed it, represented a step beyond checklists. However, like checklists, the matrices ignored anything other than first-order impacts. Recognition of the complex patterns of interaction which occur in the real world led other investigators to develop techniques which emphasize networks and the feedback among impacts.

Table 9.1 The Leopold Matrix (*from Leopold* et al., *US Geological Survey Circular 645, 1971*)

Project Actions / Environmental Characteristics and Conditions	A. Modification of regime a–m						B. Land transformation and construction a–s	C. Resource extraction a–g	D. Processing a–o	E. Land Alteration a–t	F. Resource renewal a–e	G. Changes in traffic a–k	H. Waste emplacement and treatment a–n	I. Chemical treatment a–e	J. Accidents others a–e
	a	b	c	d	e	f ... m									
A. Physical and chemical characteristics															
1. Earth															
a. Mineral resources		2/1													
b. Construction materials		6/4		4/7		3/2									
c. Soils				8/6											
d. Landform			5/1												
f.															
2. Water a–g															
3. Atmosphere a–b															
4. Processes a–i															
B. Biological condition															
1. Flora a–i															
2. Fauna a–i															
C. Cultural factors															
1. Land use a–i															
2. Recreation a–g															
3. Aesthetics and human interest a–j															
4. Cultural status a–d															
5. Man-made facilities and activities a–g															
D. Ecological relationships such as a–g															
Others															

9.4.4 NETWORKS

The intent of network techniques is to identify the chain of interactions which may be triggered by proposed development. In other words, networks recognize that identifying cause-and-effect relationships between project activities and environmental characteristics is not sufficient. A change in one environmental characteristic may lead to other environmental consequences. To illustrate, a large reservoir may change the micro-climate. Where vegetation has been existing near the margin of its tolerance threshold, a change in micro-climate may result in the demise of the plants. Without vegetation, the soil becomes susceptible to erosion, which in turn increases sediment levels in the reservoir and affects organisms in the water. It is such interactions in ecosystems that network techniques seek to trace.

While the need for network techniques has been recognized, they have proven difficult to develop. One of the early efforts in this direction was by Sorensen (1971) who developed a 'stepped' matrix designed to trace project and environment interactions. J.H. Ross (1974; 1976) also extended the matrix approach to counter the problem that 'conventional environmental matrices have, by and large, failed to recognize the dynamic nature of the environmental systems which they have attempted to describe' (Ross, 1974; 4). Modelling and simulation have also been used (Holling, 1974). Knight, Dufournaud and Mulamoottil (1983) have shown how ecological modelling and interaction matrices can be combined to trace the interactions among biophysical processes and cultural stresses.

Gibson (1976) has reviewed attempts to adapt economic models for analysis of regional environmental quality. One of the earliest studies of this type was by Isard *et al.* (1972). This study was exploratory, and sought to analyse the linkages between economic and ecologic systems. The study first reviewed the applicability of four analytical tools ((1) comparative cost approach, (2) input-output analysis, (3) activity complex analysis, (4) gravity models) for combining economic and ecological variables in planning regional development. Subsequently, input-output analysis was integrated with activity analysis to study the economic-ecological system (Whitney, 1985; 56–72).

Using the combined input-output and activity analysis technique, Isard *et al.* studied the economic feasibility and environmental consequences of establishing a recreational marina in Plymouth–Kingston–Duxbury Bay, south of Boston. The problem was stated as: 'given the alternative sites available for marina development, select that site at which the combined economic and ecological costs are minimized for a given assumed market' (Isard *et al.*, 1972; 127). Three sites were studied.

The marine complex was a hypothetical one, with the investigators using it to explore the value of their analytical approach. They were satisfied that they were able to trace through the sequence of interactions among different project activities and environmental consequences. Although their approach was limited by the assumptions made to operationalize the analysis, their study illustrates the opportunities and problems associated with a network study.

9.4.5 REVIEW

Conceptually, the network approach is superior to those based upon checklists, overlays and matrices (Table 9.2), regardless of the criteria applied. It identifies the magnitude of impacts, and may be used as a basis for determining their significance. Relationships between project activities and environmental considerations are explicitly considered. The sequence of interactions is considered, recognizing that the development process and environmental response are dynamic rather than static. Operationally, the network approach frequently falters due to lack of basic knowledge. In many instances, understanding of cause-and-effect relationships is not sufficient to predict chains of events. This situation emphasizes the value of 'pure' research for environmental impact assessment (section 9.3). Conversely, where variables and relationships are known, they frequently have been difficult to measure and monitor especially with regard to intangible aspects.

Given these problems, many investigators have turned to techniques which are conceptually less sophisticated but operationally more feasible. Checklists and/or overlays are often used during initial stages to identify environmental concerns. At subsequent stages, a

Table 9.2 Alternative techniques for environmental impact assessment (*after Warner and Preston, 1974*)

Technique	Characteristics
1. Checklists	Present a specific list of environmental considerations to be investigated. Do not require the establishment of direct cause–effect links to project activities.
2. Overlays	Rely on a set of maps of environmental characteristics (physical, social, ecological, aesthetic) for a project area. The maps are superimposed to produce a composite picture of a regional environment. Impacts are identified by noting the impacted environmental characteristics lying within the project boundaries.
3. Matrices	Incorporate a list of project activities in addition to a checklist of potentially impacted environmental characteristics. The two lists are related in a matrix which identifies first-order cause–effect relationships between specific activities and impacts.
4. Networks	Work from a list of project activities to establish cause–condition–effect networks. They recognize that a series of impacts may be triggered by a project action.

matrix or simplified network approach is used to assess the consequences of development at a specific site. No matter what criteria are used in final evaluation, each technique has strengths and limitations. The investigator must pick the one, or combination, which most closely satisfies the context and needs for a given development proposal.

9.5 POST-PROJECT ANALYSIS

One way to improve predictions of environmental impacts arising from resource development is to study developments which have been completed. Studying environmental impacts after-the-fact is a specific application of evaluation research discussed in Chapter 10. Post-project analysis has been used for many years, and has been the focus for several international conferences (Bernard and Pelto, 1972; Farvar and Milton, 1972).

Day *et al.* (1977) suggested a general framework for the hindsight evaluation of environmental impacts. This framework involves several stages (Fig. 9.2). The social values and objectives underlying project actions should be identified. Without knowing original project objectives, the investigator normally cannot differentiate between intended and unintended effects. Next, if environmental change arising from a project is to be measured, benchmark data are needed. These data about the 'project environment' are used in addressing two questions. What would the environment have been like without the project? Which changes are attributable to natural and cultural processes, and which are due to the project itself?

The third stage involves examination of legislation and administrative structures to determine responsibility for and constraints on actions. These aspects are labelled 'institutional arrangements' (Ch. 11). Subsequently, the investigator documents actual project actions with attention to type of activity (construction, operation) as well as to time and monetary expenditure required. With appreciation of values and objectives, project environment, institutional arrangements and project actions, it is then necessary to account for project impacts. The impacts may be ecological or social, and should be classified either as primary or secondary. Intended and unintended effects should be differentiated. In this manner, the investigator traces the chain of interactions caused by a project, as outlined in the network approach in pre-project analysis (section 9.4.4).

With projects identified and described, it then becomes necessary to judge the adequacy of the project and the significance of the impacts. In accounting for (in)adequacy, the analyst should study processes which have influenced the development of the project. These may range over resource allocation procedures (Ch. 4), perceptions, attitudes and behaviour (Ch. 5), institutional arrangements (Ch. 11) and policy or decision processes (Ch. 12). The final stage, as identified

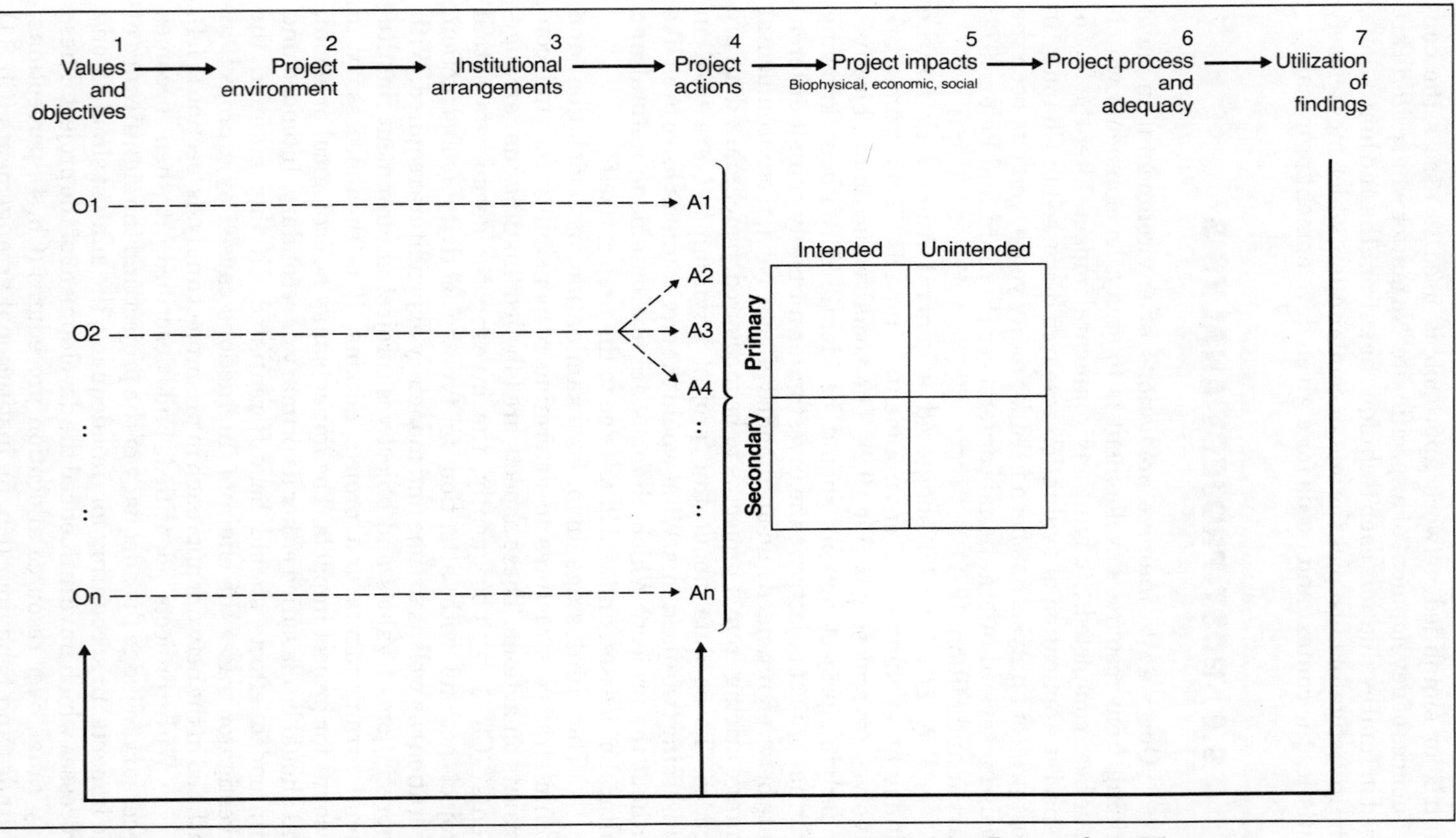

Fig. 9.2 A framework for hindsight evaluation of environmental impacts (*from Day et al., 1977*)

by Day *et al.*, is for the researchers to see in what manner their findings can be applied to improve project effectiveness. This step normally involves discussions among project evaluators, administrative agencies, and interested parties.

The framework developed by Day *et al.* (1977) indicates that resource development projects usually create a complex pattern of impacts which may arise over an extended period of time. This view was shared by Gardner (1972–1973). He felt that impacts could be triggered at several stages of development, ranging from planning, construction, operation, to termination (Fig. 9.3). As a result, he called for a 'heightened historical-temporal perspective in environmental impact research' (Gardner, 1972–1973; 155). Such a perspective often can only be obtained by monitoring a project throughout its lifetime (Bromley, 1985; 3–8). Insights gained can then be applied to estimating the impacts of future projects.

Post-project analysis has assumed greater importance following reports from around the world that resource development projects often have generated unexpected and negative results. In the field of water development, studies have shown that introduction of canals (Meyer, 1980; el Moghraby and el Sammani, 1985) and drainage (Kettel and Day, 1974; Found, Hill and Spence, 1975; 1976; Hill, 1976) may cause substantial environmental deterioration. More dramatic have been the findings from studies of the ecological and social impact of man-made lakes (Mithal, Joshi and Gohain, 1984: Olofin, 1984: Adams, 1985; Erskine, 1985).

Major reservoirs in Africa have been particularly revealing with regard to ecological and social impacts. The Kariba dam was completed in December 1958, and by July 1963 a lake covering 5,180 km^3 had formed. This area had been occupied by some 57,000 Gwembe Tonga, all of whom had to be resettled (Scudder and Colson, 1972; 41). The Volta River project in Ghana was started in 1961 and completed in 1965. Lake Volta, behind the dam, is 8,482 km^3, 402 km long and required resettlement of 80,000 people from 700 villages (Kalitsi, 1973; 77–80). Other projects were of similar scope. Scudder (1966; 99) noted that 120,000 Nubians had to be resettled as a result of the Aswan High Dam and 50,000 people from several distinct ethnic groups were relocated at the Kainji project in Nigeria. While different figures have been provided concerning numbers of people affected, agreement exists that all of these were massive projects affecting incredibly large numbers of people.

Those who have studied these projects concur that little effort was made to estimate project impacts in the planning phase (Scudder, 1965, 7; E. White, 1969, 220; Attwell, 1970, 190). After the projects reached their operational stage, numerous researchers documented significant ecological changes. Concerning the Kariba and Volta projects, investigators found that weeds became established in the reservoirs (E. White, 1969; Lawson, 1970; Kalitsi, 1973). These weeds

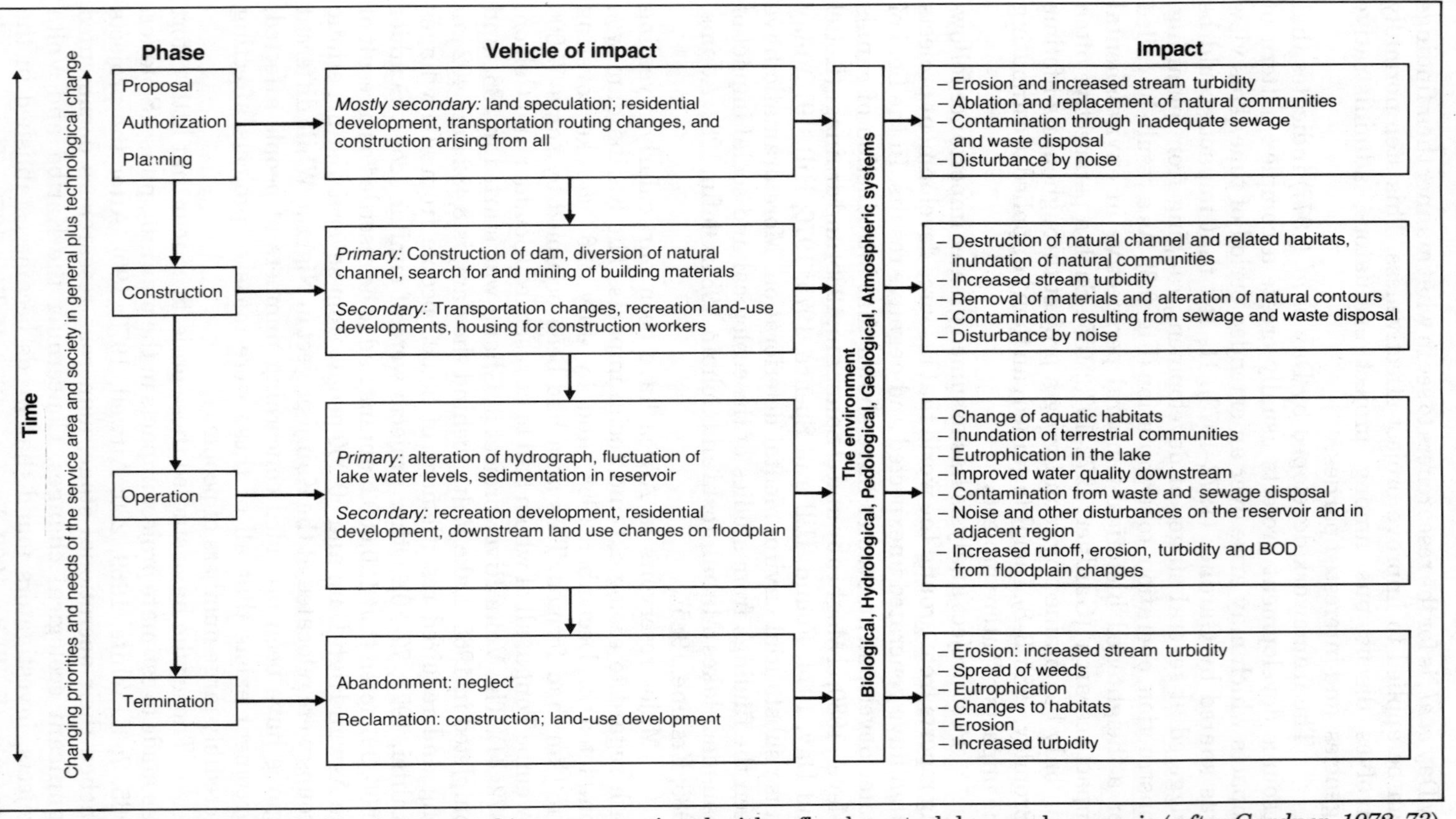

Fig. 9.3 Dynamics of environmental impact associated with a flood-control dam and reservoir (*after Gardner, 1972–73*)

provided favourable habitats for disease vectors. Thus, the weeds in Lake Volta provided a home for the *Bulinus* snail, the vector of bilharzia, and the *Mansona africana* mosquito, the vector of the yellow fever virus (Kalitsi, 1973; 84).

Other problems arose. Planners for all of the projects had to decide what to do with natural vegetation which would be drowned when the reservoirs filled. Clearing vegetation is expensive, yet numerous reasons support clearing. Absence of underwater vegetation would ensure that fishing nets did not get tangled. Lake transport would also be assisted as submerged trees represent navigational hazards.

Extensive clearing was completed at Kariba prior to flooding. At Volta, limited clearing was completed adjacent to resettlement towns to provide stump-free fishing areas (Lawson, 1970; 94). A negative side-effect occurred. Aquatic weeds quickly established themselves in the cleared areas, and the bilharzia snail vector became established. As a result, an attempt to improve fishing opportunities created adverse effects from the health point of view. A lack of appreciation for the chain of events which could be initiated by the reservoirs resulted in resource managers having to react to rather than anticipate such problems.

The impact of the reservoirs was not confined to the lakes, but also extended downstream. At Volta, Lawson (1970; 95) showed that farm land located downstream lost the benefit of silt deposition during flooding. Furthermore, irrigation systems could not function properly while the reservoir was filling, leading to drying of the earth and increased salinity. At Kariba, Attwell (1970) discovered numerous problems on the downstream floodplain. Both vegetational patterns and wildlife activity had been disrupted. These results were obvious, even though baseline data had not been assembled prior to construction of the dam. Indeed, Attwell noted that the first ecological survey of the valley below the dam was not done until three years after construction was completed.

The scale of the African man-made lakes had a substantial impact upon residents of the areas which were inundated. The resettlement programmes have attracted the interests of anthropologists and sociologists (Colson, 1963; Scudder, 1965; 1966; 1968; 1972; Scudder and Colson, 1972; Taylor, 1973). Post evaluation studies revealed that officials were preoccupied with the power generation aspects of the dam projects. Local requests for ecological surveys to identify potential resettlement areas were ignored (Scudder, 1965; 7). Senior administrators simply assumed that ample land was available for the displaced population. These studies and others have contributed to a growing interest in research on *social impacts* of development. Numerous workers have been developing procedures to identify and measure, or predict, the social consequences of developing resources (Stacey and Duchi, 1980; Andrews, Hardin and Madsen, 1981; Carley and Bustelo, 1984; McNicoll, 1984; Dillon, 1985; Finsterbusch, 1985; Green and Bone, 1985; Palinkas, Harris and Peterson, 1985).

Development of land and associated resources has attracted post-project research. Concerning agricultural development, the failure of the British-sponsored 'Groundnut Scheme' in East Africa was attributed to inadequate pre-project surveys of soils, hyrology, climate, labour sources and transportation (Matheson and Bovill, 1950; Phillips, 1959). Russell (1972) noted that virtually no ecological studies preceded selection of sites, a situation experienced in developed countries as well (Richardson, 1972). Clearing land became more costly than anticipated because of lack of understanding of the tough, woody vegetation covering the area. After clearing was completed, unanticipated problems arose concerning erosion; soil water-logging, abrasion and compaction; drought; viral (rosette) disease; and rapid growth of weeds. By 1951, a plan to cultivate 1,299,000 h for an annual production of 812,840 tonnes of groundnuts 'was a failure' (Russell, 1972; 571).

Post-project research has been conducted on other types of resource development. The consequences from development of energy resources have been studied in the Soviet Union (Izrael *et al.*, 1981), Norway (Lind, 1983), the North Sea (Manners, 1982) and Alaska (Lins, 1979; Bromley, 1985). The impact of mineral extraction also has attracted research interest (Blunden, 1985, 189–210; Hay, 1985). Furthermore, investigators have examined the impact of recreation and tourism activity, at both regional (Barker, 1982a) and local (Boggs and Wall, 1984) scales.

These studies indicate the vigour with which post-project analyses are being pursued. Such work has the potential to aid environmental impact assessments in at least two ways. By monitoring actual interactions over time, this research should improve understanding of relationships and processes in the environment. At the same time, experience and understanding acquired from earlier developments should make the design and implementation of future ones more effective.

9.6 ANALYSIS OF PROCEDURE

The preceding sections have reviewed research concerned with establishing the nature of environmental impacts arising from resource development. Another focus has considered the way in which environmental impact procedures are implemented. Ditton (1972; 140) effectively described the rationale for the latter type of study. In his words,

> Many would have us focus only on methodologies as if this was the one and only solution to our problems. It would be naive to believe that

> even with the most sharpened methods, the problems would be noticeably reduced. You must still live within the often restrictive boundaries of agency concerns, relative budgets, archaic laws and often archaic missions.

Concern with these types of problems leads to work closely related to that regarding attitudes and behaviour (Ch. 5), institutional arrangements (Ch. 11) and the policy process (Ch. 12). Environmental assessment procedures continuously are being modified. Consequently, there is little merit in providing detailed descriptions of current approaches in various countries, as such information quickly becomes outdated (Nelson and Jessen, 1981; Jammett and Madelmont, 1982; Burton, Wilson and Munn, 1983; Morgan, 1983). However, there is value in identifying the basic questions being posed and noting some investigations which have been done.

A range of questions has arisen as researchers examine procedures in different countries. Although not incorporating every question, the following identify the general issues:

1. Under what terms of reference (legislation, administrative directive) are environmental impact assessments conducted? How do these terms of reference relate to existing legislation, regulations and policies?
2. What criteria are used to determine which projects receive an environmental impact assessment? Who or what agency determines the criteria?
3. What is the prescribed content for environmental assessment statements?
4. Who, or which organization, is responsible for arranging and carrying out the environmental impact assessment for a project?
5. Who decides which projects are assessed?
6. Who decides whether an environmental impact statement is adequate?
7. Who decides whether a project will be approved or stopped?
8. What role does the public have in the environmental impact assessment procedure?
9. How many environmental impact assessments have been conducted? What types of projects have been studied?
10. How much time is required to complete an environmental impact statement?
11. How much has it cost to conduct assessments in terms of total project costs and/or pre-project feasibility costs?
12. How many projects have been rejected as a result of environmental impact assessments? How many project designs have been altered, and what adjustments have been made?
13. To what extent have environmental controls, recognized during the assessment process, been implemented and enforced?

Environmental impact assessment was first formalized in the United States by the National Environmental Policy Act of 1969. The effect of the Act was to require that Federal agencies specify the expected environmental consequences of all actions, obtain comment from other government departments and make their findings available to the public. The American approach, based upon legislation and the courts, generated a large number of environmental impact assessments and lawsuits (Liroff, 1981). This large number of assessments and court cases has provided an empirical base for numerous investigators to assess the general procedure or to analyse specific cases (White, 1972c; Bender and Clink, 1978; Simms and Thomas, 1982; Tuthill *et al.*, 1982; Daneke, Garcia and Priscoli, 1983). It also has prompted one geographer to explain what individuals should anticipate when they appear in court as expert witnesses during environmental litigation (Mitchell, J.K., 1978a).

The British took a different approach. Rather than passing legislation specific to environmental assessment, they approached the matter by an administrative route (O'Riordan, 1981). The first Minister of the Department of the Environment stated that Britain did not and would not have the equivalent of the American environmental assessment statement. In his view, such statements made 'a land fit for lawyers to live in with no great impact upon the environment itself' (Lindsay, 1972; 70). Instead, all government departments would be expected to consider environmental aspects as one of many variables when making decisions.

In Canada, the federal and provincial governments studied the American experience. Most Canadian jurisdictions rejected specific environmental assessment legislation because of a fear of generating an avalanche of assessments which would overwhelm the courts. Thus, at the federal level, an environmental assessment and review process was established by Cabinet order during December 1973. Subsequent experience led to some modifications through another Cabinet order in February 1977. In essence, the procedure gives considerable discretionary power to the ministers concerning which projects are assessed, what information is disclosed and what role the public may have. Although details vary, a similar philosophy underlies most of the provincial approaches. The main exception is Ontario which passed an Environmental Assessment Act in 1975. As in the United States, this activity has attracted research attention directed at reviews of basic procedures, studies of actual decisions or appraisals of specific agencies (Bankes and Thompson, 1980; Brassard and Harrison, 1981; King and Nelson, 1983; Gibson and Patterson, 1984; Maclaren and Whitney, 1985).

Appraisal of procedure for environmental impact assessment represents a significant research area. Ideas and concepts which appear conceptually sound may not be effective if they are not well implemented. The transition from conception to implementation of ideas is fraught with difficulties which often can only be identified and assessed by detailed studies of actual procedures and operating practices. Such work should not be left exclusively for political scientists, lawyers and management scientists. Disciplines such as geography with a strong commitment to man–environment relationships should address themselves to the issue of how environmental policies are translated into practice. Furthermore, to increase the analytical strength brought to bear on such problems, geographers should strive for joint studies with individuals from other disciplines which are concerned with policy and institutional issues.

9.7 IMPLICATIONS FOR RESOURCE MANAGEMENT

Environmental impact assessments provide an opportunity to ensure that environmental considerations are given as much attention as engineering and economic aspects. Experience has shown that too often in the past environmental considerations were either overlooked or ignored (Bernard and Pelto, 1972; Farvar and Milton, 1972). Nevertheless, advocates of environmental assessments must always remember that the environment is only one of many variables needing attention (Wall and Wright, 1977; 45).

Environmental impact assessments can be used to minimize disruption to the environment by proposed projects. Lessons may also be learned, however, by reviewing past experiences. As Allen (1972; 319) has argued, the literature usually reports 'success stories, whereas I sincerely believe that quite often more can be learned from "skeletons in the closet", if these are properly described, explained, and evaluated'.

The implications are clear. Evaluations or hindsight reviews of existing projects combined with research on fundamental processes are essential if impact predictions are to be sharpened. In this light, the general question of evaluative research is explored in more detail in Chapter 10.

A major concern about environmental impact statements is the range of their quality and the lack of standards or guidelines on which to judge their adequacy (Orloff, 1972, 32; Flamm, 1973, 203–4; Mikesell, 1974, 13; Perry, 1977, 257–8; O'Hare, 1980; Hart, Enk and Hornick, 1984). In an editorial for *Science*, Schindler (1976) emphasized some of the problems. He noted that in order to silence environmental critics, politicians were requiring funds to be made available for impact studies. In his view, the outcome often has taken the following form:

> Someone is inevitably available to receive these funds, conduct the studies regardless of how quickly results are demanded, write large, diffuse reports containing reams of uninterpreted and incomplete

descriptive data, and in some cases, construct 'predictive' models, irrespective of the quality of the data base. These reports have formed a 'gray literature' so diffused, so voluminous, and so limited in distribution that its conclusions are never scrutinized by the scientific community at large. Often the author's only scientific credentials are an impressive title in a government agency, university or consulting firm.

Although one-sided, these comments identify a serious issue demanding attention by resource managers. If environmental impact statements are to be credible, guidelines and standards are essential. Different responses have occurred. In the United States, the Council on Environmental Quality, established by the National Environmental Policy Act of 1969, has issued guidelines for preparation of statements. In Canada, the federal Environmental Assessment Review Office also has issued guidelines. In Ontario, some environmental planning and ecological consultants have organized the Ontario Society for Environmental Management. One of its long-term objectives is to establish professional standards of competence and quality to ensure self-regulation comparable to that by such professions as architecture, engineering, law or medicine. Such responses are healthy, as they reflect awareness of and concern about the types of comments offered by Schindler.

On the other hand, we should not be overly optimistic about realizing 'perfect' impact statements (Ross, 1976, 1; Wall and Wright, 1977, 3–4). White (1972c; 306–7) clearly identified the barriers against such an achievement. First, we lack knowledge about many natural and social systems. Until functions and processes are understood, it will not be possible to describe accurately the likely biophysical, economic and social consequences of decisions. Second, it usually is not possible to provide descriptions of all practicable alternatives. Such analysis often goes against the grain of agency structures and requires work cutting across disciplinary boundaries. Third, even if impacts could be identified, White is pessimistic that we are able to measure their importance to facilitate social evaluation. These represent major problems that deserve attention.

Resource managers have a number of concerns about environmental assessment which will need explicit attention in the future. One will be how to design and conduct assessments in recognition both of the uncertainty associated with the future (Kates, 1977; O'Riordan, 1979; Plotkin, 1983) and of the uncertainty regarding the response of natural and social systems to resource development (Holling, 1978). One way to address this difficult problem would be to use scenarios described in Chapter 3 to sketch possible futures (Svedin, 1979). Once the methodological problems are handled, the managers then will need to give more attention to expediting the implementation of impact assessments (Mutrie and Mulamoottil, 1980; Graybill, 1985).

Developers often view environmental assessments as one more

regulatory hurdle or obstacle to overcome. In this regard, the resource managers will have to demonstrate how such assessments can be positive ventures. Opportunities certainly are present. Reclamation of debilitated land is one area in which environmental assessments can be incorporated during pre-planning (Lautenbach, 1985). Another opportunity is presented by environmentally sensitive areas from which gains can be realized by recognizing the fragility of the ecosystems during the planning and design stages (Eagles, 1981, 1984; Fenge, 1982).

A final implication relates to costs. In other words, what expenditure of funds is required by impact assessments? Dorney (1977; 185) has addressed this issue. He noted that the necessary budget is variable, depending upon the range of disciplines represented and the detail desired. In his experience, a recurring figure was 10 per cent of an engineering or planning budget. In terms of total project costs, such engineering or planning costs frequently range between 3 to 5 per cent. As a result, environmental assessment costs often are as little as a fraction of a per cent (Pasurka, 1984). At the same time, Dorney (1973) has demonstrated that assessment studies can lead to substantial savings as they uncover problems that can be avoided. This recognition of real gains is important, especially during a recessionary period in which there often is a temptation to cut back on environmental considerations (Garner and O'Riordan, 1982).

9.8 IMPLICATIONS FOR RESEARCH

Environmental impact assessment has strong ties with the man–environment or ecological research tradition (Greenberg, Anderson and Page, 1978). It epitomizes the value of a holistic approach to studying environmental problems. To predict consequences of resource development, or appraise the impact of earlier development, it is essential to recognize a host of variables and relationships. Indeed, Commoner (1972b; xxiv–xxv) has argued that the philosophy of reductionism, which asserts that understanding of a complex system can be realized only by breaking a problem into parts and studying each in isolation, is a hindrance to analysis of vast natural systems. He regretted that reductionism is the characteristic approach of many disciplines since it may be counterproductive in environmental research.

In terms of theory and social relevance, a degree of tension exists. Environmental impact assessment is usually addressed to immediate problems. At the same time, the necessary knowledge has not always been available to provide easy or quick answers (Mikesell, 1974; 15). The time available to conduct impact assessments usually is not long, so the investigators do not have the luxury of conducting extensive investigations about processes and relationships (Lewin,

1975; 128). The result is that pure research, such as that initiated by individuals like McDonald and Kay (section 9.3), must be reviewed continuously to determine how it might assist applied studies. In this sense the most theoretical or pure research in fields concerned with biophysical processes (geomorphology, biogeography, climatology) and social processes (cultural and historical geography) has the potential to make significant contributions to environmental impact assessment work.

Given the many variables involved, a strong argument can be made for the value of a team approach to this work. While it is self-evident that individuals from the sciences (biology, soils) should be involved, social scientists also should be included. Such disciplines as anthropology, sociology and psychology should be represented, especially when social impact is deemed significant (Bernard and Pelto, 1972; 1). In addition, individuals with expertise in remote sensing (Ross and Singhroy, 1985) and geographic information systems (Griffith, 1980) are increasingly being called upon to participate in assessment studies.

While no one individual usually can evaluate all impacts for a large project, care must be taken that a team approach is treated as an integrated effort. A team approach too often ends up as a group of experts studying a project and then correlating their results. The need in environmental impact assessment is for pre-correlation, or integration of approach and findings from the outset. In this sense, an interdisciplinary approach (where objectives, methods and findings are interwoven from the outset) is preferable to a multidisciplinary one (where a group of specialists work relatively independently).

Regarding type of work being pursued, the emphasis has been upon description and prediction. The former has been pursued because of the need to identify and specify the nature of potential impacts. The latter concern underlies the rationale for estimating possible consequences. In many instances, future outcomes can be predicted even when explanations for relationships and processes are understood only poorly. In this context, Worthington (1972; 204) maintained that adequate time, funds and expertise will rarely be available to predict all consequences. The outcome is that investigators often strive to pinpoint the most critical problems.

The actual research process encounters many obstacles. Because of poor understanding of many ecosystems, as well as conflicting values held by the public and decision makers, conceptualization of the research problem is difficult. Different viewpoints result in different interpretations of what the problem is (Hare, 1985). The shortage of time often makes experimental research designs unfeasible. Measurement is frequently a problem for several reasons (Susskind and Dunlap, 1981; Ghiselin, 1982). Difficulties are encountered in quantitatively comparing different environmental features (value of an historic building versus an endangered species).

Another problem deals with identifying critical thresholds concerning deterioration, a difficulty also encountered in carrying capacity research (Ch. 7).

In many ways, research on environmental impacts represents one of de Bono's new holes. For years, environmental considerations were overlooked in resource development relative to technological and engineering concerns. By conducting research in this area, investigators are starting to produce information and understanding that never would have emerged from continuous digging in the traditional holes associated with feasibility studies. In this context, White (1972c; 307–8) suggested three areas in which geographic modes of thought could contribute to improvement of environmental impact statements. These were:

1. Research which specifies process or relationships within a natural or social system affected by a project.
2. Methods of preparing formal impact statements.
3. Methods of placing social valuations on those impacts that are identified and measured.

These three items represent important but demanding areas for inquiry. If another point, suggested by Sorenson (1972; 104) is added, a research agenda is provided which draws upon the skills of both physical and human geographers. He maintained that more attention is needed concerning the political processes associated with impact statements. In his words, 'no matter how much information or how many procedures are brought to bear in impact assessment, there will always be irreconcilable differences in values which can only be resolved in the political arena.'

These comments stress that both technical and value-laden issues must be handled in environmental impact assessment (Manheim, 1981). Geographers should not strive to be so 'systematic' and 'scientific' that they focus upon technical questions to the exclusion of basic values and aspirations (Usher, 1974).

CHAPTER 10

EVALUATION

10.1 INTRODUCTION

Several points of view have been expressed regarding evaluation research. White (1972c; 307–8) has lamented that although immense amounts of money and time are devoted to planning for the future, 'pitifully small amounts are spent on finding out what actually happened after plans were implemented'. He felt that we must know much more about what occurs after the bulldozers have withdrawn (1972b; 925). Others are more pessimistic about the need for and future of hindsight studies. Morehouse (1972; 868) observed that evaluation research 'has no determinate form, and its method is one largely of trial and error – with the emphasis on error ... There seem to be many more wrong than right ways to conduct program evaluations'. This view is shared by Schick (1971; 70) who remarked that evaluation 'tests stand accused of cultural bias; the sample was improperly drawn or just too small; the stated goals are not the real ones; the true results were ignored by the researchers; and so on'.

Despite these mixed reactions to evaluation studies, there has been an increase in their use. Recognition has been growing that assessments are needed for policies and programmes as well as for specific projects (O'Riordan and Sewell, 1981). Appreciation also has been developing with regard to the variety of resource management situations for which evaluations may be helpful. Thus, evaluations have been completed in such diverse fields as agriculture and rural land allocation (Furuseth and Pierce, 1982; Mundie, 1982; Lund, 1983; Johnston and Smit, 1985), coastal zone management (Bowen, Hoole and Anderson, 1980; Lowry, 1980; Nelson, Day and Jessen, 1981; Guy, 1983; Niedzwiedz and Batie, 1984), water management (Mitchell, 1983; Mitchell and Gardner, 1983), fisheries management (Draper, 1981; As-Sammani, 1984; Mitchell and King, 1984), energy management (Val and Nelson, 1983; Brown and Macey, 1985), forestry (McTaggart, 1983) and mountain development (Guller, 1986).

In the remainder of this chapter, issues in evaluation research will be examined. The objectives, rationale and basic problems in evaluative research are outlined in section 10.2. Subsequent sections illustrate the different approaches used in hindsight reviews: historical assessment (section 10.3), benefit-cost analysis (section 10.4) and perception and attitude surveys (section 10.5). While these approaches are discussed separately, it should be stressed that two or more may be combined during an evaluation study. The final sections consider the implications for resource management (10.6) and research (10.7).

10.2 BASIC CONSIDERATIONS

Numerous books (Suchman, 1967; Murphy, 1980; Rossi and Freeman, 1982) and articles (Roos, 1975; Pederson, 1977; Nakamoto, 1982) describe the characteristics of evaluation research. Although many terms ranging from hindsight reviews, evaluation, assessment, post-mortem analysis, to ex post facto analysis have been given to the work, general agreement exists concerning its focus. Basically, evaluations seek to determine how adequately resource policies, programmes and projects work, and what variables account for their (lack of) success. In Suchman's (1967; 31–32) classic work, the general intent of evaluative research was defined as

> the determination (whether based on opinions, records, subjective or objective data) of the results (whether desirable or undesirable; transient or permanent; immediate or delayed) attained by some activity (whether a program, or part of a program ... an ongoing or one-shot approach) designed to accomplish some valued goal or objective (whether ultimate, intermediate, or immediate, effort or performance, long or short range).

With the above purpose, the practical value of evaluation research may be rationalized on several counts. Such assessments note weaknesses in existing policies, programmes or projects which thereby might be resolved or which might be avoided in future decisions. Other, more covert motives may exist: to arbitrate or settle an internal dispute, to justify decisions already made, to support bids for power, or to postpone action (Caro, 1969; 89). On the other hand, appraisals may encounter opposition from agencies reluctant to undergo potentially self-critical analysis (Day *et al.*, 1977; 171) or from politicians fearing the 'resurrection of old skeletons which could return to haunt them' (Mitchell, 1972; 1288). Boulding (1972; 957) has expressed the motives for opposition in the following manner

> ... It's nice to be the drafter of a well-constructed plan,
> For spending lots of money for the betterment of Man,
> But Audits are a threat, for it is neither games nor fun
> To look at pleas of yesteryear and ask, 'What have we done?'
> And learning is unpleasant when we have to do it fast,
> So it's pleasanter to contemplate the future than the past.

At least four research issues deserve attention when examining evaluation studies (Mitchell, 1977; 160–75). At the *conceptualization* stage, it is desirable that the problem be formulated in such a way that data are assembled not only about *what* happened but also about *how* and *why* events transpired as they did. Concerning choice of *research design*, the classic experimental design represents the ideal since it involves comparisons through time and among control and treatment groups. These comparisons facilitate identification of cause-and-effect relationships. It is important, therefore, to determine how investigators cope with ethical and administrative problems in this design.

A third consideration involves *measurement*. Whenever a value judgement is made about a policy, programme or project, such decisions are based upon criteria, whether implicit or explicit. The analyst usually may choose from among a variety of criteria when evaluating the effectiveness of a resource management policy, programme or project. Two commonly used criteria are *efficiency* (concern with maximizing the difference between benefits and costs) and *equity* (concern with achieving fairness in the distribution of benefits and costs). Some resource development is initiated by governments to stimulate work opportunities in lesser developed regions in a country. In such circumstances, equity is given priority over efficiency, with the private sector being encouraged to locate activity in places which would not have been selected if efficiency were the first concern. The choice and operationalization of criteria is critical, since 'depending upon criteria which are picked, different conclusions may be drawn'. (Mitchell, 1975; 268). Ideally, a variety of criteria should be used when judging the adequacy of a given programme.

The fourth aspect is *timing*. Timing is always a contentious issue. If unintended negative results are to be modified, it is desirable to initiate reviews soon after implementation and to maintain continuous monitoring. Unfortunately, results may not appear immediately, and monitoring involves expenditure of time and resources. And yet, if too much time elapses before a review, negative outcomes may become too entrenched to alter. No easy answer exists for this dilemma.

10.3 HISTORICAL EVALUATION

Numerous reviews have used an approach which may be termed 'historical evaluation'. Analysis is usually based on data assembled through a combination of unstructured interviewing, field observation and library research. Cooley's (1963) study of conservation of the Alaskan salmon illustrates these characteristics. His objective was to assess salmon conservation policies and programmes. His appraisal was based upon

> a thorough examination of the written record as found in congressional hearings, committee reports, the *Congressional Record*, official

> reports of government agencies, enacted laws and policy statements, newspaper and trade journals, letters and reports of persons and organizations involved in the policy formulating process. It has been supplemented by correspondence and interviews with persons in both government and business ... A final source of information stems from personal experience, work, and travels (Cooley, 1963, xx–xxi).

Through such a procedure, the situation prior to the conception and implementation of policies and programmes was established, and subsequent events described and explained. The use of a wide variety of data sources in reconstructing the evolution of a resource management programme also ensured that cross checks were available.

Early studies using the historical approach tended to be loosely conceptualized, with little attention given to defining criteria explicitly or assessing the limitations of research designs. In terms of research designs, most inquiries adopted the one-shot case study ($\times O_1$) or the one group pretest–post-test design ($O_1 \times O_2$) described by Campbell and Stanley (1966) in Chapter 2. Only a few studies attempted to apply a time-series or longitudinal design ($O_1\ O_2\ O_3 \times O_4\ O_5\ O_6$).

Macinko (1963) completed one of the earliest systematic appraisals of a resource programme. He focused upon the Columbia Basin Project, conceived in the 1930s as the largest single irrigation project in the United States. The project area is located in the central part of Washington State, on the northwestern portion of the Columbia Plateau. Failures in dry farming during the period 1910–35 stimulated interest in irrigation. By 1948, the project was operating in an area consisting of over 1 million h, of which some 400,000 were classified as irrigable. However, slightly more than a decade after water was first brought to project lands, serious difficulties had been encountered. In Macinko's (1963; 185) words, 'development is virtually at a standstill, with less than half of the planned acreage under cultivation; and future growth is uncertain'.

In evaluating the project, he discovered a number of factors which contributed to its problems. About 30 per cent of the best irrigable land was withdrawn by farmers shortly after 1945 due to technological innovations which re-established the feasibility of dry wheat farming in the area. Ever-increasing costs represented another difficulty. Depreciation of the dollar over time was a contributing factor as well as an underestimation of drainage costs. The latter were originally estimated at $8.2 million and later were revised to $44.5 million which increased the payments expected from each participating farmer. Farm size was a third variable. Some of the smaller farms could not use the necessary capital-intensive equipment required for irrigation as effectively as larger units, and thus had low returns. Finally, all planning estimates were made on land use conditions expected to prevail when the project was at maturity. In the first decade (1949–58), hay occupied less than half the expected hectares and pastures less than one-seventh. Farmers emphasized low-value field and grain crops rather than the anticipated higher-value fruit, truck and livestock support crops.

The last factor, type of crop grown, raises the issue about timing of assessments. After the first decade, major problems had been encountered even though some positive returns had been realized. It is not known in the longer term whether the project came closer to meeting its expectations or if other problems emerged such as salts building up in soils due to increased amounts of water being applied to the land. This would only be revealed by subsequent monitoring. Thus, although in the short term the project encountered major obstacles, it may be more significant to know what happened over the longer term. This aspect emphasizes the desirability of longitudinal research designs over more time-bound appraisals.

Even though the timing of the evaluation did not facilitate conclusive findings, Macinko did suggest several guidelines based on his results. Managers must reduce the time lag between planning and implementation. The long time lag in his project area resulted in the withdrawal of 121,400 h of the best project lands. To avoid under-estimation of project costs, he recommended that means must be found to push a project along at a rapid pace after authorization. Furthermore, he recommended that project costs should not be estimated on the basis of current costs, especially when a project is to be implemented over two or even three decades as is common for many large-scale resource projects. In addition, more careful pre-project studies were recommended. He noted that detailed research on drainage problems was rejected on economic grounds. This proved to be a false saving, since subsequent drainage problems increased costs by a factor of five. Finally, he suggested that farmers should be surveyed to determine whether their future cropping strategies are in accord with what is assumed by the planners. In his study, it became apparent that even if farmers had wanted to change their cropping to take advantage of irrigation few had sufficient capital to make the transition.

Irrigation also has received considerable attention in India due to the uncertainty in the amount and timing of rainfall each year. The Government of India has made irrigation a key component in agricultural planning. Since independence in 1947, total utilization of irrigation has exceeded half the theoretical maximum limit and the goal is to reach the theoretical maximum by early in the 21st century. However, Chapman (1983) has noted that many of the existing irrigation projects, especially the larger ones, have been under-performing. He concluded that total production in irrigated areas may be only half of what could be achieved and that consequently 'it might be as important to concentrate attention on improving the effectiveness of existing canal systems as on building new ones' (Chapman, 1983; 268). This situation indicates how real gains often can be realized through systematic evaluations.

Agriculture is not the only field in which performance does not always meet expectations. Chapman (1982) has explained that oil refining and petrochemicals were given major importance in the regional development policy for Puerto Rico. Furthermore, during the 1960s that island's policy was regarded in many other developing countries as a model to emulate. As a result, Chapman decided to contrast the expectations with the actual experiences through an assessment of the policies and the outcomes.

He found that while the expectations were for the creation of 50,000 direct jobs by the 1980s, employment peaked at 5,600 in 1976. Many factors combined to create this disappointing outcome. The upheaval in the international oil market in the mid 1970s removed the cost advantage which Puerto Rico had enjoyed regarding access to raw materials. Corporate and governmental objectives, initially complementary, began to diverge. Perhaps most important was the relative lack of integrated downstream development in plastics, synthetic fibres and the like. It became clear that technological linkages in the industry do not automatically generate the establishment of related manufacturing plants since the nature of petrochemical products changes fundamentally as they pass through various stages of production.

Chapman (1982; 415) concluded that the disappointments in Puerto Rico do not mean that petrochemicals are not relevant for economic growth in developing countries. The main lesson, in his view, was that developing countries should focus upon integrating backward rather than forward and should view investment in basic facilities as an ultimate goal rather than as the starting point.

With the exception of Chapman's (1982) study, and to a lesser extent Macinko's, the preceding studies concentrated upon *what* occurred rather than considering *why* or *how* events resulted as they did. If evaluation research is to progress further in explaining as well as describing resource policies, programmes and projects, it will be necessary to devote more effort to understanding the behavioural aspects. Variables such as communications, inter-personal relationships, personalities, perceptions and attitudes and motivations are possibly significant in accounting for the relative effectiveness of resource management decisions.

Research by Draper (1977) dramatically illustrates the importance of such variables. She evaluated the establishment of an Indian cooperative fish-processing plant on a remote part of the northwestern British Columbia coast. The plant was intended to create needed jobs for Indians from seven small villages all experiencing high unemployment and few economic opportunities.

Behavioural geographers have drawn heavily on the ideas of psychologists and sociologists, but have largely ignored anthropologists who have worked in the area of resource analysis (Smith, 1977). Draper adapted an anthropological framework to account for the communications network which largely determined the problems at the processing plant (Paine, 1971). Draper suggested that in public resource management decisions, there may be a *patron–middleman–client relationship*. The patron (government) and the client (Indians) enter into a relationship in order to benefit from their transactions. However, because the two groups have different cultures, values, backgrounds and beliefs, they often find it difficult to communicate with each other. This situation requires a middleman (one or more persons or groups) who serves as an intermediary. Where the patron and client's values, messages and requests are handled honestly, the middleman is designated as a *go-between*. However, where the information is manipulated and processed to the advantage of the middleman, his role is labelled that of a *broker*. Draper suggested that one or more brokers are often involved in resource management decisions involving public funds, and that identifying them and their role is crucial to accounting for the relative success of policies, programmes or projects. In her study, a broker did emerge who almost single-handedly destroyed the newly established plant.

Identifying the broker raised interesting ethical problems for Draper. If the human variables noted previously are significant, the investigator has to reach some important decisions. Should the information be released, even if it will reflect substantial discredit upon an individual? More practically, what are the implications for libel? And, if such findings are revealed, what cooperation can be expected in future studies if respondents become aware of earlier work? In these respects, Draper's work is exciting and disturbing. Geographers evaluating resource management experiences have not before explicitly addressed the variables pursued by Draper. On the other hand, further pursuit of such work will require each individual, and perhaps the discipline as a whole, to consider more explicitly than is usually done the ethical issues which arise.

10.4 BENEFIT-COST ANALYSIS

Benefit-cost analysis is a technique to assist managers in making decisions. Resource managers must decide how much money to spend in total, how to allocate the funds among competing projects, and how the money should be allocated over time. By attempting to identify systematically the benefits and costs of alternative projects, benefit-cost analysis helps to identify those projects which are economically viable and to rank alternatives. Normally, only those projects with a benefit-cost ratio greater than 1 are considered to be viable, and preference is given to those projects with the highest ratios.

Numerous sources discuss the strengths and limitations of such analysis (Prest and Turvey, 1965; Sewell *et al.*, 1965: Pearse, 1971; Howe, 1971; Canada, Treasury Board Secretariat, 1976). They are in agreement that benefit-cost ratios must be used with caution as it is extremely difficult to express all values in monetary terms. Furthermore, different ratios may emerge depending upon choice of interest rate, discounting procedure, economic life and assumptions about secondary effects, damages and compensation, employment and taxes. Another significant concern has been noted by Sewell *et al.* (1965; viii):

> it should be emphasized that these ratios are a measure of relative merit and not of absolute merit. If there are other ways of achieving the same purpose, the fact that a project has a benefit-cost ratio greater than 1 does not necessarily imply that it should be built.

Benefit-cost analysis has been used extensively as an aid to decision making in resource management (Swartzman, Liroff and Croke, 1982). However, because of the difficulties noted above, benefit-cost studies are not always accurate. As a result, investigators have started to compare pre-project estimates with post-project benefit-cost results to see if programmes or projects have been able to deliver the originally anticipated flow of goods and services.

Small-scale water projects have attracted the interest of those conducting hindsight reviews, with attention being given to differences between planned and actual costs and benefits. Day (1974) compared the benefits and costs anticipated during pre-project planning for a dam and reservoir with those two years after dam construction. The project was a reservoir in southwestern Ontario which drained some 11 km^2 and formed a 30 ha water surface. The dam was designed to serve two major purposes: increase agricultural productivity from improved irrigation water, and improve transportation by functioning as a bridge for a new road. Other benefits foreseen were increased recreation, livestock watering, firefighting, domestic water supply, flood control and downstream summer flow. Using a 4 per cent interest rate and a 50-year amortization period, a pre-project benefit-cost ratio of 2.2 : 1 had been calculated.

Final costs increased by 15 per cent over the originally estimated costs due mainly to increased land assembly costs and increased engineering fees. While the costs went up, Day's research suggested that anticipated benefits did not fully materialize. The principal justification of the project was based on expected increases in farm productivity due to irrigation. Interviews with farmers two years after completion of the project indicated that the estimated cropping pattern was unlikely to develop mainly due to unfulfilled planning assumptions. The planners assumed a future cropping pattern typical of the entire watershed rather than confining themselves to the 310 ha directly affected. This led to a gross overrestimate of future tobacco, vegetables and strawberries as cash crops. Day further questioned the validity of the pre-project agriculture benefits since 'none of the farmers to be assisted previously experienced detrimental water shortages, none presently irrigates crops other than tobacco, and none intends to adopt vegetables or strawberries as cash crops or to irrigate corn, hay, or pasture' (Day, 1974; 26–27). Distribution of agricultural benefits was also deemed questionable as virtually all primary project benefits accrued to only four farms.

The transportation benefits were also challenged. Two routes to cross the river had been considered. In planning the reservoir, the cost of the more expensive alternative was subtracted from the cost of the adopted dam and highway plan which followed the route of the less expensive alternative. This accounting manoeuvre enhanced the feasibility of the project at a local level by transferring a large percentage (57 per cent) of conservation expenses to a transportation budget. Since the road portion of the project was subsidized by the provincial highway department, this procedure shifted costs from the local level to the provincial level. If the lower cost highway alternative route were used in the calculations, conservation costs would have been increased by 28 per cent.

Day questioned many of the other anticipated benefits. A livestock water shortage in the project area had never been experienced which cast doubt on the benefits included for livestock watering. The nearby municipality had no history of water shortages, and the local council had no intention of tapping the reservoir as a water supply source. The reservoir surface was too far from the road for rapid fire fighting purposes, and the local fire brigade did not intend to use it.

Conversely, anticipated recreation benefits had been realized in the form of new opportunities for camping, swimming, picnicking, boating and fishing. However, the extent of those benefits was seen to be doubtful. Day predicted that a popular trout fishery would be short-lived. Reservoir eutrophication would lead to more coarse game species replacing the trout after 10 years. Of even greater concern, however, was a finding that the 'dam destroyed one of the best remaining trout streams on the north shore of Lake Erie' (Day, 1974; 30). Having reviewed the experience of the dam and reservoir after two years of operation, Day concluded that the original benefit-cost ratio (2.2 : 1) had been overoptimistic. Actual experience suggested a benefit-cost ratio based on primary conservation benefits of less than 1, which prompted him to suggest changes in the way in which pre-project appraisals were evaluated.

Cecile *et al.* (1985) assessed the effectiveness of a land drainage programme in eastern Ontario through a number of stages, one of which involved benefit-cost analysis. They selected 64 drains for analysis, and first considered the ability of the drainage programme to target those lands most likely to benefit from drainage. They found that drains were built on a 'first come, first served' basis, without consideration of the characteristics of the land. The result was that only 21 of the 64 drains contained more than 70 per cent of the affected land deemed to be of the type which would benefit from drainage.

The benefit-cost analysis was viewed as an approximate appraisal since neither benefits nor costs had had time to emerge fully.

Furthermore, the analysis had to make a number of assumptions. For example, a net benefit per hectare of $71 was adopted, but this was recognized as an 'ideal' since it assumed (1) the possibility that productivity in eastern Ontario could match that in southwestern Ontario, a circumstance recognized as impossibly optimistic, (2) all drained lands would be used to grow corn and (3) the present disparity in net benefit was due solely to drainage, when it was appreciated that farmers' incomes also were affected by climate, soils, facilities, markets and individuals' skill.

Choice of interest rate also would influence the findings. Cecile *et al.* handled that problem through parallel analysis using rates of 4, 7 and 10 per cent. They also did a number of analyses in which other assumptions were modified so that the decision makers could see the different results depending upon the assumptions which had been made. They concluded that a significant number of drains under the government programme were unlikely ever to generate future benefits equal to the costs of the drains. Indeed, even using conservative assumptions, this finding applied to a *majority* of the drains.

Such reviews do not always reveal disappointing results. Ghosh (1978) used benefit-cost analysis to assess the benefits of an irrigation project in West Bengal, India. He identified two areas: one with irrigated fields and the other without irrigated fields. The irrigated area was subsequently further subdivided to control for different crops and types of irrigation systems. He then assumed that yield rate per unit of area was not affected by variation in size of farms. Given this approach, he concluded that the actual benefits were sufficient to cover the costs of irrigation as well as the costs of other inputs and services.

10.5 PERCEPTION AND ATTITUDE STUDIES

Resource analysts have often used perception and attitude studies to determine the adequacy of existing or proposed policies, plans or practices. Use of such studies raises at least two issues. For a given issue or problem, what are the best methods for obtaining input from the public? Once the input is collected, how should it be analysed to display the nature, content and extent of information received? (Clark and Stankey, 1976; 214).

A range of methods is available for obtaining input from the public in resource management. These include public hearings, opinion surveys, referenda, letters to the editor or to public officials, and statements from pressure groups. Each has strengths and limitations.

Surveys have been used in studies focused upon evaluating the value of environmental education or work programmes (O'Hearn,

1982; Birch and Schwaab, 1983; Brown and Macey, 1985; Robottom, 1985; Shepard and Speelman, 1985/86; Westphal and Halverson, 1985/86). It is important that such programmes be evaluated on a regular basis, since in recessionary periods they usually are among the first to be eliminated because their benefits are long term and intangible. Regular and systematic evaluations can be used not only to improve their design, but also to provide evidence to assist in justifying their existence.

Driver and Johnson (1983/84) conducted an assessment of the Youth Conservation Corps (YCC), a combined work and environmental education programme for youths aged 15 to 18 in the United States. They had observed that numerous investigators had surveyed selected attitudes and behaviour at the beginning and end of the four- to eight-week long summer camps. Such assessments were useful, but did not measure the duration of programme benefits over time. They decided to concentrate on perceived long-term benefits.

Some 600 enrollees and 600 parents of enrollees were surveyed three to six years after participation in the programme. The 57-question, mailed survey form asked the enrollees if they believed that they had changed regarding the listed attitudes, skills or behaviours since they had attended the YCC camp. The parents were asked the same questions regarding their perceptions of a son or daughter who had attended a YCC camp. If changes were noted, respondents were requested to rate what role the YCC camp had in those changes. Just over 42 per cent of the questionnaires were completed and returned.

The study drew upon subjective ratings by enrollees and parents some time after their involvement with YCC. Of the 16 benefit scales which were given to respondents, overall mean scores on 4 of them for former enrollees and on 7 of them for parents indicated that the YCC influenced moderately to very greatly these perceived beneficial changes in enrollees. Specifically, the YCC enrollees perceived that they had become much more environmentally aware regarding the need both to conserve and to develop natural resources. Enrollees also reported considerably improved work - and safety - related habits and skills. In addition, they believed that they had significantly increased interest in outdoor areas, particularly concerning leisure activity. Driver and Johnson concluded that more comparative work on the scope, magnitude and persistence of benefits which result from participation in youth summer programmes is needed if such programmes are to be strengthened.

The above discussion focused on means of collecting data about resource programmes, and indicated the utility of perception and attitude surveys when appraising them. Once data are collected, however, the resource analyst still must decide how to analyse them. A helpful technique for perception and attitude data is *content analysis*. A number of books describe the general characteristics of this technique (North *et al.*, 1963; Stone *et al.*, 1966; Budd, 1967; Holsti, 1968;

1969; Carney, 1972; Krippendorff, 1980; Weber, 1985). Numerous definitions exist, but its general attributes are covered in Holsti's (1969; 14) statement that content analysis is 'any technique for making inferences by objectively and systematically identifying specified characteristics of messages'.

Holsti (1969; 24) noted that the communication process is composed of six elements: a *source*, an *encoding process* producing a *message*, a *channel* of transmission, a *recipient*, and a *decoding process* (Fig. 10.1). These six elements generate three types of research questions. What is the content or characteristics of a message? What are the causes or antecedents of messages? What are the effects of communication? A number of research designs have been developed to tackle these questions (Table 10.1).

Stankey (1972) was one of the first to draw attention to the value of content analysis for resource analysis. In instances where resource managers had received large amounts of input from the public, he suggested that content analysis could be used to examine the following questions. *Who* was replying to the resource management plan or proposal (the general public? organized interest groups?) *What* were they saying? Did they agree or disagree, and were opinions coupled with significant qualifications? *Why* were they saying what they were? *Where* were responses coming from?

He and several US Forest Service colleagues analysed public response to management proposals for a wilderness area in Montana. A booklet outlining five management alternatives for the area was distributed. After receiving 500 replies, the analysts had to decide what was the basic content of the messages and who were the senders. They analysed each letter to determine (1) which alternative was favoured, (2) reasons associated with support or rejection of each alternative, (3) specific aspects considered unacceptable, (4) the affiliation of the respondent, (5) the geographical residence of the respondent and (6) whether the respondent had visited the area. After reviewing all 500 responses, categories under each of the six headings were created and the frequency of mention for each category was tabulated. The data were then sorted, tabulated and cross-classified with reference to variables of specific interest to the administrators and resource managers responsible for the wilderness area. In this way, the content of the public input was 'objectively and systematically' analysed.

The US Forest Service subsequently developed a system labelled CODINVOLVE for analysis of public input whether that input was in the form of personal letters, reports, petitions, form letters, resolutions or questionnaire responses (Clark, Stankey and Hendee, 1974; Hendee, Clark and Stankey, 1974; Clark and Stankey, 1976). The major rationale upon which CODINVOLVE is based has been described in the following manner.

> The common denominators of virtually all public input are the opinions offered *for*, *against*, or *about* the issues in question, along

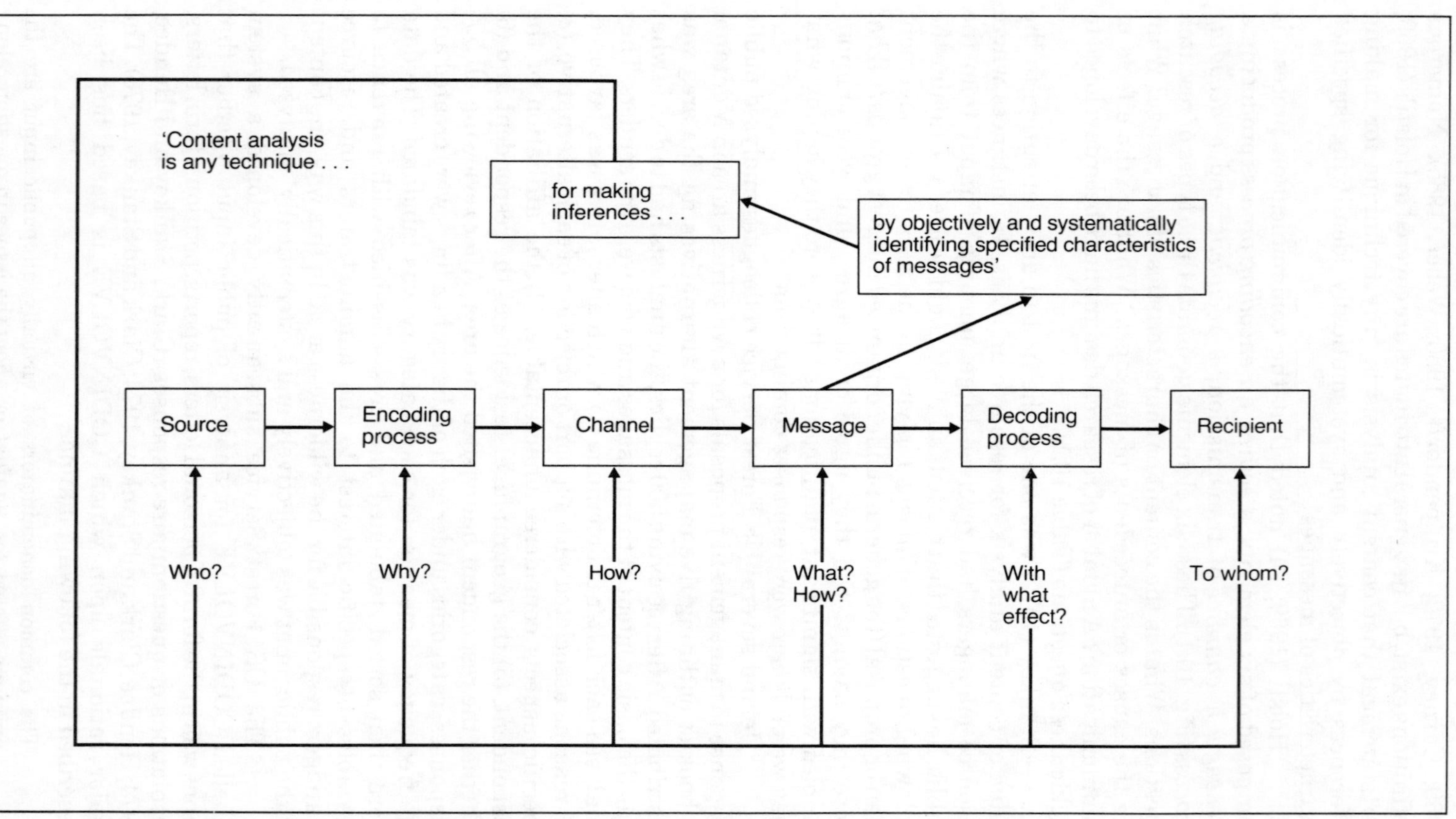

Fig. 10.1 Content analysis and the communication paradigm (*from Holsti, 1969*)

Table 10.1 Research designs for content analysis (*modified after Holsti, 1969*)

Purpose	Types of comparisons	Questions	Research problem
To describe characteristics of communication	Messages, source A 1. Variable X across time 2. Variable X across situations 3. Variable X across audiences	What?	To describe trends in communication content. To relate known characteristics of sources to messages they produce. To audit communication content against standards.
	Messages, source A Messages, source B	How?	To analyse techniques of persuasion.
	Messages/standard 1. *A priori* 2. Content 3. Non-content	To whom?	To relate known characteristics of the audience to messages produced for them. To describe patterns of communication.
To make inferences as to the antecedents of communication (the encoding process).	Messages/non-symbolic behavioural data 1. Direct 2. Indirect	Why?	To analyse traits of individuals. To secure information about preferences and needs. To infer aspects of culture and cultural change.
		Who?	To identify the characteristics of the senders.
To make inferences as to the effects of communication (the decoding process)	Sender messages/recipient messages	With what effect?	To analyse the flow of communication.
	Sender messages/recipient behavioural data		To assess responses to information.

> with any *reasons* given to support the views ... The combination of opinions and supporting reasons defines the values the public holds with regard to the issue in question (Clark and Stankey, 1976; 215).

CODINVOLVE was developed as a coding process which would provide quantitative summaries of all opinions expressed (for and against) as well as qualitative descriptions of supporting reasons. Furthermore, because many resource decisions evolve over extended time periods, the system was designed to be able to store, retrieve, add and summarize information as required.

Other investigators have used content analysis to appraise resource management practices. Grima and Dufournaud (1976) used it to code and analyse the content of public hearings held by the International Joint Commission during 1973. They reported on the affiliation of participants, content of presentations and effectiveness of presentations. Sewell and Wood (1971) analysed a public controversy over water allocation through content analysis of newspapers and other reports. Their study procedure identified the main participants in the controversy, the nature and timing of their involvement and shifts in management strategy. Needham and Nelson (1977) used content analysis to evaluate newspaper response to flooding and erosion on the north shore of Lake Erie during high water periods in 1952–53 and 1972–74. The results suggested that newspapers were not critical of adjustment strategies, with emphasis given to crisis responses. Another example is found in MacIver's (1970) study of municipal water supply decisions. Before interviewing residents of five communities about their preferences, he wished to determine the information to which they might have been exposed. To this end, he content analysed local newspapers, radio and television programmes. Content analysis was used by a team of researchers in England while studying the public inquiry process as represented by the Sizewell B Inquiry (Purdue, Kemp and O'Riordan, 1984).

In Chapter 5 it was noted that there is not always a close association between perceptions or attitudes and behaviour. It was for that reason and others that Bunting and Guelke (1979) argued that geographers should emphasize observation of actual behaviour. A study of litter control in campgrounds illustrates how covert observation can be used in evaluation of some resource management programmes.

Christensen (1981) wished to evaluate the effectiveness of information in reducing littering in campgrounds. She developed a research design and used it in Wenatchee National Forest in Washington State. Campers at randomly chosen campsites received an 'appeal-to-help' message requesting them to report any illegal littering noticed at the campground. The message was delivered by a campground employee either verbally or in the form of a cartoon. Control campers did not receive this message. Two hours after the appeal was delivered, littering was staged in sight of the subjects by a man or woman driving past a selected campsite in a car in which a radio was playing loudly. A soda or beer can was dropped from the car.

Two observers following in a second car recorded the actions of the campers: doing nothing, picking up the litter, reporting, or dealing directly with the offender. Ten minutes after the staged littering, a campground employee walked through the area to measure reporting of littering by campers.

A major goal was to determine how an appeal for assistance affected campers' reactions to littering violations. A significant difference in response was recorded between control and treatment campers. Some 83 per cent of the treatment group campers responded in some manner compared to 61 per cent of the control group campers. This finding suggested that information in the form of an appeal-for-assistance was effective, and therefore worth pursuing by campground managers. Thus, the research design generated practical evidence and avoided ethical problems since public behaviour was observed in a public place.

10.6 IMPLICATIONS FOR RESOURCE MANAGEMENT

Evaluative research serves several functions in resource management. Hindsight studies may allow managers to improve the operation of a policy, programme or project which has been implemented. A major qualification, however, is that with capital intensive resource schemes (a hydroelectric dam and reservoir) it may be difficult or even impossible to make incremental changes following establishment of basic facilities. Hindsight studies also should serve to improve the conception, design and implementation of future management approaches. By learning from previous experiences, earlier mistakes should be avoided and strengths reinforced. Again, a necessary qualification is that this advantage assumes experience may be transferred from one area to another or from one time period to another. Different cultures, technological capacities, institutional arrangements and environmental conditions may frustrate direct transfer of experiences.

Evaluations which are future-oriented also offer valuable assistance to the resource manager. Probabilistic estimates of future benefits and costs allow the manager to choose the pattern which he feels is the best approximation of the future rather than relying upon a single set of estimates. Furthermore, statements of future expectations expressed in probability terms emphasize the uncertain nature of all such estimates. At a different level, policy simulation models allow managers to study the impact of alternative policies upon resource systems or their component parts. Even where the details are not perfect, different simulated futures can indicate the major impacts of alternative approaches. Such simulations often force the manager to make explicit any values or assumptions which are held and which could influence choices.

10.7 IMPLICATIONS FOR RESEARCH

Evaluation research touches upon all of the major research traditions in geography in that resource decisions influenced by ecological, spatial or regional analysis are amenable to evaluation. Existing work demonstrates little development of theory. Much of the work is focused upon identification of critical variables. In many instances, empirical information is still to be provided concerning the variables which account for the 'success' of management decisions. Identifying such variables, let alone testing relationships or articulating theory, has proven difficult due to numerous difficulties in overcoming research barriers. This aspect has more than academic interest since methodological problems have often led to the rejection of research findings. As Schick (1971; 70) commented, 'all evaluation is vulnerable to challenge on methodological grounds. . . . Once an evaluation has been attacked, the grounds have been laid for justifiable disregard of its findings.' These views have been echoed by Morehouse's (1972; 868) observation that 'if research results do not support program aims and agency commitments, they may be simply ignored or, if acknowledged, criticized as methodologically unsound'. Much of the methodological controversy centres upon approaches to conceptualization, research design and measurement.

Hyman and Wright (1967; 754) cautioned that in conceptualizing a 'programme' the evaluator may be led astray by the term itself. Preoccupation with the programme or treatment may result in the investigator forgetting the context in which it is imbedded. They argued that most programmes are implemented by a staff. As a result, they suggested that the staff may be as important or more important than the actual programme in effecting change. For this reason, they urged greater attention in evaluative research to the role of personnel. This type of comment reinforces the approach illustrated by Draper's adaptation of a patron–broker–client framework for structuring evaluations (section 10.3).

Another concern is what is evaluated. Hyman and Wright stated that although most programmes have goals, it does not follow that they can be taken as given. They noted that most programmes have multiple objectives, which may be 'very broad in nature, ambiguously stated, and possibly not shared by all persons who are responsible for the programme'. As a result, evaluators must distinguish between that which is stated and that which is done. As we saw in Chapter 5, verbal behaviour and overt behaviour are not always interchangeable.

Choice of research design presents major problems. Ideally, evaluation should pinpoint cause-effect relationships. Only in that manner can the impact of resource decisions be explained. The classic experimental research design represents the ideal strategy for such research. Unfortunately, problems associated with control of external variables over time and ethical difficulties in identifying or manipulating control groups may be insurmountable (Morehouse, 1972, 871–2; Weiss and Rein, 1970; Campbell, 1970). The outcome is that investigators have relied upon one-shot case studies, pretest-post-test designs, or longitudinal designs. None of these facilitate unequivocal statements about cause-and-effect relationships. The prospects are not bright for a major breakthrough in development of a research design which is both theoretically sound, operationally feasible and ethically acceptable.

Measurement is the third major problem requiring attention. Evaluation implies judgement. Judgements assume standards or criteria which are operationalized through indicators and thresholds. Researchers have too often overlooked the importance of measurement, forgetting that different criteria applied to the same evidence can produce different assessments. Suchman (1967) has suggested general criteria (effort, performance, efficiency, adequacy) which are conceptually sound. If more investigators attempted to implement these, several benefits would result. General guidelines might emerge, and study results would be comparable. One of the most successful applications of Suchman's criteria in the field of resource management was done by Draper (1977). Her study represents a model which other inquiries would do well to replicate.

Concerning more general issues, evaluation research emphasizes the presence of subjectivity and compromise in research. Subjectivity is emphasized through selection of variables and criteria. Compromise is stressed by research design considerations. The ideal design can only rarely be used. Evaluation studies also reinforce the importance of de Bono's notion of lateral thinking, since such inquiries really ask whether previous or future management decisions were or will be dug in the most appropriate hole. In many ways, evaluation research represents a conscious search to determine whether or not better holes might be found, or if existing holes could be modified.

CHAPTER 11
INSTITUTIONAL ARRANGEMENTS

11.1 INTRODUCTION

As with many of the resource issues identified previously, that of institutional arrangements has a strong interdisciplinary flavour. Geographers working in this area have drawn heavily upon ideas from political science, business administration, law and economics. The objectives have included attempts to account for, assess or prescribe the means through which resource management decisions have been or might be implemented. For the geographer, the ultimate goal of obtaining such insights should be to understand spatial allocations of resources, relationships between man and his environment, or the complexity of regions. In this context, spatial scale has been significant, as geographers have sought to explore approaches adopted at local, regional, national and international levels.

In addressing the matter of institutional arrangements, this chapter first identifies some basic considerations. These include the significance and definition of the problem, the issue of research strategies and the question of measurement (section 11.2). The following section (11.3) outlines the characteristics of selected studies of institutional arrangements. Section 11.4 then considers the aspects of bargaining and negotiation which occur within institutions. The final sections consider the implications for resource management (11.5) and research (11.6).

11.2 BASIC CONSIDERATIONS

Institutional arrangements have been identified as a variable needing greater attention (Mitchell, 1975; Fernie and Pitkethly, 1985). Concerning management for energy, O'Leary (1972) argued that an institutional rather than a resource crisis was the fundamental issue. For the field of water management in the United States, reviewers of a report issued by the National Water Commisssion (1973) stated it demonstrated that the 'answer to the nation's water problem is said to lie - almost without exception - in institutional reform, broadly defined' (Bromley, Butcher and Smith, 1974, 15). In a broader context, O'Riordan (1971a; 135) observed that

> One of the least touched upon, but possibly one of the most fundamental, research needs in resource management is the analysis of how institutional arrangements are formed, and how they evolve in response to changing needs and the existence of internal and external stress. There is growing evidence to suggest that the form, structure and operational guidelines by which resource management institutions are formed and evolve clearly affect the implementation of resource policy, both as to the range of choice adopted and the decision attitudes of the personnel involved.

The importance of institutional arrangements has been reiterated by Fernie and Pitkethly (1985; vii). In their view,

> all resource problems - overpopulation, hunger, poverty, fuel shortages, deforestation - are fundamentallly *institutional* problems which warrant institutional solutions. The success or failure of resource management is intrinsically tied up with institutional structures - the pattern of agencies, laws and policies which pertain to resource issues.

The previous statements indicate that the issue of institutional arrangements is viewed as a significant research question. While interest in this problem is strong, a review of existing studies raises a disturbing fact. Little consensus has emerged regarding what is meant by 'institutional arrangements'. Individuals have developed their own operational definitions, making direct comparison of results difficult if not impossible. Lack of agreement over the nature of the research problem represents a serious weakness. Such a situation hinders replication and verification of findings.

Several studies illustrate the range of definitions which have been used. In studying water management innovations in England and Wales, Craine (1969) defined institutional arrangements as the composite of legal powers, administrative structure and financial provisions. Several years later, Craine (1971; 522) provided a more detailed interpretation:

> 'institutions' and 'institutional arrangements' refer to a definable system of public decision making, one that includes specific organizational entities and governmental jurisdictions, but transforms conventional emphasis upon definition of agency structure, per se. In addition to being concerned with component organizational entities, the term 'institutions' suggests special attention to the configuration of relationships
>
> (1) established by law between individuals and government;
> (2) involved in economic transactions among individuals and groups;
> (3) developed to articulate legal, financial and administrative relations among public agencies; and

(4) motivated by social-psychological stimuli among groups and individuals.

> Specific relationships falling in any or all of these four categories, constrained and shaped by the natural and social environment, weave a web which describes the institutional system for decision making. Thus, institutional studies focus on the linkages which tie authority and action centres together into a public decision making system which is responsive to the environment within which it must operate.

Other studies emphasize the range of definitions which have been applied. Kaynor and Howards (1971; 1119) interpreted institutional arrangements to mean 'a cluster of customs, laws, or ways of behaving and organizing behaviour around problems of life in society'. A different viewpoint was offered by Nelson (1973) who viewed them as the forms of government, agencies, legislation and other social guides established to influence human behaviour. Fernie and Pitkethly (1985; 140) provided a detailed definition. They suggested that an institutional structure involves the pattern of agencies, laws, participants and policies pertaining to a given resource. Participants or actors are marshalled within a public or private organization. Legislation allows the actors to spend money and helps to define courses of action. People in organizations create, implement, monitor and enforce policies.

While such definitions vary, they represent attempts to indicate explicitly the manner in which the term is used. Some investigations, such as those by Kristjanson (1954) and Butrico *et al.* (1971), do not define the concept. This practice is unfortunate since it makes subsequent verification next to impossible.

In a review of research on metropolitan water management institutions, Wengert (1973) succinctly noted the features of studies focused upon institutional arrangements in resource management. In addition to inconsistency in operational definitions, Wengert concluded that the literature was characterized by lack of reference to the theoretical literature on institutions. It also tended to use the concept as an umbrella term to incorporate behavioural, social and managerial variables. These attributes emphasize the need for greater care in defining the nature of the problem. Unless this fact is realized, the present trend of having a large number of idiosyncratic studies will continue, and the possibility of developing any substantive generalizations will remain slight.

The attractiveness of 'institutional arrangements' is that it facilitates study of interaction of several variables. Lawyers have completed significant studies of legislation. Policy analysts have examined policies and related processes. Economists have investigated economic and financial arrangements. Political scientists have reviewed organizational structures and political processes. Historians and others have considered the evolution of key ideas and events. Studies of institutional arrangements should make a contribution through assessing the interaction of: (1) legislation and regulations, (2) policies and guidelines, (3) administrative structures, (4) economic and financial arrangements, (5) political structures and processes, (6) historical and traditional customs and values and (7) key participants or actors. Greater understanding of the way in which these variables interact in resource management would facilitate predictions about possible futures as well as prescriptions for alterations to existing institutional patterns.

Once the matter of identifying and defining the parts of the problem is resolved, greater attention should be directed towards broadening the range of research designs and methods of measurement. Most research on institutional arrangements has relied upon one-shot case studies or the pretest-posttest research design. Concerning measurement, the same issue that arose in evaluation research (Ch. 10) appears. If judgements are to be made about the adequacy or inadequacy of institutional arrangements, researchers must make their criteria, indicators and thresholds explicit (Mitchell, 1975; 267–75). In addition, investigators must indicate which resource management *functions* are being appraised. If management functions can be broken into *surveillance* (information collection and reporting), *mediation* (developing of joint strategies and programmes, conflict resolution), and *control* (regulatory responsibility and implementing authority), different patterns of institutional arrangements may be required as various resource sectors and problems are considered (Canada–United States University Seminar, 1973; 41–42). These questions of problem definition, research designs and measurements represent major issues which require attention.

11.3 ANALYSES OF INSTITUTIONAL ARRANGEMENTS

Studies have focused upon a variety of resource sectors, topics and problems. Investigations concerned with water, fisheries, forestry, parks, hazards, coastal zone management and general environmental management are reviewed here to demonstrate different approaches to the problem of institutional arrangements.

11.3.1 WATER MANAGEMENT

Faculty members from about 20 universities and colleges in Canada and the United States worked together to analyse the institutional structures for managing land and water resources of the Great Lakes basin. A number of factors were identified as causing an imperfect response to resource problems: a diffused public interest, differing views about priorities, inadequate legislation and enforcement, special interest politics, fragmentation of responsibilities, organizational jealousies and misunderstanding of man–environment relationships. Despite these problems, the investigators concluded that an even more fundamental barrier to successful resource management was the lack of a satisfactory institutional structure. As a result, it was decided to explore 'what kinds of government organizations are needed and how these organizations should be related to each other in order to achieve the most effective management ... at the lowest possible economic, political and social costs' (Canada–United States University Seminar, 1973; 11).

After identifying the resource management problems of the Great Lakes, examining existing organizational forms (particularly the International Joint Commission), and reviewing previous research in institutional arrangements, the researchers identified a set of management functions and criteria. The functions included those mentioned earlier (surveillance, mediation, control). Nine criteria were identified, including jurisdiction, enforcement powers, fiscal adequacy, staffing adequacy, administrative discretion, flexibility, visibility, accountability and structural compatibility. The explicit recognition of functions and criteria makes this study a benchmark, even though they were used for general guidance rather than systematic analysis. They were not applied in a matrix-like fashion because the researchers concluded that the utility of each criterion depended on too many factors. For example, it was difficult to apply the criterion of 'enforcement powers' to all three management functions because the extent of necessary enforcement varied for each function. This problem was further complicated when a variety of resource management problems was included (Fig.11.1).

Using this framework, the analysts developed two options for institutional arrangements in the Great Lakes basin. The first required changes to existing arrangements, with the primary emphasis being to give the International Joint Commission a more active role in the decision process. The second alternative called for a new international organization to supplant the International Joint Commission. These findings were reported to the respective governments of the United States and Canada. From the viewpoint of resource analysis, one of the enduring contributions of this study was identification of functions and criteria. This study sets a baseline upon which future work could build.

Other studies have considered various aspects of institutional arrangements in water management (Grima, 1981; Walker, 1982; Anderson, 1983; Arnell, Clark and Gurnell, 1984; Day, 1986; Wescoat, 1986). Kromm's (1985) analysis of regional water management in England and Wales is used as the second example here. He was particularly interested in examining the advantages and disadvantages of autonomous regional districts to administer the management of water at a national level.

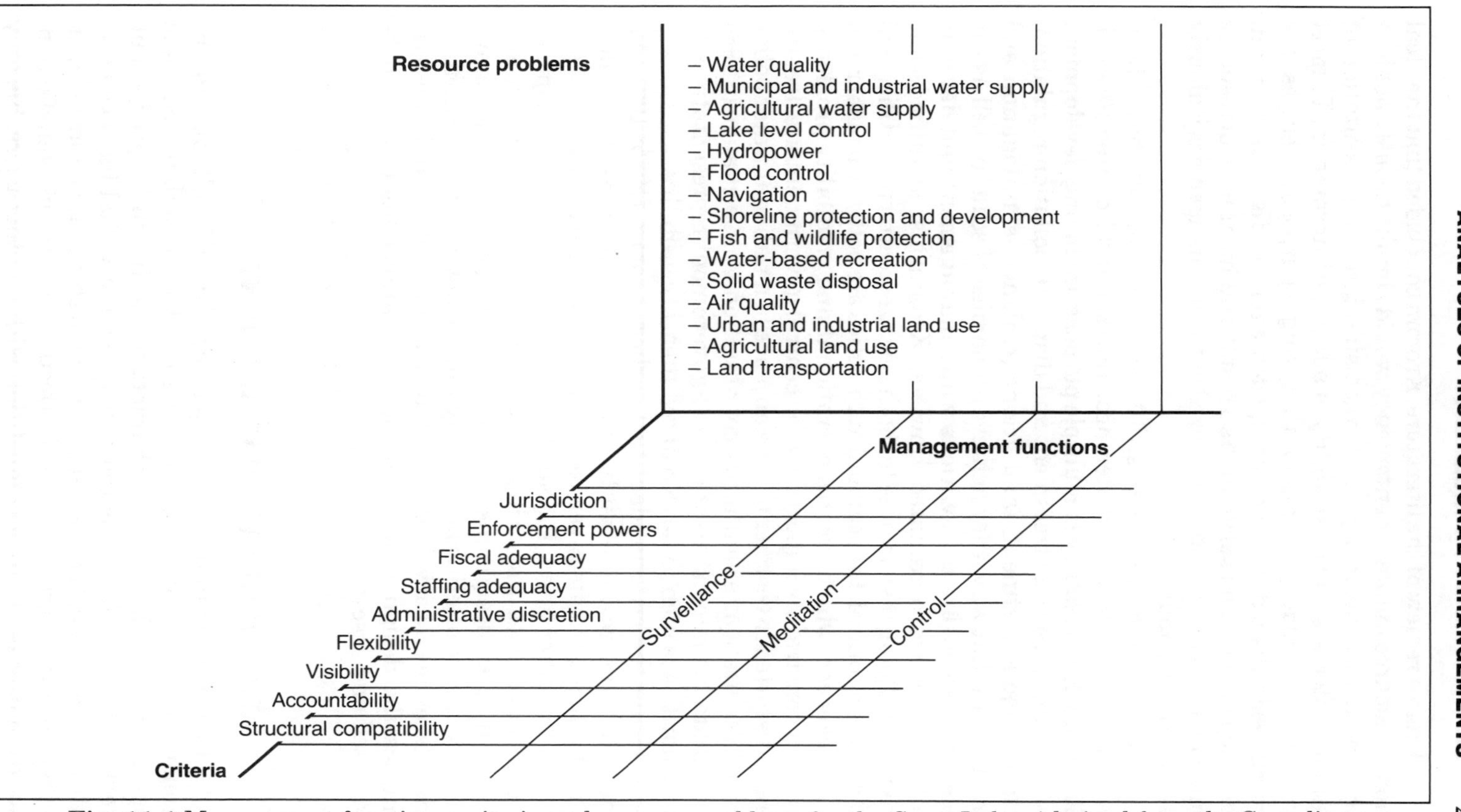

Fig. 11.1 Management functions, criteria and resource problems for the Great Lakes (*derived from the Canadian-United States University Seminar, 1973*)

From a review of the literature, Kromm concluded that the ideal regional resource management agency would simultaneously achieve efficiency, equity, desired performance standards, representation of legitimate interests and availability of adequate information. To meet these specific values, he found that single-purpose agencies are normally established. Once created, such agencies fight to maintain their independence and survival. As a result, fragmentation of resource management becomes institutionalized with various agencies jealously guarding their domain.

In England and Wales, 10 water authorities have been established on the basis of watersheds (Parker and Penning-Rowsell, 1980; 28–36). Each agency is multiple purpose, including development of water supply, sewage treatment and disposal, pollution regulation, flood damage adjustment, land drainage, fisheries, navigation and recreation. In that way, they achieve economies of scale as well as the opportunity to ensure that various water management and development activities are coordinated. However, Kromm also identified some weaknesses. Being responsible for both sewage treatment and disposal and pollution control, the regional authorities are both the poacher and the gamekeeper, which creates operational and credibility problems. Financial constraints imposed by the central government are deemed to have distorted investments. The absence of a national water policy does not facilitate inter-authority coordination. And a change in 1984 to eliminate the appointment of local government representatives to the authorities is seen to have reduced their accessibility.

Using the criteria identified earlier, Kromm (1985; 190) concluded that the regional authorities in England and Wales have realized efficiency, effectiveness and adequacy of technical information. On the other hand, the structural arrangements have impeded representation of legitimate interests. Kromm's findings illustrate how difficult it is to design institutional arrangements to meet simultaneously a mix of criteria. Usually only a few can be satisfied, so trade-offs are necessary. In that regard, it is important that the analyst identifies the design criteria so that the various trade-offs can be recognized and assessed.

11.3.2 FISHERIES MANAGEMENT

Fisheries management is particularly difficult due to the common property nature of the resource. An unregulated common property resource has several characteristics. It can be used simultaneously by more than one individual. No individual has exclusive control of the resource nor can any one person stop others from using it. Furthermore, an increase in users affects each person's satisfaction. Since each user is in direct competition with all other users, his only incentive is to obtain as large a share of the resource before others use it. Any restraint will not be rewarded as anything not taken will be claimed by others. Several consequences result. The resource is frequently depleted. In addition, excess investment usually results as each individual strives to increase his share. The outcome is an excess of capital investment, too many users, and deterioration of the resource.

With regard to fisheries, McKernan (1972; 49) observed that 'adequate institutional organizations must be formed to conserve the resources'. Research effort has concentrated upon exploring what combination of regional- or stock-based institutional arrangements would best meet the needs in different areas of the world. Management activity in the northeastern Pacific Ocean is considered in detail below, since it encompassed both regional- and stock-specific efforts at regulation.

Skud (1977) appraised the effectiveness of the International Halibut Commission, an organization responsible since 1923 for managing the halibut fishery for Canada and the United States. Research by Mitchell and Huntley (1977) confirmed Skud's findings and extended assessment to cover two other agencies. The International North Pacific Fisheries Commission attempts to influence fishing effort by Canada, Japan and the United States in the Pacific Ocean. The International Pacific Salmon Fisheries Commission was established in 1937 to regulate the harvesting by American and Canadian fishermen of sockeye and pink salmon which spawn in the Fraser River of British Columbia. The three agencies, characterized by contrasting organizational structures, target species and management problems, were selected in order to explore the relevance of criticisms made about institutional arrangements for marine fisheries.

Resource managers, fish-processing company managers, fishermen and university scientists were interviewed. Respondents were selected using positional and reputational methods (Tait, Johnson and Bokemeier, 1978). Some respondents were identified on the basis of their position in the industry revealed in trade journals, government reports, fishery journals, annual reports, newspapers and membership lists of management committees. During interviews, respondents were asked to suggest other individuals who should be contacted. This latter procedure identified individuals considered to be important by their peers even though they did not hold formal positions.

The original intention was to use a structured questionnaire which covered agency objectives, successes and weaknesses, constraints, functions and performance. A pilot study showed that this procedure was not workable, as respondents found it difficult to check or rank designated answers or reasons even when opportunity was provided for additional comments. The structured questionnaire was discarded and replaced by a procedure relying upon open-ended questions in which respondents answered in their own words. Answers were content analysed to identify common concerns. Checks on the survey responses were obtained through examination of annual reports, agency research reports, trade journals and newspapers.

Nine criticisms of international resource management organizations had been identified in the literature. The interview responses suggested they fell into two types. One type was perceived as valid but disagreement arose concerning whether the implications were positive or negative. These criticisms included concerns that institutional arrangements give limited power to agencies, give inadequate enforcement responsibility, do not provide for adequate scientific staff, discourage participation from those in the industry and encourage only presentation of recommendations known to be acceptable. A second group was perceived as valid, with agreement that substantial problems were represented. These criticisms were inability to restrict non-party countries from entering a fishery, inability to react quickly to problems, inability to obtain necessary data and inability to maintain communications.

This research identified a number of variables, considered important by those in the industry, which need attention in future efforts to modify institutional arrangements. This type of information may be useful for several reasons. Improved institutional arrangements are needed if agreements under the international treaty on the Law of the Sea are to be implemented. As W.M. Ross (1971; 326–27) has commented, 'improved management of the commons depends on the ability of the agency to formulate aims, to designate those responsible for overuse and misuse, to select the individual(s) to be restricted and to develop means of restriction and enforcement'. At a different level, these criticisms represent core issues which must be handled by a variety of resource management agencies. 'Questions associated with the nature and allocation of power, enforcement responsibility, flexibility, research procedures, communications and public involvement need consideration for a broad range of resource management organizations, functions and activities' (Mitchell and Huntley, 1977; 72).

11.3.3 FOREST MANAGEMENT

Differences often arise between that which is said and that which is done. Indeed, while resource policy is often conceived by senior officials, it is the individual in the field who implements it. In large public agencies, a major problem can be ensuring that policy intentions conceived at one level are acted upon at another. A further complication in large organizations is ensuring that the policy is implemented consistently by field personnel scattered throughout a sizeable jurisdiction. It was this relationship between broad pronouncements at senior levels and day-to-day activities in the field that stimulated Kaufman's (1960) study of the US Forest Service. He found that although field compliance in the Forest Service was not perfect, it was remarkably high in view of the many factors encouraging lack of compliance. In searching for reasons, Kaufman discovered that the US Forest Service's success in moulding the behaviour of hundreds of dispersed Rangers resulted from manipulation of perceptions, thinking and values of individuals employed by the Service.

The method of inquiry involved what Kaufman (1960; 6–7) described as the standard techniques of the political scientist. He examined administrative structure, interviewed senior officials, scrutinized statutes and government practices, reviewed histories and compiled chronologies, studied manuals, hearings and reports, and assembled other evaluations and criticisms of the agency. However, Kaufman argued that these traditional approaches and sources were useful only in helping to identify *potential* influences on field men. To assess their *actual* impact, he felt it necessary to adopt the approach of the cultural anthropologist and study individuals in their own environments. He selected five Ranger districts located in Virginia, South Carolina, Michigan, Colorado and Oregon. These represented a range of Forest Service activities and conditions under which work is conducted, as well as provided Rangers of different ages, experience and motivations.

Prior to the field research, Rangers sent the investigator information covering biographical details, employment histories, workload and financial statistics, inspection reports, work plans, organizational tables and material about the locality. With approval from US Forest Service headquarters, Kaufman visited each Ranger for a week during which time the Ranger put himself fully at the disposal of the investigator. Conversations rather than interviews involved the exchange of ideas and opinions. In this manner the investigator was able to discover details about the Ranger's behaviour beyond the relatively narrow set of questions formulated before visiting the field. These conversations were not confined to the Rangers and their families. Discussions were also held with supervisors, employees in the district and other forestry personnel. This verbal information was complemented by observation of behaviour and inter-personal relationships during visits to different management projects within each district.

The final results were based upon background reading, observations, personal interviews and visits to head ofice in Washington. Kaufman (1960; 20–21) was aware that this approach produced findings which were 'highly impressionistic'. On the other hand, he felt that the approach also had merits. In his view, 'the impressions in this study are based not merely on library sources or the word of agency leaders; whatever their shortcomings, they are rooted in relatively intensive examinations of men and conditions in the field'.

Numerous indicators suggested that the Forest Service had attained a high degree of compliance. Performance came close to goals set by the leadership. Little evidence existed regarding internal warfare or concern about sabotage of programmes. The leaders were convinced that the field men were responding to policy directives. The Rangers were inevitably supported by their superiors when the formers' decisions were challenged. Frequent personnel transfers worked successfully and were inevitably accepted by Rangers. All of these indicators, insufficient by themselves but convincing in combination, assured Kaufman that the techniques of integration had worked well.

Kaufman provided a detailed listing of factors which led to this unity, including frequency of transfers, reliance upon individuals trained primarily in one discipline (forestry), opportunity for Rangers to communicate with other professionals at different rungs in the administrative hierarchy, detailed field inspections of Ranger's performance and self-selection by the Rangers into the Service. This latter variable was considered to be highly significant. Kaufman found a remarkable degree of similarity in the Rangers. They were characterized as individuals who loved the outdoor life, were proud of the Service, viewed problems in the long term, were patient, acknowledged the rights of local users of forests, accepted the inevitability of conflict from decisions and were willing to do more than was legally expected of them in their jobs.

In terms of research design, Kaufman (1960; 229–30) realized that his approach was imperfect. To isolate the impact of influences from above and natural impulses from within individual Rangers, he suggested that an experimental design would be necessary. Some Rangers would be designated as an experimental group and exempted from the formal external influences. A panel of judges would periodically review and compare the performances of the experimental group and others chosen as a control. Only if the review demonstrated that Rangers in the experimental group deviated from announced policies would there be conclusive evidence concerning the impact of attempts to integrate field personnel behaviour. Numerous ethical and administrative obstacles would hinder such an approach. As a result, the strategy used by Kaufman is probably the only feasible one. Increased credibility for evidence is sought by searching for as many performance indicators and cross-checking data sources as possible.

Kaufman's investigation was the first of a series of studies of the United States Forest Service. Robinson (1975) completed a study of the Forest Service not only as an administrative organization, but as a focal point of the general processes, problems and controversies of public land management. Cortner and Schweitzer (1981) considered the problems of a specific piece of legislation for national planning of forest resources. Culhane (1981) studied the influence of interest groups on both the Forest Service and the Bureau of Land Management. A related study by Libecap (1981) focused entirely on the Bureau of Land Management as it moved to expand its regulatory authority.

11.3.4 PARK MANAGEMENT

The geographer Foresta (1984) analysed the National Park Service in the United States in a way similar to that used by Kaufman in his study of the US Forest Service (section 11.3.3). At a general level, Foresta (1984; 6) explained that his investigation was a case study of mission and purpose in public agencies, of how organizational goals are set and how a sense of purpose is sustained. In addition, he emphasized that two contexts were most important and therefore had to be addressed explicitly. The first was tradition and precedence. In other words, to understand the modern National Park Service it was necessary to understand a century of past attitudes, previous policies and traditional responsibilities. The second context was political power. In the United States, that involves the interaction of the National Park Service with Congress, the White House and other public agencies and private interest groups. Following examination of the two contexts of tradition and power, Foresta analysed four major areas of park policy: preservation of nature, historic preservation, urban parks and land beyond park boundaries.

Foresta was sensitive to the ethical issue of privacy, and when interviewing respondents always determined the degree of confidentiality which was wanted. Some respondents did not want to be quoted directly. Some were willing to be identified, especially regarding specific ideas or opinions. A number did not wish to be even identified as having being interviewed, and such peoples' names were omitted from the list of interviewees provided in an appendix to the study. As Foresta explained his approach, when in doubt about the degree of confidentiality he erred on the side of caution. This approach makes it difficult for other investigators to follow up or verify his findings, but it is appropriate and necessary to maintain cooperation and credibility.

Foresta's main conclusion was that the National Park Service is confused about both its purpose and the system for which it is responsible. He argued that the confusion about its mission was understandable since as a public organization the Park Service has to base its goals on society's interests and values which have changed sharply since the 1960s. He argued that the Park Service should accept that in the future it will not find a unifying vision and instead should search for different referents and philosophies for guidance regarding specific tasks. A separate and distinct set of guidelines is needed for each major area of responsibility: nature, history, cities and land beyond park boundaries.

Foresta (1984; 279–80) distinguished between ambiguous societal values and vague organizational goals. He maintained that two characteristics of an agency's goals broaden its freedom of choice. A multiplicity of goals allows for more opportunity to shift and substitute as required. Generality, ambiguity or fuzziness permit goals to be all things to all people, avoiding the identification of obvious winners and losers which arise when goals are specific. Ambiguous goals were also viewed as facilitating different courses of action as conditions change. As an institutional strategy, therefore, Foresta saw many benefits to goals stated in general or fuzzy terms, as long as the organization itself had a clear sense of purpose.

Foresta also argued that there is nothing inherently wrong or bad in shifting resources from one area of social concern to another or from policies in harmony with one perspective to those in agreement with another. As time passes, new concerns develop and old ones diminish. Strategically, he believed that it would be unwise to ignore the opportunities for potential role changes presented by changing circumstances. Thus, again Foresta differentiated between uncertainty about strategic goals and objectives, and generality in operational statements about them or willingness to change directions when new opportunities present themselves. On the surface, such actions may suggest uncertainty and unevenness in performance. However, realistically, such measures may maximize ability to take advantage of opportunities and use available resources in the best possible manner.

11.3.5 HAZARDS

In Chapter 8, research activity and resource management implications associated with hazards were reviewed. In this section, brief attention is given to what Schrecker (1984) has termed the political economy of enviromental hazards. His study dealt with both the process through which environmental hazard law and policy are made and with the frameworks which are utilized to establish objectives and strategies for controlling environmental hazards. His major conclusion was that most important decisions are made before the issues ever reach the floor of a legislature or of a public hearing room.

Schrecker (1984; 10) concluded that a particular style of agency behaviour is influenced by the legislative framework, agency resources, political and administrative context, and the attitudes and resources of constituencies. Each of these is briefly discussed in turn.

Regarding the legislative framework, at least in countries using some version of the British model of government, Schrecker suggested that most environmental hazard policy is created under enabling legislation. While providing authority to regulate certain activities, such legislation rarely specifies in detail the criteria to govern the development of regulations nor does it establish a time frame for achieving particular objectives. The outcome is that the political Minister and associated agency staff receive broad discretionary powers which can be a strength and weakness. Specific situations can be handled on a case-by-case basis, with a solution custom designed for the circumstances. This approach may save both time and money. On the other hand, questions of equity may arise since there is no standard or guideline to consult in order to establish the 'rules of the game'. This approach can create uncertainty, especially for the small business person who does not have the resources to study the issue in the same depth as the regulatory agency.

Agency resources can preclude implementation of certain actions or the ineffective application of others. For example, it frequently has been observed that inspection staffs are much too small for the number of properties (in the case of floodplains) or of workplaces (in the case of occupational health) to be monitored.

Many private firms and companies, through their activities, have considerable information about product and process characteristics, abatement technology and costs, production and effluent volumes and other factors related to environmental hazards. A public regulatory agency with limited resources often will be forced into relying on industry-generated data about an environmental hazard. As a result, even an agency with aggressive regulatory intentions may have to use a strategy involving negotiation with firms in the private sector. Sanctions may be used with a frequency and severity which is in inverse proportion to the size and wealth of the offender.

The political and administrative context creates many limitations. The introduction of a Government's political priorities into the regulatory process can weaken or otherwise alter a carefully developed action plan by an agency. In a more routine way, government officials responsible for controlling environmental hazards must compete with other agency's interests to get their concerns high on the public agenda (see Ch. 13). Departments responsible for promotion of industry, regional development or natural resource exploitation may view concerns with reduction of environmental hazards to be competitive or counter-productive to their goals and the interests of their constituents.

The relative power of constituents is also important. The distribution of benefits and costs from control of environmental hazards is not usually shared equally. Regarding control of acid rain in North America, for example, most Canadians in eastern Canada would gain directly or indirectly from its reduction. However, much of the costs in the form of unemployment or reduced tax base would be borne by the coal-mining communities in the Ohio valley of the United States. The latter interests are represented by well organized and well funded lobbyists who express the concerns of their communities in an articulate way. The average Canadian citizen, in contrast, has neither the time, expertise nor resources to present his or her views. Thus all interests are not represented equally nor equitably in most democratic government systems.

Many government departments also establish direct links with their constituents. Thus an agriculture department will often become directly involved with farmers and agricultural organizations while a mines department will become involved with its industry association, equipment suppliers and such groups. Since these groups can have a significant impact on the 'success' of the agency's programmes, the government agency will consciously cultivate relationships with the private sector. Environment departments normally do not have as well-defined constituents, and therefore can experience difficulty in the bargaining and negotiations as alternatives are examined and trade-offs are considered.

Schrecker's interest was in environmental hazards, but the conceptual framework which he developed – legislation, agency resources, political and administrative context, constituency base – are pertinent to many different resource management sectors or situations. His examination of these four attributes collectively certainly fits well into the spirit of institutional arrangements as defined in section 11.2.

11.3.6 COASTAL ZONE MANAGEMENT

The management of coastal zones has received increasing attention with the recognition that such areas too often fall between the proverbial cracks of institutional arrangements. Land-based agencies look inward and fisheries or oceans oriented agencies look seaward. At the point where the land and water meet, where there often is concentrated industrial, settlement or recreational activity, there too often have been inadequate arrangements for management of the resource.

Research on the institutional arrangements has been popular regarding the coastal zone, given the difficulty of determining which organization should take the lead role in management. Thus, studies have been completed in the United States (Ducsik, 1980; Healy and Zinn, 1985), New Zealand (Gardner, 1984) and Japan (Shapiro, 1984; Sumi and Hanayama, 1985). The illustration below considers the problems and approaches in France (French Ministry of the Environment, 1982).

Harrison and Sewell (1979) studied the development in French shoreline management strategies. Their interest was stimulated by the recognition that the sinking of the 'Torrey Canyon' off the coast of Cornwall in England in 1967 emphasized that the institutional arrangements in most countries were not adequate to deal with large environmental disasters. France faces a mix of such potential problems with coastlines adjacent to the English Channel, the Atlantic Ocean and the Mediterranean Sea. They examined the capability of the six river basin agencies and a Shoreline Trust (Conservatoire du littoral et des rivages lacustres). The purpose of the latter is to acquire saltwater or freshwater property in order to protect such areas from urban encroachment, to protect the ecological balance of this land and to enhance public access to shorelines.

As in most countries, Harrison and Sewell found that there was an abundance of legislation in France pertinent to coastal zone management, but most of it was sectoral in nature. In other words, the legislation tended to relate to specific types of problems separately, rather than to the mix of problems which might occur in a given place. Indeed, they found that as many as 20 types of institution (national, regional, local) were involved in coastal development. As a consequence, overlap could and did happen, making the need for coordination relative to the coastal zone necessary.

Harrison and Sewell (1979; 175) argued that the traditional 'line' agencies needed to be supplemented by regional groupings. The coordinating mechanisms in place - interministerial committees, consultative bodies - tended to be of a lateral nature between particular levels of the same government. Allocation of the coastal resource also required vertical coordination among various levels of government and various consumer points of view. Rather than creating additional structures, they advocated increasing the responsiveness and representativeness of existing ones. In their view, in-depth development of institutional arrangements was as necessary as in-depth development of the coastal zone.

11.3.7 ENVIRONMENTAL MANAGEMENT

Many studies have been completed regarding institutional arrangements for environmental management in general. Investigations have concentrated upon Conservation Trusts in the United Kingdom (Tunbridge, 1981), nature conservation in the four Nordic countries of Denmark, Finland, Norway and Sweden (Tivy, 1985), international agreements for the Baltic Sea (Haügerhaüll, 1980), special purpose districts in the United States (Thompson, 1986) and Canada (Carlyle, 1980), and a Conservation Council in Australia (Mercer, 1979). The approach in such work follows closely that identified during the reviews of studies about water, fisheries and forestry. As a result, only a few investigations are briefly mentioned here to provide an indication of the type of research being done.

A comparative analysis of existing value patterns and institutional structures in the United States, the Soviet Union and Japan has been completed by Kelly, Stunkel and Wescott (1976). The cogency and promise of values and institutional arrangements were viewed in a broad cultural, historical, political and economic context for such issues as population, energy and non-renewable resources, air and water pollution, solid wastes, radioactive pollution, noise and other environmental externalities.

Similar studies have been undertaken concerning other jurisdictions. Lundqvist (1974) analysed the environmental policies in Canada, Sweden and the United States. To explore the influences on policy processes and content, Lundqvist (1974; 7) considered the following components associated with institutional arrangements: (1) ideologies, values and structures of political systems, (2) historical development, habit and routine in policy making, (3) power relations among groups affected by environmental problems and policies, and (4) considerations of utility. In addition to the influence of institutional structure, Lundqvist considered the character and distribution of values, control of government and behaviour of participants in the political systems. By focusing upon these variables, he was able to identify and explain differences in the way in which the three nations approached environmental management.

At a different spatial scale, Musolf (1975) assessed the impact of the governmental system upon legislative structure and environmental policy making in British Columbia and California. Whether such studies are at local, regional, national or international scale, the approach is similar. Jurisdictions are selected either because of their common features or because of extreme differences. Library-based data sources are perused, drawing heavily upon legislation, parliamentary or legislative debates, major policy pronouncements, government reports and budgets, newspapers and other studies which have critiqued actual programmes or projects. In some instances, field work is carried out which varies from interviews of key officials to interviews with and observation of those responsible for ongoing management programmes. The overall aim is to determine the way in which institutional arrangements influence the resource management process.

11.4 BARGAINING AND NEGOTIATION

Dorcey (1986b) has noted that three types of institutional mechanisms are used in resolving disputes over resource allocation: political, judicial and market. Political mechanisms involve the different ways in which elected representatives in association with their bureaucracies deal with problems, and range from Cabinets, legislative committees, government departments, interdepartmental committees, intergovernmental agreements to task forces. The judicial mechanisms incorporate the various hierarchies of courts that interpret and apply the law. Market mechanisms use prices to guide decisions. Depending upon the circumstances, one or all of these institutional mechanisms may be used in a given situation.

However, no matter how much effort is devoted to designing appropriate institutional mechanisms, Dorcey (1986b; 10) concluded that there will always be constraints on their effectiveness. Based on research by him and his colleagues, he concluded that regardless of the potential effectiveness of the institutions, the success in handling problems will ultimately depend on the people in the process, and particularly on the manner in which they are able to interact with others. This point is an important one, because it is possible to spend too much time in attempting to design the 'perfect' institutional arrangements. Capable people can make things happen despite the system within which they work, while mediocre or incompetent individuals are unlikely to accomplish a great deal regardless of the adequacy of the institutional arrangements within which they function.

Dorcey argued that resolution of conflicts cannot occur without effective communication. In his view, this aspect involves much more than simply transmitting and receiving information in a manner suitable to the various perceptions, attitudes, needs and comprehension of those involved. It also requires the ability to challenge constructively and bargain effectively (Dorcey, 1986b, 11; Dorcey and Martin, 1986, 21–22).

From his assessment of many resource conflict situations, Dorcey concluded that unfortunately many participants have not developed these important communication skills (constructively challenging, effectively bargaining). He found that when participants challenge each other's arguments, they often do so in an adversarial manner in which the objective is destruction of the other party's argument. The basic reasons for disagreement, if present, are not identified and potential solutions are not found. In bargaining, too often participants concentrate on giving up as little as possible rather than considering a wide range of options and then searching for common ground within them. For individuals to improve their communication skills, he highly recommended reference to *Getting to Yes*: *Negotiating Agreement Without Giving In*, by Roger Fisher and William Ury (1981).

Dorcey's arguments are important since they remind the analyst that ultimately resource allocation decisions are made by people rather than institutional structures. He sees two implications. First, skills need to be improved to facilitate discussion, bargaining and negotiation. Second, innovations are needed in existing institutional arrangements to encourage greater interaction, cooperation and conflict resolution. As a beginning, he suggested that attention should be directed to three types of innovations in institutional arrangements: the structuring of innovations, their facilitation, and the appropriate incentives.

11.5 IMPLICATIONS FOR RESOURCE MANAGEMENT

For the geographer interested in resource management, studies of institutional arrangements offer several rewards. By describing, accounting for and predicting such arrangements, the analyst may be able to suggest how existing situations could be improved or else how future arrangements could be designed to take advantage of observed strengths but avoid identified weaknesses. Understanding the way in which arrangements function also provides appreciation as to how they may act as constraints upon or create opportunities for management decisions. A third reward is perhaps the most important for the geographer. By treating analysis of institutional arrangements as a means to an end rather than an end itself, new insights may be gained about spatial allocations of natural resources, man-environment relationships or the nature of regional character and complexity.

The practical value from improving institutional arrangements should be to facilitate coordination of various interests and perspectives during resource allocation decisions. As the examples above have revealed, there often is fragmentation of responsibility – vertical, horizontal, functional – of public authority regarding resource management (Platt *et al.*, 1980). Such fragmentation leads to 'boundary problems' among and within management agencies (Eddison, 1985). Assessment of institutional arrangements can contribute to improving the effectiveness in the way in which resource management decisions are reached (Stroup and Baden, 1983).

However, as Noble, Banta and Rosenberg (1977) have stressed, it is unlikely that there is any single perspective nor universally appropriate response to the coordination problem. In fact, measures taken to deal with one problem almost inevitably create problems of their own. In their words,

> The coordination problem cannot be made to disappear. If some of the ragged edges are smoothed over procedurally by treating symptoms – delay, for instance – they will crop up elsewhere. If agencies are consolidated, problems formerly handled on an interagency basis now become concerns of intraagency coordination.
>
> In sum, no coordination solution is final. Coordination is a continuous process of managing, of administering, of coping. (Noble, Banta, Rosenberg, 1977; 33)

11.6 IMPLICATIONS FOR RESEARCH

Research on institutional arrangements is in an early stage of development. While detailed studies have been completed concerning legal, administrative, economic, political and historical aspects of resource management, work is just barely underway regarding the composite impact of their interaction. The undeveloped nature of the research is highlighted by the great variety of ways in which researchers have defined the problem. Inconsistency and lack of agreement over terms are one of the first hurdles to be overcome if any cumulative knowledge is to be realized. Thus, it is premature to criticize the field for lacking a theoretical structure when it is grappling with basic operational definitions. The main priority for the immediate future should be clarification of terms of reference and identification of key independent variables.

Once these barriers have been overcome, other difficulties will still remain. Institutional arrangements represents only one of many variables which constrain or influence the resource management process. To assess the impact of this variable it is desirable to isolate its impact from other variables. Realizing this objective necessitates applying experimental research designs with their accompanying control and experimental groups. Practical, ethical and administrative factors raise major obstacles for such an approach, however, and the possibility for dramatic breakthroughs appears slim.

Measurement of cause-and-effect relations is virtually impossible until key variables and relationships are identified. Once they are identified, measurement will still be difficult for several reasons. First, many of the concepts relevant to this problem - values, customs, leadership, power, fragmentation, influence - are difficult to operationalize (Mitchell 1975; 263–7). Second, any assessment of institutional arrangements requires explicit criteria, raising the same difficulties discussed in Chapter 10. Studies such as those by the Canada–United States University Seminar (1973) are starting to come to grips with the matter of criteria, but much work remains to be done. In conjunction with clarifying criteria, work also is needed to clarify which management functions are being analyzed.

Ongoing research on institutional arrangements may be summarized in the following words. Descriptive rather than predictive. Exploratory rather than theory-based. Process rather than structure-orientated. One-shot case studies or pretest-post-test designs rather than experimental designs. Nominal and ordinal rather than interval levels of measurement. All of these characteristics suggest an emerging area of inquiry which is struggling in a new hole rather than sticking to the comfortable familiarity of an old one (De Bono, 1967). While the problems are substantial, improved insights into the resource management process will offer both practical and scholarly dividends. Simultaneously, such inquiries should strengthen insights of geographic research in resource analysis whether it be launched from the spatial, ecological or regional analysis tradition.

CHAPTER 12
POLICY MAKING

12.1 INTRODUCTION

Analysis of policy making may be related to all of the research traditions in geography. Public and private decisions influence the manner in which society adapts to or utilizes the environment, the nature of spatial, temporal and functional allocation of resources and the form of regional development. For the geographer interested in resource analysis, investigations of policy and decision processes tend to pull together many of the issues covered in previous chapters. In O'Riordan's (1971a; 109) words, 'resource management in the final analysis is a decision-making process'. As a result, he believed that studies of policy and decision making 'are significant in that they attempt to relate and to assess the *totality* of forces in operation and aid the understanding of the processes involved' (O'Riordan, 1971a; 119).

Analysis of policy making offers a numbers of returns. By studying its context, process and outcome, research provides understanding of the manner in which resources are allocated. By knowing something about the variables that shape policy, analysts should be able to predict future policies as well as to suggest how current ones might be improved. By appreciating the nature of the allocative process, analysts should be able to contribute to improving the effectiveness of citizen involvement. A cautionary note is necessary, however. Geographers should approach policy analysis as a means to an end, rather than as an end to itself. If the geographer is to gain maximum advantage from his skills and expertise, he should treat policy and decision processes as independent variables which help to account for man–environment relationships, spatial organization or regional complexity. If policy and decision processes are analysed as dependent variables, then the geographer drifts away from his areas of competence and expertise.

Despite the scholarly and practical attractiveness of policy analysis, research on this fundamental aspect is poorly developed. After reviewing the general field of policy research, Bauer (1968; 25) concluded that the problem had been inadequately conceptualized, Dror (1968; 74–75) felt that a rigorous theoretical framework was lacking, and Aucoin (1971; 33) believed that agreement still had to be reached concerning research paradigms, concepts and methodologies. Moore (1975; 13) assessed policy studies in the specific area of resources management and noted that no overall schema, paradigm or model had emerged. These assessments, completed some time ago, continue to be pertinent.

This chapter highlights some of the advances and obstacles in policy making research associated with resource management. The terms 'policy', 'policy making', 'decision' and 'decision making' are discussed (section 12.2). Attention is then directed towards efforts to establish models which either suggest how the policy process should occur or how it does occur (section 12.3). This review is based substantially upon research completed by political scientists. With this context established, the following section (12.4) examines some studies by geographers which seek to identify the nature of the policy process. In section 12.5, attention is directed to environmental mediation, a concept which emerged during the 1980s. After this appraisal of substantative studies, the final sections consider the implications for resource management (12.6) and research (12.7).

12.2 OPERATIONAL DEFINITIONS

As with the study of institutional arrangements (Ch. 11), those concerned with policy are plagued by a variety of operational definitions for basic terms. This situation is of more than academic interest since differing operational definitions make it difficult to compare results, realize cumulative knowledge or assess recommendations for change. Perhaps part of the problem is summarized by Cunningham's (1963; 229) belief that 'policy is like the elephant – you recognize it when you see it but cannot easily define it'.

A start can be made, however, in clarifying terms. Policy research generally concentrates upon conscious choice processes as opposed to habitual or unconscious/trivial choices (Kates, 1962; 17). Another way of expressing this is Sewell's (1974; 241) distinction between 'routine' and 'strategic' management issues. The former involve problems which do not include conflicts over allocation or responsibility whereas the latter involve fundamental conflicts.

If attention is focused upon conscious choices or strategic issues, then a distinction can be made between decision and policy making. Decision making is often viewed as the process of choosing from a set of competing alternatives. In contrast, policy making involves a 'pattern of action, extending over time and involving many decisions, some routine and some not so routine' (Anderson, 1975; 10). Thus, policy is viewed as a pattern of purposive or goal-oriented choice and action rather than as separate, discrete decisions. However, a further refinement is needed. When analysing the policy process, distinctions should be drawn between that which is *stated*, that which is *implied*, that which is *perceived* and that which is *done* (Aucoin, 1971; 22). These four consideratons are not always synonymous, leading to different interpretations of a given 'policy' or 'policy-making process'. The investigator must be certain which aspect of policy is being studied. Not only will this awareness avoid misunderstanding among investigators, but it will contribute towards ensuring comparability of findings.

12.3 POLICY MODELS

Many typologies of policy models have been developed. One differentiates between two types. Prescriptive or normative models seek to demonstrate how policy making should occur relative to pre-established standards. On the other hand, descriptive models document the way in which the policy process actually occurs. The two often are united when an investigator tries to determine how an existing (and imperfect) policy process can be modified to more closely approximate the ideal. In this way, both types of model have useful functions. The prescriptive ones establish an ideal towards which policy should strive; the descriptive types facilitate understanding of how the process actually works.

12.3.1 PRESCRIPTIVE MODELS

Prescriptive models are often characterized as being comprehensive and rational. Although the details vary, most models suggest that the policy process evolves through several phases:

1. A problem is clearly defined, and separated from other problems of concern to the policy maker.
2. The goals, values and objectives of the policy maker are identified; furthermore, the policy maker is able to rank the goals, values and objectives. In other words, the *ends* are known.
3. The complete range of alternative solutions to the problem is identified. In other words, the *means* for attaining the ends are known.
4. The consequences of each alternative relative to the problem, goals, values and objectives are identified, compared and ranked.
5. After comparing all of the alternative approaches or solutions, the policy maker selects the alternative that *maximizes* net expectations.

Perhaps the best known prescriptive model is that developed by Lasswell (1956; 1972) in which the policy process consists of (1) intelligence and planning, (2) recommending, (3) prescribing, (4) invoking, (5) applying, (6) appraising, and (7) terminating.

While these activities represent an ideal pattern of choice and activity, most would agree with Dror (1968; 133) that 'with a few exceptions ... pure-rationality policy-making is in fact impossible'. The most obvious reason is that these models assume the existence of people characterized as Economic Man. Not only can such individuals identify and rank goals, values and objectives, but they can choose consistently among them after having collected all the necessary data and systematically evaluating them. In many situations the necessary data are not available. Even when such information is present, the policy maker often cannot easily analyse alternatives due to the presence of intangibles.

At a more basic level, the policy maker often is not confronted with a clearly defined problem but rather with a large number of causes and effects. This often results in symptoms rather than basic causes being treated by the policy maker. A further problem is the assumption that policy makers seek to optimize or maximize in an economic sense. Other economic (distribution of benefits and costs) and non-economic (environmental or social impact) considerations may be as important in influencing choices. Thus, the number of assumptions associated with Economic Man raises problems for attainment of conditions prescribed by these models. Nevertheless, they do provide an ideal pattern against which actual policy processes may be compared.

12.3.2 DESCRIPTIVE MODELS

Many of the descriptive models reject the concept of Economic Man and rely upon Simon's (1957; 1959) idea of the 'boundedly rational' person who 'satisfices' rather than maximizes. Thus, while Economic Man maximizes, his satisficing cousin looks for a course of action that is satisfactory or 'good enough'. While Economic Man is able to cope with the complexity of the real world, Simon's satisficer or 'Administrative Man' recognizes that the world he perceives is a drastically simplified model of the buzzing, blooming confusion that constitutes the real world (Simon, 1957; XXV).

Faced with multiple problems, goals and values, Administrative Man uses adaptive behaviour in which 'the level of aspiration begins to adjust itself downward until goals reach levels that are practically attainable' (Simon, 1959; 263). In this model, alternatives are not fixed and known, goals may be vague and inconsistent, and information may be incomplete or lacking. The model also recognizes that searching for or attaining additional data may require expenditures of time, resources and effort which may be exorbitant. The outcome is that the policy maker operates in a situation in which his knowledge is incomplete and his perception of his environment is distorted (Simon, 1959; 269).

A second major difference in the descriptive models is the way in which they visualize evolution of the policy process. The prescriptive model suggests an atmosphere which is comprehensive, rational, detached and unemotional. Conversely, the descriptive models usually assume a *pluralist* society in which groups actively compete and struggle for power over the allocation of scarce resources (Bentley, 1908; Truman, 1951; Latham, 1952). As a result, policies are conceived, developed and implemented in the context of competing groups which lobby the policy makers to consider their interests. This pluralist interpretation stands in contrast to an *elitist model* developed by Dahl (1967) and Hunter (1953). Their viewpoint sees public policy as reflecting the values of a governing elite. Rather than policy being determined through the pressure and action of the general public and organized groups, public policy is determined by the ruling elite and implemented by public officials and agencies. While the elitist and Economic Man models are not synonymous, they illustrate different perspectives from those taken by most of the descriptive models.

12.3.2.1 Disjointed incrementalism

Incremental model, disjointed incrementalism and 'muddling through' are all terms associated with a model conceived by Lindblom (1959; 1968; 1979; Braybrooke and Lindblom, 1963) which has relevance for both policy and decision making. Lindblom's model, designed in reaction to some of the disadvantages associated with those based on Economic Man, has the following characterisitics:

1. The problem(s) is not clearly defined. In many instances, the major task for the policy maker is to ascertain the nature of the problem to be dealt with.
2. Goals, values and objectives may be in conflict with one another.
3. Only a limited range of alternatives are considered, and those differ only slightly or incrementally from existing policies.
4. For each alternative, only a restricted number of 'significant' consequences are identified.
5. The problem is continually redefined. Normally, we think of means being adjusted to ends (policies are sought to reach specific objectives). Under disjointed incrementalism, the reverse is often true – objectives are modified relative to means at the policy maker's disposal.
6. No correct or right solution exists. The policy maker often does not know what is wanted, but does know what should be avoided. Policies often move away from the 'bad' without necessarily heading for the 'good'. A good decision is one for which substantial agreement exists even though not everyone may think that the decision is best relative to a given objective.
7. The decision or policy process never terminates. Instead, the process is seen as a sequential chain consisting of a continuous series of incremental decisions.

With such attributes, the incremental model concentrates

attention upon familiar and better-known experiences, reduces the number of alternatives to be explored and reduces the number and complexity of variables demanding attention. In Lindblom's (1968; 27) view, while incremental strategies may appear to be indecisive, timid, inconclusive, procrastinating, cautious, narrow and patchy, they also serve as

> useful devices for stretching man's analytic capacities. ... The piecemealing, remedial incrementalist or satisficer may not look like an heroic figure. He is nevertheless a shrewd, resourceful problem-solver who is wrestling bravely with a universe that he is wise enough to know is too big for him.

The incrementalist will consciously choose a policy, knowing it is not quite adequate, in order to leave a wide range of options available rather than select a policy that appears to be on target but difficult to modify. He will sometimes solve small problems (poor seed) when he cannot solve a larger one (low agricultural productivity). He believes that policy making is serial or sequential, and as a result that continual nibbling is as adequate as a single large bite.

While proving a startlingly accurate approximation to the policy process, the incrementalist model contains weaknesses (Dror, 1968, 143–7; Anderson, 1975, 14). The major one is that it does not account for abrupt and radical changes in policy. Since the model envisages all policies or decisions as only marginally different from their predecessors, it does not explain or predict fundamental changes. If a model is supposed to have predictive capacity, such a weakness is serious. A related problem is that the model focuses upon the short term, and therefore tends to neglect longer-term social innovations. This characteristic has led to its being labelled as remedial, or a model which accounts for reactions to existing imperfections rather than indicating how future goals will be sought. Again, concerning predictive capacity, such a weakness is serious. Nevertheless, the 'muddling through' model does provide insight as to the nature of the policy process in the real world. It also reinforces the validity of Simon's idea about satisficing and bounded rationality.

12.3.2.2 Mixed scanning

The mixed-scanning model represents one of two distinct approaches for investigators who reject the concept of Economic Man, find Lindblom's alternative attractive, but are dissatisfied with the inability of the incremental model to account for fundamental changes in policy. Etzioni (1967; 1968) offered the mixed-scanning model as one which combined recognition of fundamental or 'contextual' policies and incremental or 'bit' policies. Etzioni's model is based on the assumptions that incremental decisions lead eventually to a fundamental decision and that the cumulative effect of incremental decisions is influenced by fundamental decisions.

In the actual policy process, this model suggests that the policy maker relies heavily upon a continuous series of incremental decisions. However, at the same time, the policy maker is steadily scanning a limited range of other alternatives each of which represents significant departures from present approaches. The commitment to examining fundamentally different policy alternatives is reflected by the allocation of time, resources, personnel and effort to this task. Nevertheless, the review is 'mixed' since only a few alternatives receive more than a passing appraisal. The selection of which alternatives to scan in depth and which to scan in a cursory fashion is based on an ordering of priorities. Thus, it is more systematic than the incremental model. However, like the incremental model, a restricted range of alternatives is considered, and unlike the rationalist models, maximization of net gains is not the sole criterion guiding choices. Furthermore, unlike the incremental model, commitments to alternatives are made to an extent that flexibility is lost for future choice.

Etzioni's model is conceptually attractive in that it is more comprehensive than either the rationalist or incremental models. It also emphasizes that different processes may occur depending upon the nature and magnitude of problems. On the other hand, its major shortcoming is lack of guidance concerning how to distinguish empirically between fundamental and incremental policies. No explicit guidelines are provided by Etzioni. However, by alerting analysts to the possible presence of different processes, the mixed-scanning model highlights the weaknesses of the ideas offered by rationalists and incrementalists.

12.3.2.3 Output models

A second approach is represented by the work of Lowi (1964; 1970; 1972). All of the previous approaches focused upon *inputs* to the policy process. In the spirit of a lateral thinker, Lowi found a different hole to dig and concentrated upon *outputs*. He argued that different outputs can be identified, each reflecting different processes. Three distinct policy types were noted: *distributive*, *regulatory* and *redistributive*.

Distributive policies cover situations in which particular groups receive government services on an individual basis. A group may obtain a desired output without directly competing with other groups. As Mann (1975a; 142) observed, distributive politics involve coalition-building among local interests. Through bargaining and accommodation at the local level, groups eliminate conflict and enhance their probability of achieving desired objectives from higher levels of government. This type of situation is characterized by a process labelled with terms such as logrolling, consensal politics or mutual non-interference. As each group receives a benefit specific to itself, little confrontation occurs and little in the way of 'policy' emerges. Another implication is that the taxpayers have little role. The bargaining is confined to local or regional interest and senior levels of government.

The second policy type - regulatory - represents a different situation. A conscious decision is taken to satisfy aspirations of some groups at the expense of others. With some groups indulged and others deprived, the regulatory model implies a process of overt conflict reflecting the *pluralist* school of thought (section 12.3.2). The interests are often sectoral (economic, environmental) rather than local, and are represented by national organizations (Sierra Club, industrial lobbies) which are concerned with public policy in addition to specific projects and/or programmes. With obvious winners and losers, the conflict is relatively visible, unlike in the distributive model. Conflict arises because not all interests can be satisfied without adversely affecting others. The outcome is usually a definite policy which defines the winners and losers as well as providing the departure point for future decisions.

The third type of policy was labelled as redistributive. In this category, the conflict is usually over significant class interests rather than sectoral interests. The principal issues usually involve an attempt to alter the distribution of benefits and costs in society, and frequently centre upon issues related to levels and rates of taxation, levels of public spending and subsidies. Because the conflict is based upon class interest, the major participants are often seen as belonging to either the 'elite' or ruling class and the 'counterelites' or outsiders. Participants thus become large organizations, corporations, business associations, bureaucracies and political parties.

These categories are based upon Lowi's contention that the principal concept underlying policy making is coercion. In his words

> Institutions are means of moralizing coercion. Administration is a means of routinizing coercion. Government is a means of legitimizing it. Power is simply the relative share a person or group appears to have in shaping and directing the instruments of coercion (Lowi, 1970; 314).

Following this viewpoint, all policies are interpreted as deliberate coercion since they involve attempts to define the purpose, the means, the subjects and objects of coercion. As with the other descriptive models, Lowi does not imply that his hypothesized processes are necessarily desirable, but that they account for the nature of reality. In the following sections, empirical studies drawing upon both descriptive and normative models are discussed.

12.4 POLICY MAKING AND RESOURCE MANAGEMENT

Investigators from many disciplines have studied policy making (Sabatier and Mazmanian, 1980; Dunn, 1981; House, 1982;

Brewer and de Leon, 1983; Callahan and Jennings, 1983). The relevance of policy models for environmental management in general has attracted considerable attention (Walker and Williams, 1982; Ikporuko, 1983; Ortolano, 1984; Sewell and Mitchell, 1984; Johnston and Smit, 1985). Some have concentrated upon the role of information and communications in policy making, while others have concentrated upon the influence of politics. Attention has been given to the relationship between administrative structures and policy making, as well as to developing general analytical frameworks. These aspects all appear in the following investigations which emphasize the nature of policy and decision processes.

12.4.1 PRESCRIPTIVE STUDIES

Geographers have used prescriptive models as standards against which to appraise management practices. Both Hamill (1968) and Sewell (1973) provided detailed descriptions about the nature of the ideal process (Fig. 12.1). As Sewell (1973a; 36–35) explained the process, it involves a series of interconnected steps among which there is continuous feedback. The process commences with a statement of desirable goals and identification of specific problems. Subsequent

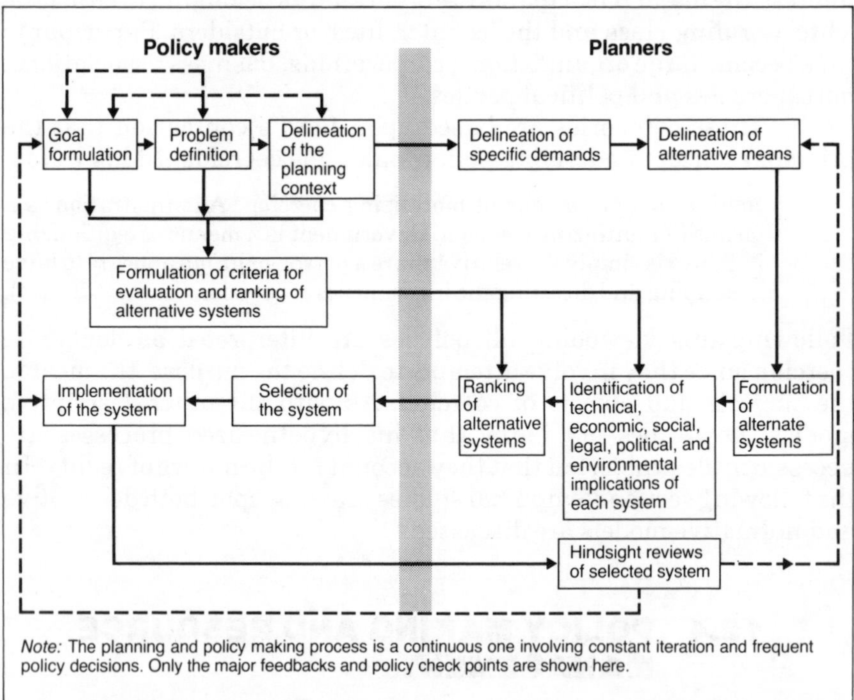

Fig. 12.1 The planning and policy-making process (*from Sewell, 1973a*)

stages include consideration of constraints (time, money, personnel), delineation of potential solutions, formulation of alternative strategies, appraisal of alternatives, selection of a solution and hindsight review following implementation.

A study of water transfers in England and Wales illustrates how a prescriptive model may be used in investigating resource policy (Mitchell, 1971; 1974b). The purpose of the inquiry was to determine the impact of the Water Resources Act 1963 upon policy and decision making. The investigation described and assessed legislative and organizational arrangements for water management in post-war England and Wales. Having established the general context for water management and having identified principal changes between 1945 and 1963, Mitchell concentrated upon case studies involving transfer of water from upland areas to urban–industrial centres. The strategy included selection of case studies which occurred before, during and after the 1963 Act to determine what changes had resulted in policy and decisions processes.

Ideally, the case studies should have been chosen in order to hold all variables constant except for the appearance of the Act. Given the many variables which influence policy, and the relatively small number of major water transfers, it was not possible to control all variables. Three case studies were examined in detail relative to a prescriptive model (Fig. 12.2). The first covered events during 1956 and 1957 when Liverpool proposed a reservoir in North Wales. This proposal aroused opposition from groups concerned with agriculture, aesthetics and Welsh culture. The second developed between 1962 and 1966 following Manchester's proposal to abstract water from existing lakes in the Lake District National Park. Criticism in this situation arose from individuals and groups opposed to such development in a national park. The third example involved the controversy which arose in 1966 when a water board in the North East sought permission to build a reservoir at Cow Green, having high amenity and scientific value and designated as a site of scientific interest.

Contrasting actual policy against the ideal suggested by the model (Fig. 12.2) revealed significant insights. The organizations proposing reservoirs and transfers defined their objectives and problems in narrow terms. In brief, the objective was to provide water to consumers at minimum cost. This approach led to dismissal of some alternatives without detailed study, as well as to preoccupation with a restricted range of solutions. In appraising alternatives, conflicting stances arose over the relationship between the scale of projects and comprehensiveness. In one case study, technical advisers urged the construction of a single, large project in order to realize savings through scale economies and to confine disruption to one site. In another case, the same technical advisers, consulting for a different authority, argued for a series of small reservoirs to maintain flexibility and to avoid overcommitment of resources. These types of arguments

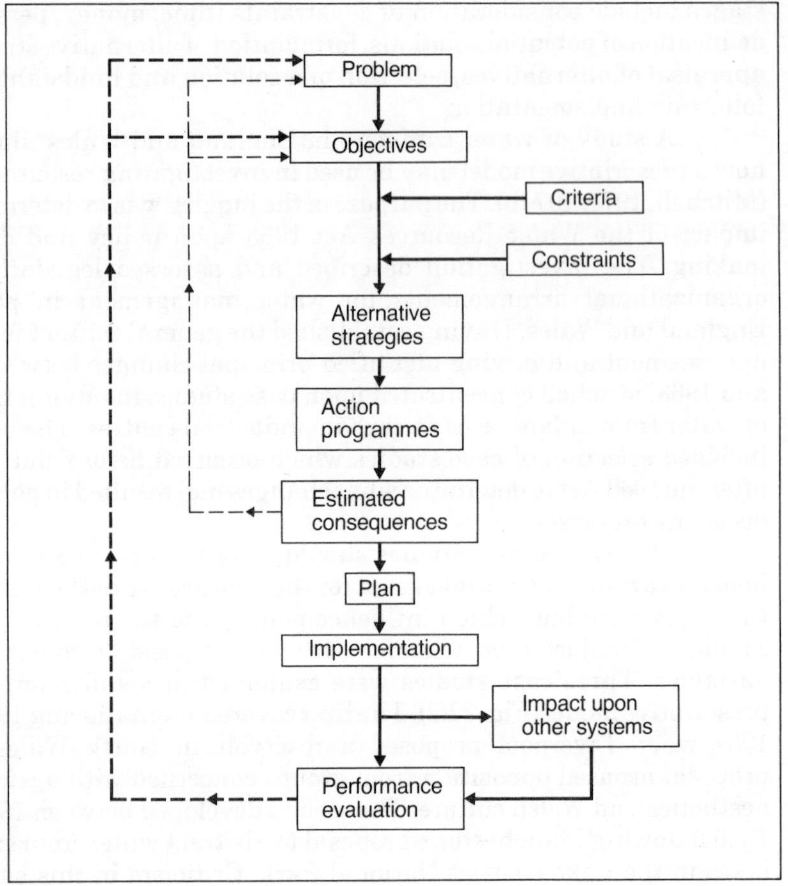

Fig. 12.2 A general model for policy and decision making (*from Mitchell, 1971*)

emphasized that rather than means being adjusted to ends, ends were often rationalized relative to available means.

The cases also illustrated that even with a narrow range of alternatives, the necessary information often was not available either because the data had not been collected or because of measurement problems. When the need for data was recognized, it was not always possible to assemble systematic evidence upon which to compare the value of a site for water developments opposed to scientific inquiry, amenity or preservation of culture. As a result, those responsible for establishing general policy or making specific decisions had to juggle arguments based upon different priorities, values and attitudes. And as one observer of the Cow Green debate noted, 'this is a debate not between right and wrong but between right and right'.

The case studies demonstrated that real world processes do not usually approach the prescriptive ideal, and especially that individuals characterized as 'Economic Man' are difficult to find. However, by establishing the sequence of steps that should be followed, the prescriptive model does highlight where weaknesses arise. For example, the model emphasizes when problems, objectives and alternatives are narrowly defined. It draws attention to needed or inadequate data, and suggests key stages at which the public could be involved in the management process. All of these features indicate that derivation of prescriptive models can be useful in attempts to improve the way in which resources are allocated.

12.4.2 DESCRIPTIVE MODELS

Geographers have devoted more attention to descriptive than prescriptive models, and White (1961; 1963) developed the basic framework which has influenced most subsequent investigators. Based largely upon his natural hazards research (Ch. 8). White sought to formulate a model which would help to describe the *actual choices* made in resource management. These choices were then contrasted with the *theoretical range of choice* to determine if and how man could make better use of, or adjustments to, the environment.

White identified six aspects associated with decision making. The first was the *perceived range of choice*, or the range of resource use recognized by the manager, whether that individual was a lay person, government official or politician. The second involved *resource estimates*, or the judgements about the quantity and quality of the physical resources. Estimates could be based on scientific inventory and appraisal and/or upon casual and highly biased perceptions. Available *technology* was a third aspect, as it influenced future demand, production and combinations of use. The fourth aspect incorporated expected *economic efficiency*, normally expressed with discount rates and benefit-cost ratios. *Spatial linkages*, or the relation of a given use to other resource uses in contiguous or functionally related areas, was the fifth concern. The sixth aspect, *social guides*, was considered to modify each of the preceding five. As White explained them, social guides incorporated the customs, attitudes, education and organizations that characterized a society.

White (1961) was explicit in stating that this framework did not necessarily explain why decisions were made. Rather, it described how decisions were reached in terms of perceived range of choice, estimated nature of the resource and practical constraints based upon economic, technological, spatial and social considerations. His framework was used as a departure point for Kates' (1962) study of adjustments to the urban flood hazard (Ch. 8) and for MacIver's (1970) study of urban water supply (Ch. 5). G. F. White (1969) also applied this framework when assessing the water management strategies which evolved in the United States. While his model served as the basis for numerous empirical studies, it also formed one of the foundations upon which a series of 'stress' models were developed.

12.4.2.1 Stress models

Several authors (Kasperson and Minghi, 1969, 431–5; Moore, 1975) have argued convincingly that political geography offers useful concepts for analysis of policy. As Kasperson and Minghi (1969; 432) noted, one focus of political geography is 'upon the role of public institutions and political conflict in the patterns and processes of environmental management'. They believed that the geographer can not only provide background analysis regarding the environment, but can also contribute to analysis of underlying issues in policy decisions. In their view (p. 432), the issues would include 'the public goals of particular actions, the assumptions upon which policy rests, the implications and probable results of particular decisions, the validity of evaluation methodologies, and policy conflicts and implementation difficulties'. They further believed that for geographers a key question would emerge from concern with spatial scale. Are costs and benefits considered for each of local, regional and national levels? Are costs and benefits spatially allocated in a pattern consistent with public objectives? They urged political geographers to apply their interests and these questions to three significant problems: environmental policy and planning, resource allocation and spatial linkages and area development.

Kasperson (1969a; 1969b) used the stress created by a drought between 1961 and 1966 in a community in Massachusetts to develop a descriptive model and to explore the role of various groups in the policy and decision processes. The city of Brockton had faced a steadily deteriorating water use/safe yield ratio in its reservoirs throughout the 1950s. When drought struck in the early 1960s, a major crisis was precipitated for city officials. By interviewing the two individuals who served as mayors over this time as well as the water superintendent, other municipal officials and the city's water consultant firm, and analysing editorials and newspaper accounts in two area papers, Kasperson (1969a) sought to examine the process by which drought became a significant issue. Simultaneously, he studied the manner in which key officals in the municipal political system perceived and responded to the stress.

The procedure of comparing actual management against a prescribed model was rejected by Kasperson. He felt such an approach does not recognize that the process of resource management is only one subsystem in a larger political system. These different subsystems compete for scarce resources. To appraise the management process, he developed a stress model which explicitly recognized the range of stresses acting upon a community as well as the shifting objectives of key officials.

The model orders or describes the process through which municipal managers evaluate and respond to stresses (Fig. 12.3). Based upon the earlier ideas of White, and Easton (1957), the model indicates that stresses are articulated to the managers by interest

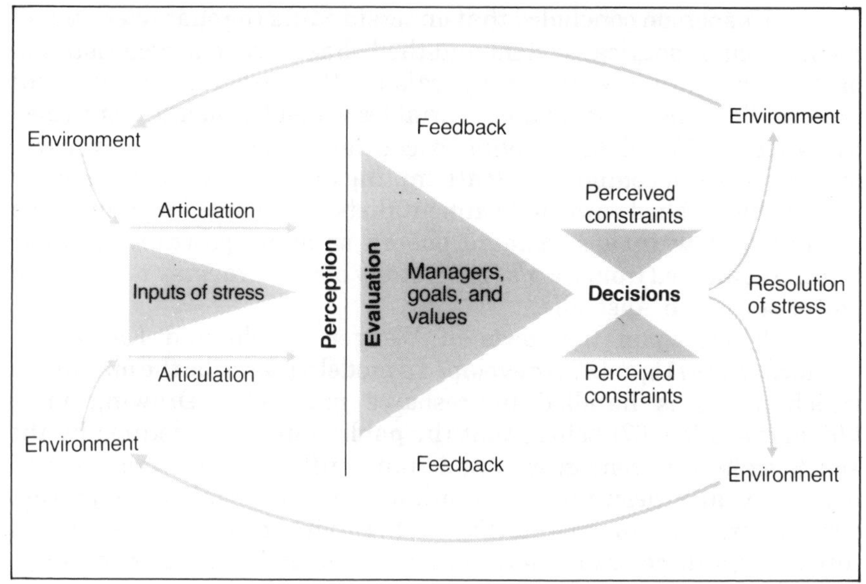

Fig. 12.3 Kasperson's model of stress management (*from Kasperson 1969a*)

groups or the media. The managers' perception of the stress is influenced by the way in which the problem is articulated. With his image of the newly identified stress, the manager seeks adaptive strategies which are rational to his limited understanding of reality and his awareness of other stresses in the system. Put in the context of his objectives, personality and perceived role, the manager acts as Simon's 'Administrative Man', making numerous incremental decisions which more often satisfice than maximize. Receiving feedback from the political system, the manager will respond to and learn from the stress and strains acting upon him.

In his analysis, Kasperson demonstrated that the lack of attention and slow response to the impending drought-induced stress was partially due to the managers' preoccupation with other stresses (school programmes, sewage treatment, transportation, urban renewal). A consulting engineering firm served as the major agent of articulation during the 1950s. It identified the increasing inability of the water supply system to meet growing needs, but its figures in a series of reports underestimated the magnitude of the problem. The first mayor, as a key actor in the drama, never perceived the deteriorating water use/safe yield ratio to be as serious as some of the other stresses demanding attention. Both he and the water superintendent genuinely confused the problems of distribution and supply. Other constraints arose through the mayor's perception of the attitude of the city council to the issue, the limitations of the municipal budget and an overly-optimistic faith in technology to resolve the problem.

Kasperson concluded that understanding the characteristics of the municipal political system and the behavioural characteristics of participants was the key to appraising the resource management process. The importance of these variables was subsequently confirmed by Wood (1976) when studying a conflict which occurred when a municipal water commissioner attempting to provide water as cheaply as possible clashed with environmentalists who wanted to maintain a minimum flow in a stream to ensure salmon spawning. Similar findings emerged from Barr's (1978) study of a controversy regarding a power station in Australia.

Based upon the ideas of Wengert (1955) and Kasperson, O'Riordan (1971b, c; 1972) developed a model to describe the manner in which stress is handled by resource managers. Drawing upon Wengert's (1955; 67) beliefs that the public interest is defined by the synthesis of different groups and that conflict is 'inevitable – even necessary and desirable', O'Riordan's model visualizes a process evolving from group struggle (Fig. 12.4). Environmental stress, either a resource shortage or deterioration, is perceived by an interest group. This stress may be passed directly to the politician or to a public

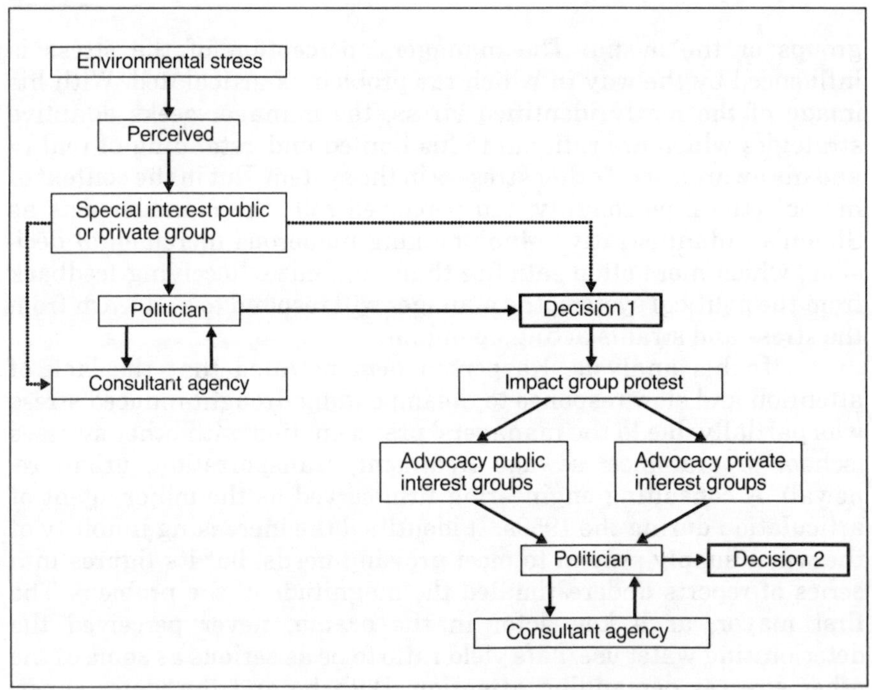

Fig. 12.4 O'Riordan's model of political conflict over environmental issues 'A Reappraisal' by Timothy O'Riordan is reprinted from *Environment and Behaviour*, Vol 3, No 2, June 1971 p. 202 by permission of the publisher, Sage Publications Inc.

agency. If the stress is acute, outside consultant advice will be sought before a decision is taken or policy announced. Since the policy or decision contains implications for the amount and distribution of societal benefits and costs, different groups will respond after the initial decision in an attempt to modify the manager's choice to improve their position. The pressure brought to bear by these groups may lead to a second decision, which in turn will lead to others.

O'Riordan's descriptive model carries several implications (1971b, 203–4). The management process is viewed as one of pluralistic group bargaining in which the public interest is a residual of conflict rather than a positive expression of conscious choice. The process also emphasizes that the public is not homogeneous, but rather consists of different segments. Indeed, drawing upon the framework first offered by Kasperson (1969b; 197), O'Riordan's (1971c; 102–3) categorized the public into two groups – the active and the inactive (Fig. 12.5). The active participants are the ones most often heard from by resource managers since they are organized and articulate. Ideological actors participate from a concern with basic principles and intellectual or moral stances regarding resource issues. In contrast, civic actors concentrate upon specific issues, especially those that have implications for their region or community, whereas private actors participate over anxiety that they will be personally affected by a policy or decision. On the other extreme, members of the public may not express their views because of being unaware, directly unaffected or fatalistic. This group, frequently the vast majority of the public, is often referred to as the 'silent majority'. It is this inactive group that the resource managers are interested in hearing from since they often represent the

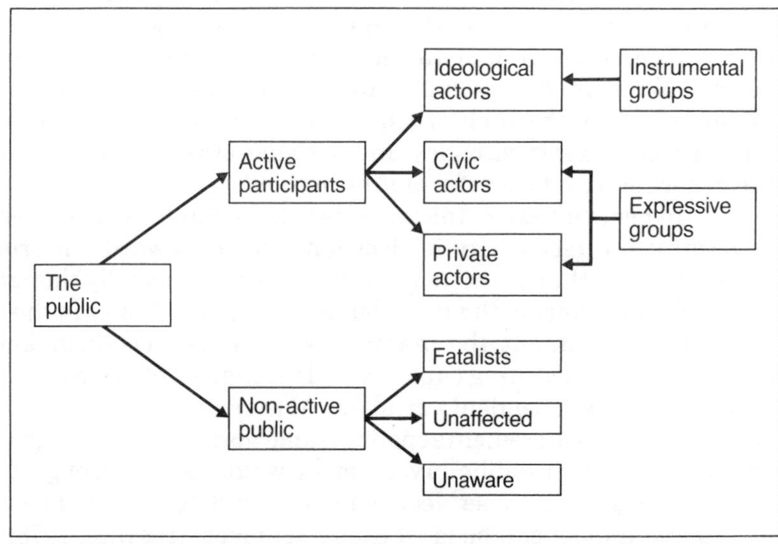

Fig. 12.5 The active and non-active public (*from Sewell, 1974*)

majority of the general public. Unfortunately, most mechanisms for citizen involvement are mainly oriented toward the active public (section 5.4.4).

From the above discussion, it is obvious that another implication of O'Riordan's model is that public input is largely associated with a variety of groups using advocacy methods. The interest groups may become involved for a variety of reasons (selfish, altruistic) and it cannot be assumed that they represent the public interest. At a different level, the structure of the model implies that professional resource managers (consultant in Fig. 12.4) have an important role which is likely to continue in the future. The outcome of the process is frequently a compromise falling between the views of the different groups (politicians, resource managers, interest groups, general public). And the outcome usually arises from a 'process of incrementalism and bargaining to achieve what is desirable rather than what is optimal' (O'Riordan, 1971b; 204). These attributes demonstrate the heavy reliance that the model places upon the ideas of Lindblom (1959, 1968) and Simon (1957) in addition to the concept of stress introduced to geographers by Kasperson.

12.4.2.2 Incremental models

While Kasperson and O'Riordan have drawn implicitly upon the incremental ideas of Lindblom, others have explicitly considered the implications of his model for resource management. Two examples are discussed here.

Ingram (1973), a political scientist, used the incremental model while studying the variables which affect the flow of information to decision makers. She appraised the National Environmental Assessment Act in the United States. The basic argument in the investigation was that incremental and fragmented processes impose serious restraints upon the flow of information. The overriding questions then become: What are the restraints upon information flows? What are the factors affecting channels of communication? What determines which facts are considered in policy and decision making? What motivates the generation and transfer of information?

In her evaluation, Ingram identified a number of considerations governing the receptivity of decision makers towards information. These included the context (e.g. water quality was usually thought of in terms of health during the 1950s but relative to aesthetics in the 1960s), the source, the content, the characteristics of the decision maker, rules and regulations, learning capacity and timing. All of these were viewed as significant independent variables. At the same time, these variables considered in an incremental policy framework were seen to generate a situation in which public involvement would occur through interest groups acting upon those 'decision points and decision makers where access and impact can be most easily achieved' (Ingram, 1973; 157).

Mitchell (1976) demonstrated that the incremental model

provided a close approximation of a fisheries management programme in British Columbia. Canadian fisheries managers implemented a four-stage programme designed to increase salmon fishermen's incomes, reduce capitalization and improve management of the resource. The programme involved introduction of licences for vessels, public purchase of vessels from individuals wishing to leave the industry, vessel standards to improve safety and quality of catches, plus examination of area and gear regulations, location of hatcheries and international issues by an advisory committee (Mitchell and King, 1984).

When first announced, the entire programme was not described. Instead, over the period of implementation, each phase was introduced separately, reaction was obtained and a final plan was established. Both the politician responsible for the programme and his resource advisers were insistent that the entire programme could not be laid out in detail at the outset. As one resource manager commented, 'it is essential in any plan to move a step at a time, review the results of that step and then move into the next' (as quoted in Mitchell, 1976; 217). This approach did not satisfy the processing companies and fishermen. The lack of guidelines and continual alterations created an atmosphere of uncertainty in which individuals found it difficult to plan for the future.

Adoption of an incremental approach caused a dilemma. The resource managers believed that the experimental and innovative nature of the programme necessitated a step-by-step, trial-and-error approach. No comprehensive outline could be provided and continuous changes were essential. In developing the different parts of the programme, consultation with groups in the industry was wanted. On the other hand, those in the industry were forced to respond to isolated proposals without any overview as to where the programme ultimately was headed. By responding in a vacuum, those offering views had no way of appraising the consequences of their views for later stages. And, after the continual alterations and changes, those in the industry could be excused for losing some of their enthusiasm for investing time and effort in articulating concerns when these often appeared to get lost during subsequent stages of 'muddling through'.

Use of an incremental approach by resource managers can thus carry serious implications concerning public involvement. In brief, incrementalism and citizen involvement do not appear to be readily compatible. The consequences of the incremental process in this regard deserve greater attention since its strengths (flexibility, recognition of limited information, simplification of problem and alternative solutions) may be seriously undermined by the difficulties it creates for obtaining public input.

12.4.2.3 Output models

Lowi's model, based upon distributive, regulative and redistributive policies, has provided a departure point for several studies of American water management (Mann, 1975b; Ingram and McCain, 1977). A study of the conflicts and coalitions that arose during water development in the Upper Colorado River basin illustrates the way in which the output model can be applied (Mann, 1975a). Mann (1975a; 141) believed that the patterns of political behaviour in the Upper Colorado River basin were consistent with the proposition that 'substantive policy is the crucial independent variable which largely determines the manner in which the actors and political institutions of American society perform'. In this context, the politics of the Colorado basin have been both distributive and regulatory.

At the end of the Second World War, the Upper Basin states were determined to exercise their claims initially made in an agreement during the 1920s to water in the Colorado River system. During 1946, the federal Bureau of Reclamation published a report in which possible development projects were catalogued. In addition, the report clearly demonstrated that not enough water existed to make all of the projects feasible. This report set the stage for subsequent distributive and regulatory politics.

A first step was formation of the Upper Colorado Compact Commission to develop an interstate agreement. The states, although in direct competition for water, had to negotiate and reach an agreement in order to approach the federal government with a unified request for funding. This procedure is one of the component parts of distributive politics (section 12.3.2.3).

One aspect of the eventual agreement was a proposed dam in Echo Park, which quickly involved regulatory politics in the allocation process. The proposed Echo Park dam made a clash with conservation groups inevitable. Upper Basin spokesmen viewed the Echo Park dam as a key component of the agreement. Conservationists totally rejected these views, reacting against construction of a dam in a national park. In Mann's (1975a, 147) words, 'this was regulatory politics in its classic mould: two major combatants linked in combat with little or no possibility of compromise on the principal issue or of disaggregating the benefits'.

Aside from opposition to the dam in the national park, little criticism arose concerning the system of storage and power dams combined with irrigation projects totalling over $1 billion. As Mann showed, there were numerous issues on which the scheme could be challenged, including interest-free funds, low interest rates, use of power rates to subsidize irrigation projects, questionable benefit-cost ratios, extended pay-out periods, opportunity costs, land values after development and costs per hectare. None of these issues was raised.

In Mann's view, the reasons were found in the nature of distributive politics. Irrigation projects financed by federal funds were part of the 'expected' output from the political system. While the West received assistance through subsidized irrigation, other regions were aided through development of inland waterways, military bases or defence contracts. Anyone who attacked the Colorado scheme invited attack on projects for his own region. Since direct competition was not involved, mutual non-interference was accepted. Furthermore, other areas might want water projects in the future. A challenge of one project would be a challenge for all, and such a conflict was better avoided, at least in the eyes of politicians.

The principal objection – the dam at Echo Park – could not be resolved behind the scenes since the opponents were criticizing from outside the system. Action was delayed for two years as the conservationists, opposed on principle, were intransigent. It was the proponents who finally backed down. With the Echo park project dropped, the agreement was approved by the House of Representatives and the President during 1956. Subsequent legislation and agreements extended this early agreement, leading to the completion of Lake Powell in 1963 and power generation in 1964, almost 20 years after the Bureau of Reclamation report which triggered the bargaining and conflict of 1946.

What are the implications of this model and the processes it identifies? Mann (1975a; 161–7) argued that water allocation processes are basically distributive in character. Only in the instance of a major battle does such policy incorporate the regulatory process. The major consequence is that many decisions are made in the spirit of mutual non-interference, facilitating authorization of inefficient and inequitable programmes and projects without the taxpayer realizing the basis upon which such approvals are granted. In the United States, Mann saw some hope in the National Water Commission's report of 1962 which declared that projects must offer definite national economic benefits rather than represent transfer of incomes among regions. In addition, in regard to water transfers, the report insisted that beneficiaries should pay the full costs of such projects, including compensation to the region exporting water.

If these guidelines were adopted, water allocation would be made on the basis of regulatory rather than distributive politics. However, Mann was not optimistic. Distributive politics involve individuals and groups who seek some benefit from a public agency. A united front is presented for the separable but common interests. From this position, the benefit from the public source is obtained without appearing to impose burdens on other interests, although the cost is usually passed on to taxpayers across the country. This procedure is attractive to regional and sectoral interests in that it obtains results, spreads the incidence of costs and minimizes open conflict. It also facilitates sidestepping of such fundamental questions as: Should demands be reassessed rather than supply? Who should determine demand? Should those who benefit directly be responsible to pay for incurred costs? Should the taxpayers of a nation carry the costs associated with a regional programme? If so, to what extent? What alternatives exist to meet demand? These and other basic questions rarely get explicitly examined in distributive politics or in the incremental process.

12.5 ENVIRONMENTAL MEDIATION

Situations may exist in which a model is developed to describe an ongoing process. However, because that process is viewed as appropriate, investigators then will attempt to develop prescriptive models which represent an improvement on the current process. Environmental mediation is an example of this situation.

In Section 11.4 a brief discussion was presented regarding the institutional aspects of bargaining and negotiation. These concepts are also pertinent to policy making, whether they are referred to as *bargaining* (Dorcey, McPhee and Sydneysmith, 1980; Bacharach and Lawler, 1981; Dorcey, 1983; 1986a; Harris, 1984), *conflict management* (Carpenter and Kennedy, 1980; 1981; Busternd, 1981; Fraser and Hipel; 1984), *dispute resolution* (Hileman, 1983; Bacow and Wheeler, 1984), *negotiation* (Rivkin, 1977; Rodwin, 1982; Ognibene, 1983; Hall and Doyle, 1984; Sullivan, 1984) or *environmental mediation* (Cormick, 1980; 1982; Lake, 1980; Curtis, 1983; Talbot, 1983).

The concept of environmental mediation arises from several ideas. First, there are increasing demands, interdependencies, complexity and uncertainty being encountered in resource allocation problems. These four attributes combine to create 'wicked problems' (Dorcey, 1986a; 90) for which traditional techniques are proving inadequate. Second, these four attributes generate conflicts which have to be resolved, and their resolution normally involves using compromises rather than relying upon cooperation, accommodation and dictation alone (Dorcey, 1983; 14).

As Carpenter and Kennedy (1981) have observed, conflict can be positive if it forces individuals and groups to re-examine values, objectives, assumptions and strategies. If handled constructively, conflict can help to broaden the range of options to be considered and can contribute to solutions in which all participants believe they have gained.

Unfortunately, too frequently unnecessary or negative conflicts are generated. This may occur when participants fail to exchange adequate information for full understanding of issues. Or participants enter the conflict with stereotypes of the other side so that they fail to appreciate the legitimacy of other viewpoints. Too often, the process results in 'winners' and 'losers' which makes it difficult to implement a decision or policy.

Dorcey (1986a; 39–40) suggests that it is important to distinguish among at least four types of conflict:

1. Cognitive conflict results from different understandings of a

situation which in turn can lead to differences in technical judgement. For example, a fisheries biologist employed by the forestry industry and a biologist working for a government fisheries agency may disagree over the probable damage caused by cutting of timber in a small watershed in which there is a valuable fishery. Both individuals may have equal concern about the damage to fish, but disagreement occurs over the probable nature of such damage.

2. Value conflict arises from different judgements regarding the ends to be accomplished by the means being considered. While both biologists may agree on the consequences of cutting timber in the watershed, the two individuals may disagree over the appropriate tradeoffs between environmental quality and economic growth.
3. Interest conflict stems from disagreement concerning the distribution of benefits and costs. Again, there may be no disagreement about the consequences of cutting timber in the watershed, but sharp disagreements may arise over who should pay for the mitigating action.
4. Behavioural conflict occurs due to the personalities and circumstances associated with the interested parties. Both sides may genuinely desire a resolution, but problems may merge as a result of historical frustration, distrust, emotionalism, political manipulation, restricted perception, posturing, or lack of communication.

Recognizing these different types of conflict is an important step towards identifying the nature of the problem, and beginning to design solutions. As indicated in Chapter 11, attention is being directed toward improving the interaction skills of individuals, improving the type and flow of information and adjusting institutional arrangements to encourage constructive bargaining.

Awareness of the existence of bargaining and tradeoffs in environmental mediation has generated attempts to describe the processes which prevail in various resource allocation situations. Recognition of the desirability of constructive negotiation leads to attempts to prescribe alternative approaches which would improve the effectiveness of negotiation and mediation. In this manner, descriptive and prescriptive models may emerge.

Increasing attention has been given to analysing alternative approaches to mediation, especially in North America where there is growing dissatisfaction with the legalistic, adversarial approach. In many ways, mediation has been built into the policy processes of those countries with a British tradition of government where there has been a longer history of using consultation and negotiation to resolve problems. In the field of resource management, applications of the mediation approach are numerous. They range from coal and related resources (Parker, 1984), power station siting (Barr, 1978), disposal of hazardous wastes (Bellman, Sampson and Cormick, 1982), water management (Caldwell, 1984a), and coastal zone management

(Muretta and Price, 1982; Nyhart, 1983; Kennedy and Breisch, 1983; Gusman and Huser, 1984; Susskind and McCreary, 1985).

12.6 IMPLICATIONS FOR RESOURCE MANAGEMENT

The question of the nature of policy making in resource management has generated research focusing on many issues. In this chapter attention has been directed towards the role of prescriptive and descriptive models in resource analysis. The implications for resource management are several. Prescriptive models establish an ideal or standard against which actual policy processes may be assessed. They help to pinpoint areas which are not being handled adequately, and thereby indicate where the resource manager should concentrate to improve the allocation process. In contrast, descriptive models indicate the nature of the actual process of resource allocation. By appreciating the reality of policy processes, the investigator should be able to make recommendations as to how a process could be made more effective. Simultaneously, such insight should enable the analyst to predict more accurately future decisions or policies. This aspect is important, since resource agencies often have to anticipate other agency policies or responses to policies. Awareness of policy and decision processes also should make the investigator more sensitive to the opportunities for and barriers against incorporating public input. Furthermore, it is becoming apparent that a key factor in the policy process is the personalities and ideologies of the key participants (Swift, 1983, 231–65; Cawley and Chaloupka, 1985). Thus, analysis of policy and decision processes contains more than scholarly benefits (Sewell and Mitchell, 1984). The outcomes can generate practical suggestions for resource managers.

12.7 IMPLICATIONS FOR RESEARCH

At the outset of this chapter, it was suggested that analysis of policy and decision processes draws upon all of the major research traditions of geography. It can be pursued as an end in itself (understand and improve the process) or as a means to an end (understand spatial allocation, man–environment relationships, regional patterns). Analysis of the policy process also touches on several of the research questions identified for resource analysis in section 1.3: understanding the variables which condition allocation and development of resources; evaluation of the impact of resource allocations.

The status of research on policy and decision making can be appraised relative to some of the issues identified in Chapters 1 and 2. General agreement exists that research in this area does not yet have a firm theoretical foundation on which to build (Dror, 1968, 74–75; Aucoin, 1971, 28). The consequences of this situation are not considered to be serious by those whose main preoccupation is to resolve pressing problems. Thus, Hamill (1968; 282) has commented regarding this area of inquiry that 'generalizations and theories are of little value' whereas Dror (1968; 129–30) suggested that politicians and policy makers, as practical people, 'regard attempts to construct normative policy making models as a waste of resources and idle daydreaming at best, and as some kind of subversive activity at worst'. Indeed, one policy maker (Drury, 1975; 89) remarked that 'less second-rate theory, and more first-rate applied work, is necessary if planning, analysis and evaluation in the field of public policy are to be useful to the elected representatives who must exercise the ultimate judgement and make the final decisions in the face of incomplete knowledge and uncertain consequences'. As a result, the investigator should be aware that many policy makers are not overly sympathetic to long-term, theoretically oriented work when they face a never-ending series of immediate problems. Hopefully, a reasonable balance may be struck between theoretical and applied research – and that some of the research cast in a theoretical framework will eventually prove to have 'practical' value.

The different assumptions associated with the descriptive models illustrate that a phenomenological research philosophy is useful for these inquiries. Recognition of 'Administrative Man' behaving in a 'boundedly rational' manner emphasizes that individuals have varying images of reality. This does not preclude utilization of a positivist approach, but does suggest that both have desirable qualities for such research.

At a different level, it is obvious that geographers do not have exclusive rights to analysis of policy making. Political scientists have been actively carrying out work in this area for many years (Caldwell, 1963; 1964; 1970) as have economists (Ciriacy-Wantrup, 1971; Herfindahl and Kneese, 1965) and management scientists (Simon, 1957; 1959). Interaction between these disciplines and geography, especially political geography (Kasperson and Minghi, 1969; Moore, 1975), will be a necessary condition for progress.

Concerning conceptual frameworks, numerous alternatives have been presented. Some of the difficulty in agreeing upon a common framework stems from perceptions as to what constitutes 'policy' and 'policy making' (section 12.2). In turn, this has created difficulty in identifying the key variables. Often, the choice of variables has been dictated by the availablility of data. In other instances even after variables are identified it is recognized that they may 'change in complexion from day to day, place to place, and issue to issue' (O'Riordan, 1976b; 241). This led a Workshop on resource management decision making at an Institute of British Geographer's annual meeting to conclude (O'Riordan, 1976a; 65)

> There are too many special factors involved to make important generalizations. ... Above all, the significance of specific personalities should be emphasized: resource decision making is not so much about organization, statutory guidelines, and coordinating arrangements, as it is about the outcome of the skill, determination, vision, or indifference, antagonism and bloody-mindedness of particular individuals in important positions with influential connections.

This type of comment suggests that much policy research is still at the stage of variable identification. Until that stage develops with more confidence, the opportunity for realizing generalizations or theories is slight.

On a more positive note, the way in which assumptions have been used demonstrates their utility in pinpointing the characterisitics of basic processes. Although all assumptions simplify and abstract, they have allowed investigators to explore the different processes which underlie policy processes. Analysts such as Lindblom and Etzioni have concentrated upon the inputs to policy, while Lowi has focused upon outputs. Although their means have been different, they have shared a common end – understanding the policy process.

In terms of research designs, there has been a heavy reliance upon the case study (Dror, 1968, 74; Moore, 1975, 13). When Campbell and Stanley's criticisms of the case study are recalled (section 2.2.2), the warning issued by the Institute of British Geographers resources management workshop that 'case studies should be taken more as unique phenomena than as illustrations of nomethetic decision models' takes on greater significance (O'Riordan, 1976a; 65). It is unlikely that the ideal experimental design with control and treatment groups will ever be feasible for such work, mainly due to ethical considerations. Nevertheless, greater use could be made of Campbell and Stanley's quasi-experimental designs, especially those involving longitudinal approaches.

Study of policies and policy processes offers substantial opportunities for geographers. Through their sensitivity to man-environment interactions, spatial dimensions and regional complexity, geographers can offer suggestions which may improve resource policies and decisions (Coppock, 1974). On the other side of the coin, geographers can examine policies to obtain insights for location decisions, ecological changes and regional development.

However, to become actively involved in the policy process, the geographer will have to make some conscious trade-offs. Whereas Hare (1974) observed that scholars are committed to long time scales, to certainty and to deferring action until understanding has been gained, the politician or policy maker cannot indulge in such luxury. The latter are preoccupied with short-term, incremental actions in which 'the concrete is preferred to the abstract, the simple to the complex, and the immediate to the ultimate glory. . . . Action must proceed when the time is ripe, and it is rarely ripe twice' (Hare, 1974; 26). These considerations suggest that geographers anxious to contribute to the policy process may have to align their research in a direction which could be distinctly different from their other scholarly work. For, as Hare (1974; 28) has stated

> Often we say that major policy issues are always interdisciplinary. This is quite wrong. They are *non*-disciplinary. They call for great feats of synthesis, acts of faith, leaps into the unknown, the laying of prodigious bets. These are not characteristic of the academic disciplines of which I have knowledge.

CHAPTER 13

RESOURCE ANALYSIS: EVOLUTION, ACCOMPLISHMENTS AND OPPORTUNITIES

13.1 INTRODUCTION

In this chapter the evolution of resource analysis in geography and related disciplines is placed in context by examining the types of questions and emphases which have prevailed over time (section 13.2). Attention is then given to highlighting the major accomplishments by geographers in resource analysis (section 13.3). In section 13.4 consideration is given to present and future opportunities in resource analysis. Discussion focuses here upon research issues and problems as well as upon research perspectives. In the final section (13.5), the relationship of geographical resource analysis to interdisciplinary inquiry is explored.

13.2 EVOLUTION OF RESOURCE ANALYSIS IN GEOGRAPHY

Geographers have had an interest in resource analysis and resource management for many decades. Research in different branches of the discipline – physical, economic, cultural, regional – has been directly relevant to resource problems and issues. In this section an overview of the evolution of geographical approaches to resource analysis is presented., The overview is not comprehensive, but instead attempts to identify pre-eminent ideas and shifts in thinking.

Whitaker (1954; 229), one of the first to identify natural resources as a focus for study which geography shared with other disciplines, believed that this field incorporated policy and action as well as theory. In his opinion, geographical interest in resources arose from at least three considerations: as part of the study of man–earth relations, as part of the practical work in land classification and inventory and as part of the analysis of economic production and trade patterns.

Whitaker suggested that geographers had contributed to resource analysis for decades through inquiries regarding the nature and distribution of resources, the appraisal of regional resources and the conservation and depletion of specific resources. Whitaker saw numerous future opportunities. Investigations of the recreational value and use of resources as well as their scenic worth would be needed. Historical physical geography had much to offer, particularly the documenting of what was happening to soils and water over considerable lengths of time. Comparative investigations of resource problems in relatively small regions were seen as vital, especially the impact of mining on other resources. In all of this work, he urged geographers not to over-emphazise physical aspects and to give due attention to cultural and human variables.

Until the early 1960s much work in geography in North America with relevance for resource analysis and management was conducted under the rubric of 'applied geography' or 'planning'. However, during the 1960s, resource management became accepted as a recognizable field of inquiry. White (1963; 1974c) reviewed the contributions of geographers to river basin development and Lucas (1966) surveyed the contributions of environmental perception research for wilderness policy.

In the late 1960s, Sewell and Burton (1967) examined research in resource management within Canada. They concluded that contributions by geographers concentrated on four major topics: distribution of resources, management of particular resources, resource development in specific regions and factors influencing decision making. They identified four types of research needing attention. These included: (1) the estimation of the quantity and quality of available resources; (2) the economic analysis of resource development, especially benefit-cost studies, assessment of risk, uncertainty, externalities and intangibles, and the spatial impact of development; (3) the influence of institutional constraints (customs, attitudes, laws, organizations) on resource development; and (4) the role of perception and attitudes in decision making.

Mikesell (1974) provided a similar review for work completed into the early 1970s by American geographers. He concluded that geographers working in different research traditions each had a contribution to offer to environmental management, and cautioned geographers not to focus exclusively upon any one tradition. In his view, the most pressing problems related to environmental quality, environmental impact studies and relationships between population and resources.

Until the 1970s the bulk of geographical research labelled as resource management was conducted in North America. Geographers in the United States and Canada generated considerable research, and often played active roles as consultants or advisers to the public and private sectors. In Britain, a concern with resource management was not as visible (Coppock and Sewell, 1975, 4–5), even though much work defined as 'applied geography' would have been labelled as resource management research on the other side of the Atlantic. However, by the late 1960s and early 1970s, a number of British geographers started to identify their work with the field of resource management.

At the International Geographical Congress held in New Delhi during November, 1968, Wise (1969) reviewed the progress made in resource studies. He called attention to the importance of resource surveys concerning both actual and potential use. Recommending the type of work done by Stamp as a model, Wise argued that while stock-taking in itself was valuable, even more important was the need to ascertain the significance of resources regarding which to develop, for what purposes, and when. In a different direction, he called for more research effort concerning the links between natural resource surveys and regional or economic planning, an idea that had been supported by geographers in North America (Whitaker, 1941; Ginsburg 1957; Zobler, 1962; Burton and Kates, 1964c).

Several years later, O'Riordan (1971a) published an appraisal of the trends and accomplishments in resource management research completed during the 1960s. He concentrated upon efforts to improve the efficiency and equity of resource allocation, attempts to evaluate intangible values of resources, the role of perceptions and attitudes and the forces and influences constraining decision processes. He identified a broad range of topics deserving attention in the future – technical, administrative, institutional, legal, social – not all of which would fall within the competence of the geographer.

Other reviews from Britain followed. Birch (1973) and Gregory (1974) both noted the empirical and problem-solving orientation of research. Coppock and Sewell (1975) provided another review, in which they suggested geographical contributions fell into five categories. The first, involving descriptive and analytical studies of specific resources, had been done since the 1930s. More recent contributions were of four kinds. One concentrated upon abstract modelling of resource systems. The few studies of this type focused upon physical parameters for water management. Another, confined primarily to North America, involved the construction of decision-making models relative to resource management. A third type, considered the best-developed in Britain, comprised case studies of particular policies. The fourth type dealt with development and application of techniques, especially benefit-cost analysis and attitudinal surveys.

In Australia, geographical research focused upon resources did not emerge as quickly as in North America and Britain. Spate and Jennings (1972) reviewed work by geographers in Australia between 1951 to 1971 and never mentioned resource management. However, as in Britain, some of the work which they noted under other categories would have been classified in North America as resource analysis, so some work was underway.

The period from 1972 to 1984 subsequently was assessed by Jeans and Davies (1984). They did not use resource analysis or management as a separate category in their review. They did find that of the books, monograph series and refereed journal articles published by geographers in that period, 8 per cent were in biogeography, nearly 7 per cent were in conservation/environment, 6 per cent were in climatology and just over 2 per cent were in recreation.

Jeans and Davies suggested that the climatic extremes in Australia had led to climatological research having strong practical connotations, especially regarding the rural environment, natural hazards (droughts, floods, storms, bushfires) and air pollution in cities. They concluded that the man–land or ecological research tradition had attracted only a few geographical scholars which likely accounted for the very modest research effort by geographers relative to resources (Jeans and Davies, 1984; 13). Those conducting research on resource analysis had addressed environmental impacts of recreation and mining developments, salinity problems associated with irrigation, human impacts on vegetation and coastal areas, and natural hazards. They were suprised that geographers had virtually ignored environmental impact studies. However, by the late 1970s and 1980s Australian geographers were addressing resource management problems in a direct and policy-oriented manner (Conacher, 1979; 1980; Crabb, 1982; Pigram, 1983; 1986; Day, 1986a; 1986b; 1987).

Geographers in Third World countries also had been developing their thinking about resource analysis. Some of their ideas were similar to their counterparts in the developed countries, whereas other considerations reflected the fundamental problems being encountered within their own countries. Ramesh (1984; 3–4) concluded that earlier studies of resources emphasized economic aspects, especially the factors influencing resource development. He believed that priority had been given to problems relating to location, production, exchange, consumption, marketing and trade, both national and international. For future research, he suggested that activity could usefully concentrate upon resource appraisal, resource utilization, resource development, spatial imbalances in the development process and over-utilization and resulting environmental problems.

While some geographers in developed countries began to focus upon landscape evaluation, social carrying capacity and behavioural aspects of resource managers and users, geographers in the Third World often concentrated upon food/population or health/disease/environment relationships in the context of regional economic development (Forbes, 1981; 1982; Kayastha, 1982; Mabogunje, 1980; 1984). Such analysts have been particularly concerned about the transfer or imposition of values from the developed world to Third World situations. Thus, Kayastha (1982; 39) argued that acceptable quality or allowable degree of environmental impact in various countries might be quite different, reflecting the perception of different values and standards of living. Furthermore, Rambo (1982; 97) expressed apprehension that environmental research could serve to divert attention from more urgent social and political problems. In his view, concern for the welfare of nature could too readily result in indifference to issues of human welfare.

As the work in resource analysis has matured, various individuals have reviewed progress, and have attempted to identify critical concerns. One aspect receiving attention has been the role of geographers in integrating various dimensions in resource analysis. The role of 'integrator' is one that geographers often attribute to themselves. However, Ferguson and Alley (1984) concluded that this role for geographers was recognized more within the discipline than it was outside the discipline. In contrast, Johnston (1983b; 132) concluded that integration by geographers was largely absent, primarily because in his view most geographical work ignores processes in either or both of physical or human geography. Furthermore, Johnston (1983b; 141) argued that integration of physical and human aspects was unlikely and unnecessary for geographers to make a significant contribution.

This review indicates that there has been a steady evolution of resource analysis in geography. Acceptance of a plurality of approaches and perspectives prevails. Different research themes or traditions in geography are recognized as offering distinctive and valuable contributions. The spatial analysis theme poses questions about the location and distribution of phenomena, interactions of phenomena over space, spatial structure and organization and associated processes. The theme of ecological analysis or man–environment relations considers the way in which individuals, groups and cultures perceive, adapt to and modify resources and the environment. In regional analysis, the focus may be upon determining the image or reality of a place and its resources, or exploring the role of resources in regional planning and development. More often than not, the geographer integrates several of these themes during a study. Indeed, it usually is the synthesis of two or more of these themes in an investigation which produces the geographer's distinctive contribution.

While the spatial, ecological and regional themes have been the dominant ones, the role of other traditions should be stressed. Physical geography often is identified as a substantive field in its own right, or as a specific application of spatial analysis (the location and distribution of landforms, climatic attributes, vegetation, wildlife, and soils plus the processes accounting for their spatial patterns). The physical geographer has much to offer resource analysis, particularly through insights about fundamental biophysical processes (Smith and Theberge, 1986). Work by cultural geographers is also important, especially with the need to understand social systems becoming increasingly significant in resource management (Mikesell, 1978). Common to both physical and cultural investigations is the idea of change over time. This aspect suggests that the perspective of the historical geographer has much to contribute (Whitaker, 1954, 231; Zobler, 1962). Awareness of the historical dimension draws attention to the concept of process, and emphasizes the gains to be realized in moving from static to dynamic analyses (Whitaker, 1941).

Regardless of the research theme or tradition, development of theory in geographical resource analysis is still in its infancy. Others have reached a similar conclusion. Zobler (1966; 281) noted that the resources field was lacking in theoretical constructs. Gregory (1974; 381) concluded that in resource management a set of theory was still to be devised.

Several reasons can be citied for the lack of theoretical orientation and development. Much of the research has been empirical in nature, focused upon specific problems in particular localities (Gregory, 1974; 381). Relatively few investigators have attempted to consider the general implications of their findings. Those who take an integrative view frequently are frustrated by the difficulty of comparing findings. As Sewell and Burton (1967; 334) commented,

> Geographical research, like social science research in the resources field in general, has lacked cohesion. Most research topics have been selected on an *ad hoc* basis, according to issues that seemed to be particularly interesting or topical at the time. Even today the effort continues to be diffused, and studies made of particular problems are seldom related to each other, and in few cases is there an attempt to develop principles which might be used in building theory.

An even more substantive difficulty for comparing findings and articulating generalizations is that for many problems the identification of critical variables still is the most pressing task. In many situations, the nature of the problem is not yet clearly defined, as investigators try to sift through a complex web of cause-and-effect relationships to differentiate symptoms from basic problems. In other situations, experience suggests the relative importance of variables but their measurement remains as a major barrier.

Given the difficulty in achieving a theoretical foundation, two questions are pertinent. Is theory needed? If it is needed, what type of theory should be sought? Regarding the first question, development of theory can contribute both to scholarly progress and to resolution of immediate, practical problems.

A basic weakness in much research in resource analysis is lack of understanding of basic processes and relationships. Environmental impact assessments are hindered by inadequate knowledge of fundamental biophysical processes. Social inquiries are weakened by inadequate understanding of perceptual and attitudinal processes. This pattern reinforces White's (1963; 436) contention that unless the geographer's studies 'provide some capacity for prediction of what will result from certain actions in the future, his work, however careful and scholarly, will be ignored'.

If theory is needed, it then should be asked what types of theory offer the greatest potential returns? Kates (1972; 519) argued that the theoretical orientation of resource management research during the 1960s was primarily economic and assumed the existence of scarcity, the correctness of growth and the conquest of nature. He argued that future work should concentrate upon developing theories which account for co-existence of hunger and gluttony, which indicates how growth could be changed into redistribution, and which define how to limit human dominance of resource systems. Kate's suggestion, offered in the early 1970s, is as pertinent now as when it was first put forward.

A search for humanistic theory to help in the allocation of resources is an important but difficult task. As O'Riordan (1976b; iii) observed, little progress has been realized in developing a theory which interrelates individual demands with collective necessities. While deserving attention, this path will demand substantial time, effort and commitment, with the prospects of frustration and disappointment along the way. A second area, perhaps more within the grasp of existing research capability, would focus upon improving the understanding of the crucial variables associated with biophysical and social processes in resource management and development. Much remains to be done in this area, given the inadequacy of our appreciation as to how natural and social systems function.

13.3 ACCOMPLISHMENTS IN RESOURCE ANALYSIS

It is relatively easy to be critical about the research in resource analysis by geographers. In many ways, the work is still in its infancy. Predictive and generalization power is modest. Investigators often are struggling at the basic level of description due to uncertainty as to which are the critical variables. In other situations, identification of cause-and-effect relationships has been frustrated by the complex set of relationships involved. Sensitivity to ethical issues has hindered the control of variables and relationships to determine basic interaction patterns. Furthermore, ethical considerations have resulted in basic questions and problems not being pursued.

Nevertheless, geographers also have significant accomplishments to their credit in resource analysis. It is important not to lose sight of these substantive achievements. Despite all of the technical, practical and ethical problems which are encountered in research, real gains are being realized and should provide encouragement for future endeavours. In addition, geographers should remember that they are not the only discipline encountering difficulties when conducting research in resource analysis. All disciplines experience problems and frustrations, many of which are shared in common. With this perspective in mind, several notable achievements can be identified.

Geographers have a substantial track record regarding resource appraisal. Under the leadership of Dudley Stamp, the World Land Use Survey was designed, and implemented in whole or in part by many countries throughout the world. The initial inventories relied primarily upon field observation and interpretation of aerial photographs. In more recent times, geographers and others have developed remote sensing techniques for application to resource inventories (Schultink, 1983; Finson and Nellis, 1986; Hill and Kelly, 1986). Remote sensing has been applied to the estimation of both existing and potential resource conditions. In conjunction with development of remote sensing, geographers can take significant credit for the development of geographic information systems (Davidson and Jones, 1986; Shields, Rosenthal and Holz, 1986; Cocks and Walker, 1987; Haefner, 1987). The computer manipulation of large data sets and the computer preparation of maps and other visual displays have been developed to a point where both the public and private sector are increasingly using geographic information systems for resource purposes.

Work by geographers in resource appraisal has reflected a concern with location, distribution and areal extent of phenomena which has been a central consideration in spatial analysis. Such considerations provide a departure point for studies focused upon the appraisal of resource supply and demand. Such inventory research incorporates questions which are important for resource management. Where are the resources located? What quantity and quality are available? What demand exists? What constraints may limit their development?

Stimulated by the research and leadership of Gilbert White, the findings of work in hazards and risk assessment have had a direct affect upon public policy in numerous countries. Indeed, the hazards research initiated by White and the resource inventories inspired by Stamp probably represented the geography discipline's most pervasive impacts upon resource management at a world scale.

Hazards research is tied to a framework of human ecology and addresses a general question. How do people adjust to risk and uncertainty in natural systems and in man-made environments? This question has been examined relative to individual hazards, combinations of hazards at a given place and man-made or technological hazards. It also has been used in cross-cultural studies of hazard adjustment strategies. A valuable contribution has been investigations which explicitly follow up the findings of the early studies (Thampapillai and Musgrave, 1985). Thus, Montz and Gruntfest (1986) have updated the early study by White *et al.* (1958) regarding nine of the seventeen cities in the original study discussed in Chapter 8. They found that structural adjustments still dominate in those cities, although a broader range of adjustments is being used.

Environmental impact assessment emerged as a substantive field during the 1970s. Impact assessment has presented many methodological issues (Preston, 1986). Geographers and others have attempted to refine methods and techniques to improve the credibilty of environmental impact statements (MacLaren and Whitney, 1985; Duinker and Baskerville, 1986; Wright and Greene, 1987). Particularly difficult issues have had to be addressed regarding predicting and monitoring impacts (Gellatly *et al.*, 1986; Aspinall and Pye, 1987; Cole, 1987). During the latter part of the 1970s, social impact assessment was developed. Ideally, social impact issues always should have been incorporated in environmental impact assessment. However, an initial preoccupation with the natural environment stimulated social scientists to develop and apply concepts, methods and techniques which were focused explicitly upon social questions (Freeman and Frey, 1986; Murdock, Leistritz and Hamm, 1986).

For geographers, ecological and regional research themes have set the context for environmental impact assessment. Under ecological analysis, investigators have concentrated upon determining the role of people in changing the face of the earth through resource use. In regional analysis, geographers have focused upon the role of resource exploitation in economic development and in environmental change within a region.

Studies of perception, attitude and behaviour, tied closely to the ecological or man–environment research tradition, have led to significant contributions. Key questions have included the following. How do people perceive the environment and resources? How do their perceptions and attitudes influence awareness and selection of strategies? What attitudinal differences exist between various groups? What are the consequences of such differences for the design and implementation of resource policies, programmes and projects?

Geographers have made a range of contributions through their behaviourally oriented research. Technical and substantive contributions have been made through research on landscape evaluation and carrying capacity. Perhaps one of the most significant contributions has been with regard to public participation in the resource management process. Geographers were among the first to advocate the importance of public participation, and have offered numerous suggestions regarding how to make it more effective in resource management.

Through their behavioural work, geographers also have made regular contributions to the evaluation of policies and resource allocation decisions (Park, 1986). Detailed case studies using a wide variety of methods and techniques have ben completed (Aiken and Leigh, 1986; Dearden, 1986; Juvik, 1986; Kliot, 1986; Smardon, 1986; Bandler, 1987). Through this ongoing evaluation of policies and decisions, an improved understanding has developed of both the structures and processes associated with resource management. As this understanding grows, the likelihood of improvements in the processes of bargaining, negotiation and mediation also grows. Work in these areas has the potential to make major improvements in resource management if more situations are to be created in which most participants can view themselves as gaining or benefiting from resource allocation decisions.

This review indicates that geographers have made numerous substantive contributions through their research to improve resource management. Particularly well-recognized contributions have been made regarding resource inventories, hazards and risk assessment. Major efforts also have been made concerning environmental and social impact assessment as well as public participation, landscape evaluation, carrying capacity and policy evaluation. In the following section attention turns from past accomplishments to present and future opportunities for resource analysis.

13.4 PRESENT AND FUTURE OPPORTUNITIES

Numerous issues have been recognized as deserving more attention from resource analysts (Munro, 1983; O'Riordan and Turner, 1983; Warren and Harrison, 1984; O'Riordan, 1985). These include issues as diverse as depletion of tropical forests, droughts and floods, acid deposition, CO_2 accumulation and climatic change, loss of productive agricultural land from salinization and urbanization, fuelwood crisis, species loss, population growth, malnutrition, control of pathogens from human waste and their aquatic vectors, and impact of hazardous substances, processes and wastes on ecosystems and people.

The relative importance of these issues has varied and will vary from time to time and place to place. As Downs (1972) suggested, there often is an 'issue-attention cycle' through which issues travel (Fig. 13.1). Issues move from attracting initial concern from research specialists to achieving recognition from the media, general public and politicians. Each issue must struggle to reach the public agenda and maintain its position. Building upon the accomplishments of geographical research, a number of these issues should receive sustained attention from resource analysts in the years ahead.

13.4.1 RESEARCH ISSUES AND PROBLEMS

Technological or human-induced hazards have become significant and are likely to remain important. These hazards include such aspects as biotechnology, noxious chemical wastes, acid rain, the greenhouse effect and climatic change, siting of nuclear power plants and nuclear winter. Attention needs to be focused upon both the products and the processes related to these different technologies. Geographical expertise should be able to consider perceptions and attitudes towards these hazards, the decision and policy processes

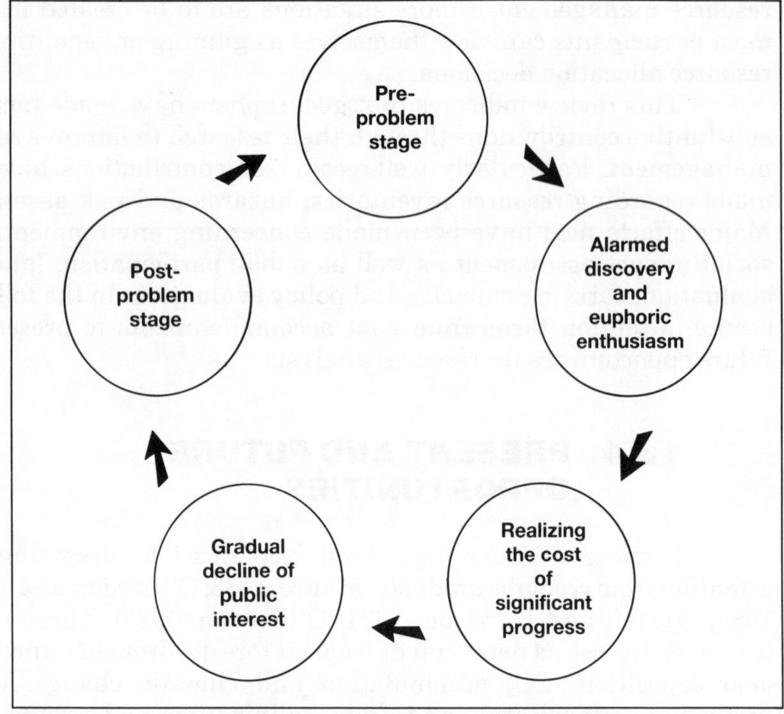

Fig. 13.1 The issue-attention cycle (*after Downs, 1972*)

associated with them, the institutional arrangements providing a context for them, and their environmental, economic and social implications.

Geographers and others already have begun to address some of these concerns. Gatrell and Lovett (1986) examined the disposal of noxious industrial wastes in England and Wales while Collins (1986) has reviewed the distribution and toxicology of lead in the environment. Acid rain and its impact have been considered by Middleton and Rhodes (1984), Rutherford (1984; 1985), Bach (1985) and Baldwin (1985). Acid rain is particularly challenging, as in addition to requiring understanding of physical processes and impacts it often requires sensitivity to international relations. For example, much of the damage to vegetation and water systems in Norway and Sweden appears to be from acid rain which originates in other European countries, and much of the impact in Canada is associated with acid rain generated in the United States. As a result, both physical and political geographers should be able to make contributions here.

The *greenhouse effect*, or the trend towards a general warming of global temperatures due to the release of various chemicals into the atmosphere, has potential major implications (Seidel and Keys, 1983; United States National Research Council, 1983; Hare, 1984). Lamb

(1981) considered the implications for food production, and more work is needed relative to this aspect since traditional agricultural production patterns could be altered significantly (Liverman *et al.*, 1986; Pittock and Nix, 1986). The implications are much broader than food production, however, and include consequences for energy consumption, coastal zones, inland water-borne transportation, and recreation activity (Kates *et al.*, 1985; Waterstone, 1985). Geographers with expertise in environmental and social impact assessment should find many substantive and methodological problems regarding climatic change.

Perhaps the ultimate technological hazard is *nuclear war* (White, 1985; White and Grover, 1985). The physical, biological and human effects from global nuclear war would be horrendous (Covey, 1985; SCOPE, 1985; United States Academy of Sciences, 1985; Bach, 1986; Grime, 1986; Peterson, 1986). The Chernobyl incident in the Soviet Union illustrated dramatically how widespread and pervasive can be the consequences from nuclear mishaps.

Emerging from research on the consequence of nuclear war has been the Nuclear Winter Hypothesis (Turco *et al.*, 1983; Greene, Percival and Ridge, 1985; Perry, 1985; Royal Society of Canada, 1985). This hypothesis suggests that following a nuclear war the smoke and dust created by explosions and fire would be transported high into the atmosphere, would block-out sunlight, and would cause a cooling of temperatures on the earth. Predictions indicate that temperatures could fall as much as 19 °C below seasonal averages. The impact on natural systems and food production would be immense. There is as much speculation as evidence to support the Nuclear Winter Hypothesis, since scientific knowledge is incomplete regarding generation, propagation and persistence of smoke in the atmosphere. Nevertheless, the impact of any nuclear war would be substantial, and it seems appropriate that geographers along with other analysts should address themselves to this ultimate technological hazard.

The *relationship between population growth and food production*, and the associated issues of *hunger and health*, will continue to be a major issue, especially in developing countries (Grigg, 1982; Wisner, Werner and O'Keefe, 1982; Manshard, 1985; Cedeño, 1986). The population/food linkage provides a departure point for analysis of fundamental aspects of carrying capacity in terms of the capability of an area to feed its own population (Peterson, 1984). Some geographers have addressed this problem, but it is one that deserves much more attention.

The trend towards intensification of agriculture deserves attention in regard to population/food relationships. As Rambo, (1982; 89) has explained, intensification through the 'Green Revolution' has created profound environmental and social consequences in developing countries. Among the most visible social impacts, in Rambo's view, have been the loss of autonomy of local communities and increased dependence on imported farm inputs, especially petroleum, fertilizers and pesticides. Disruption of traditional village welfare institutions has also occurred. Environmental impacts have included the loss of irreplaceable genetic resources as locally adapted plants are replaced with a few improved varieties which are imported, increased pest and disease problems, and contamination of soil and water from chemical pesticides. All of these problems are amenable to geographical analysis, and the different research themes in the discipline have a contribution to make.

The *impact of urbanization and industrialization* on sensitive resource lands is a problem common to developed and developing nations. As settlement and economic activity expand, pressure is placed on resources adjacent to cities (Bryant, Russwurm and McLellan, 1982). Prime agricultural lands, aggregate minerals, wetlands and other environmentally sensitive areas all experience stress. The impact of industrialization can be even more extensive, as the demands for resources in developed nations lead to pressure upon resources in developing countries (Myers, 1981; Robinson, 1985). This heartland–hinterland pattern also may emerge within countries, as the centres of high population density generate a demand for resources in the more peripheral areas. In most situations, these resources are exported from the hinterland in a relatively unprocessed state, so that the majority of the benefits from employment go to the heartland regions.

The impact of urbanization and industrialization upon resources indicates that geographical analysis drawn from the physical, urban, economic and rural branches of the discipline will all be pertinent. Since much of the concern relates to the prediction and monitoring of human activity in sensitive resource areas, both remote sensing and geographical information systems have much to offer here.

Deforestation, especially in the Third World, has been recognized as a serious problem with implications ranging from local to global scales (Allen and Barnes, 1985; Eaton, 1986). This problem has become widespread, affecting many countries and regions (Smil, 1983; Chattopadhyay, 1985; Myers, 1981; 1986; Thirgood, 1986; Myers and Tucker, 1987). A mix of factors contributes to deforestation, ranging from cutting of tropical forests to develop pasture land (Myers, 1981) to the collecting of fuelwood for domestic cooking and heating (Whitney, Dufournaud and Murck, 1985). The assessment of policies for forestry and energy becomes critical in regard to deforestation, and is an area in which resource analysts should have something to say. They also should be able to contribute to identifying and assessing environmental and soci-economic impacts of alternative development strategies. Such contributions are needed, as foresters become aware of the necessity to incorporate environmental considerations into their planning and management. (Greig, 1986).

Desertification has emerged as a major problem, with the experience in the Sahel drawing the attention of the world to this issue (Heathcote, 1983; 1987; Mabbutt, 1984). The implications for feeding and sustaining human populations in arid regions have been substantial, leading to the relocation of many people (Milas, 1984). Geographical research on adjustments to natural hazards provides a solid conceptual, methodological and empirical departure point for work related to desertification. The brunt of the problems has so far fallen on regions in the Third World. However, if predictions about climatic warming actually occur, then extension of arid regions can be anticipated in such developed countries as Australia, South Africa and the United States. Thus, geographers in various parts of the developed world may well find the process of desertification occurring in their own regions which will provide additional incentive for research (Van Ypersele and Verstaete, 1986).

Ocean resources also will provide a range of enduring resource management problems. During the 1970s the United Nations organized the Law of the Sea deliberations in an attempt to reach equitable agreements about such diverse considerations as harvesting of fishery stocks, exploitation of mineral resources from the sea bed, territorial waters, and military use of the sea bed and oceans. The outcome has been a new 'political geography of the sea', which demands careful monitoring and analysis (Glassner, 1986). Regional fisheries are also important, as they frequently are the primary source of employment for relatively immobile work forces (Jónsson, 1985) and also involve countries sending fishing fleets to the waters adjacent to other nations (Fournet, 1985). Furthermore, for some countries the fisheries are a primary source of protein. As geographers have analysed land-based resources intensively, it is appropriate that they give attention to resources associated with the oceans and freshwater aquatic systems.

Technological hazards, food/population/health linkages, urbanization and industrialization, deforestation, desertification and ocean resources all suggest the need for assessment and monitoring of environmental conditions. These and more localized problems related to wetlands and other sensitive areas have provided the motivation for preparation of *'State of the Environment' assessments*. The purpose of such reports is to provide baseline data to facilitate long-run monitoring and evaluation. 'State of the Environment' reports have been usually prepared at national scales (Organisation for Economic Co-operation and Development, 1979; 1985; Australia, 1986a; 1986b; 1987; Environment Canada, 1986; Statistics Canada, 1986). Expertise related to remote sensing, geographic information systems and environmental assessment should allow geographers to contribute to the development of methods and procedures to define, measure and monitor the state of the environment at local, regional, national and international scales.

The problems identified here are not the only ones which are amenable to geographical resource analysis. Nevertheless, they seem to have persistent and enduring characteristics which makes it highly probable that they will require sustained attention if environmentally and socially acceptable solutions are to be found. None of these problems is uniquely geographic, but the geographic research traditions (physical, ecological, spatial, regional) have important perspectives to offer. If geographers wish to enhance their credibility as resource analysts, they should be seen to be addressing these complex societal problems. No one suggests that solutions will be found readily, but it is better to tackle the really difficult problems and stumble a bit than to concentrate on relatively minor problems and come up with ready solutions.

13.4.2 RESEARCH PERSPECTIVES

In pursuing research, resource analysts should be aware of a number of perspectives which have been or should be significant in designing resource management strategies. Six of these perspectives – sustainable development, Third World viewpoints, ideologies, integration, intangibles, uncertainty – are considered here.

When the environment movement was reaching its initial peak in the late 1960s a situation developed in which those concerned about protecting the natural environment became the opponents of those concerned with economic development and growth. This polarization of views led to many confrontations between the two groups. Perhaps this was necessary in the early stages of the environmental movement if general consciousness about environmental deterioration was to be raised. However, as time went by, those supporting environmental quality issues created a credibility problem for themselves by consistently opposing development, whether it was industrial expansion, construction of highways or airports or growth of cities.

During the early 1980s, a significant shift in thinking appeared. The idea was presented that *sustained regional economic development and ecological integrity* were complementary (Kayastha, 1982; Jakeman *et al.*, 1987). This idea appeared as the core of the *World Conservation Strategy* outlined by the International Union for Conservation of Nature and Natural Resources (1980), and subsequently was elaborated upon by many others (Allen, 1980; Brown, 1981; Jacobs, 1981; Simmons, 1981; Brown and Shaw, 1982; Kundaeli, 1983; Caldwell, 1984b; Thibodeau and Field, 1984; McCormick, 1986).

The overriding purpose of the World Conservation Strategy is sustainable development through the conservation of living resources. In this context, conservation is defined as the management of human use of the biosphere so that it may yield the greatest sustainable benefit to current generations while maintaining its potential to meet the needs of future generations. A twofold focus thereby arises: maintenance and sustainability. Three specific conservation objectives are identified: (1) maintaining essential ecological processes and life-support systems, (2) preserving genetic diversity and (3) ensuring the sustainable utilization of species and ecosystems.

The World Conservation Strategy represented a significant shift in thinking by suggesting that conservation and sustainable development are mutually dependent. It has led to the preparation of national conservation strategies by many countries following its principles and guidelines (Tisdell, 1983; 1985; Munton, 1984; Young, 1984; Nelson, 1987). However, the drafters of the *Strategy* recognized that other considerations arise and noted that conservation of living resources is but one of a number of necessary conditions to ensure human survival and well-being. Other strategies would be required for world peace, a new international economic order, human rights, population, food supply and overcoming poverty. All of these strategies would be mutually reinforcing and none would be likely to succeed without the others.

The *Strategy* also recognized that conservation was by itself not sufficient to overcome problems of poverty and food supplies. It acknowledged that people facing malnutrition and poverty with little prospect of even temporary prosperity could not be expected to be sympathetic to the idea of deferring short-term needs in favour of longer-term gains. Short-term economic measures therefore had to be combined with conservation strategies. The vicious circle of poverty causing ecological degradation leading to further poverty can only be broken through development. But if the development is to create long-term benefits it must be sustainable, reinforcing the need for the *World Conservation Strategy's* interpretation of conservation. The need for combining conservation and development has been reiterated by both the Brandt (1983) and the Brundtland (World Commission on Environment and Development, 1987) inquiries.

A perspective which emphasizes the importance of keeping development and conservation in balance is enshrined in the *Gaia hypothesis* (Lovelock and Epton, 1975; Lovelock, 1979; Russell, 1982; Myers, 1984). The Gaia hypothesis suggests that the planet behaves like a living system. In other words, the physical and chemical condition of the earth, atmosphere and oceans is believed to be actively made fit and comfortable by the presence of life itself. This hypothesis conflicts with the view that life adapted to planetary conditions as it and they evolved. If this 'living earth' is to survive and flourish, and Gaia (in ancient Greece, the Goddess of the Earth) is not to be mortally stricken, the hypothesis suggests that people need to live in harmony with the environment rather than strive to subdue and conquer it.

A second important perspective relates to the position of *Third World nations* regarding resource management and development (Bintarto, 1982; Biswas and Biswas, 1982). As already noted when considering the issue of sustainable development, when people have little prospect of breaking out of a poverty trap it is unrealisitic to expect them to forgo economic development. Perhaps the primary resource management issue at a global scale is the environmental and economic viability of the least developed nations of the Third World (Mabogunje, 1980; 1984; Forbes, 1982).

With hundreds of millions of people lacking adequate food, housing, clothing, medical care, education facilities and regular employment, it is not suprising that they place tremendous stress on the natural environment in their daily struggle to collect fuelwood and water, to dispose of cooking and human waste, and to obtain sufficient food. The problems are often so fundamental and difficult that experience and strategies from developed countries are unlikely to be transferable (Rasid and Paul, 1987). New strategies will have to be developed that are sensitive to local environmental and cultural conditions (Rambo, 1982; Ramesh, 1984; Bowonder, Prasad and Unni, 1987; Kolawole. 1987). It is to be hoped that more geographers will turn their attention to these difficult problems (Joseph, 1978; Santos and Golez, 1982; Rosell, Lapid and Tolentino, 1985).

Recognition that attitudes towards resource management and development may vary between the developed and developing countries also helps to emphasize a third perspective, that of *ideologies*. Ideology represents the basic assumptions, premises or values upon which decisions are made (Sandbach, 1981; 1982). In the last decade, the emergence of the *Green Movement* on the political scene has had some impact on strategic policy making (Bahro, 1984; 1986). The Green Movement incorporates a number of viewpoints, ranging from opposition to nuclear weapons to support for environmentally compatible development. 'Deep Ecology' has been another phrase used to describe this type of thinking (Devall, 1979; Fox, 1984; Sylvan, 1985).

The Green Movement has developed to different stages in various countries, perhaps being most politically advanced in West Germany (Capra and Spretnak, 1984). However, Green parties or ecologically oriented voters are identifiable in numerous countries (McDonald, 1982; Sinh, 1985). While still minor actors on the political stage, the presence of organized political parties which advocate the basic tenets of the *World Conservation Strategy* is a significant change in the political scene. Their explicit articulation of ecologically based values and strategies is a fairly recent phenomenon on the political scene, and deserves the attention of resource analysts in the future.

A fourth perspective relates closely to the ideas espoused by the World Conservation Strategy and the Green Movement. That perspective involves a belief that a *comprehensive, unified or integrated approach* should be taken in resource management (Ahmad and Miller, 1982; Fisher, 1985; Lang, 1986). This viewpoint has arisen from concern that resource managers too frequently adopt a sectoral approach in which specific resources such as land, water, wildlife and minerals are managed or regulated in isolation from each other. The comprehensive perspective is based on the assumption that an holistic approach should lead to more effective allocation and management of resources.

The idea of an holistic approach is intuitively appealing to many people, and certainly is reinforced by the ecological research theme in geography. Nevertheless, there often appear to be problems in implementing or operationalizing the concept. One reason for this difficulty is that many people who advocate a comprehensive approach do not seem to have thought through just what it means (Mitchell 1986a, 1986b). 'Comprehensive' and 'integrated' are often used interchangeably while the two words have a distinct difference. 'Comprehensive' implies considering all elements and their interactions. 'Integration' suggests considering a selected number of elements and their interactions. It may be that a comprehensive approach is too ambitious for current skills and capabilities and that resource managers explicitly should be thinking in terms of integration, a more focused and selective approach (Mitchell, 1987).

Another problem in making a comprehensive approach effective has been the difficulty in moving from planning to action (Mitchell, 1983). In other words, there have been major problems in achieving implementation (Hjern, 1982; Mazmanian and Sabatier, 1981; 1983; Sabatier, 1986). One of the key weaknesses has been inadequate institutional arrangements (Ingram *et al.*, 1984; Gormley, 1987). A major dilemma has been to devise institutional mechanisms that overcome the 'boundary problems' which arise when there is overlap among specific resources and the agencies created to manage them (Eddison, 1985; Paterson, 1986). Too often it has been difficult to realize coordination and cooperation so that the benefits of a comprehensive approach can be realized (Brown, 1986; Nemetz, 1986). Geographers need to address these operational matters if line resource managers are to be persuaded that comprehensive or integrated approaches have practical as well as conceptual appeal (Gjessing, 1986).

The fifth perspective involves incorporation of *intangible considerations* into resource analysis and management. Aspects not lending themselves to a monetary value have always created problems in resource allocation decisions. It has been concern about this point which has motivated much of the research on landscape evaluation (Morell, 1986; Dearden, 1987). Numerous other resource issues such as those associated with air quality (Rahmatian, 1987), open space or green belts (Willis and Whitby, 1985; Croke, Fabian and Brenniman, 1986), wetlands (Danielson and Leitch, 1986; Farber and Costanza, 1987; Morris, 1987) and wildlife (Loomis and Walsh, 1986) also involve identification and measurement of intangible considerations.

Resource analysts need to continue to develop ways to incorporate intangible aspects into resource allocation procedures. Some believe that the best which can be done is to ensure that such aspects are identified and described explicitly. Other investigators believe that quantitative measures and scales should be and can be devised. Others think that the political process is the correct mechanism to handle intangible aspects. Whichever procedure is used, the resource analyst must always remember that intangible considerations are often among the core elements in resource management.

The sixth and final perspective to be considered here is the concept of *uncertainty, surprise or turbulence.* The frequently changing energy prices during the mid 1970s and throughout the 1980s emphasized the high degree of uncertainty associated with resource management and development. It often is difficult to forecast what social values, technological innovations or economic conditions will prevail five years hence. At the same time, resource managers often argue that a long-term viewpoint must be taken, and in forestry this position often implies at least 25 or 30 years.

Given the uncertainty, surprise and turbulence which are encountered, resource analysts need to spend more time considering how to handle them in order that the broadest possible range of choice is maintained. Several investigators have addressed these problems. Holling's (1978; 1981) concept of 'adaptive environmental management' was conceived in recognition of the need for resource managers to be able to anticipate and respond to changing circumstances. This concept has been refined further by Walters (1986) who has argued that understanding is more likely to be realized by viewing resource management as an ongoing, adaptive and experimental process rather than relying primarily upon basic research or development of ecological theory. He has applied his ideas to the renewable resources of fish and wildlife, and has concluded that in addition to analysing biophysical factors the resource manager must address such human factors as risk aversion and conflicting objectives.

These six perspectives – sustainable development, Third World concerns, ideologies, integration, intangibles, uncertainty – are all central in resource management, and deserve explicit attention by resource analysts. The value of resource analysis research is likely to be diminished if these fundamental aspects are not recognized and addressed in our research.

13.5 GEOGRAPHICAL ANALYSIS AND INTERDISCIPLINARY INQUIRY

The ongoing work in resource analysis reveals that the problems being studied are not the exclusive domain of one discipline or profession (Dahlberg and Bennett, 1986). Psychologists, anthropologists and sociologists share geographers' interest in the role of behavioural and cultural variables regarding human interpretation and use of resource. Architects, foresters and geographers are attracted to landscape evaluation issues. Biologists, soil scientists, foresters and physical geographers find a common interest in biophysical carrying capacity, while psychologists, systems designers, economists and geographers all study behavioural carrying capacity. Hazards and environmental impact assessment have generated interest from engineers, economists, administrators, political scientists, biologists, sociologists and geographers. Political scientists and geographers have both focused upon institutional arrangements and policy making. What are the implications for the way in which geographers should pursue their research?

The main implication carries two components. The first suggests that the geographer interested in resource analysis should have a well-defined understanding about the core concepts of the discipline, major research traditions or themes, and basic questions or hypotheses. In this manner, an individual should be able to visualize, and demonstrate to the other disciplines, what the geographer's contribution might be relative to a specific problem. This aspect should be approached not in the spirit of 'claiming' certain problems or questions for geography, but rather to indicate the nature of its contribution. As White (1963; 426) stated, as a geographer he was

> not interested in staking out professional claims in this domain of science. What does seem important is to recognize intellectual problems which call for solution and which because of their relation to spatial distributions and human adjustment to differences in the physical environment are of interest to geographers.

The second component relates to the acceptance and implementation of interdisciplinary research in resource analysis. Having identified their area of competence, the geographers should seek to build links with other disciplines and professions to ensure coverage of problems in both greater breadth and depth. Geographers have recognized this need for many years (Whitaker, 1954, 229; Dansereau, 1975, 20–21). Recognition of the value of interdisciplinary work is one thing, doing it is another. Dansereau (1975; 21) noted that disciplinary jealousies are hard to break down, and that the rewards of teamwork are less tangible than those from individual achievements. Nevertheless, interdisciplinary teams are gradually being established. This fact is encouraging. Without the pursuit of team efforts, some significant opportunities are lost. As C.P. Snow (1959; 16) commented,

> The clashing point of two subjects, two disciplines, two cultures – of two galaxies, as far as that goes – ought to produce creative chances. In the history of mental activity that has been where some of the breakthroughs came.

If interdisciplinary work is to be pursued, the question arises as to what form it should take. Jantsch (1972) provided a clear distinction between different types of teamwork which can be pursued (Fig. 13.2). In his framework, the ideal approach is represented by the concepts of interdisciplinarity or transdisciplinarity. In other words, it is not

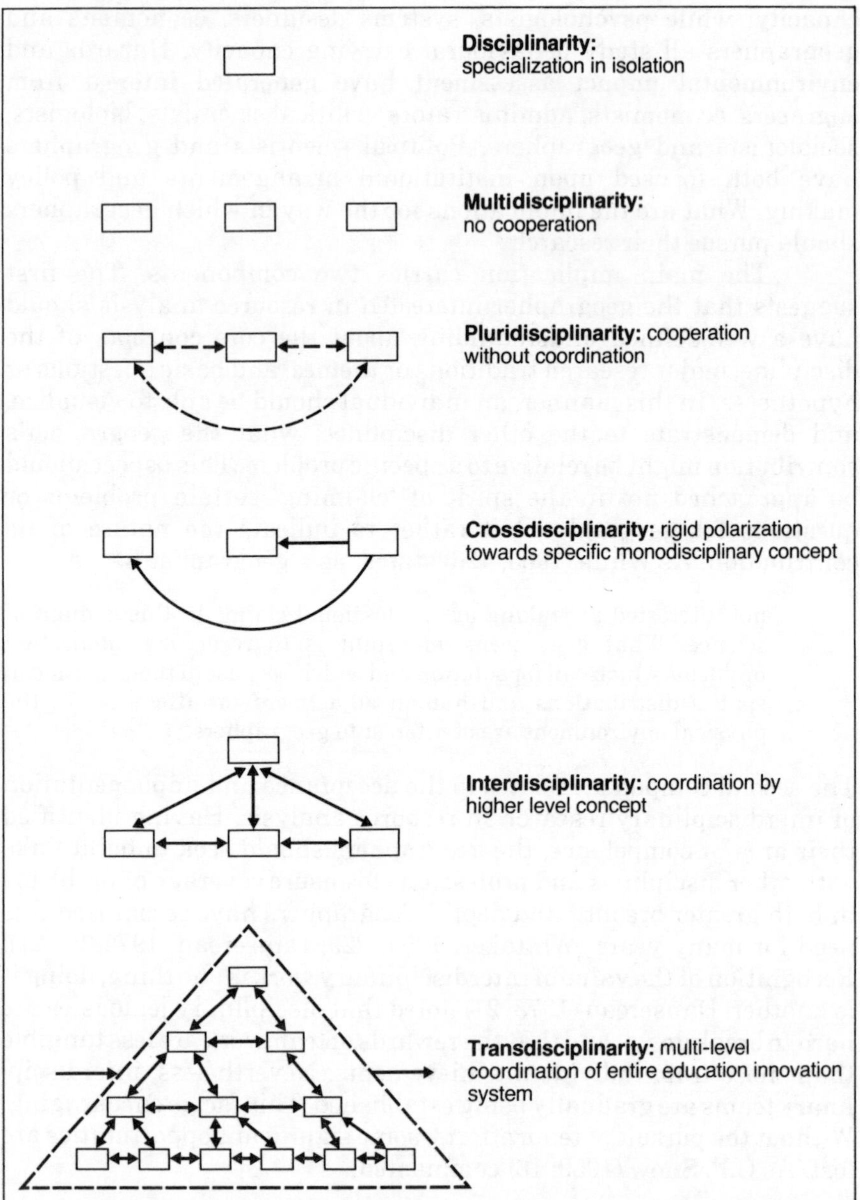

Fig. 13.2 Steps towards increasing cooperation and coordination in research (*from Jantsch, 1972*)

enough to assemble a loosely coordinated team, as indicated by his interpretation of multidisciplinarity or pluridisciplinarity. Instead, group effort should involve a team on which each member has a specific role relative to the problem under analysis. Furthermore, from the outset of any inquiry, each member must be in close touch with other team members to ensure that findings are integrated throughout. It is this approach which necessitates geographers having a well-defined conception of their role.

APPENDIX 1
METRIC (SI) CONVERSIONS

DISTANCE

1 millimetre (mm)	= 0.039 inches	1 inch	= 25.40 mm or 2.54 cm
1 centimetre (cm)	= 0.393 inches	1 foot	= 30.48 cm
1 metre (m)	= 3.28 feet or 1.09 yards	1 yard	= 0.91 m
1 kilometre (km)	= 0.62 miles	1 mile	= 1.61 km

AREA

1 hectare (ha)	= 2.47 acres	1 acre	= 0.40 ha
1 square kilometre (km^2)	= 247 acres	1 square mile	= 258.9 ha = 2.59 km^2

CAPACITY

1 litre (l)	= 0.22 Imperial gallons	1 Imperial gallon	= 4.55 l
	= 0.26 US gallons	1 US gallon	= 3.78 l

WEIGHT

1 gram (g)	= 0.035 ounces	1 ounce	= 28.35 g
1 kilogram (kg)	= 2.20 pounds	1 pound	= 453.59 g
1 tonne (t)	= 1.10 short tons	1 short ton	= 2,000 pounds = 0.907 t

REFERENCES

Abler, R., Adams, J. S. and **Gould, P. R.** (1971) *Spatial Organization: the Geographer's View of the World,* Prentice-Hall, Englewood Cliffs.

Ackerman, E. A. (1958) *Geography as a Fundamental Research Discipline,* Research Paper No. 53, Department of Geography, University of Chicago, Chicago.

Ackerman, E. A. (1963) 'Where is a research frontier?', *Annals of the Association of American Geographers,* **53,** 429–40.

Ackoff, R. L. (1953) *The Design of Social Research,* University of Chicago Press, Chicago.

Adams, R. L. A. (1973) 'Uncertainty in nature, cognitive dissonance, and the perceptual distortion of environmental information: weather forecasts and New England beach trip decisions', *Economic Geography,* **49,** 287–97.

Adams, W. M. (1985) 'The downstream impacts of dam construction: a case study from Nigeria', *Transactions, Institute of British Geographers,* New Series, **10,** 292–302.

Ad-Hoc Committee of Geography (1965) *The Science of Geography,* National Academy of Sciences – National Research Council, Washington, DC.

Aegerter, S. and **Messerli, P.** (1983) 'The impact of hydroelectric power plants on a mountainous environment: a technique for assessing environmental impacts', *Mountain Research and Development,* **3,** 157–75.

Ahmad, Y. J. and **Muller, F. G.,** eds. (1982) *Integrated Physical, Socio-Economic and Environmental Planning,* Tycooly International Publishing Ltd, Dublin.

Aiken, S. R. and **Leigh, C. H.** (1986) 'Land use conflicts and rain forest conservation in Malaysia and Australia: the Endau-Rompin and Gordon-Franklin controversies', *Land Use Policy,* **3,** 161–79.

Aldskogius, H. (1967) 'Vacation house settlement in the Siljan Region', *Geografiska Annaler,* **49**(B), 69–95.

Aldskogius, H. (1977) 'A conceptual framework and a Swedish case study of recreational behavior and environmental cognition', *Economic Geography,* **53,** 163–83.

Alexander, D. (1984) 'Housing crisis after natural disaster: the aftermath of the November 1980 Southern Italian earthquake', *Geoforum,* **15,** 489–516.

Allan, J. A. (1983) 'Natural Resources as national fantasies', *Geoforum,* **14,** 243–47.

Allen, J. C. and **Barnes, D. F.** (1985) 'The causes of deforestation in developing countries', *Annals of the Association of American Geographers,* **75,** 163–84.

Allen, R. (1980) *How to Save the World: Strategy for World Conservation,* Prentice Hall of Canada, Scarborough.

Allen, R. N. (1972) 'The Anchicaya Hydroelectric Project in Columbia: design and sedimentation problems', pp. 318–42, in Farvar, M. T. and Milton, J. P. (eds.), *The Careless Technology: Ecology and International Development,* Natural History Press, Garden City, NY.

Amir, S. (1972) 'Highway location and public opposition', *Environment and Behavior,* **4,** 413–36.

Anand, R. and **Scott, I. G.** (1982) 'Financing public participation in environmental decision making', *Canadian Bar Review,* **60,** 81–120.

Anderson, J. E. (1973) 'Pressure groups and the Canadian bureaucracy', pp. 97–104, in Kernaghan, W. O. (ed.), *Bureaucracy in Canadian Government,* Methuen, Toronto.

Anderson, J. E. (1975) *Public Policy-Making,* Praeger, New York.

Anderson, L. (1981) 'Land use designations affect perception of scenic beauty in forest landscapes', *Forest Science,* **27,** 392–400.

Anderson, L. M., Lovi, D. J., Daniel, T. C. and **Dieterich, J. H.** (1982) *The Esthetic Effects of Prescribed Burning: A Case Study,* USDA Forest Service, Research Note RM-413, Rocky Mountain Forest and Range Experiment Station, Fort Collins, Colorado.

Anderson, T. L. ed. (1983) *Water Rights: Scarce Resource Allocation, Bureaucracy, and the Environment,* Pacific Institute for Public Policy Research, San Francisco.

Andrews, W. H., Hardin, C. W. and **Madsen, G. E.** (1981) 'Social assessment indicators in water resource development', *Environment and Behavior,* **13,** 64–82.

Aniya, M. (1985) 'Landslide susceptibility mapping in the Amahata River Basin, Japan', *Annals of the Association of American Geographers,* **75,** 102–14.

Appleton, J. (1975) 'Landscape evaluation: the theoretical approach', *Transactions of the Institute of British Geographers,* **66,** 120–3.

Armand, D. L. *et al.* (1960) 'The role of geographers in the study, mapping, economic appraisal, utilization, conservation and renewal of the natural resources of the U.S.S.R.', *Soviet Geography,* **1,** 3–10.

Arnell, N. W. (1984) 'Flood hazard management in the United States and the National Flood Insurance Program', *Geoforum,* **15**, 525–42.

Arnell, N. W., Clark, M. J. and **Gurnell, H. M.** (1984) 'Flood insurance and extreme events: the role of crisis in prompting changes in British institutional arrangements', *Applied Geography,* **4,** 167–81.

Arnstein, S. (1969) 'A ladder of citizen participation', *Journal of the American Institute of Planners,* **35,** 216–24.

As-Sammani, M. D. (1984) 'Private sector and government commercial fishing in the Sudd Area, Southern Sudan', *Economic Geography,* **60,** 210–16.

Aspinall, R. J. and **Pye, A. M.** (1987) 'The effect of trampling on limestone grassland in the Malham area of North Yorkshire', *Journal of Biogeography,* **14,** 105–15.

Attwell, R. I. G. (1970) 'Some effects of Lake Kariba on the ecology of a floodplain of the mid-Zambezi Valley of Rhodesia', *Biological Conservation,* **2,** 189–96.

Aucoin, P. (1971) 'Theory and research in the study of policy-making', pp. 10–38, in Doern, G. B. and Aucoin, P. (eds.), *The Structures of Policy-Making in Canada,* Macmillan, Toronto.

Auliciems, A. and **Dick, J. H. A.** (1976) 'Factors in environmental action: air pollution complaints in Brisbane', *Australian Geographical Studies,* **14,** 59–67.

Austin, M., Smith, T. E. and **Wolpert, J.** (1970) 'The implementation of controversial facility-complex programs', *Geographical Analysis,* **2,** 315–29.

Australia, Department of Arts, Heritage and Environment (1986a) *State of the Environment in Australia.* Australian Government Publishing Service, Canberra.

Australia, Department of Arts, Heritage and Environment (1986b) *State of the Environment in Australia: Source Book.* Australian Government Publishing Service, Canberra.

Australia, Department of Arts, Heritage and Environment (1987) *State of the Environment in Australia, 1986,* Australian Government Publishing Service, Canberra.

Auty, R. M. (1983) 'High cost energy, resources and Third World growth: lessons from two oil shocks', *Singapore Journal of Tropical Geography,* **4,** 73–86.

Babb, T. A. and **Bliss, L. C.** (1974) 'Effects of physical disturbance on Arctic vegetation in the Queen Elizabeth Islands', *Journal of Applied Ecology,* **11,** 549–62.

Babcock, M. and **Mitchell, B.** (1980) 'Impact of flood hazard on residential property values in Galt (Cambridge), Ontario', *Water Resources Bulletin,* **16,** 532–7.

Bach, W. (1985) 'The acid rain/carbon dioxide threat – control strategies', *GeoJournal,* **10,** 339–52.

Bach, W. (1986) 'Nuclear war: the effects of smoke and dust on weather and climate', *Progress in Physical Geography,* **10,** 315–63.

Bacharach, S. B. and **Lawler, E. J.** (1981) *Bargaining: Power, Tactics, and Outcomes,* Jossey-Bass, San Francisco.

Bacow, L. S. and **Wheeler, M.** (1984) *Environmental Dispute Resolution* Plenum, New York.

Baggs, S. A. (1983) 'A simplified method for quantifying environmental impacts in the landscape planning/design process', *Landscape Planning,* **9,** 227–47.

Bahro, R. (1984) *From Red to Green,* Verso Books, London.

Bahro, R. (1986) *Building the Green Movement,* New Society Publishers, Philadelphia.

Bailey, R. G. (1980) 'Integrated approaches to classifying land as ecosystems', pp. 95–109 in Laban, P. (ed.), *Proceedings of the Workshop on Land Evaluation for Forestry,* International Institute for Land Reclamation and Improvement, Wageningen, The Netherlands.

Baldwin, J. H. (1985) 'Acid rain: a global perspective', *Environmental Professional,* **7,** 221–31.

Bandler, H. (1987) 'Gordon Below Franklin Dam, Tasmania, Australia: environmental factors in a decision of national significance', *The Environmentalist,* **7,** 43–53.

Banerjee, B. N. (1986) *Bhopal Gas Tragedy: Accident or Experiment?* Paribus Publishers, New Delhi.

Banerji (1985) 'Genesis of floods in West Bengal and their impact on society', *Deccan Geographer,* **23,** 39–53.

Bankes, N. and **Thompson, A. R.** (1980) *Monitoring for Impact Assessment and Management,* Westwater Research Centre, University of British Columbia, Vancouver, British Columbia.

Barber, B. and **Fox, R. C.** (1958) 'The case of the floppy-eared rabbits: an instance of serendipity gained and serendipity lost', *American Journal of Sociology,* **64,** 128–36.

Bardecki, M. J. (1984a) 'Participants' response to the Delphi method: an attitudinal perspective', *Technological Forecasting and Social Change,* **25,** 281–92.

Bardecki, M. J. (1984b) 'What value wetlands?', *Journal of Soil and Water Conservation,* **39,** 166–9.

Bardecki, M. J. (1985) *Wetland Conservation Policies in Southern Ontario: A Delphi Approach,* Geographical Monograph No. 16, Department of Geography, Atkinson College, York University, Downsview, Ontario.

Barker, M. L. (1982a) 'Comparison of parks, reserves, and landscape protection in three countries of the Eastern Alps', *Environmental Conservation,* **9,** 1–11.

Barker, M. L. (1982b) 'Traditional landscape and mass tourism in the Alps', *Geographical Review,* **72,** 396–415.

Barkham, J. P. (1973) 'Recreational carrying capacity: a problem of perception', *Area,* **5,** 218–22.

Barr, B. M. (1970) *The Soviet Wood-Processing Industry: A Linear Programming Analysis of the Role of Transportation Costs in Location and Flow Patterns,* Research Publication No. 5, Department of Geography, University of Toronto, Toronto.

Barr, L. R. (1978) 'Conflict resolution in environmental management: the Newport Power Station controversy', *Australian Geographical Studies,* **16,** 43–52.

Barrows, H. H. (1923) 'Geography as human ecology', *Annals of the Association of American Geographers,* **13,** 1–14.

Bastedo, J. D. (1986) *An ABC Resource Survey Method for Environmentally Significant Areas with Special Reference to Biotic Surveys in Canada's North,* Publication Series No. 24, Department of Geography, University of Waterloo, Waterloo, Ontario.

Bastedo, J. D., Nelson, J. G. and **Theberge, J. B.** (1984) 'Ecological approach to resource survey and planning for environmentally significant areas: the ABC method', *Environmental Management,* **8,** 125–34.

Bastedo, J. D. and **Theberge, J. B.** (1983) 'An appraisal of inter-disciplinary resource surveys (ecological land classification)', *Landscape Planning,* **10,** 317–34.

Bates, F. L., Killian, C. D. and **Peacock, W. G.** (1984) 'Recovery, change and development: a longitudinal study of the 1976 Guatemalan earthquake', *Ekistics,* **51,** 439–45.

Bates, G. H. (1935) 'The vegetation of footpaths, sidewalks, cart-tracks and gateways', *Journal of Ecology,* **23,** 470–87.

Bauer, R. A. (1968) 'The study of policy formation: an introduction', pp. 1–26 in Bauer, R. A. and Gergen, K. J. (eds.), *The Study of Policy Formation,* Free Press, New York.

Baum, A., Fleming, R., and **Davidson, L. M.** (1983) 'Natural disaster and technological catastrophe', *Environment and Behavior,* **15,** 333–54.

Baumann, D. D. (1983) 'Social acceptance of water reuse', *Applied Geography,* **3,** 79–84.

Baumann, D. D. and **Sims, J. H.** (1974) 'Human response to the Hurricane', pp. 25–30 in White, G. F. (ed.), *Natural Hazards: Local, National, Global,* Oxford University Press, New York.

Beanlands, G. E. and **Duinker, P. N.** (1984) 'An ecological framework for environmental impact assessment', *Journal of Environmental Management,* **18,** 267–78.

Beardsley, W. G., Herrington, R. B. and **Wagar, J. A.** (1974) 'Recreation site management - how to rehabilitate a heavily used campground without stopping visitor use', *Journal of Forestry,* **72,** 279–81.

Beaver, S. H. (1944) 'Minerals and planning', *Geographical Journal,* **104,** 166–93.

Beaver, S. H. (1955) 'Land reclamation after surface mineral workings', *Journal of the Town Planning Institute,* **41,** 146–52.

Beck, S. D. (1959) *The Simplicity of Science,* Penguin, Harmondsworth.

Beekhuis, J. V. (1981) 'Tourism in the Caribbean: impacts on the economic, social and natural environments', *Ambio,* **10,** 325–31.

Bell, M. (1977) 'The spatial distribution of second homes: a modified gravity model', *Journal of Leisure Research,* **9,** 225–33.

Bellman, S., Sampson, C. and **Cormick, G. W.** (1982) *Using Mediation When Siting Hazardous Waste Management Facilities,* Office of Solid Waste, US Environmental Protection Agency, Washington, DC.

Bender, A. and **Clink** (1978) 'Public involvement in the EIS process', *Environmental Management,* Vol. 2, No. 2, March, 107–12.

Bennett, W. J. and **Mitchell, B.** (1983) 'Floodplain management: land acquisition versus preservation of historic buildings in Cambridge, Ontario, Canada', *Environmental Management,* **7,** 327–37.

Benson, R. E. and **Ullrich, J. R.** (1981) *Visual Impacts of Forest Management Activities: Findings on Public Preferences,* U.S.D.A. Forest Service Research Paper INT-262, Intermountain Forest and Range Experiment Station, US Department of Agriculture, Ogden, Utah.

Benson, R. E., McCool, S. F. and **Schlieter, J. A.** (1985) *Attaining Visual Quality Objectives in Timber Harvest Areas - Landscape Architects' Education.* USDA Forest Service Research Paper INT-348, Intermountain Research Station, Ogden, Utah.

Bentley, A. (1908) *The Process of Government,* University of Chicago Press, Chicago.

Bernard, F. E. (1985) 'Planning and environmental risks in Kenyan drylands', *Geographical Review,* **75,** 58–70.

Bernard, H. R. and **Pelto, P. J.**, eds. (1972) 'Introduction', pp. 1–8, in Bernard, H. R. and Pelto P. J. (eds.), *Technology and Social Change,* Macmillan, New York.

Berry, B. J. L. (1964) 'Approaches to regional analysis: a synthesis', *Annals of the Association of American Geographers,* **54,** 2–11.

Berry, B. J. L. (1974) 'Review of H. M. Rose's *Perspectives in geography 2: geography of the ghetto, perceptions, problems and alternatives', Annals of the Association of American Geographers,* **64,** 342–5.

Berry, B. J. L. and **Horton, F. E.** (1974) *Urban Environmental Management,* Prentice-Hall, Englewood Cliffs.

Billinge, M. (1977) 'In search of negativism: phenomenology and historical geography', *Journal of Historical Geography,* **3,** 55–67.

Bintarto, R. (1982) 'Geographical relevance to the study of development', *Indonesian Journal of Geography,* **12** (43), 51–7.

Birch, J. W. (1973) 'Geography and resource management', *Journal of Environmental Management,* **1,** 3–12.

Birch, J. W. (1977) 'On excellence and problem solving in geography', *Transactions of the Institute of British Geographers,* **2** (new series), 417–29.

Birch, S. K. and **Schwaab, K. E.** (1983) 'The effects of water conservation instruction on seventh-grade students', *Journal of Environmental Education,* **14,** 26–31.

Bird, P. M. and **Rapport, D. J.** (1986) *State of the Environment Report for Canada,* Minister of Supply and Services Canada, Hull, Quebec.

Bisset, R. (1980) 'Methods of environmental impact analysis: recent trends and future prospects', *Journal of Environmental Management,* **11,** 7–43.

Biswas, A. (1981) 'The concept of ecosystem and the position of geographers', *Transactions of the Institute of Indian Geographers,* **3,** 1–12.

Biswas, M. R. and **Biswas, A. K.** (1982) 'Environment and sustained development in the Third World: a review of the past decade', *Philippine Geographical Journal,* **26,** 160–73.

Biswas, R. R. (1984) 'Landsat imagery for watershed management in Rengali River valley project', *Indian Journal of Landscape Systems and Ecological Studies,* **7,** 44–50.

Bjønness, I. M. (1980) 'Animal husbandry and grazing, a conservation and management problem in Sagarmatha (Mt. Everest) National Park, Nepal', *Norsk Geografisk Tidsskrift,* **34,** 59–76.

Bjønness, I. M. (1981) 'Outdoor recreation and its impact upon a boreal forest area – Bymarka, Trondheim, Norway', *Norsk Geografisk Tidsskrift,* **35,** 57–78.

Blacksell, M. and **Gilg, A. W.** (1975) 'Landscape evaluation in practice – the case of south-east Devon', *Transactions of the Institute of British Geographers,* **66,** 135–40.

Blalock, H. M. (1970) *An Introduction to Social Research,* Prentice-Hall, Englewood Cliffs.

Blanco, A., **Gonzales, S.** and **Ramos, A.** (1982) 'Visual landscape classification in the coastal strip of Santander, Spain', *Coastal Zone Management Journal,* **9,** 271–97.

Blaut, J. M. *et al.* (1975) 'Marxist geography', *Antipode,* **7,** 1–90.

Blunden, J. (1985) *Mineral Resources and Their Management*, Longman, London.

Board, C. (1968) 'Land-use surveys: principles and practice', pp. 29–41, in *Land Use and Resources: Studies in Applied Geography,* Special Publication No. 1, Institute of British Geographers, London.

Boggs, P. and **Wall, G.** (1984) 'Economic impacts of a recreational facility: perspectives from Canada's Wonderland', *The Operational Geographer,* **5,** 42–6.

Bonnicksen, T. M. and **Lee, R. G.** (1982) 'Biosocial systems analysis: an approach for assessing the consequences of resources policies', *Journal of Environmental Management,* **15,** 47–62.

Bouchard, A. (1974) 'Carrying capacity - management tool for parks', *Recreation Canada,* **32,** 13–19.

Boulding, K. E. (1972) 'A ballad of ecological awareness', p. 957 in Farvar, M. T. and Milton, J. P. (eds.) *The Careless Technology: Ecology and International Development,* Natural History Press, Garden City, N.Y.

Bowden, L. W. (1965) *Diffusion of the Decision to Irrigate: Simulation of the Spread of a New Resource Management Practice in the Colorado Northern High Plains,* Research Paper No. 97, Department of Geography, University of Chicago, Chicago.

Bowen, R. E., Hoole, F. W. and **Anderson, S. H.** (1980) 'Evaluating the impact of coastal zone activities: an illustration of the evaluation research approach', *Coastal Zone Management Journal,* **7,** 25–48.

Bowonder, B., Prasad, S. S. R. and **Unni, N. V. M.** (1987) 'Afforestation in India: policy and strategy reforms', *Land Use Policy,* **4,** 133–46.

Boyce, R. B. (1974) *The Bases of Economic Geography,* Holt, Rinehart and Winston, New York.

Boyer, J. C., Mitchell, B. and **Fenton, S.** (1978) *The Socio-Economic Impacts of Electric Transmission Corridors - A Comparative Analysis,* Department of Man-Environment Studies, University of Waterloo, Waterloo, Ontario.

Bradbury, J. H. (1985) 'International movements and crisis in resource oriented companies: the case of Inco in the nickel sector', *Economic Geography,* **61,** 129–43.

Bradbury, J. H. and **St. Martin, I.** (1983) 'Winding down in a Quebec mining town: a case study of Schefferville', *Canadian Geographer,* **27,** 128–44.

Bradley, J. V. (1968) *Distribution-Free Statistical Tests,* Prentice-Hall, Englewood Cliffs.

Brancher, D. M. (1969) 'Critique of K. D. Fine's landscape evaluation', *Regional Studies,* **3,** 91–2.

Brandt Commission (1983) *Common Crisis,* Pan Books, London.

Brassard, C. and **Harrison, P.** (1981) 'A la recherche d'une raison d'être - le complexe portuaire de Gros-Cacouna', *Cahiers de Géographie de Québec,* **25,** 255–68.

Bratton, S. P., Stromberg, L. L. and **Harmon, M. E.** (1982) 'Firewood gathering impacts in backcountry campsites in Great Smoky Mountains National Park', *Environmental Management,* **6,** 63–71.

Braybrooke, D. and **Lindblom, C. E.** (1963) *A Strategy of Decision Policy Evaluation as a Social Process,* Free Press, New York.

Brewer, G. D. and **de Leon, P.** (1983) *The Foundations of Policy Analysis,* Dorsey Press, Homewood, Ill.

Brière, R. (1961–62) 'Les cadres d'une géographie touristique du Québec', *Cahiers de Géographie de Québec,* **11,** 39–64.

Broek, J. O. (1965) *Geography: Its Scope and Spirit,* Charles E. Merrill, Columbus, Ohio.

Bromley, D. W., Butcher, W. R., and **Smith, S. C.** (1974) 'Policy and research implications of the National Water Commission's recommendations', *Land Economics,* **50,** 15–34.

Bromley, M. (1985) *Wildlife Management Implications of Petroleum Exploration and Development in Wildland Environments,* USDA Forest Service General Technical Report INT - 191, Intermountain Research Station, Ogden, Utah.

Bromley, P. (1981) 'The role of the public in landscape decisions: a case study in the Peak District National Park', *Landscape Research,* **6**(1), 2–6.

Bronitsky, L. and **Wallace, W. A.** (1974) 'The economic impact of urbanization on the mineral aggregate industry', *Economic Geography,* **50,** 130–40.

Brown, L. R. (1986), 'A generation of deficits', pp. 3–21 in Brown, L. R. and Wolf, E. C. (eds.), *State of the World 1986,* W. W. Norton, New York.

Brown, L. R. (1981) *Building a Sustainable Society,* W. W. Norton, New York.

Brown, L. R. and **Shaw, P.** (1982) *Six Steps to a Sustainable Society,* Paper 48, Worldwatch Institute, Washington, DC.

Brown, M. A. and **Macey, S. M.** (1985) 'Evaluating the impact of two energy conservation programmes in a midwestern city', *Applied Geography,* **5,** 39–53.

Brown, M. P. (1986) 'Environment Canada and the pursuit of administrative decentralization', *Canadian Public Administration,* **29,** 218–36.

Brown, T. C. and **Daniel, T. C.** (1984), *Modeling Forest Scenic Beauty: Concepts and Application to Ponderosa Pine,* USDA Forest Service Research Paper RM-256, Rocky Mountain Forest and Range Experiment Station, Fort Collins, Colorado.

Browning, C. E. (1974) 'The question "But is it geography?" – revisited: are there criteria for establishing the geographic content of topics?', *Professional Geographer,* **26,** 137–9.

Bryant, C. R., Russwurm, L. H. and **McLellan, A. G.** (1982) *The City's Countryside,* Longman, London.

Bryson, R. A. (1974) 'Perspective on climatic change', *Science,* **184,** 753–60.

Budd, R. W. (1967) *Content Analysis of Communications,* Macmillan, New York.

Buhyoff, G. J., Wellman, J. D., Koch, N. E., Gauthier, L. and **Hultman, S.** (1983), 'Landscape preference metrics: an international comparison', *Journal of Environmental Management,* **16,** 181–90.

Buhyoff, G. J., Williams, S. B. and **Kemperer, W. D.** (1981) 'Gravity model formulation for an extensive National Parkway site', *Environmental Management,* **5,** 253–62.

Buist, L. J. and **Hoots, T. A.** (1981) 'Recreation Opportunity Spectrum approach to resource planning', *Journal of Forestry,* **80,** 84–6.

Bunge, W. (1962) *Theoretical Geography,* C. W. K. Gleerup, Lund.

Bunting, T. E. and **Guelke, L. T.** (1979) 'Behavioural and perception geography: a critical appraisal', *Annals of the Association of American Geographers,* **69,** 448–62.

Burch, W. R. (1981) 'The ecology of metaphor – spacing regularities for humans and other primates in urban and wildland habitats', *Leisure Sciences,* **4,** 213–30.

Burchell, R. W. and **Listokin, D.** (1975) *The Environmental Impact Handbook,* Center for Urban Policy Research, Rutgers University, New Brunswick, NJ.

Burton, I. (1963) 'The quantitative revolution and theoretical geography', *Canadian Geography,* **7,** 151–62.

Burton, I. (1971) 'The social role of attitude and perception studies', pp. 1–6, in Sewell, W. R. D. and Burton, I. (eds.), *Perceptions and Attitudes in Resources Management,* Information Canada, Ottawa.

Burton, I. and **Kates, R. W.** (1964a) 'The perception of natural hazards in resource management', *Natural Resources Journal,* **3,** 412–41.

Burton, I. and **Kates, R. W.** (1964b) 'The floodplain and the seashore: a comparative analysis of hazard-zone occupance', *Geographical Review,* **54,** 366–85.

Burton, I. and **Kates, R. W.** (1964c) 'Slaying the Malthusian Dragon: a review', *Economic Geography,* **40,** 82–9.

Burton, I. and **Kates, R. W.**, eds. (1965) *Readings in Resource Management and Conservation,* University of Chicago Press, Chicago.

Burton, I., Kates, R. W., and **Snead, R. E.** (1968) *The Human Ecology of Coastal Flood Hazard in Megalopolis,* Research Paper No. 115, Department of Geography, University of Chicago, Chicago.

Burton, I., Kates, R. W., and **White, G. F.** (1968) *The Human Ecology of Extreme Geophysical Events,* Natural Hazard Research Working Paper No. 1, Department of Geography, University of Toronto, Toronto.

Burton, I., Kates, R. W., and **White, G. F.** (1978) *The Environment as Hazard,* Oxford University Press, New York.

Burton, I., Kates, R. W., and **White, G. F.** (1981) 'The future of hazard research: a reply to William I. Torry', *Canadian Geographer,* **25,** 286–9.

Burton, I., Kliman, M., Powell, D., Schmidt, L., Timmerman, P., Victor, P., Whyte, A. and **Wojick, J.** (1981) *The Mississauga Evacuation: Final Report,* Institute for Environmental Studies, University of Toronto, Toronto.

Burton, I. and **Post, K.** (1983) *The Transport of Dangerous Commodities by Rail in the Toronto Census Metropolitan Area: A Preliminary Assessment of Risk,* Railway Transport Committee, Canadian Transport Commission, Ottawa.

Burton, I. and **Pushchak, R.** (1984) 'The status and prospects of risk assessment', *Geoforum,* **15,** 463–76.

Burton, I., Wilson, J. and **Munn, R. E.** (1983) 'Environmental impact assessment: national approaches and international needs', *Environmental Monitoring and Assessment,* **3,** 133–50.

Busternd, J. (1981) 'Environmental conflict resolution: the promise of co-operative decision-making', *Environmental Science and Technology,* **15,** 150–5.

Butrico, F. A., Touhill, C. J., and **Whitman, I. L.**, eds. (1971) *Resource Management in the Great Lakes Basin,* Heath Lexington Books, Lexington, Mass.

Buttimer, A. (1986) 'Integration in geography: Hydra or Chimera?', pp. 39–67 in Guelke, L. (ed.), *Geography and Humanistic Knowledge,* Publication Series No. 25, Department of Geography, University of Waterloo, Waterloo, Ontario.

Caldwell, L. K. (1963) 'Environment: a new focus for public policy', *Public Administration Review,* **23,** 132–9.

Caldwell, L. K. (1964) *Biopolitics: Science, Ethics and Public Policy,* Yale University Press, New Haven.

Caldwell, L. K. (1970) *Environment: A Challenge For Modern Society,* Natural History Press, Garden City, NY.

Caldwell, L. K. (1984a) 'Garrison Diversion: constraints or conflict resolution', *Natural Resources Journal,* **24,** 839–63.

Caldwell, L. K. (1984b) 'Political aspects of ecologically sustainable development', *Environmental Conservation,* **11,** 299–308.

Call, C. A., Barker, J. R. and **McKell, C. M.** (1981) 'Visitor impact assessment of scenic view areas at Bryce Canyon National Park', *Journal of Soil and Water Conservation,* **36,** 50–3.

Callahan, D. and **Jennings, B.** eds. (1983) *Ethics, the Social Sciences and Policy Analysis,* Plenum Press, New York.

Campbell, D. T. (1970) 'Considering the case against experimental evaluations of social innovations', *Administrative Science Quarterly,* **15,** 110–13.

Campbell, D. T. and **Stanley, J. C.** (1966) *Experimental and Quasi-Experimental Designs for Research,* Rand McNally, Chicago.

Campbell, W. J. and **Wood, P. A.** (1969) 'Quantification and the development of theory in human geography', pp. 81–9, in Cooke, R. V. and Johnson, J. H. (eds.), *Trends in Geography: an Introductory Survey,* Pergamon Press, Oxford.

Canada, House of Commons, Standing Committee on Mines, Forests and Waters (1959) *Minutes of Proceedings,* No. 25, Queen's Printer, Ottawa.

Canada, National Energy Board (1969) *Energy Supply and Demand in Canada and Export Demand for Canadian Energy, 1966 to 1990,* Queen's Printer, Ottawa.

Canada, Treasury Board Secretariat, Planning Branch (1976) *Benefit-Cost Analysis Guide,* Minister of Supply and Services, Ottawa.

Canada-United States University Seminar (1973) *A Proposal for Improving the Management of the Great Lakes of the United States and Canada.* Water Resources and Marine Sciences Center, Cornell University, Ithaca, NY.

Cannon, W. B. (1945) *The Way of an Investigator,* W. W. Norton, New York.

Caporaso, J. A. (1973) 'Quasi-experimental approaches to social science: perspectives and problems', pp. 3–38, in Caporaso, J. A. and Roos, L. L. (eds.), *Quasi-Experimental Approaches: Testing Theory and Evaluating Policy,* Northwestern University Press, Evanston, Ill.

Capra, F. and **Spretnak, C.** (1984) *Green Politics,* E. P. Dutton, New York.

Carley, M. J. and **Bustelo, E. S.** (1984) *Social Impact Assessment and Monitoring: A Guide to the Literature,* Westview Press, Boulder, Colorado.

Carlson, A. A. (1977) 'On the possibility of quantifying scenic beauty', *Landscape Planning,* **9,** 61–74.

Carlyle, W. J. (1980) 'The management of environmental problems on the Manitoba Escarpment', *Canadian Geographer,* **24,** 255–69.

Carney, T. F. (1972) *Content Analysis,* University of Manitoba Press, Winnipeg.

Caro, F. C. (1969) 'Approaches to evaluation research: a review', *Human Organization,* **28,** 87–99.

Carpenter, S. L. and **Kennedy, W. J. D.** (1980) 'Environmental conflict management', *Environmental Professional,* **2,** 67–74.

Carpenter, S. L. and **Kennedy, W. J. D.** (1981) 'Environmental conflict management: new ways to solve problems', *Mountain Research and Development,* **1,** 65–70.

Carrothers, G. A. P. (1956) 'An historical review of the gravity and potential concepts of human interaction', *Journal of the American Institute of Planners,* **22,** 94–102.

Carson, R. L. (1962) *Silent Spring,* Houghton Mifflin, Boston.

Carter, F. W. (1985) 'Pollution problems in post-war Czechoslovakia', *Transactions, Institute of British Geographers,* New Series, **10,** 17–44.

Caviedes, C. N. (1982) 'Natural hazards in South America: in search of a method and a theory', *GeoJournal,* **6,** 101–109.

Cawley, R. M. and **Chaloupka, W.** (1985) 'James Watt and the environmentalists: a clash of ideologies', *Policy Studies Journal,* **14,** 244–54.

Cecile, C. P., Bardecki, M. J. and **Snell, E. A.** (1985) *The Eastern Ontario Subsidiary Agreement Drainage Program: Impacts on the Land Resource – An Initial Evaluation,* Environment Canada, Lands Directorate Working Paper No. 40, Minister of Supply and Services Canada, Ottawa.

Cedeño, J. E. M. (1986) 'Rainfall and flooding in the Guayas river basin and its effects on the incidence of malaria 1982–1985', *Disasters,* **10,** 107–11.

Cesario, F. J. (1975) 'A simulation approach to outdoor recreation planning', *Journal of Leisure Research,* **7,** 38–52.

Chapman, G. P. (1983) 'Underperformance in Indian irrigation systems: the problems of diagnosis and prescription', *Geoforum,* **14,** 267–75.

Chapman, K. (1980) 'Environmental policy and industrial location', *Area,* **12,** 209–16.

Chapman, K. (1981) 'Issues in environmental impact assessment', *Progress in Human Geography,* **5,** 190–210.

Chapman, K. (1982) 'Petrochemicals and economic development: the implications of the Puerto Rican experience', *Professional Geographer,* **34,** 405–16.

Chapman, K. (1983) 'The incorporation of environmental considerations into the analysis of industrial agglomerations – examples from the petrochemical industry in Texas and Louisiana', *Geoforum,* **14,** 37–44.

Chattopadhyay, S. (1985) 'Deforestation in parts of Western Ghats Region (Kerala), India', *Journal of Environmental Management,* **20,** 219–30.

Chattopadhyay, S. and **Salim, M. B.** (1985) 'Morphological classification of land and assessment of its suitability for various uses – a case study on Bavalipuzha-Aralampizna a drainage basin', *Transactions of the Institute of Indian Geographers,* **7,** 105–12.

Chepurko, N. L. and **Chizhora, V. P.** (1982) 'Regionalization of the USSR in terms of environmental protection needs', *Soviet Geography,* **22,** 744–51.

Chettri, R. and **Bowonder, B.** (1983) 'Siltation in Nizamsagar reservoir: environmental management issues', *Applied Geography,* **3,** 193–204.

Chojnicki, Z. (1970) 'Prediction in economic geography', *Economic Geography,* **46** (supplement), 213–22.

Chouinard, V. and **Fincher, R.** (1983) 'A critique of Structural Marxism and Human Geography', *Annals of the Association of American Geographers,* **73,** 137–46.

Christensen, H. H. (1981) *Bystander Intervention and Litter Control: Evaluation of an Appeal-To-Help Program,* USDA Forest Service Research Paper PNW-287, Pacific Northwest Forest and Range Experiment Station, US Department of Agriculture, Seattle, Washington.

Christensen, K. (1982) 'Geography as a human science: a philosophic critique of the positivist–humanist split', pp. 37–57 in Gould, P. and Olsson, G. (eds.), *A Search for Common Ground,* Pion, London.

Chubb, M. and **Bauman, E. H.** (1977) 'Assessing the recreation potential of rivers', *Journal of Soil and Water Conservation,* **32,** 97–102.

Chubukov, L. A., Rauner, Yu. L., Knushinova, K. V., Potapora, L. S. and **Shvareva, Yu. N.** (1982) 'Predicting the climatic consequences of the interbasin transfer of water in the Midlands Region of the USSR', *Soviet Geography,* **22,** 426–44.

Churchill, R. R. (1985) 'The Lake Erie–Niagara River ice boom', *Geographical Review,* **75,** 111–24.

Churchill, R. R. and **Hutchinson, D. M.** (1984) 'Flood hazard in Ratnapura, Sri Lanka: individual attitudes vs. collective action', *Geoforum,* **15,** 517–24.

Ciriacy-Wantrup, S. V. (1971) 'The economics of environmental policy', *Land Economics,* **47,** 36–45.

Clamp, P. (1981) 'The landscape evaluation controversy', *Landscape Research,* **6**(2) 13–5.

Clark, B. D., Bisset, R. and **Wathern, P.** (1980) *Environmental Impact Assessment: A Bibliography with Abstracts,* Mansell, London.

Clark, R. N. (1982) 'Promises and pitfalls of the ROS in resource management', *Australian Parks and Recreation,* **19,** 9–13.

Clark, R. N. and **Stankey, G. H.** (1976) 'Analyzing public input to resource decisions: criteria, principles, and case examples of the CODINVOLVE system', *Natural Resources Journal,* **16,** 213–36.

Clark, R. N., Stankey, G. H., and **Hendee, J. C.** (1974) *An Introduction to CODINVOLVE: A System For Analyzing, Storing and Retrieving Public Input to Resource Decisions,.* Pacific Northwest Forest and Range Experiment Station, Forest Service, US Department of Agriculture, Portland, Ore.

Clawson, M. (1959) *Methods of Measuring the Demand for and the Value of Outdoor Recreation,* Reprint No. 10, Resources for the Future, Washington, DC.

Clawson, M. and **Knetsch, J. L.** (1963) 'Outdoor recreation research: some concepts and suggested areas of study', *Natural Resources Journal,* **3,** 250–75.

Clawson, M. and **Knetsch, J.** (1966) *Economics of Outdoor Recreation*, Johns Hopkins, Baltimore.

Cocks, K. D. and **Walker, P. A.** (1987) 'Using the Australian Resource Information System to describe extensive regions', *Applied Geography*, **7**, 17–27.

Cole, D. N. (1981) 'Managing ecological impacts at wilderness campsites: an evaluation of techniques', *Journal of Forestry*, **79**, 86–9.

Cole, D. N. (1983a) *Assessing and Monitoring Backcountry Trail Conditions*, USDA Forest Service Research Paper INT–303, Intermountain Forest and Range Experiment Station, US Department of Agriculture, Ogden, Utah.

Cole, D. N. (1983b) *Monitoring the Condition of Wilderness Campsites*, USDA Forest Service Research Paper INT–302, Intermountain Forest and Range Experiment Station, Ogden, Utah.

Cole, D. N. (1985) *Recreational Trampling Effects on Six Habitat Types in Western Montana*, USDA Forest Service Research Paper INT–350, Intermountain Research Station, Ogden, Utah.

Cole, D. N. (1987) 'Effects of three seasons of experimental trampling on five montane forest communities and a grassland in Western Montana, USA', *Biological Conservation*, **40**, 219–44.

Cole, D. N. and **Fichtler, R. K.** (1983) 'Campsite impact on three Western Wilderness Areas', *Environmental Management*, **7**, 275–88.

Cole, M. and **Smith, R. F.** (1984) 'Vegetation as an indicator of environmental pollution', *Transactions, Institute of British Geographers*, New Series, **9**, 477–93.

Coleman, A. L. (1961) 'The second land use survey; progress and prospect', *Geographical Journal*, **127**, 168–86.

Coleman, R. (1981) 'Footpath erosion in the English Lake District', *Applied Geography*, **1**, 121–32.

Collaborative Research on Natural Hazards (1971) *Progress Report*, Natural Hazard Research Paper, Environmental Sciences and Engineering Programme, University of Toronto, Toronto.

Collins, J. (1986) 'The distribution and toxicology of lead in the environment – a review', *New Zealand Geographer*, **42**, 18–24.

Colson, E. (1963) 'Land rights and land use among the Valley Tonga of the Rhodesian Federation: the background to the Kariba resettlement program', pp. 137–56, in Biebuyck, D. (ed.), *African Agrarian Systems*, Oxford University Press, New York.

Commoner, B. (1972a) *The Closing Circle: Man, Nature and Technology*, Knopf, New York.

Commoner, B. (1972b) 'Summary of the conference', pp. xxi-xxix, in Farvar, M. T. and Milton, J. P. (eds.), *The Careless Technology: Ecology and International Development*, Natural History Press, Garden City, NY.

Conacher, A. J. (1979): 'Notes on a geographer's approach to the study of environmental problems', *Western Geographer*, **3**, 29–40.

Conacher, A. J. (1980): 'Environmental legislation in Western Australia', *Australian Geographical Studies*, **18**, 51–61.

Connor, D. M. (1978) 'Models and techniques of citizen participation', pp. 58–73 in Sadler, B. (ed.) *Involvement and Environment*, Vol. 2, Environment Council of Alberta, Edmonton.

Conover, W. J. (1971) *Practical Nonparametric Statistics,* John Wiley, New York.

Cook, T. D. and **Campbell, D. T.** (1979) *Quasi-Experimentation: Design and Analysis Issues for Field Settings,* Rand McNally, Chicago.

Cooke, H. J. (1985) 'The Kalahari today: a case of conflict over resource use', *Geographical Journal,* **151,** 75–85.

Cooke, R. U. (1984) *Geomorphological Hazards in Los Angeles,* George Allan and Unwin, London.

Cooke, R. U. and **Doornkamp, J. C.** (1974) *Geomorphology in Environmental Management,* Clarendon Press, Oxford.

Cooley, R. A. (1963) *Politics and Conservation: the Decline of Alaska Salmon,* Harper and Row, New York.

Coppock, J. T. (1974) 'Geography and public policy: challenges, opportunities and implications', *Transactions of the Institute of British Geographers* **63,** 1–16.

Coppock, J. T. and **Duffield, B. S.** (1975) *Recreation in the Countryside: A Spatial Analysis,* Macmillan, London.

Coppock, J. T. and **Sewell, W. R. D.** (1975) 'Resource management and public policy: the changing role of geographical research', *Scottish Geographical Magazine,* **91,** 4–11.

Cormick, G. W. (1980) 'The "theory" and practice of environmental mediation', *Environmental Professional,* **2,** 24–33.

Cormick, G. W. (1982) 'The myth, the reality, and the future of environmental mediation', *Environment,* **24**(7), 14–17, 36–9.

Cortner, H. J. and **Schweitzer, D. L.** (1981) 'Institutional limits to national public planning for forest resources: The Resources Planning Act', *Natural Resources Journal,* **21,** 203–22.

Corwin, R., Heffernan, P. H., Johnston, R. A., Remy, M., Roberts, J. A., and **Tyler, D. B.** (1975) *Environmental Impact Assessment,* Freeman, Cooper and Co., San Fransisco.

Covello, V. T. and **Mumpower, J.** (1985) 'Risk analysis and risk management: an historical perspective', *Risk Analysis,* **5,** 103–20.

Covey, C. (1985) 'Climatic effects of nuclear war', *Bioscience,* **35,** 563–9.

Cowley, G. (1983) 'Electricity consumption: a shift-share analysis of industrial and regional growth', *New Zealand Geographer,* **39,** 70–80.

Cox, K. R. (1965) 'The application of linear programming to geographic problems', *Tijdschrift Voor Economische en Sociale Geografie,* **56,** 228–36.

Crabb, P. (1982) 'Managing Australia's water resources', *Australian Geographical Studies,* **20,** 96–107.

Craik, K. H. (1968) 'The comprehension of the everyday physical environment', *Journal of the American Institute of Planners,* **34,** 29–37.

Craik, K. H., (1970a) 'Environmental psychology', pp. 1–121, in Newcomb, T. A. (ed.), *New Directions in Psychology,* Holt, Rinehart and Winston, New York.

Craik, K. H. (1970b) 'The environmental dispositions of environmental decision-makers', *Annals of the American Academy of Political and Social Science,* **389,** 87–94.

Craik, K. H. (1972a) 'Appraising the objectivity of landscape dimensions', pp. 292–346 in Krutilla, J. V. (ed.), *Natural Environments: Studies in Theoretical and Applied Analysis,* Johns Hopkins, Baltimore.

Craik, K. H. (1972b) 'Psychological factors in landscape appraisal', *Environment and Behavior,* **4,** 255–66.

Craik, K. H. (1976) 'The personality research paradigm in environmental psychology', pp. 55–79, in Wapner, S., Cohen, S. B., and Kaplan, B. (eds.), *Experiencing the Environment,* Plenum Press, New York.

Craik, K. H. and **McKechnie, G. E.** (1977) 'Editors' introduction to personality and the environment', *Environment and Behavior,* **9,** 155–68.

Craine, L. E. (1969) *Water Management Innovations in England,* Johns Hopkins, Baltimore.

Craine, L. E. (1971) 'Institutions for managing lakes and bays', *Natural Resources Journal,* **11,** 519–46.

Crevo, C. C. (1963) 'Characteristics of summer weekend recreational travel', *Highway Research Record,* **44,** 57–60.

Croke, K., Fabian, R. and **Brenniman, G.** (1986) 'Estimating the value of natural open space preservation in an urban area', *Journal of Environmental Management,* **23,** 317–24.

Culhane, P. J. (1981) *Public Lands Politics: Interest Group Influence on the Forest Service and the Bureau of Land Management,* Johns Hopkins University Press, Baltimore.

Cunningham, C. (1963) 'Policy and practice', *Public Administration,* **41,** 229–37.

Curtis, F. (1982) 'A checklist for the writing and presentation of environmental assessment (EA) reports', *Canadian Geographer,* **27,** 64–70.

Curtis, F. A. (1983) 'Integrating environmental mediation into EIA', *Impact Assessment Bulletin,* **2**(3), 17–25.

Dahl, R. (1967) *Pluralist Democracy in the United States,* Rand McNally, Chicago.

Dahlberg, K. A. and **Bennett, J. W.,** eds (1986) *Natural Resources and People: Conceptual Issues in Interdisciplinary Research,* Westview Press, Boulder.

Dalland, O. (1983) 'The Alta case: learning from errors made in a human ecological conflict in Norway', *Geoforum,* **14,** 193–203.

Daneke, G. A., Garcia, M. W. and **Priscoli, J. D.** (eds.) (1983) *Public Involvement and Social Impact Assessment,* Westview Press, Boulder.

Daniel, T. C. and **Boster, R. S.** (1976) *Measuring Landscape Esthetics: The Scenic Beauty Estimation Method,* USDA Forest Service Research Paper RM-167, Rocky Mountain Forest and Range Experiment Station, Fort Collins, Colorado.

Daniel, T. C. and **Vining, J.** (1983) 'Methodological issues in the assessment of landscape quality', pp. 39–84 in I. Altman and J. S. Wohlwill, eds., *Behavior and the Natural Environment,* Vol. 6, Plenum Press, NY.

Danielson, L. E. and **Leitch, J. A.** (1986) 'Private vs. public economics of Prairie wetland allocation', *Journal of Environmental Economics and Management,* **13,** 81–92.

Dansereau, P. (1957) *Biogeography: An Ecological Perspective,* Ronald Press, New York.

Dansereau, P. (1975) *Harmony and Disorder in the Canadian Environment,* Occasional Paper No. 1, Canadian Environmental Advisory Council, Minister of Supply and Service, Ottawa.

Davgun, S. K. (1980) 'Humanism in geography', *Geographical Review of India,* **42,** 211–15.

Davidson, D. A. and **Jones, G. E.** (1986) 'A land resource information system (LRIS) for land use planning', *Applied Geography,* **6,** 255–66.

Davis, R. K. (1963) 'Recreation planning as an economic problem', *Natural Resources Journal,* **3,** 239–49.

Davis, W. M. (1906) 'An inductive study of the content of geography', *Bulletin of the American Geographical Society,* **38,** 67–84.

Dawson, H. J. (1960) 'An interest group: the Canadian Federation of Agriculture', *Canadian Public Administration,* **3,** 134–49.

Day, D. G. (1986a) 'Water planning priorities and conflicts in the Hunter Valley, NSW', *Australian Geographer,* **17,** 153–69.

Day, D. G. (1986b) *Water and Coal: Industry, Environment and Institutions in the Hunter Valley, NSW,* CRES Monograph 14, Centre for Resource and Environmental Studies, Australian National University, Canberra.

Day, D. G. (1987) 'Australian natural resources policy: water and land', *Resources Policy,* **13**(3), 228–46.

Day, J. C. (1974) 'Benefit-cost analysis and multiple-purpose reservoirs: a reassessment of the Conservation Authorities Branch Deer Creek project, Ontario', pp. 23–34, in Leversedge, F. (ed.), *Priorities in Water Management,* Western Geographical Series Vol. 8, Department of Geography, University of Victoria, Victoria, BC.

Day, J. C. *et al.* (1977) 'A strategy for hindsight evaluation of environmental impacts', pp. 171–9, in Plewes, M. and Whitney, J. B. R. (eds.), *Environmental Impact Assessment in Canada: Processes and Approaches,* Institute for Environmental Studies, University of Toronto, Toronto.

Day, J. C. and **Hegadoren, B.** (1981) 'Socioeconomic mine termination policies: a case study of mine closure in Ontario', *Resources Policy,* **7,** 265–72.

Dearden, P. (1980a) 'Aesthetic encounters of the statistical kind', *Area,* **12,** 171–3.

Dearden, P. (1980b) 'Landscape assessment: the last decade', *Canadian Geographer,* **24,** 316–25.

Dearden, P. (1980c) 'A statistical technique for the evaluation of the visual quality of the landscape for land-use planning purposes', *Journal of Environmental Management,* **10,** 51–68.

Dearden, P. (1981a) 'Landscape evaluation: the case for a multi-dimensional approach', *Journal of Environmental Management,* **13,** 95–105.

Dearden, P. (1981b) 'Public participation and scenic quality analysis', *Landscape Planning,* **8,** 13–9.

Dearden, P. (1983) 'Anatomy of a biological hazard: *Myriophyllum spicatum* L. in the Okanagan Basin, British Columbia', *Journal of Environmental Management,* **17,** 47–61.

Dearden, P. (1984) 'Public perception of a technological hazard: a case study of the use of 2,4-D to control Eurasian water milfoil in the Okanagan Valley', *Canadian Geographer,* **28,** 324–40.

Dearden, P. (1985a) 'Philosophy, theory, and method in landscape evaluation', *Canadian Geographer,* **29,** 263–5.

Dearden, P. (1985b) 'Technological hazards and "upstream" hazard management strategies: the use of herbicide 2,4-D to control Eurasian water milfoil in the Okanagan Valley, British Columbia, Canada', *Applied Geography,* **5,** 229–42.

Dearden, P. (1986) 'Letters to the editor, editorials and agenda setting: a case study of newspaper response to an environmental problem', *Journal of Environmental Management,* **22,** 39–54.

Dearden, P. (1987) 'Concensus and a theoretical framework for landscape evaluation', *Journal of Environmental Management,* **24,** 267–87.

Dearden, P. and **Rosenblood, L.** (1980) 'Some observations on multi-variate techniques in landscape evaluation', *Regional Studies,* **14,** 99–110.

de Blij, H. J. and **Capone, D. L.** (1969) 'Wildlife conservation areas in East Africa: An application of field theory in political geography', *Southeastern Geographer,* **9,** 94–107.

De Bono, E. (1967) *The Use of Lateral Thinking,* Penguin, Harmondsworth.

Dee, N. *et al.* (1972) *Environmental Evaluation System for Water Resources Planning,* Report to the US Bureau of Reclamation, Batelle Memorial Institute, Columbus, Ohio.

Dee, N. *et al.* (1973) 'An environmental evaluation system for water resources planning', *Water Resources Research,* **9,** 523–35.

Deshmukh, S. N. and **Chaturvedi, A.** (1984) 'Land system mapping in Ratlam District through Landsat imagery interpretation', *Deccan Geographer,* **22,** 549–54.

Dési, I., Márton, M., Gönczi, L., Páldy, A., Király, V. and **Varga, L.** (1983) 'Epidemiological surveillance of the general population and control of nature in the prevention of diseases and environmental impairment caused by pesticides', *Geographia Medica,* **13,** 1–9.

Detwyler, T. R. (1972) 'Vegetation of the city', pp. 229–59, in Detwyler, T. R. and Marcus, M. G., (eds.), *Urbanization and Environment: The Physical Geography of the City,*Duxbury, Belmont, Calif.

Detwyler, T. R. and **Marcus, M. G.,** eds. (1972) *Urbanization and Environment: The Physical Geography of the City,* Duxbury, Belmont, Calif.

Devall, B. (1979) 'The deep ecology movement', *Natural Resources Journal,* **20,** 299–322.

Digernes, T. H. (1979) 'Fuelwood crisis causing unfortunate land use – and the other way round', *Norsk Geografisk Tidsskrift,* **33,** 23–32.

Dillon, M. C. (1985) *Social Impact Assessment and Public Policy Making: An Overview,* CRES Working Paper 1985/5, Centre for Resources and Environmental Studies, Australian National University, Canberra.

Dinsdale, E. M. (1965) 'Spatial patterns of technological change: the lumber industry of Northern New York', *Economic Geography,* **41,** 252–74.

Ditton, R. B. (1972) 'NEPA: buckling down', pp. 139–41, in Ditton, R. B. and Goodale, T. I. (eds.), *Environmental Impact Analysis: Philosophy and Methods,* University of Wisconsin Press, Madison.

Ditton, R. B. and **Goodale, T. I.** eds. (1972) *Environmental Impact Analysis: Philosophy and Methods,* University of Wisconsin Press, Madison.

Dobson, J. (1983) 'Automated geography', *Professional Geographer,* **35,** 135–43.

Dorcey, A. H. J. (1983) 'Coastal management as a bargaining process', *Coastal Zone Management Journal* **11,** 13–40.

Dorcey, A. H. J. (1986a) *Bargaining in the Goverance of Pacific Coastal*

Resources: Research and Reform, Westwater Research Centre, University of British Columbia, Vancouver.

Dorcey, A. H. J. (1986b) *The Myth of Interagency Cooperation in Water Resources Management,* Westwater Research Centre, University of British Columbia, Vancouver, BC.

Dorcey, A. H. J. and **Martin, B. R.** (1986) 'Reaching agreement in impact management: a case study of the Utah and Amax mines', in Sadler, B. (ed.), *Audit and Evaluation in Environmental Impact Assessment,* University of Calgary Press, Calgary.

Dorcey, A. H. J., McPhee, M. W. and **Sydneysmith, S.** (1980) *Salmon Protection and the B.C. Coastal Forest Industry: Environmental Regulation as a Bargaining Process,* Westwater Research Centre, University of British Columbia, Vancouver, BC.

Dorney, R. S. (1973) 'Role of ecologists as consultants in urban planning and design', *Human Ecology,* **1,** 183–200

Dorney, R. S. (1977) 'Environmental assessment: the ecological dimension', *Journal of the American Waterworks Association,* **69,** 182–5.

Downie, B. (1984) 'Reflections on the National Park zoning system', *Operational Geographer,* **3,** 15–19.

Downs, A. (1972) 'Up and down with ecology – the "issue-attention" cycle', *Public Interest,* **28,** 38–50.

Dragun, A. K. (1983) 'Hydroelectric development and wilderness conflict in South-West Tasmania', *Environmental Conservation,* **10,** 197–204.

Draper, D. (1977) *Resources Management, Socio-Economic Development and the Pacific North Coast Native Cooperative: A Case Study,* Unpublished Ph.D. dissertation, Department of Geography, University of Waterloo, Waterloo, Ontario.

Draper, D. (1981) 'Oceans exploitation: efficiency and equity questions in fisheries management', pp. 109–50 in Mitchell, B. and Sewell, W. R. D. (eds.), *Canadian Resource Policies: Problems and Prospects,* Methuen, Toronto.

Driscoll, R. S., Merkel, D. L., Radloff, D. L., Snyder, D. E., and **Hagihara, J. S.** (1984) *An Ecological Land Classification Framework for the United States,* USDA Forest Service Miscellaneous Publication 1439, US Government Printing Office, Washington, DC.

Driver, B. L. and **Johnson, L. A.** (1983–84) 'A pilot study of the perceived long-term benefits of the Youth Conservation Corps', *Journal of Environmental Education,* **15**(2), 3–11.

Driver, B. L., Brown, P. J., Stankey, G. H. and **Gregoire, T. G.** (1987) 'The ROS Planning System: evolution, basic concepts, and research needed', *Leisure Sciences,* **9,** 201–12.

Dror, Y. (1968) *Public Policymaking Reexamined,* Chandler, San Francisco.

Drury, C. H. (1975) 'Quantitative analysis and public policy making', *Canadian Public Policy,* **1,** 89–96.

Ducsik, D. W. (1980) 'Integrating coastal zone and electric facility planning: weak links in the institutional chain', *Coastal Zone Management Journal,* **8,** 263–88.

Dufournaud, C. (1982) 'On the mutually beneficial co-operative scheme: dynamic change in the pay-off matrix of international river basin schemes', *Water Resources Research,* **18,** 764–72.

Duinker, P. N. and **Baskerville, G. L.** (1986) 'A systematic approach to forecasting in environmental impact assessment', *Journal of Environmental Management,* **23,** 271–90.

Duncan, J. and **Ley, D.** (1982) 'Structural Marxism and human geography: a critical assessment', *Annals of the Association of American Geographers,* **72,** 30–59.

Dunn, W. N. (1981) *Public Policy Analysis: An Introduction,* Prentice Hall, Englewood Cliffs, N.J.

Eagles, P. F. J. (1981) 'Environmentally sensitive area planning in Ontario, Canada', *Journal of the American Planning Association,* **47,** 313–23.

Eagles, P. F. J. (1984) *The Planning and Management of Environmentally Sensitive Areas,* Longman, London.

Earle, T. R., Brownlea, A. A. and **Rose, C. W.** (1981) 'Beliefs of a community with respect to environmental management: a case study of soil conservation beliefs on the Darling Downs', *Journal of Environmental Management,* **12,** 197–219.

Easton, D. (1957) 'An approach to the analysis of political systems', *World Politics,* **9,** 383–400.

Eaton, P. (1986) 'Deforestation and forest management', *Environmental and Planning Law Journal,* **3,** 165–7.

Eddison, T. (1985) 'Managing an ecological system 5: reforming the bureaucracy', *Australian Quarterly,* **57,** 148–53.

Ehlers, E. (1982) 'Man and the environment – problems in rural Iran', *Applied Geography and Development,* **19,** 108–25.

Ehrlich, P. R. (1968) *The Population Bomb,* Ballantine, New York.

Ehrlich, P. R. (1982) 'Human carrying capacity, extinctions and nature reserves', *BioScience,* **32**, 331–3.

Elliot, N. R. (1968) 'A geographical analysis of the Tyne coal trade', *Tijdschrift voor Economische en Sociale Geografie,* **59,** 71–93.

Ellis, J. B. and **Van Doren, C. S.** (1966) 'A comparative evaluation of gravity and system theory models for state-wide recreational traffic flow', *Journal of Regional Science,* **6,** 57–70.

Elmes, G. A. (1985) 'Modeling spatial interaction of utility coal in Pennsylvania', *Annals of the Association of American Geographers,* **75,** 212–26.

el Moghraby, A. I. and **el Sammani, M. O.** (1985) 'On the environmental and socio-economic impact of the Jonglei Canal Project, Southern Sudan', *Environmental Conservation,* **12,** 41–8.

Environment Canada (1986) *State of the Environment: Report for Canada.* Minister of Supply and Services Canada, Ottawa.

Ericksen, N. J. (1975) 'A tale of two cities: flood history and the prophetic past of Rapid City, South Dakota', *Economic Geography,* **51,** 305–20.

Erickson, D. L. (1980) 'Public involvement in resource agency decision-making', *Journal of Soil and Water Conservation,* **35,** 224–9.

Erskine, W. D. (1985) 'Downstream geomorphic impacts of large dams: the case of Glenbawn Dam, NSW', *Applied Geography,* **5,** 195–210.

Etzioni, A. (1967) 'Mixed-scanning: a "third" approach to decision-making', *Public Administration Review,* **27,** 385–92.

Etzioni, A. (1968) *The Active Society,* Free Press, New York.

Evans, G. W., and **Wood, K. W.** (1980) 'Assessment of environmental aesthetics in scenic highway corridors', *Environment and Behavior,* **12,** 255–73.

Everson, P. R. (1985) 'Spatial databases in emergency planning', *Emergency Planning Digest,* April–June, 12–18.

Farber, S. and **Costanza, R.** (1987) 'The economic value of wetlands systems', *Journal of Enviromental Management,* **24,** 41–51.

Farvar, M. T. and **Milton, J. P.** eds. (1972) *The Careless Technology: Ecology and International Development,* Natural History Press, Garden City, NY.

Feimer, N. R., Smardon, R. C. and **Craik, K. H.** (1981) 'Evaluating the effectiveness of observer based visual resource and impact assessment methods', *Landscape Research,* **6**(1), 12–16.

Fenge, T. (1982) 'Towards comprehensive conservation of environmentally significant areas in the Northwest Territories of Canada', *Environmental Conservation,* **9,** 305–13.

Fenneman, N. M. (1919) 'The circumference of geography', *Annals of the Association of American Geographers,* **9,** 3–11.

Ferguson, A. and **Alley, J.** (1984) 'Resource geography: is there a shape to the terrain?', *Operational Geographer,* **5,** 36–8.

Fernie, J. and **Pitkethly, A. S.** (1985) *Resources: Environment and Policy,* Harper and Row, London.

Fesenmaier, D. R. and **Lieber, S. R.** (1985) 'Spatial structure and behavior response in outdoor recreation participation', *Geografiska Annaler,* Series B, **67B,** 131–8.

Festinger, L. (1957) *A Theory of Cognitive Dissonance,* Row, Peterson, Evanston, Ill.

Fines, K. D. (1968) 'Landscape evaluation: a research project in East Sussex', *Regional Studies,* **2,** 41–55.

Finson, K. D. and **Hellis, M. D.** (1986) 'Remote sensing of natural resources with radar', *Progress in Physical Geography,* **10,** 175–93.

Finsterbusch, K. (1985) 'State of the art in social impact assessment', *Environment and Behavior,* **17,** 193–221.

Firey, W. (1960) *Man, Mind and Land,* Free Press, Glencoe, Ill.

Fisher, D. E. (1985) 'The policy of resource use and conservation: means for its implementation', *Environmental and Planning Law Journal,* **2,** 191–9.

Fischer, D. W. and **Davies, G. S.** (1973) 'An approach to assessing environmental impacts', *Journal of Environmental Management,* **1,** 207–27.

Fischer, E. H. (1972) 'Birth planning of youth: concern about over-population and intention to limit family size', *American Psychologist,* **27,** 951–8.

Fisher, R. and **Ury, W.** (1981) *Getting to Yes: Negotiating Agreement Without Giving In,* Penguin, Harmondsworth.

Fitzgibbon, J. E., Pomeroy, J. and **Green, M. B.** (1985) 'Personal construct theory: a basis for evaluation of landscape aesthetics', *Canadian Geographer,* **29,** 267–70.

Flamm, B. R. (1973) 'A philosophy of environmental impact assessment: toward choice among alternatives', *Journal of Soil and Water Conservation,* **28,** 201–4.

Forbes, D. (1981) 'Beyond the geography of development', *Singapore Journal of Tropical Geography,* **2,** 68–80.

Forbes, D. (1982) 'Energy Imperialism and a new international division of resources: the case of Indonesia', *Tijdschrift voor Economische en Sociale Geografie,* **73,** 94–108.

Foresta, R. A. (1984) *America's National Parks and Their Keepers,* Resources for the Future, Washington, DC.

Foster, H. D. (1980) *Disaster Planning: The Preservation of Life and Property,* Springer-Verlag, New York.

Found, W. C., Hill, A. R., and **Spence, E. S.** (1975) *Economic and Environmental Impacts of Land Drainage in Ontario,* Geographical Monographs No. 6, Atkinson College, York University, Downsview, Ontario.

Found, W. C., Hill, A. R. and **Spence, E. S.** (1976) 'Economic and environmental impacts of agricultural land drainage in Ontario', *Journal of Soil and Water Conservation,* **31,** 20–4.

Fournet, P. (1985) 'Evolution et stratégie de la pêche française du thon tropical', *Les Cahiers d'Outre-Mer,* **152,** 307–30.

Fox, W. (1984) 'Deep ecology: a new philosophy of our time?' *The Ecologist,* **14,** 194–200.

Fox, L., Mayer, K. E., and **Forbes, A. R.** (1983) 'Classification of forest resources with Landsat data', *Journal of Forestry,* **81,** 283–7.

Fraser, N. M. and **Hipel, K. W.** (1984) *Conflict Analysis: Models and Resolutions,* North-Holland, New York.

Freeman, D. B. (1985) 'The importance of being first: preemptions by early adopters of farming innovations in Kenya', *Annals of the Association of American Geographers,* **75,** 17–28.

Freeman, D. M. and **Frey, R. S.** (1986) 'A method for assessing the social impacts of natural resource policies', *Journal of Environmental Management,* **23,** 229–45.

French Ministry of the Environment (1982) 'French coastal policy', *Ekistics,* **49,** 128–30.

Furuseth, O. J. and **Pierce, J. T.** (1982) 'A comparative analysis of farmland preservation programmes in North America', *Canadian Geographer,* **26,** 191–206.

Ganesh, A. (1984) 'Upper Vaigai Basin: a study on surface and groundwater resources', *Indian Geographical Journal,* **59,** 232–45.

Gardner, J. E. (1984) 'Institutional arrangements for coastal conservation in New Zealand', *Coastal Zone Management Journal,* **12,** 137–88.

Gardner, J. S. (1972–73) 'Beyond the impact statement: a discussion of the dynamics of environmental impact', Vol. 3, pp. 154–66, in *Geographical Inter-University Resource Management Seminar,* Waterloo Lutheran University, Waterloo, Ontario.

Garner, J. F. and **O'Riordan, T.** (1982) 'Environmental impact in the context of economic recession', *Geographical Journal,* **148,** 343–61.

Gatrell, A. C. and **Lovett, A. A.** (1986) 'The geography of hazardous waste disposal in England and Wales', *Area,* **18,** 275–83.

Geipel, R. (1982) *Disaster and Reconstruction: the Friuli (Italy) Earthquakes of 1976,* Allen and Unwin, London.

Gellatly, A. F., Whalley, W. B., Gordon, J. E., and **Ferguson, R. I.** (1986) 'An observation on trampling effects in North Norway: thresholds for damage', *Norsk Geografisk Tidsskrift,* **40,** 163–8.

Gerasimov, I. P. (1983) 'Land resources of the world; their use and reserves.

Definition of land quality and agricultural potential by soil survey maps', *Geoforum,* **14,** 427–39.

Ghiselin, J. (1982) 'Reaching environmental decisions: making subjective and objective judgements', *Environmental Management,* **6,** 103–8.

Ghosh, D. (1978) 'Evaluation of draft irrigation programme at Sonamukhi CADP Area: an approach to benefit-cost analysis', *Geographical Review of India,* **40,** 62–73.

Gibbons, J. D. (1971) *Nonparametric Statistical Inference,* McGraw-Hill, New York.

Gibson, J. A. (1976) 'A review of recent extensions of linear economic models to regional environmental quality analysis', *Journal of Environmental Systems,* **6,** 147–72.

Gibson, R. and **Patterson, E.** (1984) 'Environmental assessment in Canada', *Journal of Environmental Education and Information,* **3,** 230–52.

Gilg, A. W. (1974) 'A critique of Linton's method of assessing scenery as a natural resource', *Scottish Geographical Magazine,* **90,** 125–9.

Gilg, A. W. (1975) 'The objectivity of Linton type methods of assessing scenery as a natural resource', *Regional Studies,* **9,** 181–91.

Gilg, A. W. (1976) 'Assessing scenery as a natural resource', *Scottish Geographical Magazine,* **92,** 41–9.

Gill, D. and **Bonnett, P.** (1973) *Nature in the Urban Landscape: A Study of City Ecosystems,* York Press, Baltimore.

Ginsberg, N. (1957) 'Natural resources and economic development', *Annals of the Association of American Geographers,* **47,** 197–212.

Giri, H. H. (1983) 'Radicalism in geography', *Annals of the National Association of Geographers, India,* **2,** 54–9.

Gjessing, J. (1986) 'Integrated resource – geographic approach to resource and planning in the Sahel and Sudan zones of Africa', *Norsk Geografisk Tidsskrift,* **40,** 203–9.

Glacken, C. J. (1967) *Traces on the Rhodian Shore,* University of California Press, Berkeley and Los Angeles.

Gladkevich, G. I. and **Sumina, T. I.** (1982) 'Measuring the environmental impact of industrial centers in the natural–economic regions of the USSR', *Soviet Geography,* **22,** 155–63.

Glassner, M. I., ed (1986) 'Special issue: the new political geography of the sea', *Political Geography Quarterly,* **5**(1), 72 pp.

Gokhman, V. M. and **Saushkin, Yu G.** (1972) 'Present problems in theoretical geography', *Soviet Geography,* **13,** 499–517.

Gold, J. R. and **Burgess, J.** (1982) *Valued Environments,* George Allen and Unwin, London.

Goodall, B. and **Whittow, J. B.** (1980) 'The selection of scenic forest drives', *Regional Studies,* **14,** 85–97.

Goodchild, M. F. (1985) 'Geographic Information Systems in undergraduate geography: a contemporary dilemma', *Operational Geographer,* **8,** 34–8.

Gormley, W. T. (1987) 'Institutional policy analysis: a critical review', *Journal of Policy Analysis and Management,* **6,** 153–69.

Gould, P. R. (1970) 'Is statistical inference the geographical name for a wild goose?', *Economic Geography,* **46** (Supplement), 439–45.

Gray, D. H. (1972) 'Soil and the city', pp. 135–68, in Detwyler, T. R. and

Marcus, M. G. (eds.), *Urbanization and Environment: the Physical Geography of the City,* Duxbury, Belmont, Calif.

Graybill, D. L. (1985) 'If environmental impact assessment is everything, maybe it's nothing - some arguments for more attention to practical aspects of implementation', *Environmental Professional,* **7,** 344–51.

Green, J. E. (1969) 'The problem of reclamation of derelict land after coal strip mining in Appalachia', *Southeastern Geographer,* **9,** 36–47.

Green, M. B. and **Bone, R. M.** (1985) 'Measurement of socioeconomic impacts of a megaproject: the example of Norman Wells oil development and pipeline project. I: problem and measurement', *Operational Geographer,* **6,** 18–21.

Green, M. B. and **Mitchelson, R. L** (1981) 'Spatial perspectives of the flows through the Southeast Electrical Transmission Network', *Professional Geographer,* **33,** 83–94.

Greenberg, M. R., Anderson, R., and **Page, G. W.** (1978) *Environmental Impact Statements,* Resource Paper No. 78–3, Association of American Geographers, Washington, DC.

Greene, D., Percival, I. and **Ridge, I.** (1985) *Nuclear Winter,* Polity Press, Cambridge.

Greenland, D. and **Yorty, R. A.** (1985) 'The spatial distribution of particulate concentration in the Denver Metropolitan Area', *Annals of the Association of American Geographers,* **75,** 69–82.

Gregory, S. (1974) 'The geographer and natural resources research', *South African Geographer,* **4,** 371–82.

Greig, P. J. (1986) 'Forest policy developments in Victoria', *Australian Forestry,* **49,** 197–202.

Griffith, C. R. (1980) 'Geographic information systems and environmental impact assessment', *Environmental Management,* **4,** (1), 21–6.

Grigg, D. (1982) 'Counting the hungry: world patterns of undernutrition', *Tijdschrift voor Economische en Sociale Geografie,* **73,** 66–79.

Grima, A. P. (1972) *Residential Water Demand: Alternative Choices for Management,* University of Toronto Press, Toronto.

Grima, A. P. (1973) 'The impact of policy variables on residential water demand and related investment requirements', *Water Resources Bulletin,* **9,** 703–10.

Grima, A. P. (1981) 'Institutional instruments for water pollution control', *GeoJournal,* **5,** 503–11.

Grima, A. P. and **Dufournaud, C.** (1976) *Public Participation in Great Lakes Water Levels Regulation: Further Findings From the Public Hearings Held by the I.J.C. in 1973,* Institute for Environmental Studies, University of Toronto, Toronto.

Grima, A. P., Timmerman, P., Fowle, C. D. and **Byer, P.** (1986) *Risk Management and EIA: Research Needs and Opportunities,* Minister of Supply and Services, Ottawa.

Grime, J. P. (1986) 'Predictions of terrestrial vegetation response to nuclear winter conditions', *International Journal of Environmental Studies,* Section A, **28,** 11–19.

Gruntfest, E. and **Huber, T.** (1986) *The Environmental Hazards of Colorado Springs,* Working Paper No. 54, Natural Hazards Information Center, Institute of Behavioral Science, University of Colorado, Boulder.

Guelke, L. (1971) 'Problems of scientific explanation in geography', *Canadian Geographer,* **15,** 38–53.

Guelke, L. (1974) 'An idealist alternative in human geography', *Annals of the Association of American Geographers,* **64,** 193–202.

Guelke, L. (1982a) *Historical Understanding in Geography: An Idealist Approach,* Cambridge University Press, Cambridge.

Guelke, L. (1982b) 'The Idealist dispute in Anglo-American geography: a comment', *Canadian Geographer,* **26,** 51–7.

Guelke, L. ed. (1986) *Geography and Humanistic Knowledge,* Publication Series No. 25, Department of Geography, University of Waterloo, Waterloo, Ontario.

Güller, P. (1986) 'Integrated mountain development: policy, practice, and research in Switzerland', *Mountain Research and Development,* **6,** 73–82.

Gusman, S. and **Huser, V.** (1984) 'Mediation in the Estuary', *Coastal Zone Management Journal,* **11,** 273–95.

Guy, W. E. (1983) 'Florida's coastal management program: a critical analysis', *Coastal Zone Management Journal,* **11,** 219–48.

Haas, J. E., Kates, R. W., and **Bowden, M. J.** (1977) *Reconstruction Following Disaster,* MIT Press, Cambridge, Mass.

Haase, G. and **Richter, H.** (1983) 'Current trends in landscape research', *GeoJournal,* **7,** 107–19.

Haefner, H. (1987) 'Assessment and monitoring of renewable natural resources: concepts and applications', *Applied Geography,* **7,** 7–15.

Hägerstrand, T. (1952) *The Propagation of Innovation Waves,* Studies in Geography No. 4, Department of Geography, University of Lund, Lund, Sweden.

Hägerstrand, T. (1967) *Innovation Diffusion as a Spatial Process,* University of Chicago Press, Chicago.

Haggerty, J. (1974–75) 'A regional level landscape evaluation for the analysis of visual impact of high voltage transmission lines', Vol. 5, pp. 46–70, *Geographical Inter-University Resource Management Seminars,* Department of Geography, Wilfrid Laurier University, Waterloo, Ontario.

Haigh, M. J. (1984) 'Ravine erosion and reclamation in India', *Geoforum,* **15,** 543–62.

Hall, M. D. and **Doyle, K.** (1984) 'Negotiating agreements to environmental problems', *Environmental Professional,* **6,** 203–15.

Hamill, L. (1968) 'Process of making good decisions about the use of the environment of man', *Natural Resources Journal,* **8,** 279–301.

Hamill, L. (1975) 'Analysis of Leopold's quantitative comparisons of landscape esthetics', *Journal of Leisure Research,* **7,** 16–28.

Hamill, L. (1985) 'On the presence of error in scholarly communication: the case of landscape aesthetics', *Canadian Geographer,* **29,** 270–3.

Hamilton, F. E. I. (1964) 'Location factors in the Yugoslav iron and steel industry', *Economic Geography,* **40,** 46–64.

Hamilton, W. G. (1982) 'Landscape assessment: the last decade: comment No. 2', *Canadian Geographer,* **26,** 73–6.

Handmer, J. W., ed. (1987) *Flood Hazard Management: British and International Perspectives,* Geo Abstracts Ltd., Norwich.

Handmer, J. W. and **Smith, D. I.** (1983) 'Health hazards of floods: hospital admissions for Lismore', *Australian Geographical Studies,* **21,** 221–30.

Hansen, J. C. (1983) 'Regional policy in an oil economy: the case of Norway', *Geoforum,* **14,** 353–61.

Hardwick, W. G. (1964) *The Geography of the Forest Industry of Coastal British Columbia,* Tantalus, Vancouver.

Hare, F. K. (1974) 'Geography and public policy: a Canadian view', *Transactions of the Institute of British Geographers,* **63,** 25–8.

Hare, F. K. (1980) 'The planetary environment: fragile or sturdy?', *Geographical Journal,* **146,** 379–95.

Hare, F. K. (1984) 'Changing climate and human response: the impact of recent events on climatology', *Geoforum,* **15,** 383–94.

Hare, F. K. (1985) 'Future environments: can they be predicted?', *Transactions, Institute of British Geographers,* New Series, **10,** 131–7.

Harker, P. (1984) 'Mapping Canada's coal resources', *Operational Geographer,* **4,** 35–8.

Harrington, G. W., Wilson, A. D. and **Young, M. D.** (1984) *Management of Australia's Rangelands,* Commonwealth Scientific and Industrial Research Organization, East Melbourne.

Harris, C. (1971) 'Theory and synthesis in historical geography', *Canadian Geographer,* **15,** 157–72.

Harris, S. (1984) *Australian Resources Policy: Bargaining at Many Levels,* CRES Working Paper 1984/1, Centre for Resources and Environmental Studies, Australian National University, Canberra.

Harrison, P. and **Sewell, W. R. D.** (1979) 'Shoreline management: the French approach', *Coastal Zone Management Journal,* **5,** 161–80.

Hart, J. F. (1982) 'The highest form of the Geographer's art', *Annals of the Association of American Geographers,* **72,** 1–29.

Hart, S. L., Enk, G. A. and **Hornick, W. F.** (1984) *Improving Impact Assessment: Increasing the Relevance and Utilization of Scientific and Technical Information,* Westview Press, Boulder, Colorado.

Hartshorne, R. (1939, 1961 revised) *The Nature of Geography,* Association of American Geographers, Lancaster, Pa.

Hartshorne, R. (1959) *Perspective on the Nature of Geography,* Rand McNally, Chicago.

Harvey, D. (1972) 'Revolutionary and counter revolutionary theory in geography and the problem of ghetto formation', *Antipode,* **4,** 1–13, 36–41.

Harvey, D. (1973) *Social Justice and the City,* Edward Arnold, London.

Harvey, D. (1974) 'Population, resources, and the ideology of science', *Economic Geography,* **50,** 256–77.

Harvey, D. (1975) 'Review of B. J. L. Berry, *The Human Consequences of Urbanization', Annals of the Association of American Geography,* **65,** 99–103.

Harvey, D. (1983) *The Limits to Capital,* Basil Blackwell, Oxford.

Harvey, D. (1984) 'On the history and present condition of geography: an historical materialist manifesto', *Professional Geographer,* **36,** 1–11.

Hathout, S. and **Smil, V.** (1985) 'Land use and land cover in Eastern China: a Landsat analysis', *Canadian Geographer,* **29,** 137–48.

Haügerhaüll, B. (1980) 'International cooperation to protect the Baltic', *Ambio,* **9,** 183–6.

Havlick, S. W. (1984) 'The urgency of accelerated application of natural hazards research findings in human settlements', *Ekistics,* **51,** 398–405.

Hay, I. (1985) 'Some environmental incidents of alluvial gold dredging on the Grey River, Westland', *New Zealand Geographer,* **41,** 8–14.

Healy, R. G. and **Zinn, J. A.** (1985) 'Environment and development conflicts in coastal zone management', *Journal of the American Planning Association,* **51,** 299–311.

Heathcote, R. L. (1983) *The Arid Lands: Their Use and Abuse,* Longman, London and New York.

Heathcote, R. L. (1987) 'Images of a desert? Perceptions of arid Australia', *Australian Geographical Studies,* **25,** 3–25.

Heathcote, R. L. and **Thom, B. G.** eds. (1979) *Natural Hazards in Australia,* Australian Academy of Science, Canberra.

Heberlein, T. A. (1973) 'Social psychological assumptions of user attitude surveys: the case of the wilderness scale', *Journal of Leisure Research,* **5,** 18–33.

Helleiner, F. M. (1981) 'The regionalization of a waterway: a study of recreational boat traffic', *Canadian Geographer,* **25,** 60–74.

Helliwell, J. F., MacGregor, M. E. and **Plourde, A.** (1983) 'Changes in Canadian energy demand, supply and policies 1974–1986', *Natural Resources Journal,* **24,** 297–324.

Hendee, J. C., Clark, R. N., and **Stankey, G. H.** (1974) 'A framework for agency use of public input in resource decision-making', *Journal of Soil and Water Conservation,* **29,** 60–6.

Herfindahl, O. C. (1969) *Natural Resource Information for Economic Development,* Johns Hopkins, Baltimore.

Herfindahl, O. C. and **Kneese, A. V.** (1965) *Quality of the Environment,* Johns Hopkins, Baltimore.

Hewitt, K. (1983a) 'The idea of calamity in a technocratic age', pp. 3–32 in K. Hewitt (ed.), *Interpretations of Calamity,* Allen and Unwin, Boston.

Hewitt, K. (1983b) 'Seismic risk and mountain environments: the role of surface conditions in earthquake disaster', *Mountain Research and Development,* **10,** 27–44.

Hewitt, K. (1984) 'Ecotonal settlement and natural hazards in mountain regions: the case of earthquake risk', *Mountain Research and Development,* **4,** 31–7.

Hewitt, K. and **Burton, I.** (1971) *The Hazardousness of a Place: A Regional Ecology of Damaging Events,* University of Toronto Press, Toronto.

Hewitt, K. and **Hare, F. K.** (1973) *Man and Environment Conceptual Frameworks,* Resource Paper No. 20, Commission on College Geography, Association of American Geographers, Washington, DC.

Hileman, P. (1983) 'Environmental dispute resolution', *Environmental Science and Technology,* **17,** 165–8.

Hill, A. R. (1976) 'The environmental impacts of agricultural land drainage', *Journal of Environmental Management,* **4,** 251–74.

Hill, G. J. E. and **Kelly, G. D.** (1986) 'Integrating Landsat and land systems for cover maps in southern inland Queensland', *Australian Geographical Studies,* **24,** 235–43.

Hills, G. A. (1961) *The Ecological Basis for Land-Use Planning,* Research Report No. 46, Ontario Ministry of Natural Resources, Toronto.

Hills, G. A., Love, D. V., and **Lacate, D. S.** (1970) *Developing a Better Environment: Ecological Land-Use Planning in Ontario,* Ontario Economic Council, Toronto.

Hipel, K. W. (1981) 'Operational research techniques in river basin management', *Canadian Water Resources Journal,* **6,** 205–26.

Hjern, B. (1982) 'Implementation research – the link gone missing', *Journal of Public Policy,* **2,** 301–8.

Hoffman, A. J. and **Alliende, C.** (1982) 'Impact of trampling upon the vegetation of Andean areas in Central Chile', *Mountain Research and Development,* **2,** 189–94.

Hoffman, D. W. (1976) 'Soil capability analysis and land resource development in Canada', pp. 140–67 in McBoyle G. R. and Sommerville E. (eds.), *Canada's Natural Environment: Essays in Applied Geography,* Methuen, Toronto.

Hohenemser, C. (1986) 'Chernobyl: the first lessons', *Natural Hazards Observer,* **11**(1), 1–2.

Holling, C. S., ed (1974) *Modelling and Simulation for Environmental Impact Analysis,* Schloss Laxenburg, Laxenburg, Austria.

Holling, C. S., ed. (1978) *Adaptive Environmental Assessment and Management,* John Wiley, Chichester.

Holling, C. S. (1981) *Resilience in the Unforgiving Society,* University of British Columbia, Vancouver.

Holsti, O. R. (1968) 'Content analysis', Vol. 2, pp. 596–692, in Lindzey, G. and Aronson, E. (eds.), *Handbook of Social Psychology* (2nd edition), Addison-Wesley, Reading, Mass.

Holsti, O. R. (1969) *Content Analysis for the Social Sciences,* Addison-Wesley, Reading, Mass.

Homenuck, P., Durlak, J. and **Morgenstern, J.** (1978) 'Evaluation of public participation programmes', pp. 103–19 in Sadler, B. (ed.), *Involvement and Environment,* Vol. 1, Environment Council of Alberta, Edmonton.

Hoole, A. F. (1978) 'Public participation in park planning: the Riding Mountain case', *Canadian Geographer,* **22,** 41–50.

Hotelling, H. (1947) 'Letter', p. 56, quoted in Outdoor Recreation Resources Review Commission (1962) *Economic Studies of Outdoor Recreation,* US Government Printing Office, Washington, DC.

House, P. W. (1982) *The Art of Public Policy Analysis,* Sage Library of Social Research No. 135, London.

Howe, C. W. (1971) *Benefit-Cost Analysis for Water System Planning,* American Geophysical Union, Washington, DC.

Hufferd, J. (1980) 'Idealism and the participant's world', *Professional Geographer,* **32,** 1–5.

Hunter, F. (1953) *Community Power Structure: A Study of Decision Makers,* University of North Carolina Press, Chapel Hill.

Hunter, J. M. (1966) 'Ascertaining population carrying capacity under traditional systems of agriculture in developing countries', *Professional Geographer,* **18,** 151–4.

Hyman, H. H. and **Wright, C. R.** (1967) 'Evaluating social action programs', pp. 741–82 in Lazarfeld, P. F., Sewell, W. H., and Wilensky, H. L. (eds.), *The Uses of Sociology,* Basic Books, New York.

Ikporukpo, C. O. (1983) 'Environmental deterioration and public policy in Nigeria', *Applied Geography,* **3,** 303–16.

Ilberry, B. W., Foster, I. D. L. and **Donoghue, P. J.** (1982) 'Perception and water quality: a geographical perspective', *Progress in Physical Geography,* **6,** 524–40.

Ingram, H. M. (1973) 'Information channels and environmental decision making', *Natural Resources Journal,* **13,** 150–69.

Ingram, H. M., Mann, D. E., Weatherford, G. D. and **Cortner, H. J.** (1984) 'Guidelines for improved institutional analysis in water resources planning', *Water Resources Research,* **20,** 323–34.

Ingram, H. and **McCain, J. R.** (1977) 'Federal water resources management: the administrative setting', *Public Administration Review,* **37,** 448–55.

International Union for Conservation of Nature and Natural Resources (1980) *World Conservation Strategy,* IUCN, Gland, Switzerland.

International Union for Conservation of Nature and Natural Resources (1984) *National Conservation Strategies: A Framework for Sustainable Development,* IUCN, Gland, Switzerland.

Isachenko, A. G. (1973) 'On the method of applied landscape research', *Soviet Geography,* **14,** 229–43.

Isakov, Yu A. (1984) 'The protection of nature in the U.S.S.R.: scientific and organizational principles', *Geoforum,* **15,** 89–94.

Isard, W. *et al.* (1960) *Methods of Regional Analysis,* MIT Press, Cambridge, Mass.

Isard, W. *et al.* (1972) *Ecologic-Economic Analysis for Regional Development,* Free Press, New York.

Islam, M. A. (1980) 'Agricultural adjustments to flooding in Bangladesh: a preliminary report', *National Geographical Journal of India,* **26,** 50–9.

Izrael, Yu. A., Boltneva, L. I., Gasilina, N. K., Dibobes, I. K. and **Nazarov, I. M.** (1981) 'Basic principles and results of environmental impact studies of the Kansk-Achinsk lignite and power project', *Soviet Geography,* **22,** 353–60.

Jaakson, R., Buszywski, M., and **Botting, D.** (1976) 'Carrying capacity and lake recreation planning: a case study from North-Central Saskatchewan, Canada', *Town Planning Review,* **47,** 359–73.

Jackson, E. L. (1980) 'Perceptions of energy problems and the adoption of conservation practices in Edmonton and Calgary', *Canadian Geographer,* **24,** 114–30.

Jacobs, P. (1981) *Environmental Strategy and Action: the Challenge of the World Conservation Strategy,* University of British Columbia Press, Vancouver.

Jacques, D. L. (1980) 'Landscape appraisal: the case for a subjective theory', *Journal of Environmental Management,* **10,** 107–13.

Jacques, D. L. (1981) 'Landscape appraisal: The "objective/subjective" debate', *Landscape Research,* **6**(1) 32.

Jakeman, A. J., Parker, P. K., Formby, J. and **Day, D.,** eds (1987) *Resource Development and Environmental Issues: Opportunities and Constraints in the Hunter Region, N.S.W.* CRES Monograph 17,

Centre for Resource and Environmental Studies, Australian National University, Canberra.

Jammet, H. and **Madelmont, C.** (1982) 'French regulations on environmental impact assessment', *Environmental Impact Assessment Review,* **3,** 259–70.

Jantsch, E. (1967) *Technological Forecasting in Perspective,* Organisation for Economic Co-operation and Development, Paris.

Jantsch, E. (1972) *Technological Planning and Social Futures,* Halsted Press, New York.

Jeans, D. N. and **Davies, J. L.** (1984) 'Australian geography 1972–1982', *Australian Geographical Studies,* **22,** 3–35.

Jensen, J. R. (1983) 'Biophysical remote sensing', *Annals of the Association of American Geographers,* **73,** 111–32.

Johannsen, C. J. and **Barney, T. W.** (1981) 'Remote sensing applications for resource management', *Journal of Soil and Water Conservation,* **36,** 128–31.

Johnson, J. H. (1985) 'A model of evacuation - decision making in a nuclear reactor emergency', *Geographical Review,* **75,** 405–18.

Johnson, K., Olson, E. A. and **Manandhar, S.** (1982) 'Environmental knowledge and response to natural hazards in mountainous Nepal', *Mountain Research and Development,* **2,** 175–88.

Johnston, R. J. (1983a) *Philosophy and Human Geography: An Introduction to Contemporary Approaches,* Edward Arnold, London.

Johnston, R. J. (1983b) 'Resource analysis, resource management and the integration of physical and human geography', *Progress in Physical Geography,* **7,** 127–46.

Johnston, T. and **Smit, B.** (1985) 'An evaluation of the rationale for farmland preservation policy in Ontario', *Land Use Policy,* **2,** 225–37.

Johnstone, I. M., Coffey, B. T. and **Howard-Williams, C.** (1985) 'The role of recreational boat traffic in interlake dispersal of macrophytes: a New Zealand case study', *Journal of Environmental Management,* **20,** 281–93.

Jones, J. G., Hyde, J. F. C. and **Meacham, M. L.** (1986) *Four Analytical Approaches for Integrating Land Management and Transportation Planning on Forest Lands,* USDA Forest Service, Research Paper INT-361, Intermountain Research Station, Ogden, Utah.

Jones, P. (1981) 'The geography of Dutch elm disease in Britain', *Transactions of the Institute of British Geographers,* New Series, **6,** 324–36.

Jones, S. B. (1954) 'A unified field theory of political geography', *Annals of the Association of American Geographers,* **44,** 111–23.

Jónsson, S. (1985) 'The regional implications of Iceland's fisheries - 1901–1940', *Norsk Geografisk Tidsskrift,* **39,** 67–86.

Joseph, K. T. (1978) 'Geography and development in the Third World - some case studies from Malaysia', *Geographica,* **12,** 39–44.

Juvik, S. P. (1986) 'The role of the state in resource use decision-making: the case of the Moomba-Sydney gas pipeline', *Australian Geographical Studies,* **24,** 57–71.

Kairu, E. N. (1982) 'An introduction to remote sensing', *GeoJournal,* **6,** 251–60.

Kalitsi, E. A. K. (1973) 'Volta Lake in relation to the human population and some issues in economics and management', pp. 77–85 in Ackerman,

W. C. *et al.* (eds.), *Man-Made Lakes: Their Problems and Environmental Effects,* American Geophysical Union, Washington, DC.

Kamieniecki, S. (1982) 'Leaders' and citizens' attitudes towards population growth: some explanatory factors', *Journal of Environmental Management,* **14,** 35–44.

Kane, P. S. (1981) 'Assessing landscape attractiveness: a comparative test of two new methods', *Applied Geography,* **1,** 77–96.

Karan, P. P. (1980) 'Public awareness of environmental problems in Calcutta Metropolitan Area', *National Geographical Journal of India,* **26,** 29–34.

Kariel, H. G. and **Kariel, P. E.** (1982) 'Socio-cultural impacts of tourism: an example from the Austrian Alps', *Geografiska Annaler,* **64B,** 1–16.

Kasperson, R. E. (1969a) 'Environmental stress and the municipal political system', pp. 481–96, in Kasperson, R. E. and Minghi, J. V. (eds.), *The Structure of Political Geography,* Aldine, Chicago.

Kasperson, R. E. (1969b) 'Political behavior and the decision-making process in the allocation of water resources between recreational and municipal uses', *Natural Resources Journal,* **9,** 176–211.

Kasperson, R. E. and **Minghi, J. V.** (1969) 'Environment: introduction', pp. 423–35 in Kasperson, R. E. and Minghi, J. V. (eds.), *The Structure of Political Geography,* Aldine, Chicago.

Kates, R. W. (1962) *Hazard and Choice Perception in Flood Plain Management,* Research Paper No. 78, Department of Geography, University of Chicago, Chicago.

Kates, R. W. (1966–67) 'The pursuit of beauty in the environment', *Landscape,* **16**, 21–5.

Kates, R. W. (1972) 'Book review of T. O'Riordan, *Perspectives on Resource Management, 1971', Annals of the Association of American Geographers,* **62,** 519–20.

Kates, R. W. (1977) 'Assessing the assessors: the art and ideology of risk assessment', *Ambio,* **6,** (5), 247–52.

Kates, R. W. (1978) *Risk Assessment of Environmental Hazard,* SCOPE 8, John Wiley, Chichester.

Kates, R. W., Hohenemser, C. and **Kasperson, J. X.,** eds. (1984) *Perilous Progress: Technology as Hazard,* Westview, Boulder, Colorado.

Kates, R. W., Ausubel, J. H. and **Berberian, M.,** eds (1985) *Climate Impact Assessment: Studies of the Interaction of Climate and Society,* John Wiley, New York.

Kates, R. W. and **Burton, I.,** eds (1986a) *Geography, Resources, and Environment: Selected Writings of Gilbert F. White,* Vol. 1, University of Chicago Press, Chicago.

Kates, R. W. and **Burton, I.,** eds. (1986b) *Geography, Resources, and Environment: Themes from the Work of Gilbert F. White,* Vol. 2, University of Chicago Press, Chicago.

Kaufman, H. (1960) *The Forest Ranger: A Study in Administrative Behavior,* Johns Hopkins, Baltimore.

Kayastha, S. L. (1982) 'Perspectives on environment and development', *National Geographical Journal of India,* **28,** 37–43.

Kayastha, S. L. and **Singh, M. B.** (1982) 'Resources, industrial development patterns and planning in Eastern Uttar Pradesh', *Indian Geographical Journal,* **57,** 35–45.

Kaynor, E. R. and **Howards, I.** (1971) 'Limits on the institutional frame of reference in water resource decision making', *Water Resources Bulletin,* **7,** 1117–27.

Kelly, D. R., Stunkel, K. R., and **Wescott, R. R.** (1976) *The Economic Superpowers and the Environment,* W. H. Freeman, San Francisco.

Kemp, R., O'Riordan, T., and **Purdue, M.** (1984) 'Investigation as legitimacy: the maturing of the big public inquiry', *Geoforum,* **15,** 477–88.

Kemp, R., O'Riordan, T. and **Purdue, M.** (1986) 'Environmental politics in the 1980's: the public examination of radioactive waste disposal', *Policy and Politics,* **14,** 9–25.

Kennedy, M. M. (1979) 'Generalizing from single case studies', *Evaluation Quarterly,* **3,** 661–78.

Kennedy, V. S. and **Breisch, L. L.** (1983) 'Sixteen decades of political management of the Oyster fishery in Maryland's Chesapeake Bay', *Journal of Environmental Management,* **16,** 153–72.

Keogh, B. (1982) 'L'impact social du tourisme: le cas de Shédiac, Nouveau-Brunswick', *Canadian Geographer,* **26,** 318–31.

Kercher, J. R. (1982) 'An assessment of the impact on crops of effluent gases from geothermal energy development in the Imperial Valley, California', *Journal of Environmental Management,* **15,** 213–28.

Kerlinger, F. N. (1964, 1973) *Foundations of Behavioral Research* (2nd edn), Holt, Rinehart and Winston, New York.

Kessell, S. R., Good, R. B. and **Hopkins, A. J. M.** (1984) 'Implementation of two new resource management information systems in Australia', *Environmental Management,* **8,** 251–69.

Kettel, G. A. and **Day, J. C.** (1974) 'Outlet drainage in Ontario: a methodological exploration', *Journal of Environmental Management,* **2,** 331–49.

King, J. E. and **Nelson, J. G.** (1983) 'Evaluating the Federal Environmental Assessment and Review Process with special reference to South Davis Strait, northeastern Canada', *Environmental Conservation,* **10,** 293–301.

King, L. J. (1976) 'Alternatives to a positive economic geography', *Annals of the Association of American Geographers,* **66,** 293–308.

Kirby, A. and **Jacob, G.** (1986) 'The politics of transportation and disposal: hazardous and nuclear waste issues in Colorado, U.S.', *Policy and Politics,* **14,** 27–42.

Kirillova, T. B. and **Ovchinnikova, V. H.** (1975) 'Predicting the reclamation of land after surface mining in the Central Chernozem region', *Soviet Geography,* **16,** 381–9.

Kirkby, A. V. (1972) 'Perception of air pollution as a hazard and individual adjustment to it in three British cities', Paper presented to the International Geographical Union, Man and Environment Seminar, Calgary, Alberta.

Kliot, N. (1986) 'Man's impact on river basins: an Israeli case study', *Applied Geography,* **6,** 163–78.

Knight, K. D., Dufournand, C. and **Mulamoottil, G.** (1983) 'Conceptual ecological modelling and interaction matrices as tools in coastal planning', *Water Science and Technology,* **16,** 559–67.

Knudson, D. M. (1976) 'A system for evaluating scenic rivers', *Water Resources Bulletin,* **12,** 281–90.

Knudson, D. M. and **Curry, E. B.** (1981) 'Campers' perceptions of site deterioration and crowding', *Journal of Forestry,* **79,** 92–4.

Kohn, C. F. (1970) 'The 1960's: a decade of progress in geographical research and instruction', *Annals of the Association of American Geographers,* **60,** 211–19.

Kolawole, A. (1987) 'Response to natural and man-made hazards in Borno, Northeast Nigeria', *Disasters,* **11,** 59–66.

Kraft, C. H. and **Van Eden, C.** (1968) *A Nonparametric Introduction to Statistics,* Macmillan, New York.

Kraft, M. E. and **Kraut, R.** (1985) 'The impact of citizen participation on hazardous waste policy implementation: the case of Clermont County, Ohio', *Policy Studies Journal,* **14,** 52–61.

Kreutzwiser, R. D. and **Lee, A. G.** (1982) 'Rural landowner attitudes toward sport fishing access along the Saugeen and Credit Rivers, Southern Ontario', *Recreation Research Review,* **9,** 7–14.

Krippendorff, K. (1980) *Content Analysis: An Introduction to its Methodology,* Sage Publications, Beverly Hills, Calif.

Krishna, Y. S. R. and **Sastri, A. S. R. A. S.** (1980) 'Studies on the incidence of droughts over Western Rajasthan', *National Geographical Journal of India,* **26,** 44–9.

Kristjanson, K. (1954) 'Institutional arrangements in water resource development', *Land Economics,* **30,** 347–62.

Kromm, D. E. (1985) 'Regional water management: an assessment of institutions in England and Wales', *Professional Geographer,* **37,** 183–91.

Kromm, D. E., Probald, F., and **Wall, G.** (1973) 'An international comparison of response to air pollution', *Journal of Environmental Management,* **1,** 363–75.

Kromm, D. E. and **White, S. E.** (1985) *Conserving the Ogallala: What Next?,* Department of Geography, Kansas State University, Manhattan, Kansas, 16 pp.

Kromm and **White** (1987) 'Interstate groundwater management preference differences: the Ogalla Region', *Journal of Geography,* **86,** 5–11.

Krueger, R. R. and **Mitchell, B.,** eds (1977) *Managing Canada's Renewable Resources,* Methuen, Toronto.

Krueger, R. R. and **Maguire, N. G.** (1985) 'Protecting specialty cropland from urban development: the case of the Okanagan Valley, British Columbia', *Geoforum,* **16,** 287–300.

Krumpe, E. E. and **Brown, P. J.** (1982) 'Redistributing backcountry use through information related to recreational experiences', *Journal of Forestry,* **80,** 360–2.

Kumra, V. K. (1980) 'Environmental pollution and human health: a geographical study of Kanpur City', *National Geographical Journal of India,* **26,** 60–9.

Kundaeli, J. (1983) 'Making conservation and development compatible', *Ambio,* **12,** 326–31.

Kuss, F. R. and **Morgan, J. M.** (1984) 'Using the USLE to estimate the physical carrying capacity of natural areas for outdoor recreation planning', *Journal of Soil and Water Conservation,* **39,** 383–7.

Labovitz, S. and **Hagedorn, R.** (1971) *Introduction to Social Research,* McGraw-Hill, New York.

Lake, L. M., ed. (1980) *Environmental Mediation: The Search for Consensus,* Westview Press, Boulder.

Lamb, H. H. (1981) 'Climatic changes and food production: observation and outlook in the modern world', *GeoJournal,* **5,** 101–12.

Landsberg, H. H. (1964) *Natural Resources for U.S. Growth,* Johns Hopkins, Baltimore.

Lang, R., ed. (1986) *Integrated Approaches to Resource Planning and Management,* University of Calgary Press, Calgary.

LaPage, W. F. (1963) 'Some sociological aspects of forest recreation', *Journal of Forestry,* **61,** 32–6.

LaPage, W. F. and **Bevins, M. I.** (1981) *Satisfaction Monitoring for Quality Control in Campground Management,* USDA Forest Service Research Paper NE-484, Northeastern Forest Experiment Station, Broomall, PA.

LaPiere, R. T. (1934) 'Attitudes vs. actions', *Social Forces,* **13,** 230–7.

Lasswell, H. D. (1956) *The Decision Process: Seven Categories of Functional Analysis,* University of Maryland, College Park.

Lasswell, H. D. (1972) 'Communications research and public policy', *Public Opinion Quarterly,* **36,** 301–10.

Latham, E. (1952) *The Group Basis of Politics,* Cornell University Press, Ithaca, NY.

Laubier, L. (1980) 'The Amoco Cadiz oil spill: an ecological impact study', *Ambio,* **9,** 268–76.

Lautenbach, W. E. (1985) *Land Reclamation Program 1978–1984,* Regional Municipality of Sudbury, Sudbury, Ontario.

Law, C. S. and **Zube, E. H.** (1983) 'Effects of photographic composition on landscape perception', *Landscape Research,* **8**(1), 22–3.

Lawson, G. W. (1970) 'Lessons of the Volta – a new man-made lake in tropical Africa', *Biological Conservation,* **2,** 90–6.

Lawson, M. P. and **Stockton, C. W.** (1981) 'Desert myth and climatic reality', *Annals of the Association of American Geographers,* **71,** 527–35.

Learmonth, A. T. A. and **Akhtar, R.** (1984) 'The malaria resurgence in India, 1965–76: towards a diffusion model', *Annals of the National Association of Geographers, India,* **4,** 23–69.

Leatherberry, E. C. and **Lime, D. W.** (1981) *Unstaffed Trail Registration Compliance in a Backcountry Recreation Area,* USDA North Central Forest Experiment Station Research Paper NC-214, United States Department of Agriculture, St. Paul, Minnesota.

LeDrew, E. F. and **Franklin, S. E.** (1985) 'The use of thermal infrared imagery in surface current analysis of a small lake', *Photogrammetric Engineering and Remote Sensing,* **51,** 565–73.

Lee, N. (1982) 'The future development of environmental impact assessment', *Journal of Environmental Management,* **14,** 71–90.

Lee, N. (1983) 'Environmental impact assessment: a review', *Applied Geography,* **3,** 5–28.

Lee, T. R. (1969) *Residential Water Demand and Economic Development,* Research Publications, Department of Geography, University of Toronto, Toronto.

Leinbach, T. R. (1976) 'Networks and flows', pp. 180–207, in Board, C. *et al.* (eds.), *Progress in Geography,* Edward Arnold, London.

Leitch, J. A. and **Leistritz, F. L.** (1984) 'Delphi analysis: a technique for identifying and ranking environmental and natural resource policy issues', *Environmental Professional,* **6,** 32–40.

Leonard, R. E., McMahon, J. L. and **Kehoe, K. M.** (1985) *Hiker Trampling Impacts on Eastern Forests,* USDA Forest Service Research Paper NE-555, Northeastern Forest Experiment Station, US Department of Agriculture, Durham, New Hampshire.

Leopold, L. B. (1969a) 'Landscape esthetics', *Natural History,* **78,** 37–44.

Leopold, L. B. (1969b) *Quantitative Comparison of Some Aesthetic Factors Among Rivers,* US Geological Survey Circular 620, US Government Printing Office, Washington, DC.

Leopold, L. B. (1974) 'The use of data in environmental impact assessment', pp. 27–34, in Dickert, T. G. and Domeny, K. R. (eds.), *Environmental Impact Assessment: Guidelines and Commentary,* University of California Press, Berkeley.

Leopold, L. B. and **Marchand, M. O.** (1968) 'On the quantitative inventory of the riverscape', *Water Resources Research,* **4,** 709–17.

Leopold, L. B. *et al.* (1971) *A Procedure for Evaluating Environmental Impact,* US Geological Survey Circular 645, US Government Printing Office, Washington, DC.

Levins, R. (1968) *Evolution in Changing Environments,* Princeton University Press, Princeton, New Jersey.

Lewin, J. (1975) 'Geomorphology and environmental impact statements', *Area,* **7,** 127–9.

Libecap, G. D. (1981) *Locking Up the Range: Federal Land Controls and Grazing,* Pacific Institute for Public Policy Research, San Francisco.

Lime, D. W. and **Stankey, G. H.** (1971) 'Carrying capacity: maintaining outdoor recreation quality', pp. 174–84, *Recreation Symposium Proceedings,* Northeastern Forest Experiment Station, Forest Service, U.S. Department of Agriculture, Upper Darby, Pa.

Lind, T. (1983) 'The environmental impact assessment process and offshore oil and gas exploration and production in Norway', *Environmental Impact Assessment Review,* **4,** 457–72.

Lindblom, C. E. (1959) 'The science of "muddling through"', *Public Administration Review,* **19,** 79–88.

Lindblom, C. E. (1968) *The Policy Making Process,* Prentice Hall, Englewood Cliffs.

Lindblom, C. E. (1979) 'Still muddling, not yet through', *Public Administration Review,* **39,** 517–26.

Lindell, M. K. and **Earle, T. C.** (1983) 'How close is close enough: public perceptions of the risks of industrial facilities', *Risk Analysis,* **3,** 245–53.

Lindsay, S. (1972) 'Conversation with Britain's Environmental Chief', *Saturday Review,* **55,** 64–70.

Lins, H. F. (1979) 'Energy development at Kenai, Alaska', *Annals of the Association of American Geographers,* **69,** 289–303.

Linstone, H. and **Turoff, M.,** eds (1975) *The Delphi Method: Techniques and Applications,* Addison-Wesley, Reading, Mass.

Linton, D. (1968) 'The assessment of scenery as a natural resource', *Scottish Geographical Magazine,* **84,** 219–38.

Liroff, R. A. (1981) 'NEPA litigation in the 1970's: a deluge or a dribble?', *Natural Resources Journal,* **21,** 315–30.

Litton, R. B. (1968) *Forest Landscape Description and Inventories: A Basis for Land Planning and Design,* USDA Forest Service Research Paper PSW-49, Pacific Southwest Forest and Range Experiment Station, Berkeley, Calif.

Litton, R. B. (1972) 'Aesthetic dimensions of the landscape', pp. 262–91 in Krutilla, J. V. (ed.), *Natural Environments: Studies in Theoretical and Applied Analysis,* Johns Hopkins, Baltimore.

Litton, R. B. (1974) 'Visual vulnerability of forest landscapes', *Journal of Forestry,* **72,** 392–7.

Litton, R. B. and **Tetlow, R. J.** (1978) *A Landscape Inventory Framework: Scenic Analyses of the Northern Great Plains,* USDA Forest Service, Research Paper PSW-135, Pacific Southwest Forest and Range Experiment Station, Berkeley, California.

Liverman, D. M., Terjung, W. H., Hayes, J. T. and **Mearns, L. O.** (1986) 'Climatic change and grain corn yields in the North American Great Plains', *Climatic Change,* **9,** 327–47.

Loomis, J. B. and **Walsh, R. G.** (1986) 'Assessing wildlife and environmental values in cost-benefit analysis: state of the art', *Journal of Environmental Management,* **22,** 125–31.

Lopatina, Y. B. *et al.* (1971) 'The present state and future tasks in the theory and method of an evaluation of the natural environment and resources', *Soviet Geography,* **12,** 142–51.

Lovelock, J. E. (1979) *GAIA: A New Look at Life on Earth,* Oxford University Press, Oxford.

Lovelock, J. E. and **Epton, S.** (1975) 'The quest for Gaia', *New Scientist,* **65,** 304–6.

Lowe, P. and **Goyder, J.** (1983) *Environmental Groups in Politics,* George Allan and Unwin, London.

Lowenthal, D. (1966) 'Assumptions behind the public attitudes', pp. 128–37 in Jarrett, H. (ed.), *Environmental Quality in a Growing Economy,* Johns Hopkins, Baltimore.

Lowenthal, D., ed. (1967) *Environmental Perception and Behavior,* Research Paper No. 109, Department of Geography, University of Chicago, Chicago.

Lowenthal, D. (1968) 'The American scene', *Geographical Review,* **58,** 61–88.

Lowenthal, D. (1972a) 'Editor's introduction', *Environment and Behavior,* **4,** 251–4.

Lowenthal, D. (1972b) 'Research in environmental perception and behavior: perspectives on current problems', *Environment and Behavior,* **4,** 333–42.

Lowenthal, D. (1975) 'The place of the past in the American landscape', pp. 89–118, in Lowenthal, D. and Bowden, M. J. (eds), *Geographies of the Mind: Essays in Historical Geography,* Oxford University Press, New York.

Lowenthal, D. (1977) 'The Bicentennial landscape: a mirror held up to the past', *Geographical Review,* **67,** 253–67.

Lowenthal, D. (1978) *Finding Valued Landscapes,* Environmental Perception Research Working Paper No. 4, Institute of Environmental Studies, University of Toronto, Toronto.

Lowenthal, D. (1981) 'Conclusion: dilemmas of preservation', pp. 213–37, in Lowenthal, D. and Binney, M. (eds), *Our Past Before Us: Why Do We Save It?,* Temple Smith, London.

Lowenthal, D. and **Prince, H. C.** (1964) 'The English landscape', *Geographical Review,* **54,** 309–46.

Lowenthal, D. and **Prince, H. C.** (1965) 'English landscape tastes', *Geographical Review,* **55,** 186–222.

Lowenthal, D. and **Prince, H. C.** (1976) 'Transcendental experience', pp. 117–31, in Wapner, S., Cohen, S. B., and Kaplan, B. (eds.), *Experiencing the Environment,* Plenum Press, New York.

Lowery, R. C., Hepburn, M., Dixon, R. D. and **Sabella, J.** (1983) 'Perceptions of resource regulation: a comparison of North Carolina fishermen and managers', *Coastal Zone Management Journal,* **10,** 387–405.

Lowry, G. K. (1980) 'Policy-relevant assessment of coastal zone management programs', *Coastal Zone Management Journal,* **8,** 227–55.

Lowi, T. (1964) 'American business, public policies, case studies and political theory', *World Politics,* **16,** 677–715.

Lowi, T. (1970) 'Decision making vs. policy making: toward an antidote for technocracy', *Public Administration Review,* **30,** 314–25.

Lowi, T. (1972) 'Four systems of policy, politics and choice', *Public Administration Review,* **32,** 298–310.

Lucas, R. C. (1964) 'Wilderness perception and use: the example of the Boundary Waters Canoe Area', *Natural Resources Journal,* **3,** 394–411.

Lucas, R. C. (1966) 'The contribution of environmental research to wilderness policy decisions', *Journal of Social Issue,* **22,** 116–26.

Lucas, R. C. (1981) *Redistributing Wilderness Use through Information Supplied to Visitors,* USDA Forest Service Research Paper INT-277, Intermountain Forest and Range Experiment Station, US Department of Agriculture, Ogden, Utah.

Lucas, R. C. (1983) *Low and Variable Visitor Compliance Rates at Voluntary Trail Registers,* USDA Forest Service Research Note INT-326, Intermountain Forest and Range Experiment Station, Ogden, Utah.

Lucas, R. C. (1985) *Visitor Characteristics, Attitudes, and Use Patterns in the Bob Marshall Wilderness Complex, 1970–82,* USDA Forest Service Research Paper INT-345, Intermountain Research Station, Ogden, Utah.

Lucas, R. C. and **Kovalicky, T. J.** (1981) *Self-Issued Wilderness Permits as a Use Measurement System,* USDA Forest Service Research Paper INT-270, Intermountain Forest and Range Experiment Station, Ogden, Utah.

Lukermann, F. (1964) 'Geography as a formal intellectual discipline and the way in which it contributes to human knowledge', *Canadian Geographer,* **8,** 167–72.

Lukermann, F. and **Porter, P. W.** (1960) 'Gravity and potential models in economic geography', *Annals of the Association of American Geographers,* **50,** 493–504.

Lulla, K. (1983) 'The Landsat satellites and selected aspects of physical geography', *Progress in Physical Geography,* **7,** 1-45.

Lund, R. (1983) 'The need for monitoring and result evaluation in a development project – experiences from the Mahaweli Project', *Norsk Geografisk Tidsskrift,* **37,** 171–86.

Lundqvist, L. J. (1974) *Environmental Policies in Canada, Sweden, and the United States: A Comparative Overview,* Sage Publications, Beverly Hills, Calif.

Lysyk, K. M. (1978) 'Public inquiries and the protection of the public interest in resource development projects', *Journal of Natural Resource Management and Interdisciplinary Studies,* **3,** 2–9.

Mabbutt, J. A. (1968) 'Review of concepts of land classification', pp. 11–28, in Stewart, G. A. (ed.), *Land Evaluation,* Macmillan of Australia, Melbourne.

Mabbutt, J. A. (1984) 'A new global assessment of the status and trends of desertification', *Environmental Conservation,* **11,** 103–13.

Mabogunje, A. L. (1980) 'The dynamics of centre-periphery relations: the need for a geography of resource development', *Transactions of the Institute of British Geographers,* New Series, **5**(3), 277–96.

Mabogunje, A. L. (1984) 'The poor shall inherit the earth: issues of environmental quality and Third World development', *Geoforum,* **15,** 295–306.

Macgill, S. (1983) 'Exploring the similarity of different risks', *Environment and Planning B,* **10,** 303–30.

Macgill, S. M. and **Snowball, D. J.** (1983) 'What use risk assessment?', *Applied Geography,* **3,** 171–92.

Macinko, G. (1963) 'The Columbia basin project: expectations, realizations, implications', *Geographical Review,* **53,** 185–99.

MacIver, I. (1970) *Urban Water Supply Alternatives: Perception and Choice in the Grand Basin, Ontario,* Research Paper No. 126, Department of Geography, University of Chicago, Chicago.

Mackney, D. (1974) 'Land use capability classification in the United Kingdom', pp. 4–11, in *Land Capability Conference Proceedings,* Technical Bulletin 30, Ministry of Agriculture, Fisheries and Food, London.

Maclaren, V. W. and **Whitney, J. B.,** eds (1985) *New Directions in Environmental Impact Assessment in Canada,* Methuen, Toronto.

MacLeod, G. (1981) 'Some public health lessons from Three Mile Island: a case study in chaos', *Ambio,* **10,** 18–28.

Maggiotto, M. A. and **Bowman, A.** (1982) 'Policy orientations and environmental regulation: a case study of Florida's Legislators', *Environment and Behavior,* **14,** 155–70.

Maher, R. V. and **Wightman, J. F.** (1985) 'A design for Geographic Information Systems training', *Operational Geographer,* **8,** 43–6.

Malini, B. H. (1981) 'Patterns of aridity, spread and severity of drought in Andhra Pradesh', *Indian Geographical Journal,* **56,** 30–6.

Manheim, M. L. (1981) 'Ethical issues in environmental impact assessment', *Environmental Impact Assessment Review,* **2,** (4), 315–34.

Mann, D. E. (1975a) 'Conflict and coalition: political variables underlying water resource development in the Upper Colorado River Basin', *Natural Resources Journal,* **15,** 141–69.

Mann, D. E. (1975b) 'Political incentives in U.S. water policy: relationships between distributive and regulatory politics', pp. 94–123, in Holden, M. and Dresang, D. L. (eds), *What Government Does,* Sage Publications, Beverly Hills, Calif.

Manners, I. R. (1982) *North Sea Oil and Environmental Planning: the United Kingdom experience,* University of Texas Press, Austin, Texas.

Manshard, W. (1985) 'The world's food and energy requirements – a global conflict for resources', *Natural Resources and Development,* **21,** 120–7.

Mansikkaniemi, H. (1982) 'Soil erosion in areas of intensive cultivation in southwestern Finland', *Fennia,* **160,** 225–76.

Marcus, M. G. (1979) 'Coming full circle: physical geography in the Twentieth Century', *Annals of the Association of American Geographers,* **69,** 521–32.

Marsh, G. P. (1864) *Man and Nature or Physical Geography as Modified by Human Action,* Scribner, New York.

Marsh, J. (1985) 'Postcard landscapes: an exploration in method', *Canadian Geographer,* **29,** 265–7.

Marshall, H. (1966) 'Politics and efficiency in water development', pp. 291–310, in Kneese, A. V. and Smith, S. C. (eds), *Water Research,* Johns Hopkins, Baltimore.

Marten, G. G. and **Sancholuz, L. A.** (1982) 'Ecological land use planning and carrying capacity evaluation in the Jalapa Region (Veracruz, Mexico)', *Agro-Ecosystems,* **8,** 83–124.

Martinson, T. L. (1980) 'The most perfect example of an alien ecology ever constructed', *Professional Geographer,* **32,** 471–7.

Maruyama, M. and **Dator, J. A.** (1971) *Human Futuristics,* Social Science Research Institute, University of Hawaii, Honolulu.

Massa, I. (1985) 'Hydroelectricity and development in Northern Finland and Northern Quebec', *Fennia,* **163,** 465–77.

Matheny, A. R. and **Williams, B. A.** (1985) 'Knowledge vs. NIMBY: assessing Florida's strategy for siting hazardous waste disposal facilities', *Policy Studies Journal,* **14,** 70–80.

Mather, A. S. (1982) 'The changing perception of soil erosion in New Zealand', *Geographical Journal,* **148,** 207–18.

Matheson, J. K. and **Bovill, E. W.** (1950) *East African Agriculture,* Oxford University Press, London.

Mathieson, A. and **Wall, G.** (1982) *Tourism: Economic, Physical and Social Impacts,* Longman, London.

Matley, I. M. (1976) *The Geography of International Tourism,* Resource Paper No. 76–1, Association of American Geographers, Washington, DC.

May, P. J. and **Williams, W.** (1986) *Disaster Policy Implementation: Managing Programs under Shared Governance,* Plenum, New York.

Mazmanian, D. and **Sabatier, P.** eds (1981) *Effective Policy Implementation,* D. C. Heath, Lexington, Mass.

Mazmanian, D. and **Sabatier, P.** (1983) *Implementation and Public Policy,* Scott Foresman and Co, Chicago.

McCarty, H. H. (1963) 'The geographer and his intellectual environment', *New Zealand Geographer,* **19,** 1–6.

McCool, S. F. and **Stankey, G. H.** (1986) *Visitor Attitudes Toward Wilderness Fire Management Policy – 1971–1984,* USDA Forest

Service Research Paper INT-357, Intermountain Research Station, Ogden, Utah.

McCormack, R. J. (1971) 'The Canada land-use inventory: a basis for land-use planning', *Journal of Soil and Water Conservation,* **26,** 141–6.

McCormick, J. (1986) 'The origins of the World Conservation Strategy', *Environmental Review,* **10,** 177–87.

McDonald, A. and **Kay, D.** (1981) 'Enteric bacterial concentrations in reservoir feeder streams: baseflow characteristics and response to hydrograph events', *Water Research,* **15,** 961–8.

McDonald, A., Kay, D. and **Jenkins, A.** (1982) 'Generation of fecal and total coliform surges by stream flow manipulation in the absence of normal hydrometeorological stimuli', *Applied and Environmental Microbiology,* **44,** 292–300.

McDonald, J. R. (1982) 'Environmental concern and the political process in France: patterns of the 1981 elections', *Environmental Professional,* **4,** 15–21.

McDonnell, M. J. (1981) 'Trampling effects on coastal dune vegetation in the Parker River National Wildlife Refuge, Massachusetts, U.S.A.', *Biological Conservation,* **21,** 289–301.

McHarg, I. L. (1968) 'Comprehensive highway route selection method', *Highway Research Record,* **246,** 1–15.

McHarg, I. L. (1969) *Design With Nature,* Doubleday, Garden City, NY.

McKernan, D. (1972) 'World fisheries world concern', pp. 35–51, in Rothschild, B. (ed.), *World Fisheries Policy: Multidisciplinary Views,* University of Washington Press, Seattle.

McLellan, A. G. (1975) 'The aggregate dilemma for surface mining in Canada - the conflicts of public sentiment and industrial conscience', *Bulletin of the Conservation Council of Ontario,* **22,** 12–20.

McLellan, A. G. (1983) 'The geographer as practitioner: the challenges, opportunities, and difficulties faced by the academic consultant', *Canadian Geographer,* **27,** 62–7.

McLellan, A. G. (1985) 'Government regulatory control of surface mining operations - new performance guideline models for progressive rehabilitation', *Landscape Planning,* **12,** 15–28.

McNicoll, I. (1984) 'The pattern of oil impact on affected Scottish rural areas', *Geographical Journal,* **150,** 213–20.

McTaggart, W. D. (1983) 'Forestry policy in Bali, Indonesia', *Singapore Journal of Tropical Geography,* **4,** 147–61.

Meadows, D. H., Meadows, D. L., Randers, J. and **Behrens, W. W.** (1972) *The Limits to Growth,* 2nd edn, Signet Books, New York.

Mensching, H. (1982) 'Applied geomorphology: examples of work in the Tropics and Subtropics', *Applied Geography and Development,* **19,** 87–96.

Mercer, D. (1979) 'Victoria's Land Conservation Council and the Alpine Region', *Australian Geographical Studies,* **17,** 107–30.

Mercer, D. (1983) 'Conflict over a high voltage power line: a Victorian case study', *Australian Geographer,* **15,** 292–307.

Mercer, D. C. (1971) 'The role of perception in the recreational experience: a review and discussion', *Journal of Leisure Research,* **3,** 261–76.

Mercer, D. C. (1972) 'Behaviourial geography and the sociology of social action', *Area,* **4,** 48–52.

Mercer, D. C. and **Powell, J. M.** (1972) *Phenomenology and Related Non-Positivistic Viewpoints in the Social Sciences,* Monash Publications in Geography No. 1, Monash University, Melbourne.

Meredith, T. C. (1983) 'Geography and the environmental impact assessment process', *Operational Geographer,* **1,** 12–14.

Meyer, G. (1980) 'Effects of the "New Valley" Project upon the development of the Egyptian Oases', *Applied Geography and Development,* **15,** 96–116.

Middleton, P. and **Rhodes, S. L.** (1984) 'Acid rain and drinking water degradation', *Environmental Monitoring and Assessment,* **4,** 99–103.

Midttun, A. and **Baumgartner, T.** (1986) 'Negotiating energy futures: the politics of energy forecasting', *Energy Policy,* **14,** 219–41.

Mikesell, M. W. (1974) 'Geography as the study of environment: an assessment of some old and new commitments', pp. 1–23, in Manners, I. R. and Mikesell, M. W. (eds.), *Perspectives on Environment,* Publication No. 13, Association of American Geographers, Washington, DC.

Mikesell, M. W. (1978) 'Tradition and innovation in cultural geography', *Annals of the Association of American Geographers,* **68,** 1–16.

Milas, S. (1984) 'Population crisis and desertification in the Sudano-Sahelian Region', *Environmental Conservation,* **11,** 167–9.

Miller, T. (1973) 'Military airfields and rural planning', *Town Planning Review,* **44,** 31–48.

Mints, A. A. and **Kakhanovskaya, T. G.** (1974) 'An attempt at a quantitative evaluation of the natural resource potential of regions in the USSR', *Soviet Geography,* **15,** 554–65.

Mitchell, B. (1971) *Water in England and Wales: Supply, Transfer and Management,* Research Paper No. 9, Department of Geography, University of Liverpool Press, Liverpool.

Mitchell, B. (1972) 'Hindsight evaluation: the Tryweryn Reservoir in Wales', No. 2, pp. 1288–90 in Adams, W. P. and Helleiner, F. M. (eds), *International Geography 1972,* University of Toronto Press, Toronto.

Mitchell, B. (1974a) 'Three approaches to resolving problems arising from assumption violation during statistical analysis in geographical research', *Cahiers de Géographie de Québec,* **18,** 507–24.

Mitchell, B. (1974b) 'Value conflicts and water supply decisions', pp. 37–59 in Leversedge, F. M. (ed.), *Priorities in Water Management,* Western Geographical Series Vol. 8, Department of Geography, University of Victoria, Victoria.

Mitchell, B. ed. (1975) *Institutional Arrangements for Water Management: Canadian Experiences,* Publication No. 5, Department of Geography, University of Waterloo, Waterloo, Ontario.

Mitchell, B. (1976) 'Decision-making and consultation in resource management: the B.C. salmon fishery', *Journal of Environmental Management,* **4,** 211–23.

Mitchell, B. (1977) 'Hindsight reviews: the B.C. licence programme', pp. 148–86, in Ellis, D. V. (ed.), *Pacific Salmon: Management for People,* Western Geographical Series Vol. 13, Department of Geography, University of Victoria, Victoria.

Mitchell, B. (1983) 'Comprehensive river basin planning in Canada: problems and opportunities', *Water International,* **8,** 146–53.

Mitchell, B. (1986a) 'The evolution of integrated resource management', pp. 13–26 in Lang, R. (ed.), *Integrated Approaches to Resource Planning and Management,* University of Calgary Press, Calgary.

Mitchell, B. (1986b) 'Integrated river basin management: Canadian experiences', in *Hydrology and Water Resources Symposium 1986: River Basin Management,* Institution of Engineers, Australia, Barton, A.C.T.

Mitchell, B. (1987) *A Comprehensive-Integrated Approach for Water and Land Management,* Occasional Paper 1, Centre for Water Policy Research, University of New England, Armidale, NSW, Australia.

Mitchell, B. and **Draper, D.** (1982) *Relevance and Ethics in Geography,* Longman, London.

Mitchell, B. and **Draper, D.** (1983) 'Ethics in geographical research', *Professional Geographer,* **35,** 9–17.

Mitchell, B. and **Gardner, J. S.,** eds (1983) *River Basin Management: Canadian Experiences,* Publication Series No. 20, Department of Geography, University of Waterloo, Waterloo, Ontario.

Mitchell, B. and **Huntley, H. M.** (1977) 'An analysis of criticisms of international fishery organizations with reference to three agencies associated with the Canadian West Coast fishery', *Journal of Environmental Management,* **5,** 47–73.

Mitchell, B. and **King, P.** (1984) 'Resource conflict, policy change and practice in Canadian fisheries management', *Geoforum,* **15,** 419–32.

Mitchell, B. and **Leighton, P. H.** (1977) 'A comparison of multivariate and trend forecasting estimates with actual water use', *Water Resources Bulletin,* **13,** 817–24.

Mitchell, B. and **Priddle, G. B.** (1981) 'The long-term economic and behavioral impact of an electrical power transmission corridor on the rural environment: reality and perception', pp. 370–384 in Finsterbusch, K. and Wolf, C. P. (eds.), *Methodology of Social Impact Assessment,* 2nd edn, Hutchinson Ross, Stroudsburg, Pennsylvania.

Mitchell, B. and **Turkheim, R.** (1977) 'Environmental impact assessment: principles, practices and Canadian experiences', pp. 47–66 in Krueger, R. R. and Mitchell, B. (eds.), *Managing Canada's Renewable Resources,* Methuen, Toronto.

Mitchell, J. K. (1974a) 'Natural hazards research', pp. 311–41, in Manners, I. R. and Mikesell, M. W. (eds.), *Perspectives on Environment, Publication* No. 13, Commission on College Geography, Association of American Geographers, Washington, DC.

Mitchell, J. K. (1974b) *Community Response to Coastal Erosion: Individual and Collective Adjustments to Hazard on the Atlantic Shore,* Research Paper No. 156, Department of Geography, University of Chicago, Chicago.

Mitchell, J. K. (1978a) 'The expert witness: a geographer's perspective on environmental litigation', *Geographical Review,* **68,** 209–14.

Mitchell, J. K. (1978b) 'Impact of offshore oil and gas development on the coastal zone: reforming the impact assessment process', *Coastal Zone Management Journal,* **4,** (3), 299–328.

Mitchell, J. K. (1984) 'Hazard perception studies: convergent concerns and divergent approaches during the past decade', pp. 33–59 in Saarinen, T. F., Seamon, D. and Sell, J. L. (eds), *Environmental Perception and*

Behavior: An Inventory and Prospect, Research Paper No. 209, Department of Geography, University of Chicago, Chicago.

Mithal, R. S., Joshi, B. C. and **Gohain, K.** (1984) 'Environmental impact of the Ramganga Dam project', *National Geographical Journal of India,* **30,** 81-91.

Mohammad, N. (1978) 'Impact of economic factors on diffusion of agricultural innovations in central Trans-Ghaghara Plain', *Geographical Review of India,* **40,** 266–80.

Mohan, H. S. R. and **Subrahmanyam, V. P.** (1980) 'Drought climatology of the semiarid zone of Tamil Nadu', *Indian Geographical Journal,* **55,** 12–21.

Monmonier, M. S. (1982) 'Cartography, geographic information, and public policy', *Journal of Geography in Higher Education,* **6,** 99–107.

Montz, B. and **Gruntfest, E. C.** (1986) 'Changes in American urban floodplain occupancy since 1958: the experience of nine cities', *Applied Geography,* **6,** 325–38.

Moore, P. W. (1975) *Public Decision-Making and Resource Management: A Review,* Discussion Paper Series No. 17, Department of Geography, University of Toronto, Toronto.

Moore, T. R. (1983) 'The problem of soil erosion in semi-arid Kenya', *Kenyan Geographer,* **5,** 61–71.

Morehouse, T. A. (1972) 'Program evaluation: social research versus public policy', *Public Administration Review,* **32,** 868–74.

Morell, M. G. (1986) 'Needs for landscape planning: landscape and environmental problems in the Dominican Republic', *Landscape and Urban Planning,* **13,** 419–28.

Morgan, J. P. (1974) 'A.D.A.S. (lands) physical agricultural land classification', pp. 80–9, in *Land Capability Conference Proceedings,* Technical Bulletin 30, Ministry of Agriculture, Fisheries and Food, London.

Morgan, R. K. (1983) 'The evolution of environmental impact assessment in New Zealand', *Journal of Environmental Management,* **16,** 139–52.

Morrill, R. L. (1968) 'Waves of spatial diffusion', *Journal of Regional Science,* **8,** 1–18.

Morrill, R. L. (1970) *The Spatial Organization of Society,* Wadsworth, Belmont, California.

Morrill, R. L. (1974) 'Review of D. Harvey's Social justice and the city', *Annals of the Association of American Geographers,* **64,** 475–7.

Morrill, R. L. (1984) 'The responsibility of geography', *Annals of the Association of American Geographers,* **74,** 1–8.

Morrill, R. L. and **Symons, J.** (1977) 'Efficiency and equity aspects of optimum location', *Geographical Analysis,* **9,** 215–25.

Morris, J. (1987) 'Evaluating the wetland resource', *Journal of Environmental Management,* **24,** 147–56.

Moss, R. P. (1970) 'Authority and charisma: criteria of validity in geographical method', *South African Geographical Journal,* **52,** 13–37.

Muckleston, K. W., Turner, M. F. and **Brainerd, R. T.** (1981) *Floodplain Regulations and Residential Land Values in Oregon,* WWRI-73, Water Resources Research Institute, Oregon State University, Corvallis, Oregon.

Mumphrey, A. J., Seley, J. E., and **Wolpert, J.** (1971) 'A decision model for locating controversial facilities', *Journal of the American Institute of Planners,* **37,** 397–402.

Mumphrey, A. J. and **Wolpert, J.** (1973) 'Equity considerations and concessions in the siting of public facilities', *Economic Geography,* **49,** 109–21.

Mundie, R. M. (1982) 'Evaluating the effectiveness of local government farmland protection programs', *GeoJournal,* **6,** 573–7.

Munro, R. D. (1983) 'Environmental research and management priorities for the 1980s', *Ambio,* **12,** 60–3.

Munton, R. (1984) 'Resource management and conservation: the UK response to the World Conservation Strategy', *Progress in Human Geography,* **8,** 120–6.

Murck, B. W., Dufournaud, C. M. and **Whitney, J. B. R.** (1985) 'Simulation of a policy arrived at the reduction of wood use in the Sudan', *Environment and Planning A,* **17,** 1231–42.

Murdoch, S. H., Leistritz, F. L. and **Hamm, R. R.** (1986) 'The state of socio-economic impact analysis in the United States of America: limitations and opportunities for alternative futures', *Journal of Environmental Management,* **23,** 99–117.

Muretta, P. and **Price, W.** (1982) 'Environmental mitigation of dredge and fill projects: a case study of Coos Bay/North Bend, Oregon', *Coastal Zone Management Journal,* **10,** 233–54.

Murphy, J. T. (1980) *Getting the Facts: A Fieldwork Guide for Evaluators and Policy Analysts,* Goodyear Publishing Co, Santa Monica.

Murphy, P. E. and **Rosenblood, L.** (1974) 'Tourism: an exercise in spatial search', *Canadian Geographer,* **18,** 201–10.

Murtha, P. A. and **Harding, R. A.,** eds (1984) *Renewable Resources Management: Applications of Remote Sensing,* American Society of Photogrammetry, Falls Church, Virginia.

Musolf, L. D. (1975) *Legislatures, Environmental Protection, and Development Goals: British Columbia and California,* Sage Publications, Beverly Hills, Calif.

Mutrie, D. and **Mulamoottil, G.** (1980) 'Environmental supervision of construction: linking environmental planning and implementation', *Plan Canada,* **20,** (3-4), 195–203.

Myers, N. (1981) 'The Hamburger Connection: How Central America's forests became North America's hamburgers', *Ambio,* **10,** 3–8.

Myers, N. ed. (1984) *GAIA: An Atlas of Planet Management,* Doubleday, Garden City, New York.

Myers, N. (1986) 'Environmental repercussions of deforestation in the Himalayas', *Journal of World Forest Resource Management,* **2,** 63–72.

Myers, N. and **Tucker, R.** (1987) 'Deforestation in Central America: Spanish Legacy and North American consumers', *Environmental Review,* **11,** 55–71.

Nag, P. (1980) 'Perception of technological hazard in an urban environment: the case of power crises in Calcutta (India)', *National Geographical Journal of India,* **26,** 174–84.

Nag, P. (1983) 'Perception of the environment: issues and challenges', *National Geographical Journal of India,* **29,** 217–31.

Naganna, C. and **Barai, D. C.** (1982) 'Drought mitigation strategy – a case study in the Kolar Region, Karnataka', *Transactions of the Institute of Indian Geographers,* **4,** 125–31.

Nagel, E. (1961) *The Structure of Science,* Harcourt, Brace and World, New York.

Nair, N. G. N., Nair, N. J. K. and **Kutty, M. N.** (1984) *Resource Atlas of Kerala,* Centre for Earth Science Studies, Trivandrum, India.

Nair, N. J. K., Chattopadhyay, S., Shravan Kumar, V., Saravanan, E. and **Sukumar, B.** (1985) *Environmental Mapping – An Aid for Long-Term Planning,* Resources Analysis Division, Centre for Earth Science Studies, Trivandrum, India.

Nakamoto, T. (1982) 'The changing field of evaluation', *Journal of the American Planning Association,* **48,** 515–17.

Nakos, G. (1983) 'The Land Resource Survey of Greece', *Journal of Environmental Management,* **17,** 153–70.

Nash, R., ed. (1968) *The American Environment: Readings in the History of Conservation,* Addison-Wesley, Reading, Mass.

Nassauer, J. I. (1983) 'Oil and gas development in a coastal landscape: visual preferences and management implications', *Coastal Zone Management,* **18,** 323–38.

Nassauer, J. I. and **Benner, M. K.** (1984) 'Visual preferences for a coastal landscape including oil and gas development', *Journal of Environmental Management,* **18,** 323–38.

Natural Hazards Research Working Paper No. 16 (1970) *Suggestions for Comparative Field Observations on Natural Hazards,* Department of Geography, University of Toronto, Toronto.

Needham, R. D. and **Nelson, J. G.** (1977) 'Newspaper response to flood and erosion hazards on the North Lake Erie Shore', *Environmental Management,* **1,** 521–40.

Nelson, J. G. (1973) 'Canadian national parks and related reserves: research needs and management', pp. 348–79, in Nelson, J. G. *et al.* (eds), *Canadian Public Land Use in Perspective,* Social Science Research Council, Ottawa.

Nelson, J. G. (1982) 'Public participation in comprehensive resource and environmental management', *Science and Public Policy,* **9,** 240–50.

Nelson, J. G. (1987) 'National Parks and Protected Areas, National Conservation Strategies and sustainable development', *Geoforum,* **18**(3), 291–319.

Nelson, J. G., Day, J. C. and **Jessen, S.** (1981) 'Regulation of environmental protection: the Nanticoke Industrial Complex, Ontario, Canada', *Environmental Management,* **5,** 385–95.

Nelson, J. G. and **Fenge, T.** (1982) 'A human ecological perspective on large scale industrial development in rural areas: the Nanticoke complex, Southern Ontario, Canada', *Science and Public Policy,* **9,** 144–53.

Nelson, J. G. and **Jessen, S.** (1981) *Scottish and Alaskan Offshore Oil and Gas and the Canadian Beaufort Sea* Canadian Arctic Resources Committee, Ottawa.

Nelson, J. G., Needham, R. D., and **Mann, D. L.** eds (1978) *International Experience With National Parks and Related Reserves,* Publication No. 12, Department of Geography, University of Waterloo, Waterloo, Ontario.

Nemetz, P. N. (1986) 'The Fisheries Act and federal-provincial environmental regulation: duplication or complementarity?', *Canadian Public Administration,* **29,** 401–24.

Newman, J. L. (1974) 'The use of the term "hypothesis" in geography', *Annals of the Association of American Geographers,* **63,** 22–7.

Nicholson, N. L., Cornwall, I. H. B., and **Raymond, C. W.** (1961) *Canadian Land Use Mapping,* Geographical Paper No. 31, Queen's Printer, Ottawa.

Niedzwiedz, W. R. and **Batie, S. S.** (1984) 'An assessment of urban development into coastal wetlands using historical aerial photography: a case study', *Environmental Management,* **8,** 205–13.

Nieman, T. J. (1980) 'The visual environment of the New York coastal zone: user preferences and perceptions', *Coastal Zone Management Journal,* **8,** 45–61.

Noble, J. H., Banta, J. S. and **Rosenberg, J. S.** (1977) *Groping Through the Maze,* The Conservation Foundation, Washington, DC.

North, R. C. *et al.* (1963) *Content Analysis: A Handbook,* Northwestern University Press, Evanston, Ill.

Nyhart, J. D. (1983) 'Negotiating conflicts over marine resources: the use of multiparty models', *Environmental Impact Assessment Review,* **4,** 557–60.

Ofori-Sarpong, E. (1983) 'The drought of 1970–77 in Upper Volta', *Singapore Journal of Tropical Geography,* **4,** 53–61.

Ognibene, P. J. (1983) 'Environmental negotiation', *Electric Perspectives,* Fall, 21–7.

O'Hare, M. (1980) 'Improving the use of information in environmental decision making', *Environmental Impact Assessment Review,* **1,** 229–50.

O'Hearn, G. T. (1982) 'What is the purpose of evaluation?', *Journal of Environmental Education,* **13**(4), 1–3.

Ohlhorst, C. W. (1981) 'The use of Landsat to monitor Deep Water Dumpsite 106', *Environmental Monitoring and Assessment,* **1,** 143–53.

O'Leary, J. F. (1972) 'Resource vs. institutional crisis', pp. 238–40, in Murphy, J. J. (ed.), *Energy and Public Policy - 1972,* Conference Board Report No. 575, The Conference Board, Inc., New York.

Olofin, E. A. (1984) 'Some effects of the Tiga dam on valleyside erosion in downstream reaches of the River Kano', *Applied Geography,* **4,** 321–32.

Olsson, G. (1965) *Distance and Human Interaction: A Review and Bibliography,* Bibliography Series No. 2, Regional Science Research Institute, Philadelphia.

Olsson, G. (1968) *Verification in Geography,* Paper presented to the Faculty Seminar in Geography, University of Michigan, January 1968, mimeo.

Organisation for Economic Co-operation and Development (1979) *The State of the Environment in OECD Member Countries,* OECD, Paris.

Organisation for Economic Co-operation and Development (1985) *OECD Environment Data: Compendium 1985,* OECD, Paris.

O'Riordan, T. (1971a) *Perspectives on Resource Management,* Pion, London.

O'Riordan, T. (1971b) 'Public opinion and environmental quality: a reappraisal', *Environment and Behavior,* **3,** 191–214.

O'Riordan, T. (1971c) 'Towards a strategy of public involvement', pp. 99–110, in Sewell, W. R. D. and Burton, I. (eds), *Perceptions and Attitudes in Resources Management,* Information Canada, Ottawa.

O'Riordan, T. (1972) 'Decision-making and environmental quality: an analysis of a water quality issue in the Shuswap and Okanagan Valleys, British Columbia', pp. 1–111, in *Okanagan Water Decisions,* Western Geographical Series Vol. 4, Department of Geography, University of Victoria, Victoria.

O'Riordan, T. (1973) 'Some reflections on environmental attitudes and environmental behavior', *Area,* **5,** 17–21.

O'Riordan, T. (1976a) 'Workshop on resource management decision making', *Area,* **8,** 65.

O'Riordan, T. (1976b) *Environmentalism,* Pion, London.

O'Riordan, T. (1979) 'The scope of environmental risk management', *Ambio,* **8,** 260–4.

O'Riordan, T. (1981) 'Beware binding commitments: the British approach to EIA', *Environmental Impact Assessment Review,* **2,** 89–102.

O'Riordan, T. (1982) 'Risk-perception studies and policy priorities', *Risk Analysis,* **2,** 95–100.

O'Riordan, T. (1984) 'The Sizewell B Inquiry and a national energy strategy', *Geographical Journal,* **150,** 171–82.

O'Riordan, T. (1985) 'Research policy and review 6: future directions for environmental policy', *Environment and Planning A,* **17,** 1431–46.

O'Riordan, T. (1986) 'Coping with environmental hazards', pp. 272–309 in Kates, R. W. and Burton, I. (eds), *Geography, Resources and Environment, Volume II: Themes from the Work of Gilbert F. White,* University of Chicago Press, Chicago.

O'Riordan, T. and **Sewell, W. R. D.,** eds (1981) *Project Appraisal and Policy Review,* John Wiley, Chichester.

O'Riordan, T. and **Turner, R. K.** (1979) 'Recycling and householder attitudes: a survey of Norwich', *Resources Policy,* **5,** (1), March, 42–50.

O'Riordan, T. and **Turner, R. K.** eds (1983) *Progress in Resource Management and Environmental Planning,* Vol. 4, Wiley, Chichester.

Orloff, N. (1972) 'Suggestions for improvement of the environmental impact statement program', pp. 29–41, in Ditton, R. B. and Goodale, T. I. (eds.), *Environmental Impact Analysis: Philosophy and Methods,* University of Wisconsin, Madison.

Ortolano, L. (1984) *Environmental Planning and Decision Making,* John Wiley, New York.

Osunade, M. A. A. (1979) 'Methodological framework for rural land evaluation', *National Geographical Journal of India,* **25,** 167–79.

Oyeleye, D. A. (1982) 'The diffusion of agricultural cooperatives in Western Nigeria', *Singapore Journal of Tropical Geography,* **3,** 69–85.

Paine, R., ed (1971) *Patrons and Brokers in the East Arctic,* University of Toronto Press, Toronto.

Palinkas, L. A., Harris, B. M. and **Peterson, J. S.** (1985) *A Systems Approach to Social Impact Assessment: Two Alaskan Case Studies,* Westview Press, Boulder, Colorado.

Park, C., ed. (1986) *Environmental Policies: A Review,* Croom Helm, London.

Parker, D. J. and **Penning-Rowsell, E. C.** (1980) *Water Planning in Britain,* George Allen and Unwin, London.

Parker, D. J. and **Penning-Rowsell, E. C.** (1982) 'Flood risk in the urban environment', pp. 201–39 in Herbert, D. T. and Johnston, R. J. (eds.), *Geography and the Urban Environment: Progress in Research and Applications,* Vol. 5, Wiley, Chichester.

Parker, P. (1984) *Crisis Management in the Hunter Valley: Infrastructure Provision by Protest not Plan,* CRES Working Paper 1984/11, Centre for Resource and Environmental Studies, Australian National University, Canberra.

Parkes, J. G. M. (1973) *Public Perceptions of Water Quality and Their Effect on Water-Based Recreation,* Social Science Series No. 8, Information Canada, Ottawa.

Parsons, J. J. (1985) 'On Bioregionalism' and 'Watershed Consciousness', *Professional Geographer,* **37,** 1–6.

Pasqualetti, M. J. and **Pijawka, K. D.,** eds (1984) *Nuclear Power: Assessing and Managing Hazardous Technology,* Westview Press, Boulder.

Pasurka, C. A. (1984) 'The short-run impact of environmental protection costs on U.S. product prices', *Journal of Environmental Economics and Management,* **11,** 380–90.

Paterson, J. (1986) 'Co-ordination in government: decomposition and bounded rationality as a framework for "user friendly" statute law', *Australian Journal of Public Administration,* **45,** 95–111.

Pattison, W. D. (1964) 'The four traditions of geography', *Journal of Geography,* **63,** 211–16.

Paul, B. K. (1984) 'Perception of and agricultural adjustment to floods in Jamnna floodplain, Bangladesh', *Human Ecology,* **12,** 3–19.

Peace, J. R. (1985) 'Collecting land use data', *Journal of Soil and Water Conservation,* **39,** 361–4.

Pearce, S. R. and **Waters, N. M.** (1983) 'Quantitative methods for investigating the variables that underlie preference for landscape scenes', *Canadian Geographer,* **21,** 73–8.

Pearce, D. W. (1971) *Cost-Benefit Analysis,* Macmillan, London.

Pearse, P. (1968) 'A new approach to the evaluation of non-priced recreational resources', *Land Economics,* **44,** 87–99.

Pécsi, M. (1979) 'Landslides at Duneföldvár in 1970 and 1974', *Geographia Polonica,* **41,** 7–12.

Pederson, K. H. (1977) 'A proposed model for evaluation studies', *Administrative Science Quarterly,* **22,** 306–17.

Peet, R. (1975) 'Inequality and poverty: a Marxist-geographic theory', *Annals of the Association of American Geographers,* **65,** 564–71.

Peet, R. (1977) 'Editorial: interaction of the environmental and spatial contradictions during late capitalism', *Antipode,* **9.**

Peet, R. (1985) 'The social origins of environmental determinism', *Annals of the Association of American Geographers,* **75,** 309–33.

Penning-Rowsell, E. C. (1975) 'Constraints on the application of landscape evaluations', *Transactions of the Institute of British Geographers,* **66,** 149–55.

Penning-Rowsell, E. C. (1981a) 'Assessing the validity of landscape evaluations', *Landscape Research,* **6**(2), 22–4.

Penning-Rowsell, E. C. (1981b) 'Fluctuating fortunes in gauging landscape value', *Progress in Human Geography,* **5,** 25–41.

Penning-Rowsell, E. C. and **Hardy, D. I.** (1973) 'Landscape evaluation and planning policy: a comparative survey in the Wye Valley Area of Outstanding Natural Beauty', *Regional Studies,* **7,** 153–60.

Penning-Rowsell, E. C., Parker, D. J. and **Harding, D. M.** (1986) *Floods and Drainage: British Policies for Hazard Reduction, Agricultural Improvement, and Wetland Preservation,* Allen and Unwin, Winchester.

Perry, A. H. (1985) 'The nuclear winter controversy', *Progress in Physical Geography,* **9,** 76–81.

Perry, R. W. and **Greene, M. R.** (1982) 'Emergency management in volcano hazards: the May 1980 eruptions of Mt. St. Helens', *Environmental Professional,* **4,** 340–51.

Perry, T. L. (1977) 'The Skagit Valley controversy: a case history in environmental politics', pp. 239–61, in Krueger, R. R. and Mitchell, B. (eds.), *Managing Canada's Renewable Resources,* Methuen, Toronto.

Petersen, M. E. (1985) *Improving Voluntary Registration through Location and Design of Trail Registration Stations,* USDA Forest Service Research Paper INT-336, Intermountain Forest and Range Experiment Station, Ogden, Utah.

Peterson, J. (1984) 'Global population projections through the 21st century: a scenario for this issue', *Ambio,* **13,** 134–41.

Peterson, J. (1986) 'Scientific studies of the Unthinkable: the physical and biological effects of nuclear war', *Ambio,* **15,** 60–9.

Phillips, J. (1959) *Agriculture and Ecology in Africa,* Praeger, New York.

Pierce, J. T. and **Furuseth, O. J.** (1983) 'Assessing the adequacy of North American agricultural land resources', *Geoforum,* **14,** 413–25.

Pigram, J. J. J. (1972) 'Resource reappraisal and resistance to change: an Australian example', *Professional Geographer,* **24,** 132–6.

Pigram, J. J. J. (1983) *Outdoor Recreation and Resource Management,* St Martin's Press, New York.

Pigram, J. J. (1986) *Issues in the Management of Australia's Water Resources,* Longman Cheshire, Melbourne.

Pittock, A. B. and **Nix, H. A.** (1986) 'The effect of changing climate on Australian biomass production – a preliminary survey', *Climatic Change,* **8,** 243–55.

Platt, R. H. (1981) 'Farmland conversion: national lessons for Iowa', *Professional Geographer,* **31,** 113–21.

Platt, R. H. ed. (1987) *Regional Management of Metropolitan Floodplains,* Program on Environment and Behavior Monograph 45, Institute of Behavioral Science, University of Colorado, Boulder.

Platt, R. H., McMullen, G. M., Paton, R., Patton, A., Grahek, M. and **English, M. R.** (1980) *Intergovernmental Management of Floodplains,* Institute of Behavioral Science, University of Colorado, Denver.

Plotkin, S. E. (1983) 'Incorporating the risk of control failure into environmental assessments', *Environmental Impact Assessment Review,* **4,** 155–72.

Pocock, D. C. (1973) 'Environmental perception: process and product', *Tijdschrift voor Economische en Sociale Geografie,* **64,** 251–7.

Pomeroy, J. W., Green, M. B. and **Fitzgibbon, J. E.** (1983) 'Evaluation of urban riverscape aesthetics in the Canadian Prairies', *Journal of Environmental Management,* **17,** 263–76.

Popper, F. J. (1983) 'LP/HC and LULU's: the political uses of risk analysis in land-use planning', *Risk Analysis,* **3,** 255–63.

Powell, M. (1981) 'Landscape evaluation and the quest for objectivity', *Landscape Research,* **6**(2), 16–18.

Prasad, S. R. (1984) 'Malaria in project areas: a study on Nagarjunasagar and Srisailam project areas, India', *Indian Geographical Journal,* **59,** 18–21.

Prasad, S. N. (1985) 'Impact of grazing, fire and extraction on the bamboo (*Dendrocalamus strictus* and *Bambusa arudinacea*) populations of Karnataka', *Agriculture, Ecosystems and Environment,* **14,** 1–14.

Prasartseree, M. (1982) 'A conceptual development of quantitative environmental impact assessment methodology for decision-makers', *Journal of Environmental Management,* **14,** 301–8.

Pratap, D. and **Sheda, M. D.** (1983) 'Land use and forest cover types in Dehra Tehsil and adjacent Siwaliks – an application of remote sensing methods', *Annals of the National Association of Geographers, India,* **3,** 15–23.

Prest, A. and **Turvey, R.** (1965) 'Cost-benefit analysis: a survey', *Economic Journal,* **75,** 683–735.

Preston, B. J. (1986) 'Adequacy of environmental impact statements in New South Wales', *Environmental and Planning Law Journal,* **3,** 194–207.

Preston, V., Taylor, S. M. and **Hodge, D. C.** (1983) 'Adjustment to natural and technological hazards: a study of an urban residential community', *Environment and Behaviour,* **15,** 143–64.

Price, M. F. (1985) 'Impacts of recreational activities on alpine vegetation of Western North America', *Mountain Research and Development,* **5,** 263–77.

Priddle, G. B. (1979–1980) 'Public participation in park planning: the Algonquin experience in 1979', Vol. 10, pp. 67–89, *Geographical Inter-University Resource Management Seminars,* Department of Geography, Wilfrid Laurier University, Waterloo, Ontario.

Privalovskaya, G. A. (1984a) 'The concept of the spatial organization of resource use in Soviet industry', *Soviet Geography,* **25,** 312–27.

Privalovskaya, G. A. (1984b) 'Regional development and the natural resources of the U.S.S.R.', *Geoforum,* **15,** 39–48.

Prowse, T., Owens, I. F. and **McGregor, G. R.** (1981) 'Adjustment to avalanche hazard in New Zealand', *New Zealand Geographer,* **37,** 25–31.

Purdue, M., Kemp, R. and **O'Riordan, T.** (1984) 'The context and conduct of the Sizewell B Inquiry', *Energy Policy,* **12,** 276–82.

Pushchak, R. and **Burton, I.** (1983) 'Risk and prior compensation in siting low-level nuclear waste facilities: dealing with the NIMBY syndrome', *Plan Canada,* **23,** 68–79.

Radtke, K. W. H. (1983) *Living More Safely in the Chaparral-Urban Interface,* USDA Forest Service General Technical Report PSW-67, Pacific Southwest Forest and Range Experiment Station, US Department of Agriculture, Berkeley, California.

Raghavswamy, V. and **Vaidyanadhan, R.** (1980) 'Land use studies from aerial photographs: a case study of Visakhapatnam and its environs', *Geographical Review of India,* **42,** 1–15.

Rahmatian, M. (1987) 'Component value analysis: air quality in the Grand

Canyon National Park', *Journal of Environmental Management,* **24,** 217–23.

Rajotte, F. (1975) 'A locational analysis of recreational facilities in the Quebec City Region', *Revue de Géographie de Montréal,* **29,** 69–74.

Ramanaiah, Y. V. and **Reddy, N. B. K.** (1983) 'Carrying capacity of land in Andhra Pradesh', *Indian Geographical Journal,* **58,** 107–18.

Rambo, A. T. (1982) 'Human ecology research on tropical agroecosystems in South-east Asia', *Singapore Journal of Tropical Geography,* **3,** 86–99.

Ramesh, A., ed. (1984) *Resource Geography,* Heritage Publishers, New Delhi.

Ramesh, A. and **Tiwari, P. S.,** eds (1983) *Basic Resource Atlas of Tamil Nadu,* Department of Geography, University of Madras, Madras, India.

Ramesh, A., Barai, D. C. and **Hyma, B.** (1984) 'The scope and limitations of insecticide spraying in rural sector control programmes in the state of Karnataka and Tamil Nadu, India', *Indian Geographical Journal,* **59,** 89–97.

Rao, K. N. and **Vaidyanadhan, R.** (1981) 'Land-use capability studies from aerial photo interpretation – a case study from Krishna Delta, India', *Geographical Review of India,* **43,** 226–38.

Rasid, H. and **Paul, B. K.** (1987) 'Flood problems in Bangladesh: is there an indigenous solution?', *Environmental Management,* **11,** 155–73.

Rees, J. (1985) *Natural Resources: Allocation, Economics and Policy,* Methuen, London.

Rees, J. A. (1973) 'Demand for water in S.E. England', *Geographical Journal,* **139,** 20–36.

Rees, J. A. (1974) 'Water management and pricing policies in England and Wales', pp. 163–99, in Leversedge, F. M. (ed.), *Priorities in Water Management,* Western Geographical Series Vol. 8, Department of Geography, University of Victoria, Victoria.

Rees, J. A. and **Rees, R.** (1972) 'Water demand forecasts and planning margins in South-East England', *Regional Studies,* **6,** 37–48.

Rees, R. (1973) 'Geography and landscape painting: an introduction to a neglected field', *Scottish Geographical Magazine,* **89,** 147–57.

Rees, R. (1976) 'Images of the Prairie: landscape painting and perception in the Western Interior of Canada', *Canadian Geographer,* **20,** 259–78.

Rees, W. E. (1977) *The Canada Land Inventory in Perspective,* Lands Directorate, Canada Department of Fisheries and Environment, Ottawa.

Reilly, W. J. (1929) 'Methods for the study of retail relationships', *University of Texas Bulletin,* No. 2944.

Relph, E. (1970) 'An inquiry into the relations between phenomenology and geography', *Canadian Geographer,* **14,** 193–201.

Relph, E. (1984–85) 'The instant landscape machine', Vol. 15, pp. 100–14, *Geographical Inter-University Resource Management Seminar,* Department of Geography, Wilfrid Laurier University, Waterloo, Ontario.

Ribe, R. G. (1982) 'On the possibility of quantifying scenic beauty – a response', *Landscape Planning,* **9,** 61–75.

Richardson, B. (1972) *James Bay,* Sierra Club, San Francisco.

Ris, H. (1982) 'Integrating visual management into the coastal zone planning process: the Massachusetts experience', *Coastal Zone Management Journal,* **9,** 299–311.

Rivkin, M. D. (1977) *Negotiated Development: A Breakthrough in Environmental Controversies,* The Conservation Foundation, Washington, DC.

Robinson, G. O. (1975) *The Forest Service: A Study in Public Land Management,* Johns Hopkins University Press, Baltimore.

Robinson, J. B. (1982a) 'Backing into the future: on the methodological and institutional biases embedded in energy supply and demand forecasting', *Technological Forecasting and Social Change,* **21,** 229–40.

Robinson, J. B. (1982b) 'Bottom-up methods and low-down results: changes in the estimation of future energy demands', *Energy,* **7,** 627–35.

Robinson, J. B. (1982c) 'Energy backcasting: a proposed method of policy analysis', *Energy Policy,* December, 337–44.

Robinson, J. B. (1983) 'Pendulum policy: natural gas forecasts and Canadian energy policy, 1969–1981', *Canadian Journal of Political Science,* **16,** 299–319.

Robinson, M. H. (1985) 'Alternatives to destruction: investigations into the use of tropical forest resources with comments on repairing the effects of destruction', *Environmental Professional,* **7,** 232–9.

Robottom, I. (1985) 'Evaluation in environmental education: time for a change in perspective', *Journal of Environmental Education,* **17**(1), 31–6.

Rodda, R. P. C. (1980) 'Soil erosion and conservation in Britain', *Progress in Physical Geography,* **4,** (1), March, 24–47.

Rodwin, M. (1982) 'Can bargaining and negotiation change the administrative process?' *Environmental Impact Assessment Review,* **3,** 373–86.

Rogerson, C. M. and **Kobben, S. M.** (1982) 'The locational impact of the Environment Planning Act on the clothing and textiles industry of South Africa', *South African Geographer,* **10,** 19–32.

Roos, L. L. (1975) 'Quasi-experiments and environmental policy', *Policy Sciences,* **6,** 249–65.

Rosell, D. Z., Lapid, F. M. and **Tolentino, A. S.** (1985) 'Conservation of natural resources: a vital environmental issue in the Philippines', *Philippine Geographical Journal,* **29,** 1–8.

Ross, D. I. and **Singhroy, V.** (1985) 'The application of remote sensing technology in the environmental assessment process', pp. 144–78 in Maclaren, V. W. and Whitney, J. B. (eds), *New Directions in Environmental Impact Assessment in Canada,* Methuen, Toronto.

Ross, J. H. (1974) *Quantitative Aids to Environmental Impact Assessment,* Occasional Paper No. 3, Lands Directorate, Environment Canada, Ottawa.

Ross, J. H. (1976) *The Numeric Weighting of Environmental Interactions,* Occasional Paper No. 10, Lands Directorate, Environment Canada, Ottawa.

Ross, W. G. (1967) 'Encroachment of the Jeffrey Mine on the town of Asbestos, Quebec', *Geographical Review,* **57,** 523–37.

Ross, W. M. (1971) 'The management of international common property resources', *Geographical Review,* **61,** 325–37.

Ross, W. M. and **Marts, M. E.** (1975) 'The High Ross Dam project: environmental decisions and changing environment attitudes', *Canadian Geographer,* **19,** 221–34.

Rossi, P. H. and **Freeman, H. E.** (1982) *Evaluation: A Systematic Approach,* (2nd edn) Sage Publications, Beverly Hills, Calif.

Rossi, P. H., Wright, J. D., Weber-Burdin, E. and **Pereira, J.** (1983) *Victims of the Environment: Loss from Natural Hazards in the United States, 1970–1980,* Plenum, New York.

Roudabush, R. D., Herriman, R. C., Barmore, R. L., and **Schellentrager, G. W.** (1985) 'Use of Landsat multispectral scanning data for soil surveys on Arizona rangeland', *Journal of Soil and Water Conservation,* **40,** 242–5.

Royal Society of Canada, Committee on Environmental Consequences of Nuclear War (1985) *Nuclear Winter and Associated Effects,* Royal Society of Canada, Ottawa.

Rubec, C. D. A., ed. (1979) *Applications of Ecological (Biophysical) Land Classification in Canada,* Minister of Supply and Services, Hull, Quebec.

Rubec, C. D. A. (1981) *Characteristics of Terrestrial Ecosystem Impinged by Acid Precipitation across Canada,* Environment Canada Lands Directorate Working Paper No. 19, Supply and Services Canada, Ottawa.

Rudzitis, E. (1982) 'Resolution of an oil–shrimp environmental conflict', *Geographical Review,* **72,** 190–9.

Runkel, P. and **McGrath, J.** (1972) *Research on Human Behavior: A Systematic Guide to Method,* Holt, Rinehart and Winston, New York.

Russell, E. W. (1972) 'The impact of technological developments on soil in East Africa', pp. 567–76, in Farvar, M. T. and Milton, J. P. (eds), *The Careless Technology: Ecology and International Development,* Natural History Press, Garden City, N.Y.

Russell, P. (1982) *The Awakening Earth: The Global Brain,* Ark, London.

Rutherford, G. K. (1984) 'Toxic effects of acid rain on aquatic and terrestrial ecosystems', *Canadian Journal of Physiological Pharmacology,* **62,** 986–90.

Rutherford, G. K. (1985) 'The influence of acid precipitation on the Canadian biosphere', pp. 23–45 in Atkinson, K. and McDonald, A., *Planning and the Physical Environment in Canada,* Regional Canadian Studies Centre, University of Leeds, Leeds.

Saarinen, T. F. (1966) *Perception of the Drought Hazard on the Great Plains,* Research Paper No. 106, Department of Geography, University of Chicago, Chicago.

Saarinen, T. F. (1969) *Perception of Environment,* Resource Paper No. 5, Commission on College Geography, Association of American Geographers, Washington, DC.

Saarinen, T. F. (1971) 'Research approaches and questionnaire design', pp. 13–25, in Sewell, W. R. D. and Burton, I. (eds), *Perceptions and Attitudes in Resources Management,* Information Canada, Ottawa.

Saarinen, T. F. (1974) 'Problems in the use of a standardized questionnaire for cross-cultural research on perception of natural hazards', pp. 180–4, in White, G. F. (ed.), *Natural Hazards: Local, National, Global,* Oxford University Press, New York.

Saarinen, T. F. (1976) *Environmental Planning: Perception and Behavior,* Houghton Mifflin, Boston.

Saarinen, T. F. (1984) 'Some reasons for optimism about environmental perception research', pp. 13–24 in Saarinen, T. F., Seamon, D. and Sell, J. L. (eds.), *Environmental Perception and Behavior: An Inventory and Prospect,* Research Paper No. 209, Department of Geography, University of Chicago.

Saarinen, T. F., Seamon, D. and **Sell, J. L.,** eds (1984) *Environmental Perception and Behavior: An Inventory and Prospect,* Research Paper No. 209, Department of Geography, University of Chicago.

Saarinen, T. F. and **Sell, J. L.** (1980) 'Environmental perception', *Progress in Human Geography,* **4,** 525–48.

Saarinen, T. F. and **Sell, J. L.** (1981) 'Environmental perception', *Progress in Human Geography,* **5,** 525–47.

Saarinen, T. F. and **Sell, J. F.** (1985) *Warning and Response to the Mount St. Helens Eruption,* State University of New York Press, Albany.

Saarinen, T. F., Sell, J. L. and **Husband, E.** (1982) 'Environmental perception: international efforts', *Progress in Human Geography,* **6,** 515–46.

Sabatier, P. (1986) 'Top-down and bottom-up approaches to implementation research', *Journal of Public Policy,* **6,** 21–48.

Sabatier, P. A. and **Mazmanian, D.** (1980) 'The implementation of public policy: a framework for analysis', *Policy Studies Journal,* **8,** 538–560.

Sadler, B., ed., (1978) *Involvement and the Environment,* 2 volumes, Environment Council of Alberta, Edmonton.

Sadler, B., ed., (1981) *Public Participation in Environmental Decision-Making,* Environment Council of Alberta, Edmonton.

Sadler, B. and **Carlson, A.,** eds (1982) *Environmental Aesthetics,* Western Geographical Series Volume 20, Department of Geography, University of Victoria, Victoria, British Columbia.

Salter, C. L. and **Lloyd, W. J.** (1977) *Landscape in Literature,* Resource Papers for College Geography No. 76–3, Association of American Geographers, Washington, DC.

Salter, L. A. (1967) *A Critical Review of Research in Land Economics,* University of Wisconsin Press, Madison.

Sandbach, F. (1980) *Environment, Ideology and Policy,* Basil Blackwell, Oxford.

Sandbach, F. (1982) *Principles of Pollution Control,* Longman, London.

Santos, T. M. and **Golez, F.** (1982) 'The role of the Philippine copper industry in national development', *Philippine Geographical Journal,* **26,** 116–36.

Sauer, C. O. (1925) 'The morphology of landscape', *University of California Publications in Geography,* **2,** 19–53.

Sauer, C. O. (1938) 'Theme of plant and animal destruction in economic history', *Journal of Farm Economics,* **20,** 765–75.

Sauer, C. O. (1941) 'Foreward to historical geography', *Annals of the Association of American Geographers,* **31,** 1–24.

Sauer, C. O. (1952) *Agricultural Origins and Dispersals,* American Geographical Society, New York.

Sauer, C. O. (1956) 'The education of a geographer', *Annals of the Association of American Geographers,* **46,** 287–99.

Sawyer, S. W. (1983) 'Water conservation: conflicting attitudes of planners and utility managers', *Environmental Professional,* **5,** 124–33.

Sawyer, S. W. and **Feldman, S. L.** (1981) 'Technocracy versus reality: perceptions in solar policy', *Policy Sciences,* **13,** 459–72.

Saxena, M. R., Saxena, P. R. and **Vidhyanath, V.** (1984) 'Land use planning using remote sensing technology in Dindi reservoir basin', *Indian Journal of Landscape Systems and Ecological Studies,* **7,** 56–64.

Schaefer, F. K. (1953) 'Exceptionalism in geography: a methodological examination', *Annals of the Association of American Geographers,* **43,** 226–49.

Schick, A. (1971) 'From analysis to evaluation', *Annals of the American Academy of Political and Social Science,* **394,** 57–71.

Schiff, M. R. (1971) 'The definition of perceptions and attitudes', pp. 7–12 in Sewell, W. R. D. and Burton, I. (eds.), *Perceptions and Attitudes in Resources Management,* Information Canada, Ottawa.

Schiff, M. R. (1977) 'Hazard adjustment, locus of control, and sensation seeking: some null findings', *Environment and Behavior,* **9,** 233–54.

Schindler, D. W. (1976) 'Editorial: the impact statement boondoggle', *Science,* 192.

Schlesinger, B. and **Daetz, D.** (1973) 'A conceptual framework for applying environmental assessment matrix techniques', *Journal of Environmental Science,* **16,** 1–16.

Schrecker, T. F. (1984) *Political Economy of Environmental Hazards,* Minister of Supply and Services Canada, Ottawa.

Schroeder, H. W. and **Daniel, T. C.** (1980) 'Predicting the scenic quality of forest road corridors', *Environment and Behavior,* **12,** 349–56.

Schultink, G. (1983) 'Integrated remote sensing and information management procedures for agricultural production potential assessment and resource policy design in developing countries', *Canadian Journal of Remote Sensing,* **9,** 4–18.

Schuörmann, H. (1981) 'The effects of international tourism on the regional development of Third World countries', *Applied Geography and Development,* **18,** 80–93.

Schuster, E. G., Frissell, S. S., Baker, E. E. and **Loveless, R. S.** (1985) *The Delphi Method: Application to Elk Habitat Quality,* USDA Forest Service Research Paper INT-353, Intermountain Research Station, Ogden, Utah.

Scientific Committee on Problems of the Environment (1985) *Environmental Consequences of Nuclear War,* 2 vols, Scope 28, John Wiley, Chichester.

Scott, A. J. (1971) *An Introduction to Spatial Allocation Analysis,* Resource Paper No. 9, Commission on College Geography, Association of American Geographers, Washington, DC.

Scudder, T. (1965) 'The Kariba case: man-made lakes and resource development in Africa', *Bulletin of the Atomic Scientist,* **21,** 6–11.

Scudder, T. (1966) 'Man-made lakes and population resettlement in Africa', pp. 99–108, in Lowe-McConnell, R. H. (ed.), *Man-Made Lakes,* Academic Press, London.

Scudder, T. (1968) 'Social anthropology, man-made lakes and population relocation in Africa', *Anthropological Quarterly,* **41,** 168–76.

Scudder, T. (1972) 'Ecological bottlenecks and the development of the Kariba Lake Basin', pp. 206–235, in Farvar, M. T. and Milton, J. P. (eds), *The Careless Technology: Ecology and International Development,* Natural History Press, Garden City, N.Y.

Scudder, T. and **Colson, E.** (1972) 'The Kariba Dam project: re-settlement and local initiative', pp. 40–69, in Bernard, H. R. and Pelto, P. (eds), *Technology and Social Change,* Macmillan, New York.

Seddon, G. and **Pike, J.** (1979) 'Landscape studies in Australia', *Landscape Planning,* **6,** 255–69.

Seidel, S. and **Keyes, D.** (1983) *Can We Delay a Greenhouse Warming?* US Government Printing Office, Washington, DC.

Seley, J. and **Wolpert, J.** (1974) 'A strategy of ambiguity in locational conflicts', pp. 275–300, in Cox, K. R., Reynolds, D. R., and Rokkan, S. (eds), *Locational Approaches to Power and Conflict,* Halsted Press, New York.

Sell, J. L., Taylor, J. G. and **Zube, E. H.** (1984) 'Toward a theoretical framework for landscape perception', pp. 61–83 in Saarinen, T. F., Seamon, D. and Sell, J. L. (eds), *Environmental Perception and Behavior: An Inventory and Prospect,* Research Paper No. 209, Department of Geography, University of Chicago, Chicago.

Sewell, W. R. D. (1971a) 'Environmental perceptions and attitudes of engineers and public health officials', *Environment and Behavior,* **3,** 23–59.

Sewell, W. R. D. (1971b) 'Integrating public views in planning and policy making', pp. 125–31, in Sewell, W. R. D. and Burton, I. (eds.), *Perceptions and Attitudes in Resources Management,* Information Canada, Ottawa.

Sewell, W. R. D. (1973) 'Broadening the approach to evaluation in resources management decision-making', *Journal of Environmental Management,* **1,** 33–60.

Sewell, W. R. D. (1974) 'Perceptions, attitudes and public participation in countryside management in Scotland', *Journal of Environmental Management,* **2,** 235–57.

Sewell, W. R. D. and **Bower, B. T.** (1968) 'Problems and procedures', pp.18–42, in Sewell, W. R. D. and Bower, B. T. (eds), *Forecasting the Demands for Water,* Queen's Printer, Ottawa.

Sewell, W. R. D. and **Burton, I.** (1967) 'Recent innovations in resource development policy', *Canadian Geographer,* **11,** 327–40.

Sewell, W. R. D. and **Burton, I.,** eds (1971) *Perceptions and Attitudes in Resource Management,* Information Canada, Ottawa.

Sewell, W. R. D., Davis, J., Scott, A. D., and **Ross, D. W.** (1965) *Guide to Benefit-cost Analysis,* Queen's Printer, Ottawa.

Sewell, W. R. D. and **Foster, H. D.** (1976) *Images of Canadian Futures: The Role of Conservation and Renewable Energy,* Report No. 13, Office of the Science Advisor, Environment Canada, Ottawa.

Sewell, W. R. D. and **Mitchell, B.** (1984) 'Geographers, the policy process and education', *Operational Geographer,* **5,** 23–8.

Sewell, W. R. D. and **Phillips, S. D.** (1979) 'Models for the evaluation of public participation programmes', *Natural Resources Journal,* **19,** 337–58.

Sewell, W. R. D. and **Roueche, L.** (1974) 'Peak load pricing and urban water management: Victoria, B. C., a case study', *Natural Resources Journal,* **14,** 383–400.

Sewell, W. R. D. and **Wood, C. J. B.** (1971) 'Environmental decision making and environmental stress: the Goldstream controversy', pp. 33–44 in, *Annual Meeting of the Canadian Association of Geographers: Proceedings,* Department of Geography, University of Waterloo, Waterloo, Ontario.

Shafer, E. L., Hamilton, J. E., and **Schmidt, E. A.** (1969) 'Natural landscape preferences: a predictive model', *Journal of Leisure Research,* **1,** 1–19.

Shafer, E. L. and **Tooby, M.** (1973 'Landscape preferences: an international replication', *Journal of Leisure Research,* **5,** 60–5.

Shapiro, H. A. (1984) 'Coastal area management in Japan: an overview', *Coastal Zone Management Journal,* **12,** 19–56.

Sharma, S. C. and **Sharma, R.** (1980) 'Land capability classification and landuse planning: Block Padrauna, District Deoria (Uttar Pradesh) – a case study', *Geographical Review of India,* **42,** 31–40.

Shepard, C. L. and **Speelman, L. R.** (1985/86) 'Affecting environmental attitudes through outdoor education', *Journal of Environmental Education,* **17**(2), 20–3.

Sheskin, I. M. (1978) 'Alaska natural gas: which route to market?' *Professional Geographer,* **30,** 180–9.

Shields, P. G., Rosenthal, K. M. and **Holz, G. K.** (1986) 'The use of a computer in detailed land resource assessment', *Journal of Environmental Management,* **23,** 75–88.

Shoard, M. (1981) 'Why landscapes are harder to protect than buildings', pp. 83–108 in Lowenthal, D. and Binney, M. (eds.), *Our Past Before Us: Why Do We Save It?* Temple Smith, London.

Shopley, J. B. and **Fuggle, R. F.** (1984) 'A comprehensive review of current environmental impact assessment methods and techniques', *Journal of Environmental Management,* **18,** 25–48.

Shrubsole, D. A. (1986) 'The context of environmental mediation within the field of conflict resolution', pp. 11–26 in Dorney, R. S. and Smith, L. E. (eds), *Environmental Mediation,* Working Paper No. 19, School of Urban and Regional Planning, University of Waterloo, Waterloo, Ontario.

Shuttleworth, S. (1979–80) 'The evaluation of landscape quality', *Landscape Research,* **5**(1), 14–20.

Siegel, S. (1956) *Nonparametric Statistics,* McGraw-Hill, New York.

Simmons, I. G. (1981) 'Resource management and conservation', *Progress in Human Geography,* **5,** 93–6.

Simms, D. L. and **Thomas, J. F. A.** (1982) 'Integrated monitoring – principles and practice', *Environmental Monitoring and Assessment,* **1,** 405–12.

Simon, H. A. (1957) *Administrative Behavior,* Macmillan, New York.

Simon, H. A. (1959) 'Theories of decison-making in economic and behavioral science', *American Economic Review,* **49,** 253–83.

Simpson-Lewis, W., Moore, J. E., Pocock, N. J., Taylor, M. C. and **Swan, H.** (1979) *Canada's Special Resource Lands: A National Perspective of Selected Land Use,* Minister of Supply and Services Canada, Ottawa.

Sims, J. H. and **Baumann, D. D.** (1972) 'The tornado threat: coping styles of the North and South', *Science,* **176,** 1386–92.

Sims, J. H. and **Baumann, D. D.** (1975) 'Interdisciplinary, cross-cultural research: double trouble', *Professional Geographer,* **27,** 153–9.

Sims, J. H. and **Baumann, D. D.** (1983) 'Educational programs and human response to natural hazards', *Environment and Behavior,* **15,** 165–89.

Singh, A. (1983) 'Patterns of industrial location and environmental pollution in the National Capital Region, India', *National Geographer,* **18,** 69–76.

Singh, J. (1971) 'Optimum carrying capacity of land, caloric density and intensity of population pressure changes in Punjab, 1951–1960', *National Geographical Journal of India,* **7,** 31–49.

Singh, O. P. and **Pande, D. C.** (1982) 'Man–land ratio: a resource appraisal of Kashipur Tuhsil, Nainital', *Indian Geographical Journal,* **57,** 68–70.

Singh, S. R., Pofali, R. M. and **Batt, R. K.** (1985) 'Quantitative analysis of the Hiran catchment for land resources development and management: a case study based on aerial photo interpretation', *National Geographical Journal of India,* **31,** 10–17.

Sinh, D. (1985) *The Eco-Vote: People's Representatives and Global Environment,* Prentice-Hall of India, New Delhi.

Sivasubramanian, S. (1983) 'Environmental health management – a systematic view', *Indian Geographical Journal,* **58,** 69–71.

Skud, B. E. (1977) 'Jurisdictional and administrative limitations affecting management of the halibut fishery', *Ocean Development and International Law Journal,* **4,** 121–42.

Slater, D. (1975) 'The poverty of modern geographical inquiry', *Pacific Viewpoint,* **16,** 159–76.

Slater, D. (1977) 'Resources and class structure: notes on an alternative Marxist perspective', *Antipode,* **9,** 68–70.

Smardon, R. C. (1986) 'Historical evolution of visual resource management within three federal agencies', *Journal of Environmental Management,* **22,** 301–17.

Smardon, R. C. and **Fellman, J. P.** (1982) 'The quiet revolution in visual resources management: a view from the coast', *Coastal Zone Management Journal,* **9,** 211–24.

Smil, V. (1983) 'Deforestation in China', *Ambio,* **12,** 226–32.

Smit, B. E. (1981) 'Prime land, land evaluation and land use planning', *Journal of Soil and Water Conservation,* **36,** 209–12.

Smit, B. and **Brklacich, M.** (1985) *Feasibility of Constructing a Multisector Land Evaluation System: The New Brunswick Pilot Study,* Working Paper No. 42, Lands Directorate, Environment Canada, Minister of Supply and Services Canada, Hull, Quebec.

Smith, C. L. (1977) 'The failure of success in fisheries management', *Environmental Management,* **1,** 239–47.

Smith, D. I. (1981) 'Actual and potential flood damage: a case study for urban Lismore, N.S.W., Australia', *Applied Geography,* **1,** 31–9.

Smith, D. I. and **Handmer, J. W.,** eds., (1986) *Flood Warning in Australia: Policies, Institutions and Technology,* Centre for Resource and Environmental Studies, Australian National University, Canberra.

Smith, D. and **Irwin, A.** (1984) 'Public attitudes to technological risk: the contribution of survey data to public policy-making', *Transactions, Institute of British Geographers,* New Series, 9, 419–26.

Smith, L. G. (1982) 'Mechanisms for public participation at a normative planning level in Canada', *Canadian Public Policy,* **8,** 561–72.

Smith, L. G. (1983a) 'Electric power planning in Ontario: public participation at a normative level', *Canadian Public Administration,* **26,** 360–77.

Smith, L. G. (1983b) 'The evaluation of public participation in water resources management: a Canadian perspective', pp. 235–44 in J. W. Frazier, B. J. Epstein, M. Bardecki and H. Jacobs, eds., *Papers and Proceedings of Applied Geography Conferences,* Vol. 6. Department of Geography, Ryerson Polytechnical Institute, Toronto.

Smith, P. G. R. and **Theberge, J. B.** (1986) 'A review of criteria for evaluating natural areas', *Environmental Management,* **10,** 715–34.

Smith, S. L. J. (1983) *Recreation Geography,* Longman, London.

Smith, S. J. (1984) 'Practicing humanistic geography', *Annals of the Association of American Geographers,* **74,** 353–74.

Smith, V. K. (1981) 'Congestion, travel cost recreational demand models, and benefit evaluation', *Journal of Environmental Economics and Management,* **8,** 92–6.

Snow, C. P. (1959) *The Two Cultures and the Scientific Revolution,* Cambridge University Press, Cambridge.

Sorensen, J. C. (1971) *A Framework for Identification and Control of Resource Degradation and Conflict in the Multiple Use of the Coastal Zone,* Department of Landscape Architecture, University of California, Berkeley.

Sorenson, J. C. (1972) 'Some procedures and programs for environmental impact assessment', pp. 97–106, in Ditton, R. B. and Goodale, T. I. (eds), *Environmental Impact Analysis: Philosophy and Methods,* University of Wisconsin, Madison.

Sorg, C. F. and **Loomis, J. B.** (1984) *Empirical Estimates of Amenity Forest Values: A Comparative Review,* USDA Forest Service, General Technical Report RM-107, Rocky Mountain Forest and Range Experiment Station, Fort Collins, Colorado.

South, R. R. (1986) 'Environmental legislation and the locational process', *Geographical Review,* **76,** 20–34.

Spate, O. H. K. and **Jennings, J. N.** (1972) 'Australian geography, 1951–1971', *Australian Geographical Studies,* **10,** 113–40.

Spoehr, A. (1956) 'Cultural differences in the interpretation of natural resources', pp. 93–102, in Thomas, W. L. (ed.), *Man's Role in Changing the Face of the Earth,* University of Chicago Press, Chicago.

Stacey, G. S. and **Duchi, M. L.** (1980) 'Analysing socioeconomic effects of large energy projects', *Environmental Impact Assessment Review,* **1,** 267–86.

Stafford, H. A. (1985) 'Environmental protection and industrial location', *Annals of the Association of American Geographers,* **75,** 227–40.

Stamp, L. D. (1931) 'The Land Utilization Survey of Britain', *Geographical Journal,* **78,** 40–53.

Stamp, L. D. (1948, 1962 3rd edn) *The Land of Britain: Its Use and Misuse,* Longman Green, London.

Stamp, L. D. (1958) 'Measurement of land resources', *Geographical Review,* **48,** 1–15.

Stamp, L. D. (1960) *Applied Geography,* Penguin, Harmondsworth.

Stankey, G. H. (1972) 'The use of content analysis in resource decision making', *Journal of Forestry,* **70,** 148–51.

Stankey, G. H. (1976) *Wilderness Fire Policy: An Investigation of Visitor Knowledge and Beliefs,* USDA Forest Service Research Paper INT-180, Intermountain Forest and Range Experiment Station, Ogden, Utah.

Stankey, G. H. (1980) 'Wilderness carrying capacity: management and research progress in the United States', *Landscape Research,* **5**(3), 6–11.

Stankey, G. H., Cole, D. N., Lucas, R. C., Petersen, M. E. and **Frissell, S. S.** (1985) *The Limits of Acceptable Change (LAC) System for Wilderness Planning,* USDA Forest Service General Technical Report INT-176, Intermountain Forest and Range Experiment Station, Ogden, Utah.

Statistics Canada, (1986) *Human Activity and the Environment: A Statistical Compendium,* Minister of Supply and Services Canada, Ottawa.

Staudt, T. L. and **Harris, G. R.** (1985) 'Environmental attitudes: a comparison of waste managers and citizens in Northern New York', *Environmental Professional,* **7,** 27–38.

Steila, D. (1983) 'Quantitative vs. qualitative drought assessment', *Professional Geographer,* **35,** 192–4.

Stewart, J. Q. (1950) 'The development of social physics', *American Journal of Physics,* **18,** 239–53.

Stewart, T. R., Dennis, R. L. and **Ely, D. W.** (1984) 'Citizen participation and judgment in policy analysis: a case study of urban air quality policy', *Policy Sciences,* **17,** 67–87.

Stone, P. J. *et al.* (1966) *The General Inquirer: A Computer Approach to Content Analysis,* MIT Press, Cambridge, Mass.

Street, J. M. (1969) 'An evaluation of the concept of carrying capacity', *Professional Geographer,* **21,** 104–7.

Stroup, R. L. and **Baden, J. A.** (1983) *Natural Resources: Bureaucratic Myths and Environmental Management,* Pacific Institute for Public Policy Research, San Francisco.

Stynes, D. J., Spotts, D. M. and **Strunk, J. R.** (1985) 'Relaxing assumptions of perfect information in park visitation models', *Professional Geographer,* **37,** 21–8.

Suchman, E. A. (1967) *Evaluative Research: Principles and Practice in Public Service and Social Action Programs,* Russell Sage Foundation, New York.

Sullivan, T. J. (1984) *Resolving Development Disputes Through Negotiations,* Plenum, New York.

Sumi, K. and **Hanayama, K.** (1985) 'Existing institutional arrangements and implications for management of Tokyo Bay', *Natural Resources Journal,* **25,** 167–93.

Susskind, L. E. and **Dunlap, L.** (1981) 'The importance of nonobjective judgements in environmental impact assessments', *Environmental Impact Assessment Review,* **2,** 335–66.

Susskind, L. E. and **McCreary, S.** (1985) 'Techniques for resolving coastal resource management disputes through negotiation', *Journal of the American Planning Association,* **51,** 365–74.

Svedin, U. (1979) 'Technology, development and environmental impact: an introduction to the scenarios', *Ambio,* **8,** 48–51.

Swaminathan, E., Dhanapal, D. and **Murugesan, N.** (1985) 'Spread of parthenium plant and environmental hazard in Madurai City: a study on perceptions of public', *Indian Geographical Journal,* **60,** 9–16.

Swanston, D. N. (1981) *Watershed Classification Based on Soil Stability Criteria,* Cooperative Extension, Washington State University, Pullman, Washington.

Swartzman, D., Liroff, A. and **Croke, K. G.** (1982) *Cost-Benefit Analysis and Environmental Regulations: Politics, Ethics, and Methods,* The Conservation Foundation, Washington, DC.

Swift, J. (1983) *Cut and Run: The Assault on Canada's Forests,* Between the Lines, Toronto.

Sylvan, R. (1985) *A Critique of Deep Ecology,* Discussion Papers in Environmental Philosophy, No. 12, Philosophy Departments, Australian National University, Canberra.

Taafe, E. J. (1974) 'The spatial view in context', *Annals of the Association of American Geographers,* **64,** 1–16.

Taher, M. A. (1980) 'Applicability of "land system" method of land classification: a case study of Agri Valley, Italy', *Oriental Geographer,* **24,** 41–56.

Tait, J. L., Johnson, A. H., and **Bokemeier, J. L.** (1978) 'Identifying community power actors for rural development', *Journal of Soil and Water Conservation,* **33,** 270–3.

Talbot, A. (1983) *Settling Things: Six Case Studies in Environmental Mediation,* The Conservation Foundation, Washington, DC.

Taylor, B. W. (1973) 'People in a rapidly changing environment: the first six years of Volta Lake', pp. 99–107, in Ackerman, W. C. *et al.* (eds.), *Man-Made Lakes: Their Problems and Environmental Effects,* American Geophysical Union, Washington, DC.

Taylor, G. D. (1965) 'An approach to the inventory of recreational lands', *Canadian Geographer,* **9,** 84–91.

Teitz, M. B. (1968) 'Toward a theory of urban public facility location', *Papers, Regional Science Association,* **21,** 35–52.

Thampapillai, D. J. and **Musgrave, W. F.** (1985) 'Flood damage mitigation: a review of structural and nonstructural measures and alternative decision frameworks', *Water Resources Research,* **21,** 411–24.

Thibodeau, F. and **Field, H.** eds (1984) *Sustaining Tomorrow: A Strategy for World Conservation and Development,* University Press of New England, Hanover, NH.

Thie, J. and **Ironside, G.,** eds., (1976) *Ecological (Biophysical) Land Classification in Canada,* Lands Directorate, Environment Canada, Ottawa.

Thirgood, J. V. (1986) 'The Barbary forests and forest lands: environmental destruction and the viscissitudes of history', *Journal of World Forest Resource Management,* **1,** 137–84.

Thom, D. J. and **Martin, N. L.** (1983) 'Ecology and production in Baringo-Kerio Valley, Kenya', *Geographical Review,* **73,** 15–29.

Thomas, J. K., Gill, D. and **Adams, C. E.** (1984) 'Environmental perceptions of licensed Texas hunters', *Environmental Professional,* **6,** 255–62.

Thomas, W. A. (1976) 'Attitudes of professionals in water management toward the use of water quality indices', *Journal of Environmental Management,* **4,** 325–38.

Thomas, W. L., ed. (1956) *Man's Role in Changing the Face of the Earth,* University of Chicago Press, Chicago.

Thompson, S. A. (1986) 'Urbanization and the Middle Rio Grande Conservancy District', *Geographical Review,* **76,** 35–50.

Thovez, J. P. and **Singh, B.** (1984) 'Perception and attitudes to air pollution in an asbestos mining town', *GeoJournal,* **8,** 123–8.

Tillman, S. E., Upchurch, S. B., and **Ryder, G.** (1975) 'Land use site reconnaisance by computer-assisted derivative mapping', *Geological Society of America Bulletin,* **86,** 23–34.

Tips, W. E. J. (1984) 'A review of landscape evaluation in Belgium and some implications for future research', *Journal of Environmental Management,* **18,** 57–72.

Tisdell, C. A. (1983) 'An economist's critique of the World Conservation Strategy, with examples from the Australian experience', *Environmental Conservation,* **10,** 43–52.

Tisdell, C. (1985) 'World conservation strategy, economic policies and sustainable resource - use in developing countries', *Environmental Professional,* **7,** 102–7.

Titzer, D. R. and **Moser, J. W.** (1982) 'Indiana's Outdoor Recreation Management Information System', *Journal of Environmental Management,* **14,** 139–48.

Tivy, J. (1985) 'Nature conservation in the Nordic countries: consensus rather than conflict', *Geoforum,* **16,** 239–55.

Tiwari, A. K. and **Singh, J. S.** (1984) 'Mapping forest biomass in India through aerial photographs and nondestructive field sampling', *Applied Geography,* **4,** 151–65.

Tobin, G. A. (1982) 'Natural hazards and urban planning', pp. 157–201 in D. T. Herbert and R. J. Johnston, eds. *Geography and the Urban Environment,* John Wiley, Chichester.

Tomlinson, R. F., ed. (1972) *Geographical Data Handling,* 2 vols, IGU Commission on Geographical Data Sensing and Processing, Ottawa.

Tomlinson, R. F. (1984) 'Geographic Information Systems - a new frontier', *Operational Geographer,* **5,** 31–6.

Torry, W. I. (1979) 'Hazards, hazes, and holes: a critique of *The Environment as Hazard* and general reflections on disaster research', *Canadian Geographer,* **33,** 368–83.

Townshend, J. R. G. (1981a) 'The spatial resolving power of earth resource satellites', *Progress in Physical Geography,* **5,** 32–55.

Townshend, J. R. G., ed. (1981b) *Terrain Analysis and Remote Sensing,* Allen and Unwin, London.

Trilsbach, A. and **Hulme, M.** (1984) 'Recent rainfall changes in central Sudan and their physical and human implications', *Transactions, Institute of British Geographers,* New Series, **9,** 280–98.

Truman, D. (1951) *The Governmental Process,* Knopf, New York.

Tuan, Yi-Fu (1967) 'Attitudes toward environment: themes and approaches', pp. 4–17, in Lowenthal, D. (ed.), *Environmental Perception and*

Behavior, Research Paper No. 109, Department of Geography, University of Chicago, Chicago.

Tuan, Yi-Fu (1968a) *The Hydrologic Cycle and the Wisdom of God: A Theme in Geoteleology,* University of Toronto Press, Toronto.

Tuan, Yi-Fu (1968b) 'Discrepancies between environmental attitude and behaviour: some examples from Europe and China', *Canadian Geographer,* **12,** 176–91.

Tuan, Yi-Fu (1971a) 'Geography, phenomenology and the study of human nature', *Canadian Geographer,* **15,** 181–92.

Tuan, Yi-Fu (1971b) *Man and Nature,* Association of American Geographers, Washington, DC.

Tuan, Yi-Fu (1973) 'Ambiguity in attitudes toward environment', *Annals of the Association of American Geographers,* **63,** 411–23.

Tuan, Yi-Fu (1974) *Topophilia: A Study of Environmental Perception, Attitudes and Values,* Prentice-Hall, Englewood Cliffs.

Tuan, Yi-Fu (1976) 'Humanistic geography', *Annals of the Association of American Geographers,* **66,** 266–76.

Tunbridge, J. E. (1981) 'Conservation trusts as geographic agents: their impact upon landscape, townscape and land use', *Transactions of the Institute of British Geographers,* New Series, **6,** 103–25.

Turco, R. P., Toon, O. B., Ackerman, T. P., Pollack, J. B. and **Sagan, C.** (1983) 'Nuclear winter: global consequences of multiple nuclear explosions', *Science,* **222,** 1283–1300.

Turner, J. R. (1975) 'Applications of landscape evaluation: a planner's view', *Transactions of the Institute of British Geographers,* **66,** 156–61.

Tuthill, C., Schutte, W., Frank, C. W., Santolucito, J. and **Potter, G.** (1982) 'Retrospective monitoring: a review', *Environmental Monitoring and Assessment,* **1,** 189–211.

Udall, S. L. (1963) *The Quiet Crisis,* Holt, Rinehart and Winston, New York.

Ullman, E. L. (1957) *American Commodity Flow,* University of Washington Press, Seattle.

Ullman, E. L. and **Volk, D. J.** (1962) 'An operational model for predicting reservoir attendance and benefits: implication of a location approach to water recreation', *Papers of the Michigan Academy of Science, Arts and Letters,* **47,** 473–84.

United States Academy of Sciences, National Research Council, Committee on the Atmospheric Effects of Nuclear Explosions (1985) *The Effects on the Atmosphere of a Major Nuclear Exchange,* National Academy Press, Washington, DC.

United States, Environmental Protection Agency, Region X (1973) *Environmental Statement Guidelines,* US Environmental Protection Agency, Seattle, Washington.

United States, Land Committee (1941) *Land Classification in the United States,* US Government Printing Office, Washington, DC.

United States National Research Council, Carbon Dioxide Assessment Committee, (1983) *Changing Climate,* National Academy Press, Washington, DC.

United States, National Water Commission (1973) *Water Policies for the Future,* US Government Printing Office, Washington, DC.

Usher, P. J. (1974) 'Northern development: some social and political considerations', *Alternatives,* **4,** 21–5.

Val, E. and **Nelson, J. G.** (1983) 'Offshore petroleum and commercial fishery interactions: the case of Long Point, Port Dover, Lake Erie', *GeoJournal,* **7,** 247–60.

Vale, T. R. and **Parker, A. J.** (1980) 'Biogeography research opportunities for geographers', *Professional Geographer,* **32,** 149–57.

Vallentyne, J. R. (1984) 'Towards a symbol for the World Campaign for the Biosphere', *Environmental Conservation,* **11,** 309–12.

Van Valkenburg, S. (1950) 'The World Land Use Survey', *Economic Geography,* **26,** 1–5.

Van Ypersele, J. P. and **Verstraete, M. M.**, eds (1986) 'Climate and desertification: special issue', *Climatic Change,* **9**(1/2), 258 pp.

Vaughan, A. V. (1973–74) 'A visual analysis system', Vol. 4, pp. 41–66, *Geographical Inter-University Resource Management Seminar,* Department of Geography, Wilfrid Laurier University, Waterloo, Ontario.

Vaux, H. J., Gardner, P. D. and **Mills, T. J.** (1984) *Methods for Assessing the Impact of Fire on Forest Recreation,* USDA Forest Service General Technical Report PSW-79, Pacific Southwest Forest and Range Experiment Station, US Department of Agriculture, Berkeley, California.

Veblen, T. T. and **Stewart, G. H.** (1982) 'The effects of introduced wild animals on New Zealand forests', *Annals of the Association of American Geographers,* **72,** 372–97.

Wadley, D. (1981) 'Cost, price, and revenue differentials in electricity supply: Queensland and Australia', *Australian Geographical Studies,* **19,** 25–46.

Walker, R. (1982) 'The illusion of effluent charges, or regulatory dilution is no solution to pollution', *Antipode,* **14,** 12–20.

Walker, R. A. and **Williams, M. J.** (1982) 'Water from power: water supply and regional growth in the Santa Clara Valley', *Economic Geography,* **58,** 95–119.

Wall, G. (1976) 'National coping styles: policies to combat environmental problems', *International Journal of Environmental Studies,* **9,** 239–45.

Wall, G. (1978) 'Competition and complementarity: a study in park visitation', *International Journal of Environmental Studies,* **13,** 35–41.

Wall, G. (1982) 'Cycles and capacity: incipient theory or conceptual contradiction', *Tourism Management,* **3,** 188–92.

Wall, G. and **Wright, C.** (1977) *The Environmental Impact of Outdoor Recreation,* Publication Series No. 11, Department of Geography, University of Waterloo, Waterloo, Ontario.

Wall, W. D. and **Williams, H. L.** (1970) *Longitudinal Studies and the Social Sciences,* Heinemann, London.

Wallace, B. C. (1974) 'Landscape evaluation and the Essex coast', *Regional Studies,* **8,** 299–305.

Walmsley, D. J. (1974) 'Positivism and phenomenology in human geography', *Canadian Geographer,* **18,** 95–107.

Walsh, S. J. (1985) 'Geographic information systems for natural resource management', *Journal of Soil and Water Conservation,* **40,** 202–5.

Walters, C. J. (1986) *Adaptive Management of Renewable Resources,* Macmillan, New York.

Warren, A. and **Harrison, C. M.** (1984) 'People and the ecosystem: biogeography as a study of ecology and culture', *Geoforum,* **15,** 365–81.

Waterstone, M. (1985) 'The equity aspects of carbon dioxide-induced climate change', *Geoforum,* **16,** 301–6.

Watts, M. (1983) 'Hazards and crises: a political economy of drought and famine in Northern Nigeria', *Antipode,* **15,** 24–34.

Webb, E. J. *et al.* (1966) *Unobtrusive Measures: Nonreactive Research in the Social Sciences,* Rand McNally, Chicago.

Webb Edmunds, C. M. (1984) 'The politics of public participation and the siting of power plants in Japan', *Environmental Professional,* **6,** 293–302.

Weber, R. P. (1985) *Basic Content Analysis,* Sage Publications, Beverly Hills, Calif.

Weiss, R. S. and **Rein, M.** (1970) 'The evaluation of broad-aim programs: experimental design, its difficulties, and an alternative', *Administrative Science Quarterly,* **15,** 97–109.

Welch, H. W. and **Lewis, G. D.** (1976) 'Assessing environmental impacts of multiple land use management', *Journal of Environmental Management,* **4,** 197–210.

Wengert, N. (1955) *Natural Resources and the Political Struggle,* Doubleday, New York.

Wengert, N. (1973) 'What do we mean by "Metropolitan Water Management Institutions"?', *Water Resources Bulletin,* **9,** 512–21.

Wengert, N. (1976) 'Citizen participation: practice in search of a theory', *Natural Resources Journal,* **16,** 23–40.

Werner, K. (1973) 'Reclamation of land damaged by open-cast mining – methods and results', *Biological Conservation,* **5,** 277–80.

Werner, R. G., Leonard, R. E. and **Crevelling, J. O.** (1985) *Impact of Backcountry Recreationists on the Water Quality of an Adirondack Lake,* USDA Forest Service, Research Note NE-326, Northeastern Forest Experiment Station, Durham, New Hampshire.

Wescoat, J. L. (1986) 'Impacts of Federal salinity control on water rights allocation patterns in the Colorado River Basin', *Annals of the Association of American Geographers,* **76,** 157–74.

West, P. C. (1981) *On-Site Social Surveys and the Determination of Social Carrying Capacity in Wildlife Recreation Management,* USDA Forest Service Research Note NC-264, North Central Forest Experiment Station, St Paul, MN.

Westing, A. H. (1981) 'A world in balance', *Environmental Conservation,* **8,** 177–83.

Westphal, J. M. and **Halverson, W. F.** (1985/86) 'Assessing the long-term effects of an environmental education program: a pragmatic approach', *Journal of Environmental Education,* **17**(2), 26–30.

Whitaker, J. R. (1941) 'Sequence and equilibrium in destruction and conservation of natural resources', *Annals of the Association of American Geographers,* **31,** 129–44.

Whitaker, J. R. (1954) 'The geography of resources', pp. 226–39, in James, P. E. and Jones, C. F. (eds), *American Geography: Inventory and Prospect,* Syracuse University Press, Syracuse.

White, E. (1969) 'Man-made lakes in tropical Africa and their biological potentialities', *Biological Conservation,* **1,** 219–24.

White, G. F. (1942) *Human Adjustment to Floods: A Geographical Approach to the Flood Problem in the United States,* Research Paper No. 29, Department of Geography, University of Chicago, Chicago.

White, G. F. (1961) 'The choice of use in resource management', *Natural Resources Journal,* **1,** 23–40.

White, G. F. (1963) 'Contributions of geographical analysis to river basin development', *Geographical Journal,* **129,** 412–36.

White, G. F. (1966) 'Formation and role of public attitudes', pp. 105–27, in Jarrett, H. (ed.), *Environmental Quality in a Growing Economy,* Johns Hopkins, Baltimore.

White, G. F. (1969) *Strategies of American Water Management,* University of Michigan Press, Ann Arbor.

White, G. F. (1972a) 'Geography and public policy', *Professional Geographer,* **24,** 101–4.

White, G. F. (1972b) 'Organizing scientific investigations to deal with environmental impacts', pp. 914–926, in Farvar, M. T. and Milton, J. P. (eds.), *The Careless Technology: Ecology and International Development,* Natural History Press, Garden City, NY.

White, G. F. (1972c) 'Environmental impact statements', *Professional Geographer,* **24,** 302–9.

White, G. F. (1973) 'Natural hazards research', pp. 193–216, in Chorley, R. J. (ed.), *Directions in Geography,* Methuen, London.

White, G. F. (1974a) 'Natural hazards research: concepts, methods, and policy implications', pp. 3–16, in White, G. F. (ed.), *Natural Hazards: Local, National, Global,* Oxford University Press, New York.

White, G. F., ed. (1974b) *Natural Hazards: Local, National, Global,* Oxford University Press, New York.

White, G. F. (1974c) 'Role of geography in water resources management', pp. 102–21, in James, L. D. (ed.), *Man and Water: The Social Sciences in Management of Water Resources,* University Press of Kentucky, Lexington.

White, G. F. (1984) 'Environmental perception and its uses: a commentary', pp. 93–6 in Saarinen, T. F., Seamon, D. and Sell, J. L. (eds.), *Environmental Perception and Behavior: An Inventory and Prospect,* Research Paper No. 209, Department of Geography, University of Chicago, Chicago.

White, G. F. (1985) 'Geographers in a perilously changing world', *Annals of the Association of American Geographers,* **75,** 10–16.

White, G. F. and **Grover, H. D.** (1985) 'Toward understanding the effects of nuclear war', *BioScience,* **35,** 552–6.

White, G. F. and **Haas, J. E.** (1975) *Assessment of Research on Natural Hazards,* MIT Press, Cambridge, Mass.

White, G. F. *et al.* (1958) *Changes in Urban Occupance of Flood Plains in the United States,* Research Paper No. 57, Department of Geography, University of Chicago, Chicago.

Whitney, J. B. R. (1985) 'Integrated economic-environmental models in environmental impact assessment', pp. 53–86 in Maclaren, V. W. and Whitney, J. B. (eds.), *New Directions in Environmental Impact Assessment in Canada,* Methuen, Toronto.

Whitney, J. and **Dufournaud, C.** (1982) 'Ecological input-output models', pp. 135–60, in White, R. and Burton, I. (eds.), *Ecoville: Urbanization in the Context of Ecodevelopment,* Institute for Environmental Studies, University of Toronto, Toronto.

Whitney, J. B. R., Dufournaud, C. M. and **Murck, B. W.** (1985) *Energy Use and the Environment in the Sudan,* Project Ecoville Working Paper, No. 22, Institute for Environmental Studies, University of Toronto, Toronto, Ontario.

Whyte, A. V. T. (1986) 'From hazard perception to human ecology', pp. 240–71 in Kates, R. W. and Burton, I. (eds.), *Geography, Resources and Environment: Volume II, Themes From the Work of Gilbert F. White,* University of Chicago Press, Chicago.

Whyte, A. V. and **Burton, I.,** eds (1980) *Environmental Risk Assessment,* SCOPE 15, John Wiley, Chichester.

Wilcock, D. N. (1979) 'Post war land drainage, fertilizer use and environmental impact in Northern Ireland', *Journal of Environmental Management,* **8,** 137–49.

Willhite, R. G., Bowles, D. R., and **Tarbet, D.** (1973) 'An approach to resolution of attitude differences over forest management', *Environment and Behavior,* **5,** 351–66.

Williams, A. V. and **Zelinsky, W.** (1970) 'On some patterns in international tourist flows', *Economic Geography,* **46,** 549–67.

Willis, K. G. and **Whitby, M. C.** (1985) 'The value of green belt land', *Journal of Rural Studies,* **1,** 147–62.

Wilson, M. G. A. (1967) 'The coal traffic of Eastern Australia', *Economic Geography,* **43,** 128–42.

Winkel, G. H. (1971) *Theory and Method in Behavioural Geography,* Paper presented to the Annual Meeting of the Canadian Association of Geographers, University of Waterloo, Waterloo, Ontario, mimeo.

Wise, M. J. (1969) 'On the utilization of resources', *Geography,* **54,** 257–70.

Wisner, B., Weiner, D. and **O'Keefe, P.** (1982) 'Hunger: a polemical review', *Antipode,* **14,** 1–16.

Wohlwill, J. F. (1982) 'The visual impact of development in coastal zone areas', *Coastal Zone Management Journal,* **9,** 225–48.

Wolfe, R. I. (1966) 'Recreational travel: the new migration', *Canadian Geographer,* **10,** 1–14.

Wolpert, J. (1970) 'Departures from the usual environment in locational analysis', *Annals of the Association of American Geographers,* **60,** 220–9.

Wolpert, J. (1976) 'Regressive siting of public facilities', *Natural Resources Journal,* **16,** 103–16.

Wong, S. T. (1972) 'A model of municipal water demand: a case study of Northeastern Illinois', *Land Economics,* **48,** 34–44.

Wood, C. J. B. (1976) 'Conflict in resource management and the use of threat: the Goldstream controversy', *Natural Resources Journal,* **16,** 137–58.

Wood, L. J. (1970) 'Perception studies in geography', *Transactions of the Institute of British Geographers,* **50,** 129–42.

Wood, L. J. and **Kirkpatrick, J. B.** (1984) 'The allocation of rights to public forests in Tasmania: a geographical critique', *Applied Geography,* **4,** 215–34.

Woodcock, C. E., Strahler, A. H. and **Franklin, J.** (1983) 'Remote sensing for land management and planning', *Environmental Management,* **7,** 223–37.

Woods Gordon (1981) *Study on the Economic Impact of Electric Transmission Corridors on Rural Property Values: Final Report,* Woods Gordon, Toronto.

Wooldridge, S. W. and **Beaver, S. H.** (1950) 'The working of sand and gravel in Great Britain: a problem in land use', *Geographical Journal,* **115,** 42–57.

World Book Dictionary (1975) Doubleday, Chicago, 2 vols.

World Commission on Environment and Development (1987) *Our Common Future,* Oxford University Press, Oxford.

Worthington, E. B. (1972) 'The Nile catchment – technological change and aquatic biology', pp. 189–205 in Farvar, M. T. and Milton, J. P. (eds), *The Careless Technology: Ecology and International Development,* Natural History Press, Garden City, NY.

Wright, D. S. and **Greene, G. D.** (1987) 'An environmental impact assessment methodology for major resource developments', *Journal of Environmental Management,* **24,** 1–16.

Wright, J. K. (1947) 'Terrae incognitae: the place of the imagination in geography', *Annals of the Association of American Geographers,* **37,** 1–15.

Yapa, L. S. (1977) 'The Green Revolution: a diffusion model', *Annals of the Association of American Geographers,* **67,** 350–9.

Yapa, L. S. (1979) 'Ecopolitical economy of the Green Revolution', *Professional Geographer,* **31,** 371–6.

Yin, R. K. (1981) 'The case study crisis: some answers', *Administrative Science Quarterly,* **26,** 58–65.

Yool, S. R., Eckhardt, D. W., Estes, J. E. and **Cosentino, M. J.** (1985) 'Describing the brushfire hazard in Southern California', *Annals of the Association of American Geographers,* **75,** 417–30.

Young, A. (1968) 'Natural resource surveys for land development in the Tropics', *Geography,* **53,** 229–48.

Young, J. and **Sukhwal, B. L.** (1984) 'Radical geography: a new philosophical approach in the development of geographic thought in the United States', *Indian Geographical Journal,* **59,** 183–95.

Young, R. W. (1984) 'A national conservation strategy for Australia: living resource conservation for sustainable development', *Australian Geographical Studies,* **22,** 146–9.

Zaring, J. (1977) 'The romantic face of Wales', *Annals of the Association of American Geographers,* **67,** 397–418.

Zeigler, D. J., Brunn, S. D. and **Johnson, J. H.** (1981) 'Evacuation from a nuclear technological disaster', *Geographical Review,* **71,** 1–16.

Zeigler, D. J., Johnson, J. L. and **Brunn, S. D.** (1983) *Technological Hazards,* Association of American Geographers, Washington, DC.

Zelinsky, W. (1975) 'The demigod's dilemma', *Annals of the Association of American Geographers,* **65,** 123–43.

Zelinsky, W. (1985) 'Review of *GAIA: An Atlas of Planet Management,* edited by N. Myers, Doubleday, Garden City, NY, 1984', *Geographical Review,* **75,** 365–8.

Zimmermann, E. W. (1933, 1951 revised) *World Resources and Industries,* Harper and Brothers, New York.

Zipf, G. K. (1949) *Human Behaviour and the Principle of Least Effort,* Addison-Wesley Press, Cambridge, Mass.

Zobler, L. (1962) 'An economic-historical view of natural resource use and conservation', *Economic Geography,* **38,** 189–94.

Zobler, L. (1966) 'Review of I. Burton and R. W. Kates, *Readings in resource management and conservation,* (1965)', *Economic Geography,* **42,** 281–2.

Zube, E. H. (1970) 'Evaluating the visual and cultural landscape', *Journal of Soil and Water Conservation,* **25,** 137–41.

Zube, E. H. (1974) 'Cross-disciplinary and intermode agreement on the description and evaluation of landscape resources', *Environment and Behavior,* **6,** 69–89.

Zube, E. H. (1976) 'Perception of landscape and land use', Vol. 1, pp. 87–121, in Altman, I. and Wohlwill, J. F. (eds), *Human Behavior and Environment,* Plenum Press, New York.

Zube, E. H. and **Pitt, D. G.** (1981) 'Cross-cultural perceptions of scenic and heritage landscapes', *Landscape Planning,* **8,** 69–87.

Zube, E. H., Sell, J. L. and **Taylor, J. G.** (1982) 'Landscape perception: research, application and theory', *Landscape Planning,* **9,** 1–33.

INDEX